SEEING INDIANS

SEEING INDIANS

A STUDY OF RACE, NATION, AND POWER IN EL SALVADOR

VIRGINIA Q. TILLEY

UNIVERSITY OF NEW MEXICO PRESS   ALBUQUERQUE

10   09   08   07   06   05   1   2   3   4   5   6   7

Library of Congress Cataloging-in-Publication Data

Tilley, Virginia.
Seeing Indians : a study of race, nation,
and power in El Salvador / Virginia Q. Tilley.
p.   cm.
Includes bibliographical references and index.
ISBN 0-8263-3925-5 (pbk. : alk. paper)
1. Indians of Central America—El Salvador—History.
2. Indians of Central America—El Salvador—Ethnic identity.
3. Indians of Central America—Cultural assimilation—
El Salvador.   4. Ethnic conflict—El Salvador.
5. El Salvador—Race relations.
6. El Salvador—Ethnic relations. I. Title.
F1505.T55 2005
305.897'0728—dc22
2005020760

Design and composition: Melissa Tandysh

To my parents,

And to the memory of Segundo Montes

CONTENTS

Preface and Acknowledgments | ix

A Note on Terminology | xvii

Introduction: A Conqueror's Vision | 1

Chapter 1: "There are No Indians in El Salvador":
Indigeneity, the State, and Power | 7

Chapter 2: El Salvador's Ethnic Landscape/s | 26

Chapter 3: "What is an Indian?" | 42

Chapter 4: In the Shadow of the Maya | 61

Chapter 5: Remembering Cuscatlán | 83

Chapter 6: From Colonial Rule to Independence | 103

Chapter 7: The Matanza:
Genocide, Ethnocide . . . Auto-ethnocide? | 137

Chapter 8: Assimilated or Erased?: Ethnocide by Statistics | 169

Chapter 9: Being Mestizo: The Twisted Logics of Mestizaje | 189

Chapter 10: Celebrating Indians | 218

Notes | 241

Bibliography and Sources | 274

Index | 290

PREFACE AND ACKNOWLEDGMENTS

This exploration of imagery, ideas, and power surrounding Indians in El Salvador represents one political scientist's foray into a theoretical field—racial and ethnic politics in Central and Latin America—largely defined and certainly dominated by scholars in other disciplines. I therefore draw copiously and gratefully on studies especially in anthropology and history, and I owe much to wonderful conversations with friends in these disciplines and the humanities. But my own work remains firmly planted in theories from political science, focusing on how evolving state interests such as international security and nation building have contributed to indigenous marginality by shaping local ethnic perceptions and values. Hence this study combines approaches common to many fields—especially, an appreciation for discourse in the Foucauldian sense—with the more structural theories of statehood, nationhood, and the international system developed in political science. In rather brutal shorthand, I could sum up my method here as examining the discourse of indigeneity in order to illuminate the workings of state hegemony (in the Gramscian sense) as it has played out in an evolving international normative environment of a constructed international system.

Additionally, a Geertzian appreciation for culture resides behind this approach, as I assume a priori that ethnic politics on the ground is always shaped by individuals' personal negotiations within "webs of meaning" generated and sustained through complex social interactions. Yet in analyzing indigeneity, I take those very webs as outcomes of diverse historical processes that have been swept up and given new meaning by grand political narratives invented by nationalists to serve state authority. This book therefore probes the extent—greater than many people commonly realize—to which ethnic perceptions are products of the framing condition of nation building and the state-led discursive projects that nation building always inspires.

My focus on nation-building discourse shapes the trajectory of this inquiry in several ways. First, I do not attempt to provide a comprehensive portrait of racial thought but rather to highlight a few evolving state doctrines regarding Indians. Readers familiar with the actual complexity of ethnic experience on the ground will recognize that these doctrines greatly oversimplify local ethnic perceptions and relations. But such oversimplifications are precisely my interest. State elites, in their attempts to gain hegemonic power, commonly distill complex popular ideas into public mantras in order to galvanize broad popular support for particular policies (e.g., "we are all mixed"). People encounter these distilled doctrines through schooling and other nationalist reiterations and subsequently weave them into their own local webs of meaning. As the state's interests change, local domestic ethnic perceptions and values are periodically reconstructed and reinforced (although incompletely) in ways favorable to state hegemony. That such official narratives overwrite and abuse local complexities makes them more important to examine rather than less, for such overwriting is precisely their purpose, as this book attempts to demonstrate.

Second, certain broad and blurry categories emerge from this approach that are common in political science, like "state elites" and "nationalist intellectuals." No false conflation of internal complexities is intended in such terms: rather, they reflect a political scientist's structural view of the nation-state as an ideational framework whose institutional arrangements, security imperatives, and economic needs tend forcibly to enlist individuals—whatever their diverse motives or methods—in certain bracketed political roles. Terms like "nationalist intellectuals" are therefore intended to highlight the state's impact both in inspiring certain common concerns among intellectuals and in distilling their complex debates into categories serving state and nation building.

Finally, my historical approach to *mestizaje*, the doctrine of racial mixture, and indigeneity might risk seeming overdetermined, especially in focusing on a few famous voices like Manuel Gamio and José Vasconcelos. In offering their writings as illustrations, I do not mean to imply that such intellectuals drove later hegemonic ethnic beliefs in any linear way. Rather I seek to expose the contradictions and coloration of certain threads of ethnic thought that eventually gained impressive cognitive force throughout the continent and came to circumscribe indigenous political options in ways overwhelmingly favorable to state authority. Recognizing the state's crude but formative role in inspiring such intellectual fashions may fill out our understanding of ethnic thought more broadly and perhaps inspire some new conversations about the theory of racial formation.

But my academic colleagues, valued as they are, are not my primary intended audience here. Since its discursive and heavily historical approach may make this less than obvious, let me alert them that this book is concerned with practical policymaking in the present day. It is therefore written neither for scholars nor for policymakers, precisely, but for that broader educated readership interested in (and, in their aggregate beliefs about Indians, complicit in forming) the background ideas that form the superstructure of power. My primary concern is to expose and examine the empirical presumptions, tacit values, and larger worldview of those who control the doors to the halls of power and who determine who can speak, who is authentic, and who is worthy of political access. This book opens with some vignettes intended to demonstrate the material power of such ideas, which I observed determining so graphically who was able to get political access and funding in Washington, D.C., by defining who is a real Indian. In sharing my own political experience as a launching point, perhaps I take on the formidable challenge expressed by Charles Hale (1996:54) and Les Field (2002:4), among many: bridging our analysis of discourse (or cultural theory, a first-cousin project) to real-world problem solving. Aside from this preface, this book is therefore deliberately directed to any reader or student ready to explore this fascinating field of Latin American mestizaje, with the hope of influencing the ideas—or at least the questions—which comprise the larger political terrain on which indigenous people must maneuver.

The first requirement of such a project is, obviously, readability. This book attempts, in nonspecialist language, to demonstrate rather than directly theorize how the discourse of indigeneity interweaves national historical myth with concepts of ethnicity, race, nationhood, civilization, modernity, progress, and state security. I therefore explain things that, within the academy, probably do not need explanation; I also glide over academic debates that some might consider incumbent. The result is doubt-less semisuccessful: it has been no easier for me than for most of us to shift gears from the formal internecine debates of academia to the wider global conversations where ideas about Indians actually percolate and turn into policymaking. I will therefore be grateful to specialists for their patience through some reiterations of established knowledge necessary to the tale, and to nonspecialists for their tolerance of my strategic interweaving of disparate sources aimed at illuminating, at least in some dimensions, the nexus of images that compose racial politics in El Salvador.

One final note: this book conspicuously omits the indigenous voice, and so risks implying that I did not attend to those voices, or that I consider indigenous people mere passive objects or victims of state-led discourse rather than architects of their identity and politics. On the contrary, I spent months in 1995–96 and in 1998 primarily in the company of the Nahua, in Izalco, Santo Domingo de Guzmán, and especially in the Nahuizalco *cantones*: in individual interviews, political discussions during visits to their homes, and in group meetings with their organizations. (I did not work with the so-called eastern "Lenca" simply because of lack of time and resources; their core remaining territory is at the opposite end of the country, and security conditions in Morazán were then much more difficult. I managed only one visit to Miguel Amaya Amaya in Morazán, enough to suggest a fascinating second study if later opportunity arises.) In the late 1980s and early 1990s, too, I collaborated extensively with the transnational indigenous movement, an experience that informs my discussion in chapter 10. In twenty years of work, both activist and academic, I have always assumed as incontestable that indigenous people are protagonists of their epic history and subjects of their political relations to nonindigenous others.

However, I have considered it my particular contribution to indigenous struggles not to express their voices (they do not need me to do that) but instead to exploit my own position as a white, middle-class, North American academic to illuminate certain logics within the discourse of state builders: especially, the influence of international norms of the emerging North-Atlantic state system that has shaped, and continues periodically to reshape, Salvadoran state security and trade interests, nationalist discourses, and indigeneity. Beyond describing some indigenous public platforms and internal political debates, especially in chapters 1 and 10, to help expose the impact of ladino and foreign thought on material struggles, I leave indigenous voices to indigenous people. I rely on later researchers—especially anthropologists, strangely absent from these fascinating communities—to work more collaboratively with the Nahua and Lenca in producing works that express more fully their own lives and experience. This book instead focuses on how state interests have played into the perceptions and values of the dominant society by generating a Gramscian "hegemonic bloc" of officially sponsored doctrines, highlighting the hubris and violence embedded in those doctrines that have reshaped the discursive terrain in which indigenous people must negotiate "being Indian" or "being indigenous."

Some material in this book raised the possibility of physical danger to some of my informants, and for this reason I have kept my most valuable informants anonymous here. I trust that those familiar with such difficulties in Latin America will understand this predicament and ask that they view the relatively thin sources especially in chapters 1 and 10 in that light. I can extend my public and deepest thanks to Epifania Tepas, who accompanied me on many trips around the Nahuizalco cantones, and to all the Nahua (and Miguel Amaya Amaya of the Ulua/Lenca) for their patient and extensive help. Samuel Aguirre in Nahuizalco also offered instruction, guidance, and friendship.

Aside from its debt to the hard work of many scholars in Central America, indicated in the footnotes and bibliography, this study could not have been completed without some lucky breaks. For one thing, I had the good fortune to have in hand the recently completed dissertations of historians Aldo Lauria-Santiago, Patricia Alvarenga, and Erik Ching, whose groundbreaking findings had freshly transformed our understanding of late-nineteenth- and early-twentieth-century Salvadoran history. Without their exhaustive archival work and careful analysis, the historical reading I present here would have been greatly curtailed and my errors plentiful. Nor could I have made sense of all these sources without the ongoing conversations of that marvelous Salvadoran historian, Knut Walter, and my old friend, Javier Molina, whose hospitality, good conversations, and support in San Salvador are forever remembered with gratitude.

I also could not have had greater luck than to collaborate at one stage with Erik Ching, whose superb quality as a historian was matched only by his marvelous humor and warm spirit. Moreover, my work in the Salvadoran national archives would have been far less fruitful had Erik not carefully boxed and labeled for any subsequent researcher the most valuable documents from his exhaustive work on the crisis in 1932, a gesture consistent with his always generous professional vision.

This book's comparative framework also benefited greatly from brilliant anthropologists and linguists with whom I connected partly through the good graces of the Centro de Investigación Regional de Meso-América (CIRMA) in Antigua, Guatemala. I remain especially grateful for the invaluable guidance of Judy Maxwell, R. McKenna Brown, Walter Little, and the "third musketeer," Carol Hendrickson. Generous in both hospitality and ideas, Richard Adams was a senior mentor in the finest spirit. Gail Ament was, of course, a comrade in arms, whose touchstone good sense was a constant corrective and whose friendship was a staunch support through the fun times as well as the harder ones. Our connection is lasting.

Here as in all my academic work, my gratitude to my graduate advisor, Crawford Young, has only deepened with time, as his teachings and guidance still help to open intellectual vistas at every turn. Similarly lasting has been the influence of Mark Beissinger and Michael Barnett, who illuminated my appreciation of international-relations theory and cross-regional comparison, as well as Frank Salomon, Steve Stern, Ben Marquez, and other mentors at the University of Wisconsin-Madison. The John D. and Catherine T. MacArthur Foundation provided funds for my work in Guatemala and El Salvador and for the UW-Madison Global Scholars Program and the Cultural Pluralism Working Group that so greatly informed and enhanced my own interdisciplinary approach. Finally, I am very grateful for comments and corrections especially by Les Field, whose insights inspired important revisions, as well as Lynn Stephen, Jim Spates, and several anonymous reviewers influential to the manuscript's long journey.

This book also rests on the support of priceless friends whom I could call at all hours for intellectual guidance, theoretical brainstorming, and, not least, a shared political rant. In my early research, Bruce Magnusson's constant friendship, insight on politics of all stamps, and tactful incisions on my free-flying ideas were invaluable, a compass in the trenches. Patricia Billings and Dunbar Moodie continue regularly to inform and enrich my intellectual universe.

Finally, my lasting love to my friend Jake, who provided comfort and delight through tough times and most of this project: we will meet again.

A NOTE ON TERMINOLOGY

In this book, I frequently use "Indian" to refer to indigenous peoples in the Americas. This term may be controversial in some contexts, but in each case I used it deliberately to evoke its socially constructed and political character.

I also use "Nahua" to embrace the indigenous people of the western coffee zone of El Salvador, not because the term is the most common in the area (which it is not, the local term being simply *indígena*) but for three other reasons. First, many indigenous political activists in the region do call themselves Nahua (as in the formula "Maya-Nahuat," deployed especially by ANIS), so the usage here is supported by some contemporary indigenous terminology. Second, distinguishing the western Nahua from the generic *indígena* is important to avoid conflating the Nahua-language group with the Ulua indigenous people of eastern El Salvador (often called the Lenca), whose historical experience is very different and not included in this book. Third, for reasons explained in chapters 5 and 6, both history and collective memory link the indigenous populations in Sonsonate Department to the preconquest indigenous society, belonging to the Nahua language group, which established the city-state of Cuscatlán. Highlighting that legacy is, I propose, useful here.

My use of "Nahua" might face at least three objections, however. First, some scholars familiar with the region might object to my not using the long-established term "Pipil" for the western indigenous communities, breaking with scholarly tradition and familiar literature. Second, by implying that

"Nahua" is itself a bounded ethnic identity, I may wrongly suggest a unitary subject that is, on the ground, not only fluid but fraught with internal ethnic schisms tracing to before the Spanish arrival, especially between populations centered on the Izalcos, the Nonualcos, and the eastern region of Cuscatlán. (Neglect of these important ethnic divisions extends beyond my own, however; indigeneity in El Salvador cries out for attention by ethnographers.) Third, "Nahua" might even suggest a conflation, not intended, of the Nahua in El Salvador with the Nahua of Nicaragua. Given all these concerns, my use of "Nahua" might suggest an irresponsible neologism—even wrong-headed capitulation to current indigenous political rhetoric at the expense of scholarly integrity.

Even within scholarship, however, "Nahua" is not a neologism. "Nahua" or "Nahoa" was employed by some turn-of-the-century Salvadoran scholars to describe the western indigenous ethnicity and has lingered in scholarship drawing from these sources. Moreover, the provenance of "Pipil" might be seen as more dubious. "Pipil" was a term adopted by the Spanish upon the initial contact with the people of Cuscatlán and later translated as "childish" or "child-like." The common idea, drawn from this putative etymology, that the preconquest Nahua were a culturally backward, inconsequential, and simple people is not insignificant to their lowly standing in the Salvadoran national narrative—although recent research on the term has discredited such demeaning notions (see chapter 5). Hence my use of "Nahua" might help here to cast the western indigenous peoples of El Salvador as new subjects, as in other cases of indigenous renaming— although I do not suggest "Nahua" over "Pipil" as a "politically correct" usage for others.

Whatever its controversies, at least I adopt the term "Nahua" after pondering all these complexities. That the question can engage so many controversies is itself an illustration of some of the arguments in this book.

INTRODUCTION

A CONQUEROR'S VISION

ON A JUNE DAY IN 1524, THE SPANISH CONQUEROR PEDRO DE ALVARADO
sat on his horse overlooking a battlefield.[1] He may well have been sitting
in a steamy downpour, as it was the rainy season. He was certainly in
tremendous pain. In their first major battle six days earlier with the people he knew as "Pipiles," his army had entirely wiped out a defending
Pipil army to the last man. But an obsidian-tipped Pipil spear or arrow
had shattered a bone in his leg, and the ruthless conqueror of the
Guatemalan highlands had been forced to his tent for five days, unable
to proceed further. (The wound would heal slowly and badly, perhaps
with obsidian fragments embedded in the bone; his leg would remain
some four inches shorter than the other.) When he could climb into the
saddle, his army advanced to the next confrontation, a day's march east.
But he was still unable to fight, and he had ridden up a hill (probably with
an aide-de-camp) to watch the battle now preparing on the rain-soaked
plain below.

Facing him across the field, the Pipiles themselves must have been
apprehensive as they faced the Spanish forces: thousands of their kin and
countrymen had just been slaughtered by these strange Spanish invaders,
with their marvelous weapons and horses, on a scale previously unimag-
inable. Nevertheless, what remained of their once-formidable army had
assembled to face that invader again: thousands of warriors in thick cotton armor, the nobles emblazoned with brilliant silver chest emblems and
plumed war crests. Alvarado viewed in consternation the "terrifying"

spectacle of their spears, each thirty hands long and standing upright like a forest over the Pipil ranks. The Pipiles also bore cudgels and powerful throwing devices, forming an impressive wall of weaponry.

Facing that spectacle, Alvarado's own army had stopped altogether. On his right, his kinsman Diego waited at the head of thirty Spanish horsemen, ready to advance but stalled at the edge of the grassland. They were reluctant to ride forward over what looked like a marsh, fearing their horses would founder and leave them helpless targets of Pipil attack. On his left, Alvarado's other kinsman Gomez waited with twenty horsemen in the same predicament.

In between these two flanks, the main part of Alvarado's force stood similarly immobilized: a hundred Spanish foot soldiers, with some five thousand indigenous troops. Some of these indigenous allies were Mexica, from the famous Aztec city of Tenochtitlán (recently conquered by Cortéz). As was common among indigenous powers throughout the Spanish conquest, the Mexica had allied with their Spanish invader in the hope of mutual gain, initially to seize the Mayan territories. In the Mayan highlands, the Maya-Kaqchikel had also allied with Alvarado, hoping to dominate their historical rivals, the Maya-K'iche'. (This alliance would backfire later, when the Kaqchikeles became disgusted with Spanish abuses and rebelled, and Alvarado enlisted the freshly offended K'iche' to help crush them.) The Kaqchikeles were also hopeful that Alvarado would help them to overcome their other great rivals, the Pipiles of the Pacific lowlands, with whom they had openly battled in recent decades over control of the rich cacao lands of Los Izalcos. Thus Spanish, Maya, and Mexicans had marched together toward the coast with dreams of grasping the wealth of the great coastal state of Cuscatlán. But now the Mayan and Mexican infantry also stood motionless, clutching their war weapons in the drizzle, facing the daunting Pipil line.

At last, the Spanish determined that the ground was solid and the two mounted flanks moved forward over the sloppy field (we can imagine the horses' hooves splashing through the shallow water, tossing up clumps of sod and mud). The foot troops also surged forward, and battle was joined (and we can imagine the cacophony: explosions of muskets, screamed orders, cries of the fallen, flailing swords and spears). But the battle quickly became a rout. Six days earlier, Alvarado had already seen that the Pipiles' cotton armor, three fingers thick and reaching nearly to their feet, was so cumbersome and heavy that, once thrown down, the warriors could not easily get up again. (Armor so immobilizing seems a strange arrangement for foot fighters, but it was an excellent defense against arrows. Perhaps the Pipiles had made it extra thick to face the Spanish forces, hoping it would repel bullets. Perhaps the rain contributed to its debilitating weight.) In any case, that cotton armor and the great spears were now lethal burdens in the warriors' desperate flight back across the sodden fields. The Spanish and Kaqchikel forces pursued them for a league and finally cut them down, slaughtering even those who tried to surrender, committing "great massacre and punishment."

It was the last major battle in Pipil territory. As a fighting force, the great standing army of Cuscatlán, which had guarded this affluent and densely populated region for four centuries, was shattered and would never assemble again. Those Pipil fighters left alive fled into the surrounding mountains; some later reassembled as a guerrilla force.

The next day, Alvarado rode on with his army toward the central Pipil city of Cuscatlán, but met no more resistance. A few days later, in a town he thought was called Atehuan, they were met by a delegation. The ambassadors of Cuscatlán announced their surrender, presented themselves as Spanish vassals, and indicated that Alvarado would be received graciously, as conqueror, in Cuscatlán itself. Two days later, he entered the city, where the entire population had turned out to greet him. Chroniclers mention thousands of people lining the roads, offering turkeys and "great piles of fruit and other food." He entered the city in triumph.

But here the story diverges. In his own report to Cortéz, Alvarado said that he quickly realized that something was amiss: except for some notables, there was a conspicuous absence of men. The Pipil fighters, he realized, had remained in the hills. He sent out messengers. If the warriors returned, and accepted rule by the Spanish Crown, they would not be harmed, only brought to serve God and the Crown. The answer came back: they recognized no one, would not come, and if anything was wanted of them, they would be waiting where they were, with their arms. To Alvarado, this signaled that the "surrender" was a deception; the Pipiles were undefeated and unrepentant. Perhaps they were lying in wait, or preparing to strike the Spanish while they relaxed in the falsely welcoming city. So Alvarado sent out a second message: against such "traitors," he would launch a last war which would certainly be another bloody rout, and would enslave anyone taken alive, but those who swore fresh loyalty he would treat gently, as vassals. It didn't work; no one came back. So Alvarado sent troops out into the mountains and high valleys to find them. But now the densely forested mountains, rugged ravines, and bad weather gave the advantage to Pipil guerrilla warfare, and Spanish and Kaqchikel casualties mounted to no avail. To add more pressure, Alvarado seized a Pipil noble and sent him out to demand his people's surrender, but again the answer was the same.

So in terminal frustration and anger at the useless loss of his friends' lives, his leg probably still giving him serious pain (it remained infected for eight months), Alvarado denounced the entire population as traitors. He sentenced all the nobles, and all the prisoners taken in battle, to death (by strangulation, some reports said). Then he declared the rest of the population slaves, branded them, and forced them to pay, from their own sale as slaves if necessary, for the eleven horses that had been killed in the fighting, as well as the arms and other things used in their own conquest. He stayed in the city for sixteen days. Finally, with the Pipil forces still undefeated in the mountains, he went back to Guatemala and the Kaqchikel court, planning to return after the rainy season.

So ended the first Spanish expedition. Or at least, this was how Alvarado reported events in his letter, written a month later from the Kaqchikel court in the Mayan highlands, to Hernando Cortéz (his commander and the conqueror of the Aztec, who was still stationed in Tenochtitlán, in Central Mexico). But word of quite a different scenario trickled back to Spanish authorities from other observers, and these reports—like many similar ones—eventually reached the desk of someone who was making a career of collecting them. The one-time conquistador and later Dominican priest Bartolomé de Las Casas would go down in history as an impassioned defender of Indians against the brutalities of his own people, although his own view of "Indians" was as innocent children, needing paternal Spanish protection. We might imagine Las Casas sitting at his desk piled high with correspondence and reports from all quarters of the realm, his brow dark with fury, his secretary handing him additional reports as he wrote his famous treatise, *The Destruction of the Indies*. Certainly his language is steeped in outrage as he provides, from other eye witnesses, a different account altogether:

Of the infinite horrible deeds that were committed by this wretched tyrant and his brothers in their rule, because his captains were no less wretched and callous than he along with the others who helped him, there was one truly noteworthy, that happened in the province of Cuzcatlán, near the city of San Salvador, which is a very happy land, with all the southern sea coast that extends for forty or fifty leagues; and in the city of Cuzcatlán, which was the head of the province, they gave him a grand reception, and twenty or thirty thousand Indians were waiting for him laden with fowl and food. Having arrived and received the gift, he ordered that each Spanish take from that great number of people all the Indians that he desired for whatever days they were there, so that they should make full use of them and take charge of bringing them whatever they needed. Each took a hundred or fifty, or those which seemed sufficient to their being very well served, and the innocent lambs suffered the division and served with all their might, short only of worshiping them. Meanwhile, that captain asked the nobles [señores] to bring him much gold, because he had come principally for this. The Indians responded that they were glad to give all the gold they had, and they gathered a great quantity of gilded copper hatchets (which they used, which served them well enough), which appears gold, because that they did have. He put it to the test, and seeing it was copper he said to the Spanish: "To hell with this land; let's go, since there's no gold, and each one, the Indians who have to serve you, throw them in chains and I'll order them branded and sold as slaves." They did this and branded as slaves with the king's iron all they could tie up, and I saw the son of the principal lord of that city branded. The Indians who got loose and the rest of all that land seeing such wickedness began to join together and arm themselves. The Spanish did them great ruin and massacre and returned to Guatemala . . ."[2]

A few years later, in 1529, formal charges were brought against Alvarado for what were even then considered war crimes in the conquest of Guatemala and Cuscatlán, so Las Casas's version was probably more true. In any case, Alvarado reaped no great rewards for the venture that cost him the health of his leg; a few years later, he fell from his horse and died in a battle with Mayan warriors in the Yucatán.

But little good any Spanish court procedures would do the Pipiles, the Nahuat-speaking civilization that had built one of the great city-states of Mesoamerica. Either version gives us a dire picture: their leadership was decimated, and the capital's population was maimed and traumatized. The death of so many thousands of men in the first two battles must have wrought incalculable damage to family and town economies, aside from the emotional trauma and political devastation to the whole society. Still, things would get far, far worse. In the forests, from some strongly fortified bases, the indigenous people did sustain a lively guerrilla resistance for years, and a second Spanish expedition came and went in 1525, similarly unsuccessful. But a third expedition in 1528, led by Alvarado's kinsman Diego, established a permanent Spanish settlement, and over the following decade completed the region's subjugation. Within a few years after the Spanish arrival, Cuscatlán was entirely destroyed: its political and social institutions stripped away, its once-affluent and highly centralized society of nobles, commoners, and slaves converted into a population of vassals, in effective slavery.

In other words, the Pipiles were turned into "Indians"—the new identity, and grim material experience, imposed by Spanish rule. For three centuries, they would comprise the laboring base for Spanish colonial settlement: their culture shattered and transformed, their towns and cities appropriated and ruined. Through the first century of El Salvador's independence, they would continue to live mostly in miserable poverty. Yet they would also reconstitute themselves in villages and hamlets, harboring their transformed culture in new institutions, and nursing an oral tradition of unjust conquest. And in the early twentieth century, those old sentiments would flare into mass rebellion, in one of the last great Indian revolts in the Americas. The effort would unleash state repression on a scale exceeding all other outbreaks of modern Central American ethnic violence until the Guatemalan state's genocidal attacks on the Maya, in the 1980s. Decimated, they fled back to their hamlets and a protected obscurity.

Shortly afterward, they were "erased" altogether.

CHAPTER 1

"THERE ARE NO INDIANS
IN EL SALVADOR"

INDIGENEITY, THE STATE, AND POWER

There is a legend current in Central America that San Salvador has no Indians. Before my first visit several people advised me that the chief difference I would find, in moving there from Guatemala, was the absence of these aborigines, and I remember my first day in the city when a Costa-Rican friend for whose courtesy I am grateful took me about town to show me its sights. In the midst of the market-place, between the stalls where Indians in droves with naked brown children at their feet were selling their wares, I was again told, "You notice there are no Indians in this city, as in Guatemala."

"What are all these?" I asked, with a vague sweep of my arm.

He seemed embarrassed by the question and finally answered, "All I know is that you won't find any Indians here in the capital." It is curious how readily an accepted legend will triumph over observation, under the most unfavorable circumstances. The eager traveler sometimes learns more by keeping his ears shut.

—Louis J. Halle, 1936

The Indian-Free Nation

IT IS 1995. I AM ENTERING, PASSIVELY, INTO EVERY INTERNATIONAL RESEARCHER'S automatic first interview: the taxi driver from the international airport. We are winding slowly up the four-lane highway into the coastal mountain range toward the capital of San Salvador. Dropping behind us is the steamy coastal zone where, with unrequited faith in the beach's appeal for international tourism, the government chose to locate the National Airport, rendering it convenient to nothing. The ancient Fiat's worn engine is whining audibly with the grade and our ascent is modest; we pass only handcarts and pickup trucks billowing smoke, and are occasionally whipped by the wind of passing BMWs—the surreal apparitions of this deeply stratified country's elite class. It's stretching into an hour-plus ride, long enough for us both to be a bit bored. He asks over his shoulder what I'm doing in El Salvador and I tell him that I'm here to study the situation of the indigenous people: *los indígenas*.

"Oh no," he says. "We have no indígenas here. They all disappeared, long ago. In Guatemala, yes, they have many indígenas." He waves vaguely northward. "But not here. Here everyone is mestizo." Mixed race.

But I have done my reading, and this is not my first time in the country. "I thought there were still some indígenas in Panchimalco." A famous Indian community south of the capital, somewhere in the misty hills to the left of the highway.

"Yes, there are many in Panchimalco."

"And in Nahuizalco? and Izalco?" Towns in the west.

"Yes, many in Izalco and Nahuizalco. And in some other towns in that area . . ." He's warming to his subject, enjoying his expertise. "Santo Domingo de Guzmán, also, has many indígenas."

"I understand there are indígenas in Morazán, too . . ." The northeast of the country.

"Yes, some. The Lenca, yes."

"So if there are all these indígenas, how is it that people say El Salvador has no Indians?"

Brief pause. "Well, yes, there are indígenas, but they have lost their customs, see? They don't wear their typical dress or speak their language. Like in Guatemala. You go to Guatemala, you will see them, in their typical dress, and they have their languages. Here no. There are some indígenas, yes, but only a few old people, and they don't have their customs any more. They lost their ethnicity."

By the road looms an enormous billboard, sporting a forty-foot yellow rooster, grinning and brandishing a machete. *"Pollo Indio"*—Indian Chicken—trumpets the billboard, promoting the famous brand. Indian chicken, after all, has more flavor.

"How did they 'lose' their ethnicity?"

Another pause, but now the conversation is loaded in another way, in this country where the fight against "communists" cost sixty years of misery. "Well, you see, back in 1932 the communists organized a rebellion, and tried to take the land. And they fooled the indígenas into rebelling, see? And the indígenas rebelled, because they were fooled into following the communists, and many were killed. Thirty thousand were killed. And after that, they gave up their dress and their language, see? So they lost their ethnicity. And now there are no indígenas. Well, just those few old people, see? So because of this, in El Salvador we are all mestizo. Everyone is mestizo. El Salvador is the most mestizo country in Latin America."

With time to chat at length, my driver has just given me all the story pieces about El Salvador's vanished Indians—the account I would hear from people all over El Salvador. According to his own account, somewhere in the hills to our left—a tumble of second-growth woods, crumbled bluffs of rock, and half-seen road scars—Indians still live quietly: tens or even hundreds of thousands of them, unseen in their backwoods hamlets. Somewhere in those same hills, just seventy years ago, their parents or grandparents launched what may have been the last great Indian uprising of the continent. And in the days that followed, for a few weeks in February and March of 1932, tens of thousands of Indians fled and fell, mowed down by firing squads, hauled from their homes and shot, tied to fences and slaughtered with machetes. No one denies the scale, or the trauma. What became known as the *Matanza* (massacre) remains a bloody turning point in the national memory.

Yet in El Salvador, no sense of national moral responsibility about that trauma, or even glancing concern, lingers in the national conscience. No one thinks of compensation for the massacre's survivors, or truth commissions, or any of the measures that today, in other countries, surround the aftermath of ethnic cleansing. People laboring so hard to reconstruct the Salvadoran nation, after its crippling civil war, do not think of inquiring about how postwar democratization might take hold among people whose collective ethnic memories still resonate with the 1932 massacre. They do not consider the psychology of people participating in elections who lost family members to that massacre, who still live near the people who promulgated it, and whose town governments remain dominated by some of the descendents of those who directed it. They don't think of survivors at all. The Matanza is admitted to have targeted and terrified an entire ethnic population. But the ethnic group targeted in that massacre is presumed to have disappeared. The taxi driver was very clear on that. There *are* Indians in El Salvador, he readily admitted. But at the same time, he was quite clear: there are no Indians in El Salvador.

Ethnic Ideas in the Halls of Power

I first encountered the enigmatic case of El Salvador's indigenous people when I was living in Washington, D.C. in the late 1980s. Working in a small nongovernmental organization (NGO) concerned with international cases of state-sponsored racial discrimination, I was temporarily in charge of the section on indigenous peoples. It was an extraordinary time. Small and painfully underfunded delegations of indigenous peoples from all over the world were beginning to come to Washington to lobby the U.S. Congress, the World Bank, the human rights groups, seeking help to defend their lands and cultures against rapacious mining companies, settlers, and governments. It was a difficult mission. The human rights networks were then still steered by leftist ideologies that left little room for ethnic issues. Most leftists still saw ethnic politics as less important than class: specifically Indian politics were seen as outmoded if not outright divisive, best channeled into campesino coalitions. Major North American funders—the churches, the development agencies—still tended to see indigenous peoples as microminorities on the brink of social extinction. The supposed indigenous delegations (I was told privately) were doubtless just some opportunistic individuals trying to capitalize on the recent faddish ascent of North American Indian politics.

But change was percolating. The major environmental organizations had discovered that indigenous peoples could be valuable assets in save-the-rainforest campaigns, and ushered the delegations into their glittering offices. This prestigious backing soon provided a true wedge into the Washington power structure. The Human Rights Caucus of the U.S. Congress listened to the delegations and sometimes offered its mahogany tables for formal meetings. The World Bank offered similar tables and began to compose toothless but symbolically significant policy statements. The better-run delegations sometimes gained a few thousand dollars and perhaps a decent hotel room, but, most importantly, some vital first-world allies in their long-frustrated efforts to lobby their own unresponsive (or openly repressive) governments.

It was during this period that the Salvadoran delegation arrived in Washington, looking for grant money. The delegation was formally embraced by local Native American activists, and their itinerary was assisted by kind hands; they made the usual rounds. But they achieved nothing. Among the environmental organizations, doors didn't open. Bureaucratic blandishments veiled a conspicuous lack of interest and access at the Congress, at the World Bank. The reason? Word had floated quietly around the higher echelons of power. "There are no Indians in El Salvador," said the experts, so these people can't really represent anyone. They can't even be real Indians. Of course, no one said this to the delegation's face. After it left town (richer for some $75), I sat over dinner with an Apache friend who had done his best for them. It seems that the Salvadorans had trouble getting recognized as Indians, I ventured.

He looked at me askance. "Well," he confessed, "for us too, we had some trouble, although we didn't want to say so. We weren't really sure either. No one has ever been sure of the Salvadorans. *Are* they Indians?"

Seeing "Indians"

To anyone familiar with the question of "Indian-ness" in the Americas, the obstacles facing the Salvadoran indigenous delegation will immediately ring familiar. Ethnic identities are sometimes clear and obvious, but just as often they are not. Even within the group, people may differ about who is truly a member. Criteria for membership may actually vary, depending on class, age, gender, or where people are working (for example, it may be acceptable to abandon the group's typical dress when outside the village, but a suspicious sign of assimilation if one fails to wear it at home).

Arguments about identities and boundaries can also reflect political interests, as groups argue about which people have legitimate claims to, say, political representation, wages, water, or land. And defining some group right out of existence—by claiming they have assimilated, or perhaps that they are not a *racial* group but an *ethnic* identity rapidly dwindling in importance—is an especially tidy way to deny their collective claims. A sordid massacre, as in El Salvador (or Turkey, or other states with genocidal histories), may therefore motivate a national society to retool not only its history but its racial and ethnic definitions. And throughout the world, few such identities have been as frequently reconfigured, redefined, and hotly argued, for so long a time and with such political baggage, as "Indian."

Sorting out the enigma of the supposedly vanished Indians of El Salvador therefore requires our considering a whole complex of ideas and debates about "Indian-ness" itself, which the first part of this book explores. Chapter 2 offers a snapshot portrait of El Salvador's basic ethnic dilemma: a country whose majority population sustains a blanket denial of any Indian presence even while recognizing that a significant minority does consider itself indígena. But that portrait is just the springboard for our understanding the country's local images of Indians, which are actually nested in pan-continental debates, images, and values dating back five centuries.

"Indian" is, of course, an identity created during the first moments of Spanish arrival in the Americas, at the end of the fifteenth century, ascribed to the supposed native peoples of "India" as a whole. Later, Spanish colonial law confirmed the term Indian as a juridical category requiring a special body of laws, and North American settlers and governments picked up the term as well. Within a century, Indian became a pan-American label embracing thousands of (vastly diverse) cultures throughout the hemisphere—although understood quite differently under the imperialist doctrines of Spanish, French, and English governments. After the old empires broke up into independent states, the old category of Indian fed into new state policymaking about Indians (often, "our Indians") and fresh waves of transnational philosophizing about Indians. These discussions fed into local thinking about Indians everywhere, and they still linger in popular ideas and imagery regarding Indians in El Salvador.

And yet, that pan-American label, and related official legal provisions, were always adapted by people in local settings to make sense of various versions of "being Indian," such as social and labor relations regarding Indians and the local dress, language, customs, or residence understood to make someone Indian. Indianness or *lo indio* therefore has always differed markedly from place to place. Chapter 3 highlights those differences by comparing some common Central American images about Indians to very different North American imagery.

One quality, however, has always pervaded ideas about being Indian in the Americas: its racial character. Whatever else it may be, "Indian" is a *racial formation* in the sense that it is a social identity based on ideas of biological descent, historically imagined by a dominant society to secure a vulnerable labor force (or to exclude a savage Other), yet transcending strictly economic interests by generating durable patterns of social prejudice and discrimination.[1] Any visitor to El Salvador will find just such a population: people identified by a complex of physical and behavioral criteria, who as a group—at least in their own view—are still oppressed by a classic racial pattern of discrimination, marginalization, and exploitation.

And yet, in El Salvador, it is precisely the existence of any such group that is disputed, through a panoply of arguments impressive in their range and complexity. Most basically, Latin American thought today generally understands the term Indian not as a racial identity but as an ethnic one, signaled by behavior rather than by physical criteria. Denial of any Indian presence in El Salvador therefore rests on ethnic (behavioral) criteria: that the country's self-described indígenas are not really Indians because they lack the key practices—mainly, dress and language (as my cab driver maintained)—which are understood to signal deeper cultural matters, like spiritual beliefs and ethnic cohesion. Having lost these signal practices, indígenas are understood to have assimilated into a generic mestizo (mixed-race) identity and culture, distinguished only by their lingering poverty. Chapter 3 also lays out these arguments—and their less obvious political use in "decapitating" indigenous politics—in more detail. But the struggling indigenous movement firmly disagrees with these assumptions, arguing for a version of being Indian that does not rest on dress and language and explaining the indigenous communities' poverty as, in fact, a product of ethnoracial discrimination.

It hardly seems appropriate for outsiders to judge these competing claims. Local disagreements about ethnic identities suggest tactful neutrality by third parties (or by scholars, who may retreat to the higher ground of an enlightened detachment about such social constructions). But policymakers do not enjoy such postmodern privileges, for indigenous movements routinely make claims on material state resources: teachers and textbooks for bilingual education, funds for cultural revival, land reform, new credit structures. Rival ethnic claims therefore require some concrete assessment. But how can policymakers—or outsiders watching those policymakers—assess arguments about ethnic identities?

Chapter 4 illustrates the difficulties of attempting any such assessment by pointing out the slippery nature of supposedly hard ethnic data, through a comparison of the Guatemalan Maya and the Salvadoran Nahua. To mobilize people and to matter politically, ethnic identities must indeed be recognizable through observable behaviors understood as definitive, like language, dress, religion, food, and family organization. Researchers could usefully develop a "trait list" that seems to mark an Indian population: the ethnographic sketch offered in chapter 2 cites such studies.[2] Or researchers could take a more statistical approach by simply counting the number of people showing hallmark practices, such as the number of native-language speakers or people wearing "typical" indigenous dress. Some researchers have done this as well, and their findings are detailed in chapter 4.

But how can we be certain that practices like dress and language are so definitive of being Indian when it is precisely those definitions that people dispute? Even in neighboring Guatemala, among the famous Maya, such practices are less subject to argument. Does an Indian truly become mestizo when he or she stops speaking an indigenous language? Or must the person also abandon indigenous traditional dress? Or move out of the indigenous community into the central (ladino-dominated) town? Maya themselves differ sharply about these questions, and whose view should the researcher consider authoritative? Moreover, ethnic politics pervades even basic statistics: indigenous activists are often motivated to favor higher counts of Indians, while ladinos may be motivated to favor lower ones. Can some outside arbiter be found? Salvadoran scholars, who are (supposedly) intimately familiar with the domestic situation, may not be immune from local ladino bias. Foreign researchers, who have (supposedly) no axe to grind, have less local experience. United Nations declarations or human rights conventions may reflect international consensus that does not apply well locally. All these sources can be challenged—and they disagree in any case.

Establishing any objective authority on who is Indian is not only daunting. It is misguided. Ethnic identities are not objectively definable by practices in themselves, which can be established, measured, and tested by outside researchers. Rather, ethnicity is a collective sense of group identity, which matters to people—to the point of violence—even while measurable criteria and exact boundaries remain murky.

Hence for government census-takers in recent decades, the only workable way to check ethnic identities has been to rely on self-reporting: if a person believes herself to belong to a group, she is listed as belonging. On those grounds, a census would find that Indians certainly exist in El Salvador in that somewhere between 2 and 10 percent of the country's people consider themselves to be indígenas—and believe they are worse off because they are indígenas.

But such a survey would not get us far. For one thing, a range from 2 to 10 percent signifies a vast difference in numbers (and no more solid numbers are available, for reasons laid out in chapter 8). Worse, in El Salvador, any such poll would only return us to the ethnic standoff in the country: the basic denial, by other Salvadorans, that these supposed Indians are really Indians or deserve any political recognition as such.

Ethnic Metaconflict

In confronting that ethnic standoff, we confront a dilemma that lies at the heart of many ethnic conflicts: a metaconflict—that is, a contest among rivals to define the very nature of the conflict, or even whether any conflict exists at all. Metaconflicts are common in ethnic conflict. For example, René Lemarchand confronted one in his 1996 study of the small central African country of Burundi. Like Rwanda (famous for its 1994 genocide of Tutsis by the dominant Hutu party), neighboring Burundi has periodically been convulsed by mass ethnic violence between Tutsis and Hutus.[3] But Lemarchand found that political rhetoric by these rival groups was focusing not so much on material grievances as on arguments about the very nature of the groups themselves. Hutu activists were arguing that "Hutu" and "Tutsi" were distinct ethnic groups, that Hutus were suffering from long-standing discrimination by Tutsis, and that Hutus therefore deserved and required remedial state policies. The dominant Tutsis, who controlled the government, were arguing that the supposed Hutu-Tutsi ethnic division was actually superficial: a colonial invention with no real substance. Therefore, the Tutsis maintained, no state action to provide for Hutu rights was necessary or even proper—a conclusion obviously very convenient for the Tutsis. Lemarchand recognized that the metaconflict in Burundi was manipulative and an impediment to more practical efforts at reconciliation. But he also saw that, precisely because of this effect, the metaconflict was fundamental to the conflict. It was not just that Hutu-Tutsi rivalry to control the dominant discourse about their own group identities, thereby controlling the basic nature of the conflict, had obvious policy consequences. Even more importantly, individual behavior and ethnic passions sprang from rival "cognitive maps":

> It is one thing for a reasonably dispassionate observer to try to assess the roots of the Hutu-Tutsi problem; but how members of each community perceive their predicament, what each attempts to suppress as well as to invent, is an altogether different matter. In Burundi—as in South Africa—political actors share radically different cognitive maps, each connecting past and present through divergent paths. No attempt to demystify the Burundi situation can fail to appreciate the chasm that separates the reality of ethnic conflict from the manner in which it is perceived, explained, and mythologized by the participants.[4]

Competing ideas about Indians in El Salvador comprise just such a metaconflict. Different and competing ideas about "what is an Indian"— which underlie beliefs about whether the Indians admitted to live in El Salvador are still *really* Indians—represent different cognitive maps: what people believe they know, what they see, and what meanings they attach to what they see. Those meanings go far beyond the narrow question of what makes someone Indian. Ideas about Indians are emotionally and politically charged because they have much broader implications: national absolution from any responsibility for redressing the Matanza, for one thing, but also El Salvador's very claim to national unity—even its profile on the international stage. To appreciate these broader implications, and how they feed back into ideas about Indians, we need to consider just how politically adaptable and useful the concept of Indian actually is.

Ethnic Identities and the State

Although ethnic identities often run very deep in people's thinking, they are actually fluid and adaptable concepts, changing over time. They can even change quite suddenly under new political conditions (just as "Indian" was created by European conquest). Of course, they are not fluid in the sense that any politician can alter them at will; new political rhetoric must resonate with older ideas and perceptions in order to have any influence.⁵ Still, political agendas do regularly infiltrate and deliberately alter people's cognitive maps—their engrained perceptions and values regarding ethnic identities. Especially when new economic or political conditions require new state policy-making involving indigenous peoples, we typically find new political arguments about Indians being forwarded by all kinds of players: e.g., government bureaucrats, the security forces, churches, local landowners, local indigenous leaders and shamans, non-indigenous campesino leaderships, artisans and merchants, and intellectuals on all sides.⁶

Among all this diversity, however, only ideas favorable to state elites (both economic and political) will normally gain official endorsement and be promoted through various state-controlled media: especially school textbooks, as well as newspaper editorials, national symbols, and public rhetoric generally. Public imprimatur and wide diffusion tend to grant the state's version of a given ethnic reality a special force of authority or at least a tactical advantage. And over time (if promoted successfully), such an official doctrine typically gains sway at least among its target audiences. But when people's ethnic perceptions and values are more tenacious, or counter-arguments are persistent, new state-promoted doctrines can couple onto older ideas rather than replace them entirely: for example, an individual may be inspired by, and fully believe, some new doctrine of (glorified) racial fusion with Indians while at the same time fully sustaining older ideas about Indian racial inferiority. Over the decades and centuries, such layering can leave a deep sediment of ideas and meanings, some compatible and others contradictory, embedded in an identity like Indian.

Recognizing this layered historical character of ethnic identities, our questions about Salvadoran Indians can shift away from fruitless efforts to establish objective criteria for who is Indian. Instead, we can examine how, and under what political conditions, competing sets of criteria took shape. What were the evolving state-elite interests that inspired evolving official doctrines and definitions of Indian as an identity? Just how and why have those definitions changed over the centuries, and who benefited? What interests, perspectives, and goals have fed into leftist doctrines about Indians? And how do indigenous counter-definitions therefore reflect—and impact—all those interests? It is one thing to ask whether Indians still live in El Salvador; it is much more illuminating to ask why and exactly how the presence of Indians is so strongly denied by some and so firmly defended by others.

Answering those questions requires a more archaeological approach: excavating ideas laid down at different historical periods; probing their original purposes and logics; and identifying how older elements interplay in present values and images regarding Indians. In short, to explain both the 1932 Matanza and its aftermath of silence and denial, we need to explore the ethnopolitical history of being Indian in El Salvador.

Excavating Indigeneity

Part 2 of this book undertakes that archaeological project by digging into the origins, early logics, and changing motives behind Salvadoran ethnic ideas. Beginning with the conquest, we will trace how the conception of being Indian in El Salvador has been built not only from centuries of ethnohistory but from the dominant society's collective memory of that ethnohistory. The indigenous communities were certainly transformed by colonial rule and by life in the independent nation-state: chapter 6 traces some of those transformations. But their lives were also periodically reconfigured by popular doctrines originally concocted by colonial scholars and later nationalist intellectuals, who endeavored to imagine and formulate for policymaking what Indians have been, what they are, and what they should be.

Especially important to ethnic politics in the 1990s—and to the Matanza myth of Indian disappearance—were debates in the early twentieth century, when nationalist intellectuals throughout Latin America were striving afresh to determine what role Indians should or could play in their modernizing nation-states. Their debates generated racial doctrines and revisions of history that were then diffused into textbooks, public rhetoric, public monuments, and eventually oral tradition. In El Salvador, such doctrines eventually fused with local ethnic experience to naturalize the policy first to disparage and ignore the indigenous communities and then to deny that they exist at all.

In other words, Indianness—"indigenous-ness," indigeneity—is a discourse, in the sense described by Michel Foucault: something that seems to have objective existence (here, Indians) but which is actually a *set of ideas and practices about that object*: the body of beliefs, perceptions, values, institutions, and social relations strategically assembled over time to compose Indianness. In Foucault's view, a discourse is a mutually reinforcing interplay of ideas and behaviors. Indians are understood to have a certain characteristic look, a certain political configuration in the nation, and are associated with certain places and lifestyles. People accordingly understand Indianness in ways that shape their attitudes and daily behavior; those practices then make Indianness something material and apparently real. Thus reinforced on all sides, Indianness becomes something people think they see as an objective reality: something natural or given. They will therefore find any counter-ideas strange or absurd. In other words, as Foucault famously put it, the discourse of indigeneity has become a "regime of truth."[7]

But in El Salvador, again, that regime of truth is not fully hegemonic. It is contested by the very people it defines. For Indians throughout the Americas, in fact, being Indian is a matter of constant renegotiation, selective adaptation, and (generally wearying) rejection of the dominant discourse. As Fernando Mires wrote, "The Indian 'discovered,' invented and reinvented by the 'non-Indian,' converted into 'the other' or into a simple object, has found himself obliged to discover himself."[8] Through centuries of internal discussions and survival strategies, Indian peoples have thus generated counter-discourses, their own versions of being Indian.

Indigenous counter-discourses have been equally entangled with politics. For example, a new set of claims about being Indian may be deployed by activists trying to muster mass participation in a liberation movement; or ideas may be cultivated more quietly within a community to cultivate, under pressure, a collective sense of dignity and solidarity. These counter-discourses may be kept hidden and covert, to protect the new ideas from attack, subversion, or appropriation by the dominant society.[9] But sometimes they are deployed publicly, especially in times of open revolt, resistance, or new political campaigns, to legitimize Indian claims and galvanize popular support. In recent decades, indigenous counter-discourses have extended to affirming their rights as distinct peoples and nations in order to reclaim their unjustly extinguished sovereignty within their ancestral territories, a shift traced in chapter 10.

Hence states and indigenous movements are often locked in metaconflicts, which are indeed battles over truth and which can become violent.[10] For changing the regime of truth about Indians always threatens to alter, erode, or overturn established power hierarchies, with unpredictable consequences. For example, if it truly threatens to gain political reform, even a nonviolent indigenous counter-discourse can threaten economic elites by wrecking cheap labor arrangements that exploit Indians. Facing elite outrage and damaged export earnings, state governments therefore often react immediately and harshly to the first suggestion of such indigenous counter-discourses. Violent state reaction also traces to older ideas, however, for dominant societies in the Americas have lived for five centuries in apprehension of Indian rebellions.[11]

In El Salvador, the last such crisis came in the 1932 uprising and Matanza. In that year, the dominant society's discourse of indigeneity was altering dramatically, and the indigenous communities in the western coffee region rose up to reject its new material terms (loss of their lands and collective ethnic leverage) and to affirm their own. In response, the state launched massive and brutal repression; ladino landowners, brandishing slogans of race war and the national welfare, carried the violence much further. Chapter 7 plunges deeply into that crisis, probing its events but especially its discursive dimensions: the terms by which the indigenous people launched what might qualify as the last major Indian uprising in American history.

Afterward, the Salvadoran discourse of indigeneity would never be the same. As chapter 8 traces, in subsequent decades the very existence of any indigenous population would be erased from the municipal civil records. By 1958, the Salvadoran legislature would claim simply that "in our country indigenous populations do not exist."[12] But Indians still understood themselves as Indians, and their immediate neighbors understood them as Indians. So why this sweeping claim? If political containment was the goal, why not some other solution, such as the tokenistic ethnic pluralism promoted in Mexico?

Chapter 9 explains how El Salvador's domestic conditions favored a different trajectory: wholesale adoption of the regional discourse of racial mixture (mestizaje), which—under the banner of enlightened inclusion—actually translated into ethnic denial and erasure. But in exploring how mestizaje transformed the Salvadoran discourse of indigeneity, a close focus on El Salvador is no longer sufficient. Salvadoran mestizaje was not designed in a vacuum; it emerged in the wider context of Latin America's historical political experience. Indeed, some of El Salvador's most formative challenges—the Spanish conquest, early independence struggles, Liberal reforms and the rise of export agriculture of the late nineteenth century, anticommunist military dictatorship in the twentieth century—were shared by many states and societies throughout Latin America. The "Indian problem" was no exception.

The Discourse of Mestizaje

Latin America's great political discourse of mestizaje—racial fusion—has recently been illuminated by a number of groundbreaking works revealing how it has functioned in modern nation-building projects. Exemplary among these (and originally inspirational to this book) is Alan Knight's (1990) magisterial essay, "Racism, Revolution, and *Indigenismo*: Mexico, 1910–1940." Knight traced the adoption of mestizaje to the immediate aftermath of the Mexican Revolution, when Mexico's new nation builders were facing a cluster of governance challenges. He was hardly the first to probe this nationalist context of Mexican mestizaje: Martin Stabb had addressed many of the same issues in 1959, as had T. G. Powell in 1968, among others. But Knight probed mestizaje not only as evolving racial thought of Mexican scholars trying to understand and theorize about indigeneity in order to prescribe social policies, although certainly such motives were key to its invention. He identified mestizaje also as a discursive maneuver deployed by the Revolution's intellectuals partly to acknowledge and dignify the nation's ethnic pluralism but also to appropriate and defuse indigenous ethnopolitics within Mexico's modernizing national narrative. In other words, Knight identified mestizaje as a nation-building doctrine, driven by a concern for state authority, which had a mixed impact on the Indians (and other groups) it discursively absorbed.

Knight's work joined a rapidly growing wave of scholarship rediscovering the politics of race and ethnicity in Latin America, mostly in countries where indigeneity was easily recognizable as a major issue: Mexico, Guatemala, Bolivia, Ecuador, Peru.[13] But some scholars were also probing racial politics in areas where indigeneity was commonly believed to have vanished, and discovering that mestizaje itself was complicit in some major cover-ups. An early landmark in this vein was Jeff Gould's "'Vana Ilusión!' The highland Indians and the myth of Nicaraguan mestizaje, 1880–1925" (followed in 1998 by his book on the same subject). Like

Knight, Gould found that mestizaje was less the consensus of a society actually experiencing changing racial mixture than it was a strategic discursive shift, adopted in Nicaragua to facilitate a transfer of land from Indian to ladino hands. His work dovetailed with explorations of mestizaje by a cluster of scholars of indigeneity (especially in Peru, Central America, and Mexico) and of blackness (especially in Brazil and the Caribbean), which together indicated a pattern.[14] For all its diverse applications, mestizaje had always emerged at a crucial political juncture when the national society and identity discourse were both in flux, and it always functioned—whatever its ostensible celebration of indigenous (or black) identity and cultures—to appropriate and defuse indigenous (or *africano*) ethnopolitics.

For all its important revelations, however, the new literature on mestizaje tended toward a certain parochialism, for two reasons. First, close focus by scholars on local settings allowed rich detail but impeded their addressing the extent to which mestizaje and new ideas about indigeneity were flowing transnationally through elite intellectual networks and global indigenous consultations. Without serious consideration of those networks, neither the timing nor the exact terms of each country's doctrine of mestizaje (or later indigenous ethnic resurgences) could be fully explained. Second, researchers of mestizaje and indigeneity have overwhelmingly been historians, anthropologists, and linguists. Contributions by political scientists have remained notably—and shamefully—scarce.[15] This has been a loss, because political science holds useful theoretical keys to mestizaje, partly through its extensive attention to a subject less well explored by other disciplines: the modern state as an entity of the international system.

The Geopolitics of Mestizaje

In the early twentieth century, nationalist doctrines of mestizaje were indeed formulated and deployed in an international system awash with geostrategically crucial doctrines about race. Claims of "white" or "Anglo-Saxon" racial superiority were then explicitly linked, by European intellectuals and propagandists, to European and U.S. imperialist missions and manifest destiny. Mestizaje was accordingly imagined by Latin American intellectuals to redefine—and redignify—mixed-race Latin America in respect to the Anglo-Saxon racial bloc. Certainly mestizaje's central claim of racial fusion was imagined partly to further a sense of national unity among domestic populations (although unevenly so, varying with demographic conditions). But it was also a foreign relations claim, invented to conceive "Latin America" itself as a racially defined security community. Hence racial thought became a geopolitical maneuver, designed to reposition Latin America in a global order of rival racial blocs (as chapter 9 illustrates). In this tense international context, mestizaje quickly became loaded with mass popular anti-imperialist political passions—and so spun inward with added energies to inform domestic racial thought. Indians now became problematic in a new way: where they manifested as racially distinct communities, they not only manifested as "backward" impediments to national progress but also eroded the mixed-race or "cosmic-race" claim that buttressed the nation's dignified global standing in a racially defined international system.

Hence images and ideas about Indians also became linked to El Salvador's *international* identity. Indigenous ethnicity was reimagined to have evaporated partly because its evaporation confirmed the country's standing as truly mestizo—and therefore a civilized, modern, exemplary member of Latin America and of the global international community. And yet, that claim to a grand or "cosmic" racial fusion actually rejected any persistently distinct racial identities. Chapter 9 traces these xenophobic logics in Salvadoran mestizaje, which were also expressed as entrenched negrophobia and, for a time, a vicious Sinophobia.

Today, Salvadoran mestizaje still carries those old political agendas like old baggage: it is a discourse woven of multiple voices, with contradictory layers, implicated in multiple (and partly outdated) political concerns and values. But chapter 10 shows a final irony. El Salvador's entrenched discourse of mestizaje is now running afoul of new international thinking by the very authorities which originally inspired it: the "standards of civilization" promoted by European and U.S. voices, which have come to emphasize not racial unity but ethnic pluralism. In the past, a strong nation was understood to draw its spiritual character and cohesive strength from its racial homogeneity. Today, a nation is considered modern and progressive if it celebrates ethnic diversity as an intrinsic national resource. As a result, today Salvadoran state denial of any Indian presence in the nation manifests to international human rights observers not as progressive antiracism but as backward ethnic rejectionism. In the mid-1990s, UNESCO and the

European Union introduced just such new standards into El Salvador, which—although directly at odds with established Salvadoran rejectionist arguments about Indians—swayed Salvadoran government policy to alter its discourse of indigeneity, if largely through the leverage of conditional grants.

And yet, chapter 10 also describes how this discursive shift brought troubles of its own to El Salvador's Indians, by importing a new transnational model for being indigenous. It became politically imperative for the Salvadoran indígenas to manifest as indigenous not so much to the state as to the international organizations that were self-appointed to assist the new identity formula, "indigenous and tribal peoples." Hence the irony that sympathetic external actors, wielding a hegemonic transnational discourse of indigeneity, actually exerted unwelcome and even damaging pressure on the Salvadoran indigenous movement by making the Salvadoran Indians, yet again, seem not truly Indian.

Conclusion

With their historical layers exposed, their inner logics laid out, arguments against any Indian presence in El Salvador today assume a very different aspect. The contest is not merely between two domestic rival camps about "who is Indian," or "who gets what." Both domestic and international pressures led Salvadoran nationalists, in the early twentieth century, to orchestrate the Indians' official erasure. A nationalist doctrine implicated also in the country's foreign relations brought the entire society to naturalize the Indians' disappearance as a central point of distinction for the national identity. Certainly a deep history of local ethnic relations underlies today's metaconflict about indigeneity in El Salvador, but a global history of international tension has added weight to that conflict. Hence indigeneity is only one thread in a much larger tapestry. Pulling on that thread immediately twists the discourses of nationhood and statecraft in which it is wound. No wonder the opposing camps are so firmly set; a great deal is implicitly at stake.

In this larger context, the enigmatic situation of the Salvadoran indigenous peoples emerges as a provocative case through which to probe the covert political motives of racial ideas in a modern nation-state. Today, in their humble stick and mud-brick homes, on the quiet footpaths through the backwoods that link their hamlets, Salvadoran Indians have been living out their part in Salvadoran nationalist doctrine by remaining unseen and unheard. Denied, erased from public vision, they enable the nationalist claim of complete racial fusion and associated modernity and dignity. Tucked conceptually into an unreachable past, they absolve the nation of any collective guilt or further action following the Matanza. El Salvador's claim of national unity as well as impunity indeed partly depend on their staying in that past— quaint relics, at most, of a glorified national mythohistory.

This book traces the crumbling foundations of that claim. For, like many indigenous peoples throughout the continent, they are no longer content to manifest as relics. They are emerging with fresh claims on the nation's future.

CHAPTER 2

EL SALVADOR'S ETHNIC LANDSCAPE/S

Still they resist in their sorrow in Cacaopera, in Panchimalco, in Santo Domingo de Guzmán, in Nahuizalco, in Tacuba, in Guaymango, in Ataco, in Nahulingo, in Izalco.
      —*Pedro Escalante, Salvadoran scholar, 1992*

DO SIGNIFICANT INDIGENOUS COMMUNITIES TRULY STILL LIVE IN EL Salvador? It might seem that straight empirical data would answer that question, but the answer actually depends on the lens that each person brings to it. A few specialists—anthropologists, mostly—wave the question aside: they "know" that indigenous communities do persist, based on the criteria they bring to such matters, just as they "know" that hard definitions are elusive. But because most travelers to El Salvador do not *see* any Indians—as they expect Indians to look—they tend to believe that Indians (or at least real Indians) no longer live there. Salvadoran ladinos also tend to believe that Indians do not live there, as a given fact, and so do not look for any. A very different view is of course shared by activists within the Salvadoran indigenous movement, who—from their bases in the denser indigenous population among the western and northeastern cantones (hamlets)—argue that an indigenous population does exist and moreover is suffering from lasting discrimination. A quick survey of the ethnic landscape of El Salvador is our first step toward exploring this metaconflict. But as that metaconflict itself suggests, we do not find one such landscape in El Salvador. Looking through different lenses, we find several.

26

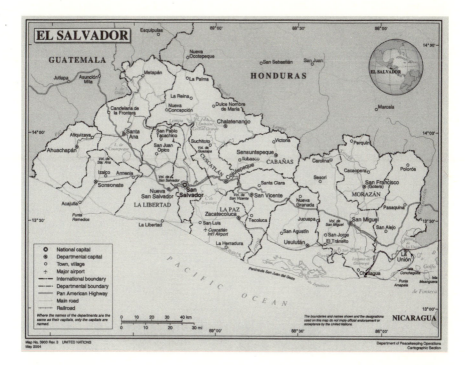

MAP 1. Map of El Salvador. (Courtesy of the United Nations Department of Cartography).

The Mestizo Republic

Looking at the country through the lens of mainstream (ladino) public life and symbols, anything "Indian" is indeed impressively absent from El Salvador. Until the late 1990s, no newspaper coverage, mainstream political discussions, cultural celebrations, or university forums in El Salvador even mentioned Indians. The country's legislation has not been concerned with Indians since the late nineteenth century. (The national legislature did ratify two international conventions on indigenous rights, but specified that El Salvador was doing so only on principle, because it had no such "tribal" populations.[1]) The fiery political debates of left and right, through the civil war of the 1970s and 1980s, made almost no mention of Indians or indeed any other racial or ethnic group. El Salvador is, not only in claim but in most public life, an entirely mestizo republic.

FIGURE 1. Nahua activist Epifania Tepas and her mother, from the Nahuizalco cantón of Pushtán, 1996. (Photo by author.)

FIGURE 2. Nahua women on market day, on the path network among cantons east of Nahuizalco. (Photo by author.)

Nor does the country's national art make reference to Indians. Government buildings (except the national airport) are strictly Greco-Roman or modern, lacking the pre-Columbian motifs showcased in other Central American capitals. Private art is similarly unforthcoming. Some Salvadoran painters from the 1910s through the 1940s did use indigenous imagery. But the two principal artists who did so, José Mejia Vides and Camino Minero, both drew their inspiration from the *indigenista* movement in Mexico (where both artists lived for brief periods). Some studies of Salvadoran subjects might strike a visitor as alluding to Indians, such as the dark-skinned "Sleeping Child" by Julio Hernández Alemán. But such works reflect not *indigenismo* but *costumbrismo*: a school concerned with the daily realities or customs of ordinary Salvadoran people, understood as consisting of a mestizo ethnicity rather than an Indian one.[2] Nor has the Salvadoran Indian inspired modern popular poetry. For example, the country's most famous popular poet, Roqué Dalton, made no reference to Indians even in his most richly textured descriptions of Salvadoran popular life.

So, beyond an occasional odd reference—some Nahua word forms celebrated as distinguishing Salvadoran Spanish from that of other regions,

FIGURE 3. Julio Hernández Alemán, *Sleeping Child*. (Photo by author.)

or the originally indigenous *pupusa* (a thick tortilla with relish) lauded in government publicity as El Salvador's "national dish"—indigenous peoples and cultures do not appear on the nation's public stage. Nor is their absence viewed with any apparent regret. The Salvadoran national narrative seems to suggest that El Salvador's ultimate progress as a nation is indeed due partly to its absence of the poverty-stricken (racially inferior) Indian communities that so "plague" Guatemala. Salvadorans sometimes hopefully compare the country's racially homogeneous and hard-working national population to the Japanese. If the country has floundered through decades of authoritarian rule, class strife, cold-war interventions, and civil war, at least its prospects for national unity are believed free of any racial division or divisive ethnopolitics. Being a mestizo republic is therefore not simply a fact but a point of satisfaction.

Every lens has its supporting evidence—or legends. The supposed absence of any Indian presence in El Salvador is commonly explained, by ladinos, by one pivotal belief about the country's history: that Indians assimilated and vanished as an ethnic group after 1932, in the wake of the notorious Matanza (massacre). The Matanza itself is, of course, no legend. In January of that year, a communist movement did try to mobilize the rural peasantry to revolt against the government. The indigenous communities of the western departments, a Nahuat-speaking people, did rise up in coordination with communist activists, seizing several towns. In repressing the revolt (the story proceeds), the army launched a concerted attack on anything "Indian," massacring tens of thousands and subsequently making indigenous dress and language illegal. Traumatized by some 20,000–30,000 deaths, the terrified survivors gave up their native language and dress in order to escape further repression.

Whatever the truth of this story (explored later), in the decades after the Matanza the Salvadoran government dropped racial categories from the census and eliminated racial notations from the civil registry. A great official silence fell.[3] By the 1950s, the 300,000 people identified by mid-century surveys as "Indian" were officially conflated into a generic "peasant" identity—except for those "few old people" admitted to live somewhere out in the western towns.[4]

This monumental denial held sway for the rest of the century. In the 1970s, one isolated indigenous organization emerged in the western coffee zone and clamored for recognition, but remained ineffectual and was ignored by mainstream politics. Scholarly disagreement also made little dent. Some ethnographies in the 1950s and 1970s described significant indigenous communities persisting in the southwest and northeast.[5] In 1990, Mac Chapin updated those studies in a serious and thoughtful survey focusing mostly on the western Nahua, later summarized in a 1994 article, "The 500,000 Invisible Indians of El Salvador."[6] But these studies, too, remained isolated and marginalized from mainstream knowledge and political thought. By the 1980s, the international community was becoming more politically sensitive to the presence of indigenous peoples (see chapter 10), and by the 1990s writers offering general profiles of the country often dutifully noted that some indigenous communities and even ethnopolitics persisted among the western coffee zones. Even in these sources, however, references to the indigenous presence were typically isolated in a special section on ethnicity or society, with Indians appearing nowhere else in the text.[7] Writers inspired to analyze El Salvador by its ruinous civil war of the 1980s, or its painful reconstruction in the 1990s, tended to omit race or ethnicity altogether even when they were explicitly concerned with explaining the emergence or origins of rural insurrection.[8] So as political players, as subjects of social science, and as factors in the country's political analysis, Indians have not really existed either.

But by the early 1990s, cracks in this mestizo edifice were appearing. In 1994, a much broader indigenous movement emerged, insisting on recognition. At the same juncture, indígenas suddenly reappeared on the public stage through the most unlikely vector: Salvadoran government rhetoric.

State Rhetoric: Indigeneity as National Window-Dressing

In the early 1990s, in an unprecedented shift, the Salvadoran government began officially to celebrate El Salvador's indigenous peoples as valued components of the Salvadoran nation. For one thing, Indians had suddenly become lucrative because they were attracting international tourists. For another, indigeneity was enlisted for the country's postwar project to redesign and redignify the war-battered Salvadoran national identity, in order to help the democratization process (see chapter 10). Both projects reflected domestic interests but also external ones: some international voices were calling for recognition of the indigenous presence, and the government was responding strategically.

This is our first moment to consider the role of outside authority in shaping local ethnic and racial ideas. As noted above, prior academic studies recognizing the indigenous presence had remained largely marginal to mainstream racial thought and had little political impact. Nor, by the late 1980s, had the indigenous movement gained more than the most isolated bit of political ground. But by the early 1990s, UNESCO (United Nations Economic and Social Council) and the European Union added greatly to government interest in the indigenous communities by offering special funding for indigenous cultural-revival projects. By mid-decade, the Rigoberta Menchú Foundation had also offered support for related population surveys. All this activity both reflected and fostered the Salvadoran indigenous movement; in the 1990s a larger constellation of indigenous political organizations emerged as from nowhere, arguing for recognition of their communities and gaining occasional headlines in mainstream national newspapers. Hence the shift in government rhetoric played out in the context of multiple voices—and major financial incentives (like the UNESCO grant money).

The main government voice in that shift was the National Council for Culture and the Arts (CONCULTURA), established in 1991 as a special agency of the Education Ministry and the prime agent of UNESCO's "Culture of Peace" project. Soon housed in a three-story complex of glass and steel, with a large staff equipped with an array of computers and telephones impressive by the country's standards, by the mid-1990s CONCULTURA had assumed the role of nerve center for a range of national "cultural" projects, ranging from the promotion of concerts and cultural festivals to national poster campaigns. At the community level, CONCULTURA also assumed directorship of the pre-existing *Casas de la Cultura* (cultural centers), established in towns around the country a decade earlier as community centers for cultural education activities. CONCULTURA's new doctrines about Indians therefore had nationwide impact, extending to the local level. CONCULTURA's formal mission was to promote national culture, including fresh celebration of El Salvador's pre-Columbian cultural "roots," focusing mostly on archaeological sites and precolonial art. In the mid-1990s, this revival mission spun off to unprecedented celebration of the present-day indigenous communities. In 1994, CONCULTURA established an Office of Indigenous Affairs and a Center for Cultural Revival, both of which promoted indigenous artisan crafts and, crucially, even recognized some indigenous movement organizations.[9] CONCULTURA's research center also attracted some serious social scientists, who brought new energy to exploring and mapping the long-ignored indigenous communities.

Politically, however, all these gestures remained very confined. State doctrine that the country had no Indians still guided policy in every other government ministry, such as Labor or Economy. CONCULTURA itself made no effort to consider the indigenous communities' urgent material needs, or even to admit that their shadowy presence called for a population count. The director of CONCULTURA's Indigenous Affairs office (a Salvadoran anthropologist) repeatedly urged surveys, consultation with indigenous activists, and inclusion of the indigenous communities in development programs, to no avail. (Some research funds did come from the Rigoberta Menchú Foundation, but CONCULTURA acted as a magnet and beneficiary, rather than initiator, of such efforts.) In its own discourse, CONCULTURA promoted the indigenous peoples rather as cultural relics: "The Past in the Present," as phrased in a national poster campaign, valued for the much-needed cachet it could lend to what one observer has called the *ningunidad* ("nothingness") of the ladino nation.[10]

But what were the implications of all this symbolic activity for the relics themselves: the country's indigenous peoples?

The Indigenous Peoples

As noted above, the sufficient condition for ethnopolitics is simply that local people believe ethnic identities to be politically relevant. That condition certainly holds in El Salvador. Over the past fifty years, occasional scholars have noted that a marginalized portion of El Salvador's population—locked in poverty in rural villages and urban barrios—still blamed its misery on enduring discrimination against indígenas.[11] In the 1990s, in the southwest and northeast of El Salvador, I found that significant numbers of people remained "Indians" in the sense that they consider themselves to be Indians and believed they were worse off because they were Indians. Estimates varied about how many people held this identity, ranging from 60,000 to 500,000 or about 2–10 percent of the national population, with the government offering the low estimate (see details in chapter 8). But aside from such attitudes, is there more "solid" evidence to support the idea that indigenous people do live in El Salvador . . . and deserve political rights as such?

In this study of conflicting authorities over ethnicity, it might seem impossible to assert anything objective or quantifiable about indigenous identities in El Salvador. But disagreements do not mean that no "real" ethnic experience can be established. Ethnographic surveys, scholars of the country's deeper ethnohistory, and local testimony by people considering themselves to be indígena all agree that the territory of El Salvador presently embraces two groups of indigenous peoples: the western Nahua (historically and by social scientists often called "Pipiles") and the eastern communities commonly known as Lenca. Tracing their history to the famous precolonial indigenous society of Cuscatlán, the Nahua speak a dialect of Nahuatl, the language of the Aztecs (reflecting old migrations from the north, as discussed later) and live mostly in the western coffee-producing highlands and the southwestern coastal region. It was from the Nahua communities that indigenous activists launched the 1932 uprising and suffered the subsequent brutal massacre (the infamous Matanza). The Nahua are therefore the primary focus of this book.

The Lenca communities are clustered at the opposite end of the country, in the northeast departments (primarily Morazán) centered politically on Cacaopera. (Historically, they occupied most of the eastern region; the Lempa River is traditionally understood to represent the western boundary of their historical territory. They reputedly lost most of their coastal lands only in the mid-twentieth century.[12]) Although they have been called "Lenca" for centuries, they actually speak Ulua (divided into the dialects of Potón and Cacaopera), which belongs to the Macro-Chibchan language group and is shared by some communities in Nicaragua (reflecting older migrations from the south). But because "Lenca" has held on so firmly in chronicles and general references, the name will be used here.

The Nahua and Lenca communities share long-standing connections to the Maya, and regional trade and pilgrimage has infused common cultural and religious references through the region, although traditional dress patterns and other cultural practices between the Lenca and Nahua have differed sharply. Certainly both populations share a perception of being oppressed as "Indians." Nevertheless, the Nahua and Lenca are politically divided not only by their ethnic differences and physical distance but by their respective experiences in a country long torn by conflict. The eastern Lenca communities were mostly unaffected by the 1932 Matanza, yet suffered from major land loss in the mid-twentieth century and terrible military violence during the civil war in the 1980s. The western Nahua (perhaps because their collective memory remained seared by the Matanza) were slower to mobilize in the civil war of the 1980s. (Partly for this reason, leftist militancy during the civil war ultimately had to move north and east.) Hence, although they suffered some ugly massacres in the civil war's early years, the Nahua ultimately escaped the worst of the later violence.

Outside these known indigenous areas, many more indigenous communities may persist than are known even to indigenous organizations (see map in chapter 8). Some communities are actually urban; indigenous barrios survive, for example, in the outskirts of the capital city of San Salvador. But the great majority of people who still consider themselves indígena live in rural areas, primarily in the cantones scattered through the wooded countryside around central towns. Many of these cantones are substantial communities, holding thousands of people and, in the aggregate, greatly exceeding the population of the mostly ladino towns. In heavily indigenous Nahuizalco, for example, 84 percent of the municipality's population lives in the cantones.

Through their backwoods networks of footpaths, these indigenous communities are in constant touch with each other, sustaining an ethnic world generally invisible to outsiders.[13] Hence El Salvador's indigenous landscape—unlike the distinct village which forms such an important public signal of being Indian in countries like Guatemala—is here invisible to outsiders because it is fragmented and obscured in a forested countryside.

How "Indian" are these Indians? The awkward question again raises the interminable question of definition: which practices are Indian and which are not? Ethnographic studies by outsiders are both scarce and woefully dated; the only full-scale ethnographic study of heavily indigenous Panchimalco was conducted in the early 1960s, and the last serious ethnographic survey in the western Sonsonate (Nahua) region was conducted in the early 1970s.[14] But a few illustrative practices can be cited which tend to suggest, for travelers, a "genuine" indigenous presence. First, among the western cantones, many women do wear characteristic Nahua dress, and people do regularly use words and phrases of Nahuat: the extent of these practices is described further in chapter 4. Second, the

1970s surveys of the Nahua found that they sustained a distinct cosmology, including a pantheon of good and evil spirits, the magic of the moon in planting and harvest, human transmutation into animals, distinct marriage and mortuary customs, and spiritually informed knowledge of medicinal plants.[15] In the mid-1990s, in unstructured conversations with western Nahua, I found that almost all these beliefs, especially religious ones, were still current. Another hallmark feature of the indigenous communities is the *cofradía* or Catholic religious brotherhood. Dozens or possibly hundreds of cofradías still exist, although they have suffered in recent decades from poverty and war (aggravating the illegal sale of icons, essential to cofradía rituals). Indigenous people and observers alike consider the cofradía to be the organizational linchpin of indigenous life (see also chapter 6).[16]

How important is the indigenous/ladino division in these areas? Socially, ethnic boundaries are porous; ladino/indígena intermarriage is common. Even in Los Izalcos, locally famous for its continuing ethnic tensions, the distinctions between "upper" (ladino) and "lower" (indígena) towns are eroding noticeably. But the ethnic divide remains very important in Los Izalcos as it does in Nahuizalco, Santo Domingo de Guzmán, and other towns. Sometimes the divide is bitter and open (as in Los Izalcos's interminable water disputes), but more often it is subtle, expressed as lingering ethnic prejudices, resentments, and mutual caution. Certainly regarding national politics, ethnic sentiment resonates deeply. Any electoral candidate today recognizes the need to address indigenous solidarities and perceptions when campaigning in the western Nahua zone. It is from this ethnic base—Nahuat in the west, Ulua in the east—that an eclectic group of indigenous organizations arose in the 1990s and obtained the appearance of a coherent movement.[17]

The Indigenous Movement

The oldest indigenous organization in El Salvador, and by far the best known, is ANIS (National Association of Indigenous Salvadorans). ANIS is based in San Ramón (outside the major town of Sonsonate) and is headed by self-proclaimed spiritual leader and *cacique* Adrian Esquino Lizco. Esquino Lizco claims that ANIS dates to 1954, but other former members report that it was founded in 1965 (it obtained its *personeria jurídica* or legal standing in 1980).[18] Whatever its age, it was the only indigenous organization of any national note in 1983 when a major army massacre on the ANIS cooperative land brought the organization a flood of national and international publicity. Its sudden posture of open indigenous opposition to state brutality quickly attracted widespread support from indígenas throughout the country, both Nahua and Lenca—possibly even the 40,000 followers that ANIS still claims.

As *"primer cacique espiritual de las tres naciones Mayas, Lencas y Nahuat"* ("first spiritual leader of the three nations Maya, Lenca and Nahuat," his own formula), Adrian Esquino Lizco remains the only internationally known indigenous leader in the country. He regularly attends the major international conferences, including the United Nations Working Group on Indigenous Populations in Geneva, and donations have floated in to ANIS from multiple foreign sources. Tours abroad also brought him into regular contact with North American Indian nations, who contributed small but vital funds: hence ANIS's construction of several "sweatlodges"

FIGURE 4. Adrian Esquino Lizco in front of his "sweat lodge." (From an ANIS poster.)

(of unique and distinctly un-Nahua design), each capable of holding dozens of international visitors.

But international funding and fame generated the usual internal trouble. By 1990, Esquino Lizco was under growing criticism even by other members of ANIS for his autocratic behavior ("cacique for life," in one former member's words, or "slavemaster cacique" for another). He was also charged with embezzlement: he now owns several homes and a bus fleet, which he is suspected of having purchased with international funds (international visitors to San Ramón are taken to his old mud-brick home outside of town, not his new gilt one in the center). On the cooperative, some violent internecine clashes in the early 1990s further eroded ANIS's support. Eventually, a series of defections by ANIS members generated a new phalanx of organizations. In 1994, twelve of these organizations came together to form the National Coordinating Council of Indigenous Salvadorans (CCNIS), which launched a bitter competition with ANIS for domestic and international recognition and funds (see chart 1).[19]

In 1996, the origins and composition of the CCNIS group ran the political and organizational gamut. It was not without some solid footing. Of the twelve, MAIS had a long history of solid projects and grassroots organizing. ADESCOIN was well based in the heavily Nahuat town of Santo Domingo de Guzmán, with a substantial and stable membership and several solid projects to its name. Although most of the organizations were composed of kin networks, this feature in itself is probably more legitimizing than otherwise, as kin connections remain a staple of Salvadoran indigenous communal life in every sphere.

And yet, the profiles of several CCNIS organizations were of a kind to foster considerable skepticism in observers. Two were husband-wife teams (RAIS and CONAIS), one of which was actually composed of ladinos (RAIS). The "women's organization," COMUPRIN, was set up explicitly as a fundraising magnet by Victor Ramos, president of ACOCPINSA and of CCNIS, who installed his wife as president. The only "Lenca" organization (CODECA) was originally set up as a ladino-campesino organization promoting sustainable development, and shifted to an indigenous profile only when major international funding seemed imminent. ADMIS, based in Santa Ana, went dormant because the president's husband would not let her travel. By the mid-1990s, ADTAIS (in the Nonualco region) was in disarray with the arrest and imprisonment of its president

Chart 1: Indigenous Movement in El Salvador, 1965–1996

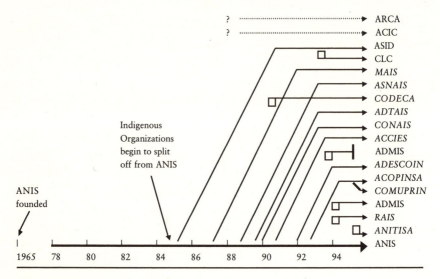

KEY: Organizations in italics: CCNIS members

    Organization closed.

    Organizations whose principal founders include former ANIS members

    Organizations with origins autonomous from ANIS

ACIC	Cojutepeque	??
ACCIES	Sonsonate	Asoc. Coordinadora de Comunidades Indígenas de El S.
ACOPINSA	San Ramón	Asoc. Coordinadora de Comunidades y Pueblos Ind. de El S.
ADMIS	Santa Ana	Asoc. Democrática de Mujeres Indígena Salvadoreña
ADESCOIN	Sto Domingo de Guzman	Asoc. de Desarrollo Comunal Indígena Nahuat
ADTAIS		Asoc. Democratica de Trabajadores Agropecuarios Ind.de El S.
ASNAIS	San Julián	Asoc. Nacional de Indígenas de El Salvador
ANIS	Sonsonate	Asoc. Nacional Indígena Salvadoreña
ANITISA	Texistepeque	Asoc. Nacional Indígena Tierra Sagrada
ARCA	Sonsonate	??
ASID	Santa Tecla	Asoc. Salvadoreña Indígena Democrática
CLC	Cacaopera	Asoc. Comunal Lenca
CODECA	Guatajiaqua	Coorda. de Comunidades para el Desarrollo de Cacahuatique
COMUPRIN	Nahuizalco	Consejo de Mujeres Principales Nahuat
CONAIS	Nahuizalco	Consejo Nacional Indio Salvadoreño
MAIS	Panchimalco	Movimiento Autóctono Indígena Salvadoreño
RAIS	San Salvador	Instituto para el Rescate Ancestrales Indígena Salvadoreña
MAIS	Ilopango	Movimiento Autóctono Indígena Salvadoreño

on charges of corruption. Even the so-called membership organizations, although they had some following, lacked any lists or other hard evidence that they had a stable membership (ACOCPINSA, ANITISA, ASNAIS, ACCIES, even MAIS and ADESCOIN).

Hence the frequent comment, by observers (both indígena and ladino) who had contact with the CCNIS group that "these people don't represent anybody."[20] The whole movement appeared to some observers in a baldly gold-digging light. Esquino Lizco's Navajo-style dances in loincloth, and his daily white "indigenous" dress (actually Filipino imports), were seen by some professionals and journalists as so blatantly false and imitative as to entirely delegitimize any ethnic claim he might make.

For their part, these indigenous organizations viewed CONCULTURA with at least equal skepticism. Internally, indigenous activists shared a candid and bitter criticism that the state's new celebration of their cultures was simply an effort to commodify and exploit indigenous culture for its own gain. Although cautiously accepted as a tactical ally, CONCULTURA was identified as a state tool created specifically to angle for international funding. The Salvadoran indigenous organizations also recognized that the state's discourse actually brought pressure on them to conform to a model of being Indian that would suit international funding parameters. Hence their central dilemma: resisting that pressure would preserve their integrity as representatives of unique cultural communities but would risk their access to international funding and public-political recognition. Yet bowing to that pressure might only further delegitimize the movement, by alienating its own constituency—the local indigenous communities—while making it seem to be mimicking models for being Indian taken from outside the country.

This dilemma brings us back to the central issue in El Salvador: that the ethnic conflict in El Salvador is really a metaconflict founded on competing definitions of "what is an Indian." How Salvadoran ladinos and indígenas understand indigeneity itself—in ethnic, racial, or class terms—is our next subject.

CHAPTER 3

"WHAT IS AN INDIAN?"

"Who are the Indians? Paradoxically, and after a half century of international indigenismo, we don't know."
—*Andres Medina, Mexican anthropologist, 1988*

"What you believe is what you see is what you are is what you do."
—*Stanley Fish, 2002*

Defining Indians

WHAT OR WHO IS AN INDIAN? THE PUZZLE IS HARDLY UNIQUE TO EL Salvador. Over the last five hundred years, state policymakers throughout the Americas have debated it, and indigenous peoples too have grappled with it. Certainly the continent's settler-colonial societies have expounded various definitions while probing what they long called the "Indian problem," because finding the right policy to address the Indian problem always required defining "Indian" in the first place.

And so intellectual debates have rolled down the centuries, and are still tangled today. Are Indians just obsolete cultural relics of an earlier age? In that case, the state should assimilate them, by proper schooling (forcibly relocating their children into Christian missionary schools if necessary), so that they cease to suffer the poverty and backwardness that Indianness generates. Or are Indians simply poor rural peasants, locked in poverty due to their own ignorance, labor exploitation, and state neglect? Then they should be "uplifted," through job training and employment which will give them better incomes and let them move to the city—again, cease to be "Indians." Or are they imbued with mystical insights and ancient environmental knowledge? Then they should be preserved like museum pieces as the potential salvation of alienated and self-destructive Western culture. Or are they simply ethnic groups, with unusually specific cultural needs, who deserve special festivals or even a special subcommittee in the state legislature? Or are they actually nations unto themselves, who require their own legislatures? Or are such claims of nationhood ridiculous, because Indians are so clearly an ignorant and self-destructive subclass, whose "wasted" land should be seized and turned over to commercial agribusinesses—in which the Indians themselves might, again, gain decent wage employment? Debates about these questions have proved tortuous and run deep in national histories. *But they have also operated in reverse.* If someone wants a particular policy, like seizing Indian land, that goal may require and inspire them to redefine Indians as merely ignorant impoverished peasants.

In Latin America, periodic debates about what it means to be an Indian have interplayed with hard material interests since the conquest. In the earliest decades of Spanish settlement, some thinkers sought to legitimize the enslavement of Indians by proposing that Indians lacked souls and could therefore be freely abused and even killed. The same arguments denied the Church's authority regarding these "beasts." Church voices, of course, argued that Indians had souls, partly to protect the indigenous people but partly also to consolidate the Church's political role in Spanish America; the famous works of Bartolomé de las Casas are much cited today as having established, for Spanish colonial policy, the indigenous peoples' essential humanity.[1] But major arguments about what is Indian were not exhausted with such sixteenth-century colonial debates. Even in the twentieth century, Mexican state builders were still arguing about whether the Indian had the mental capacity to be educated (see chapter 9).

Arguments over the last century, however, have shared a few consistent threads. No one disagrees that Indian was an identity conceived by Europeans upon their arrival in the Americas, which grouped the greatly diverse indigenous peoples of the continent into a single subordinate category. Nor that this Indian identity was the object of political, economic, juridical, and social discrimination throughout the colonial period. Nor that colonial rule left a legacy of marginalization that endured for indigenous communities living in Latin America's independent nation-states.

Beyond that very basic framework, however, people disagree about almost everything: for example, whether Indian today is an *ethnic* or *racial* identity, or simply a *class* designation or, in any case, only an anachronism, a mere vestige of colonial rule. These arguments become especially heated when they engage sensitive national issues: for example, whether the national economy has truly transcended the old colonial racism or actually still rests on some kind of racial caste system. Arguments may also implicate far broader issues, also emotionally loaded: nationalist discourses of progress, civilization, modernity, racial superiority, and of Latin America itself. It is through such discourses, fraught with values, dreams, and self-images, that people everywhere perceive and understand their world, their collective and individual identity, and their nation. Any change in definitions of Indian tugs at these visions, and so ripples far through the national fabric. It is therefore no small matter to define the Indian, but a project of power: over knowledge, over ethics, over state policy, over "who gets what"—as well as national cohesion and pride, even the state's legitimacy.

Competing definitions of Indian are therefore promoted adamantly and emotionally, by Indians and non-Indians, in speeches, print, ceremonies, and song. But as lived by people in their daily experiences, discourses of indigeneity are also quiet matters, embedding in people's perceptions from early ages. Forming an uninterrogated backdrop, such ideas come to seem natural to people, making related state policies also seem natural and right. And in such a background position, they are very difficult to challenge or change. Hence in El Salvador, ladinos understand indio or indígena in ways that make any case for their presence in the country seem strained, plain wrong, or even ridiculous. This embedded rejection is indeed the main political obstacle faced by the indigenous movement.

But just which ideas and images about Indians come to mind, when Salvadorans think of the Indians that the country supposedly lacks? Throughout the Americas, ideas about what is Indian involve perceptions, attitudes, and practices developed in that particular place over time. Each local definition seems basic and certain, the innate nature of Indianness. But not everyone knows and experiences Indianness the same way, and the

Salvadoran model is only one of many. The actually wide range of possibilities for being Indian indeed raises new questions about why that model is internally configured the way it is. Dreamed up by the settler colonial societies that encountered American native peoples in the fifteenth and sixteenth centuries, Indianness today incorporates disparate threads from the ensuing five centuries: the ruthless savage, the noble savage, the humble peon, the wise and spiritual guardians of nature . . . sometimes all of these at once. But different threads matter more in different regions. Most dramatically, Indianness varies dramatically between North American and Latin America. And we can begin to probe the politics of being Indian by reviewing some ideas that whites (or "Anglos") and ladinos have loaded onto "Indian"—ideas which Indians themselves have been forced to deflect, adapt, exploit, or continually renegotiate.

Being Indian in the United States

In the United States, many white people, or Anglos, associate the term "Indian" first with images drawn largely from movies: a line of warriors on spotted ponies lining a cliff's edge or whooping through the sagebrush after the stagecoach, fighting white settlers and cavalry.[2] Eagle-feather war bonnets, loincloths, beads. Teepees, canoes, bows and arrows, hatchets. Perhaps longhouses. Perhaps totem poles. In recent years, more sympathetic visions have altered these older ones, but are not really more complex. Old Lodgeskins or Kickingbird smoking thoughtfully in the family teepee. Or even the dark bits of limbs and shapeless bulks protruding from the snow at Wounded Knee. All these images focus closely on certain details, forget and erase many others. Taken together, they contribute to characterizing (and simplifying) "what is Indian" in ways that allow Anglos to conceptualize Indians' identity, political rights, and social needs. Anglos have even used such images to add romance and mystique to their own self-image: playing Indian by dressing up in eclectic Indian garb (war bonnet, tomahawk) is an old American practice.[3]

These stereotypes also tend to cast "Indian" as something belonging properly to the past. Yet, again, that past selectively omits far more than it includes. For example, movies have rendered the classic Indian landscape also as a certain type: buffalo moving across the prairie; sagebrush desert; the stunning rock formations of Monument Valley. White people thinking about Indians don't usually think of the pastoral villages and rich fruit orchards of the Seneca among the Finger Lakes of western New York. Or the farming communities of the Cherokee in Georgia, with their barns and fences and crops, not to mention their constitution, courts, and literature. They might think of Iroquois canoes carrying furs through the waterways of Canada (the films *Black Robe* and *Last of the Mohicans* helped with this). But they don't usually remember the elaborate fishing nets of the Hoopa arching over rivers in the Pacific Coastal Range, or the extensive maple sugar factories of the Ojibwa of northern Wisconsin, or the whaling longboats of the Makah on the Northwest coast. They might not know these heavily agricultural and fishing cultures ever existed.

Strategically brought together, these selective images of Indianness construct a version of history that has crucial political effects. For example, a narrow association of Indians with western desert landscapes and the great horse cultures of the Great Plains suggests that Indians never cultivated crops, never built towns—and so never used land in ways directly in competition with white settlers. It suggests rather that Indians merely roamed over the land, chasing game, and so were never exactly "civilized." This is a very old, and very important, political idea. In the last century, it was used by the U.S. government to justify expelling the Indian nations from their ancestral lands (since God obviously intended such rich land to be used more productively).[4] Today, it lingers as a sense of inevitability, drawing on ideas of social Darwinism: that, as savages (even if noble savages), Indians were always doomed before the dispassionate onslaught of civilization and progress. (Progress is also a discourse, replete with its own images, values, and assumptions. Among its countless political functions, it is frequently used to justify or explain the demolition of indigenous cultures.) Their dispossession and ruin might be sad, and their preconquest cultures viewed with some nostalgia for the lost life of nature. But their time has gone, superceded by white culture. And here is the punch line: because their dispossession (and pending extinction) was inevitable, whites needn't feel particularly guilty or worried about it. The United States does not really have an unhealed sore at its national core.

These images (exotic, romantic, tragic, obsolete) juxtapose uncomfortably with perceptions of Indians today. Pickup trucks instead of ponies, T-shirts and jeans instead of buckskins. Casinos, of course. For the tourist, Indianness is trinketized as turquoise jewelry or prayer circles strung with feathers and shells, suggesting something earthy, exotic, mysterious, infused with spiritual and ecological wisdom that can be purchased and experienced vicariously for a few dollars.[5] By contrast, social workers or white neighbors of some reservations might hold grimmer images: housing projects on some bleak expanse, surrounded by fragments of dead cars and appliances. Poverty, alcoholism, impressions of despair. For those sympathetic to Indians' historical experience, these same images might bring value-laden associations of government abuse and mismanagement, and perhaps FBI persecution. For others, the same images might simply reinforce the idea that Indianness is an anachronism, an outdated culture enduring a prolonged and miserable process of extinction, not precisely confined to the past, but making cultural sense only in the past, unable to handle the present, and lacking any meaningful future.

Still, in the U.S., "Indian" is not entirely confined to the past, or to poverty, or to the reservation. "Indian" can also embrace the college-educated Navajo women staffing the reservation health clinic, or the Apache lawyer in the state capital, or the Mohawk professor at the research university. In North America, "Indian" today is an identity determined by descent, and can embrace such professional roles. Nor does being Indian require that Native Americans wear typical "Indian" dress. Wearing jeans and T-shirts, or even business suits, does not ipso facto signify loss of Indianness (although some tensions can arise, and Native American professionals may add some symbol, like a bead necklace, partly to confirm their Indian identity to themselves and others). Native language is not mandatory, either. Speaking only English does not, in itself, make someone "not a real Indian." Racial type is also flexible. Even very white-looking people can get away with claiming that they are Indian—if they dress and act right. These are the more flexible social parameters of indigeneity in the U.S.

Being Indian in El Salvador

Now let us briefly consider some commonplace ideas about indigeneity in El Salvador, and in Guatemala, its close neighbor, which heavily shapes the Salvadoran model (all discussed in more detail later, especially in chapter 4). Here "Indian" still means the native peoples, and racial images are similar: the darker skin, the glossy straight black hair, the broad high cheekbones.

But for ladinos (non-Indians, a term also explored later), the term indio (Indian) or even indígena (indigenous) does *not* bring to mind native peoples fighting white settler (Spanish) invaders, as in the U.S. stereotype. Instead, it carries an explicit class association: the subordinated and usually poverty-stricken workers of the society—the maids, gardeners, road workers, coffee pickers, and other so-called black labor. The ladino's stereotypical image of what is Indian may be a loose line of men laboring with hand tools on the road's edge, or the maid in the kitchen, or whole families picking coffee on a mountainside or waiting on the road for the "chicken bus." This version of Indianness cannot include the lawyer or professor. Indians are poor by definition; professionals are therefore by definition not Indian. So heavily associated with manual labor and the misery that goes with it, "indio" is actually a derogatory term, rather like "nigger." "Stupid Indian!" or "beastly Indian!" (*¡indio bruto!*) are generic insults.

Everything else associated with Indianness is infused with this class stigma, signaling a touch of quaintness but primarily backwardness, primitivity, ignorance, misfortune, and oppression. For example, the banner emblem of Indianness in Central America is dress: especially, the women's dress, a brightly colored blouse (*huipil*) and long colorful skirt (*corte*). But no serious artistic value is attached by ladinos to these richly complex weavings; they do not adorn their homes, as do foreign tourists, with samples of such "backward" lives. A second ethnic emblem is the indigenous languages, but these are deemed to signal only the insulated and backward world of the peasantry, outmoded and inadequate to modern needs, lacking any literary capacity or worth.

A third emblem is the indigenous landscape: classically, the "Indian village," the cluster of one-story houses of mud brick, adobe, sod, or sticks in the highlands or along the Atlantic Coast, quaint but poor, a vestige of an older but also more primitive social order. As in North America, this landscape reinforces ideas of Indian culture and place in the larger social order, but here as agriculturalists and peasants, framed within the closed corporate communities.[6] Regarding such villages, "Indian" may signify "culture" in the folk sense of drum and flute, dance or religious procession.[7] But it also signifies *lack* of culture in what is deemed a higher sense: painting, sculpture, philosophy, and literature in the European tradition.[8] Some quaint charm but no serious value, mystery, or wisdom is believed to dwell in Indian folk culture. Rather, the dress, languages, and villages are seen as manifestations of the closed and marginal worldview of the peasantry, associated with ignorance, illiteracy, and superstition. To be Indian is to have these traits.

In fact, so insulting is the word Indian that the polite term among ladinos—and the term adopted by Indian movements throughout Latin America—is "indigenous," indígena in Spanish. Politically, this is not simply a change of term. Like the deliberate shift in U.S. political language from "colored" to "negro" to "black" to "African American," the shift from "Indian" to "indigenous" reconfigures its focus: emphasizing the peoples' original habitation in the territory, their prior and unjustly extinguished sovereignty, and therefore their right to self-determination. Hence the term "pueblos indígenas" (indigenous peoples) links Indianness to strategies of nationalist political mobilization and territorial claims. By contrast, for most ladinos, "indígena" invokes none of these dimensions. It is simply a polite term for indio: still associated with poverty, manual labor, illiteracy, and an entrenched underclass. In this view, the Mayan lawyer or professor in Guatemala City still has great trouble gaining ladino acceptance that she is actually indígena, or that she can be a legitimate spokesperson for indígenas.

Native peoples, of course, have always had their own discourses of Indianness (and of "whiteness" and "ladino-ness"), which have developed in reaction but also opposition to white or ladino discourses. But sorting out how to select among multiple threads of being Indian becomes a complicated and deeply personal project for Indian individuals because it is so loaded politically. Each person's choices about dress, hair, ornaments, spiritual practice, home, profession, and myriad other behaviors are informed by how those choices function socially as a kind of graphic *text*—that is, visual signals, seen and read by others. The smallest practice can indicate to a community the native person's particular relation to her people's history, to its way of life, to its land, to clan or tribe—and to non-Indians. But such vital meanings have not evolved autonomously; they are informed by centuries of tense and violent interactions with Europeans. For example, pressure from ladino or white society for indigenous people to give up their native dress or long hair—on the grounds that such practices are backward—may heavily feed the political importance, within the indigenous community, of continuing to wear both.

So being Indian involves a complicated range of ideas, images, and choices, each with different payoffs. Tourists see Indians within their own webs of meaning—mysterious, exotic, wise, ancient, close to the land, close to nature—and playing into those expectations brings Indians vital infusions of money. Human rights activists cast Indians as unfairly abused by federal mismanagement, or as outright targets of state violence, to be protected and helped to gain political voice—and to be brought vital resources: funding, networking, and publicity. Social scientists may endorse arguments that indígenas are actually indigenous *nations* with legitimate claims to sovereignty in their ancestral territories—and bring the authority of their disciplines to support indigenous movements in reclaiming autonomy within those territories. With so many ideas at work, "Indian" may mean different things not only to different people, but to the same person depending on whether she is dealing with indigeneity in the college classroom, the human rights office, the street, the coffee plantation, the reservation, or the tourist shop.[9]

But the terms Indian and indígena are composed not just of present-day images and perceptions. They carry unseen threads of older ideas, reflecting their social meanings and debate by scholars and policymakers through the centuries. And one such thread—indeed, the very woof of the fabric—is race. This claim might seem too broad. In North America, Indian is commonly understood as a racial identity (partly because tribal membership still depends legally on various "blood" percentages). But in Latin America, any argument that indígena is a racial identity typically encounters brisk rejection; it is instead commonly considered an ethnic identity, and has been treated in much social science simply as a variation on the central matter of class (typically, Indians vanish into "peasants").[10] But in the recent past, indígena was openly understood in Latin America too as a racial identity; it was redefined as ethnic only recently. Such an ethnicization of race—redefinition of racial identities as ethnic ones—has indeed been a common way for states throughout the world to deny that any racial discrimination endures. We can therefore learn much about Indianness—and about Salvadoran indigeneity—by exploring such claims more closely.

Indian as a Racial Identity

To explore the racial dimension of being Indian, we must define yet another concept: what is a race, and how are racial and ethnic identities distinguished from each other? Race is a much-debated concept, and a vast literature exists on it, but a simple definition can serve us here: a race is an intergenerational group identity signaled by readily visible somatic features (like skin color, eye and nose shape, hair texture, and so forth), associated with a geographic region of origin and often understood to suggest essential mental or physical characteristics. Of course, races are socially constructed categories. We are not born knowing such categories; we learn from our families and peers that certain markers, like eye shape or skin color, signify a particular group, like "Asian" and "black." But once these ideas are internalized, races seem real to most people, partly because their signals are physical and therefore seem objective.

Races also seem real because the geographic regions with which they are associated seem physical and therefore real. Actually, if we look at them closely, units like "Europe" or "Africa" are also imagined in that they have uncertain boundaries or unexpected internal diversity. But zones like Europe or Africa are nevertheless understood to have provided racial groups (whites or blacks) with certain environmental conditions and a generally common history. In racist thought, this collective experience is believed to imbue each race with essential traits or a typical psychology (like intelligence or stupidity, laziness or industry, aggression or passivity, and so forth). In practice, racism springs from the idea that markers like skin color are reliable signals of such traits, and that individuals can therefore legitimately be treated according to them. Racial hierarchies, like slavery or caste systems, are sustained and rationalized on the basis of such ideas. Races are indeed imagined partly to generate and legitimize such hierarchies.[11]

Racial identities work in complicated ways to define people. For one thing, a racial identity tends to obscure ethnic identities within the racial category, effectively undefining people as distinct ethnic groups (as, for example, "black" in North America has overridden and largely erased identities like "Yoruba" and "Ibo").[12] As mentioned earlier, the identity Indian homogenized the culturally diverse peoples of the Americas into one overarching racial identity based solely on their continental origin. For another thing, racial thinking can also persist even when strict genetic determinism is set aside. For example, people who disparage Indians may well deny (when challenged) that some genetic attribute determines the negative qualities they associate with Indian, like poverty and filth. Yet people still attribute "Indian" with essential qualities in fully racialist ways: for instance, Indians are regularly deemed noble or backward, pitiable or despised, mystical and/or tragic, postcolonial subjects, or the salvation of humanity.[13] All these ascriptions associate social qualities (culture, poverty, illiteracy, marginality, environmental wisdom, spiritual superiority) with an identity rooted in ideas of biological descent.[14]

Ethnic identities, by contrast, are believed to involve only behavior. In this view, if a newborn baby is taken out of one ethnic group and put into another, she will grow up with the second group's identity. Still, many ethnic identities also have physical markers, which can make such transformations difficult. For example, in Central America, someone with the tall stature, fair skin, light blonde hair, and long face associated with the Swedes would find it effectively impossible to be accepted socially as Indian even if born and raised among Indians. In this book, the term "ethnoracial" will signal this interplay.

So is Indian a racial or an ethnic category? Latin American arguments that Indian is not a racial identity have been important to denying that indigenous peoples are targets of racial discrimination—and to arguing that they are well incorporated into their respective nation-states. Those arguments fall into several categories. Michael Omi and Howard Winant have offered a trenchant critique of how the racial experience of blacks in the United States is sometimes reinterpreted in nationalist, ethnic, or class-based paradigms in ways that miss essential characteristics of racial thought.[15] Similarly, common arguments that "Indian" is not a racial identity build on three paradigms all of which support the assertion that indígenas no longer exist within El Salvador's boundaries:[16]

(1) the *"racial fusion" paradigm*: that racial intermixture throughout the continent has advanced so far that formerly distinct racial groups have melted together into one mixed (mestizo) identity, and the old distinct racial categories have vanished;

(2) the *class paradigm*: that "Indian" is essentially a class designation, identified with subsistence agriculture, rural poverty, and low-end urban service jobs (like maids);

(3) the *ethnicity paradigm*: that "Indian" is defined by various customs, which may be quaint or charming but are largely backward and outmoded, are certainly politically insubstantial, and are largely disappearing.

The Racial Fusion Paradigm

The racial fusion argument denies that Indian is a racial category by arguing that any racial division in Latin America has been eliminated, over the centuries, through interbreeding. As a result, no one in Latin America supposedly cares about race anymore because distinct races no longer exist. This claim is, of course, well justified—in a sense. In much of Latin America, people have mingled into a broad mestizo (mixed race) spectrum that lacks precise internal boundaries. Indian-Spanish mixture lies at the core of the mestizo ideologically, but the actual contribution includes all of Latin America's immigrants: diverse European ethnic groups, Africans, Greeks, Arabs, Jews, Chinese, and so forth. Reflecting this blend, a wide range of skin tones and facial features marks the great middle stratum of Latin American societies, offering no particular obstacle to marriage, friendships, or other social relations. Within this stratum, at least, the mixed-race claim does seem generally to hold; no one perceives racial differences or looks for them. In Spanish, this racial mixture is termed mestizaje (mes-tee-*sah*-heh).

But it is one thing to assert a universal mestizaje and quite another to say that physical features associated with the old racial categories have no social weight. For one thing, a certain physical type is powerfully associated with Indianness: shorter stature, darker skin, broad cheekbones, black glossy hair. Although Indian and mestizo appearances may blur together, the Indian stereotype has boundaries, excluding (as an extreme example) the Nordic features mentioned above. For another thing, biases tracing to the old racial types still infuse the mestizo category: even within the mestizo spectrum, Latin American societies are quite sensitive to skin color, sustaining a wide variety of terms for different shades, formalized in such official venues as passports. (In El Salvador, official terms include, in increasing order of darkness, *blanco*, *trigueño*, *moreno claro*, *moreno oscuro*, and *negro*).[17] The darker end of the color spectrum slips out of mestizo into Indian (in El Salvador, blacks are presumed not to exist at all: see chapter 9). A dark-purplish cast to a baby's skin, particularly around the buttocks (*el rabo morado*), marks her definitively as Indian. Certainly hair and stature are also very important: straight, black, glossy hair and short build are associated with indios. These somatic features comprise the racial component of being Indian, and their social stigma cannot be escaped simply through ethnic assimilation (ladinization).

All these distinctions carry heavy social and normative weight. Dark skin is considered to be intrinsically uglier than light skin, and skin color is often a consideration in marriage. Salvadoran media images of ideal female beauty—as portrayed in television commercials or calendar posters—are usually blonde, always fair of skin, and generally Western European of feature. That these preferences are not seen as racial, but merely as aesthetic, would only reinforce their intrinsically racist character to people whose racial sensibilities were trained in North America. Moreover, these values still include echoes of earlier belief that "whitening" the nation "improves" it. Darkness still carries an aura of inferiority and degeneration.

Further evidence of a racial order is that very short, dark-skinned, Indian-looking people are almost never seen—except as servants—in elite clubs, theatres, wealthy private homes, or the higher ranks of political power. The exceptional Indian-looking individual who does gain access to elite social levels—and to whom mestizos may point to show the absence of racial barriers—will be a target for private mestizo mockery. (Take, for example, the poignant situation of a dark, short, Indian-looking young woman working in San Salvador as a trainer in an elite spa. Despite her conformity with the mestizo female standard—sophisticated clothing, makeup—she was socially ignored by the female clientele and, behind her back, called by patrons and other employees "la pipil."[18]) The powerful racial order is also indicated in rampant prejudice against blacks (*negros* or *africanos*).[19] In earlier periods, the Chinese (*chinos*, *asiatecos*, sometimes *amarillos*—yellows—in census reports) were also targeted, sometimes violently—a history reviewed in chapter 9.

Finally, and hardly of least importance, indigenous people perceive many mestizos in equally essentializing and racial terms, especially those of more European phenotype who are identified with Europe, Spain, and the dominant society, and therefore as living representatives of ongoing conquest and dispossession.[20] Each identity—Indian (or indígena) and mestizo (or ladino)—therefore engages the other in classically racial dynamics of subordination, public and hidden transcripts, mutual disdain and suspicion, and sometimes open contest.

So indigeneity today still carries strong racial dimensions. But if race and class always interplay, as they seem to do, perhaps the real problem is class. If so, should indigenous peoples simply fight for better schooling and job opportunities, and governments alleviate indigenous poverty and marginalization simply through antipoverty programs and democratization?

The Class Paradigm

In the class paradigm, indigenous peoples persist only because they have been so marginalized, economically and politically. In this view, indigenous cultures collapsed and vanished completely at the time of the conquest. Today's indigenous peoples are new ethnic formations resulting from colonial discourse: centuries of deliberate political exclusion, economic marginalization, protections, isolation, and class oppression. In this model, they are rightly conflated under that great amorphous label that too many politicians and scholars slap on anyone in the countryside: "peasants" (campesinos in Spanish). Peasants may sometimes also be Indians, but in mainstream social science literature, Indian ethnicity is incidental to being a peasant. Indianness is sometimes recognized as steering a behavior worth noting (like additional motives to participate in a leftist uprising), but otherwise is not considered important and is often not mentioned at all.[21]

Certainly the class paradigm accurately identifies a central element of the Latin American racial system—almost by definition. Throughout Latin America, indigeneity is indeed associated (by indigenous peoples and ladinos alike) with images of the rural poor, the illiterate manual laborer, the subsistence farmer. Arduous manual labor and service jobs (maids, trash collectors, road workers) is called "black" or "Indian" labor, whatever the ethnoracial identity of the person who actually performs such jobs. Indio in Spanish indeed takes much of its pejorative flavor from this class-based association. Throughout Central America, the ladino's classic image of the Indian is the downtrodden laborer by the roadside or the market woman in her typical dress, perhaps grappling with a heavy basket of produce. Both images evoke illiteracy, ignorance, and backwardness, but primarily poverty.

In El Salvador, the class paradigm is further reinforced by the white-skinned poor population in the northern department of Chalatenango. In the late eighteenth century, European immigrants were brought in to fill the labor shortage resulting from the decimation of the indigenous communities (by indigo production). Locally, this white population today still performs all the manual, dirty jobs that elsewhere are performed by Indians. They are casually referred to as indios, and their work understood as Indian jobs. They have even picked up many Nahuat words and customs, such that they have been called *indios cheles* ("honky Indians").[22]

Perhaps most significantly, a class definition of indigeneity appears, on first brush, to be fairly total among the indigenous population as well. For example, when in conversation with western Nahua I asked them "what does it mean to be Indian?" [*qué significa ser índio?*], they would immediately answer "poor" [*pobre*]. In the mid-1990s, CCNIS representatives (see chapter 2) were indeed clarifying with each other that indígenas are different from campesinos in being *more* poor than campesinos, because campesinos have campo (land) and indígenas do not.[23] This argument might be viewed as an effort to imagine and instill ethnic consciousness in a constituency where ethnic identity is weak. But outside the CCNIS organizations I found similar views. The fundamental and enduring split in the society, from the perspective of those indígenas with whom I spoke, is between the ladinos who have land, businesses, and especially power, and the poor indígenas who have nothing. "Having nothing" also has a certain look to it; indígenas live in stick or mud-thatch houses, grow corn if they have a bit of land, work as day laborers if they don't. There is a quasi-primordial quality perceived in this condition: Indians are and always have been poor, and ladinos are and always have been rich.[24]

But any assumption that these ideas signify a purely, or even primarily, class definition of indígena among the Nahua would be misplaced. When, in dozens of exchanges, I asked, "How do you know who is Indian?" the answer was never "poor." Answers focused immediately on physical appearance, names, and accent. Like native Americans in the U.S. and Canada, the Nahua perceive "Indian" and "non-Indian" according to physical and behavioral signals that far transcend class—and are not always easy to articulate (especially to outsiders), as illustrated in the following exchange with a gathering of about ten Nahua in a Nahuizalco *cantón*:

Q. What does it mean to be Indian?
A. [in chorus] Poor.
Q. So Indians are poor? To be Indian is to be poor?
A. Yes, we are always poor. We have nothing.
Q. Rich people are not Indians?
A. No, never.

Q. But what if some Indian becomes rich? What if some Indian makes a lot of money, like Adrian [Esquino Lizco]? Would he stop being Indian?

A. [bemused smiles] No, he would still be Indian.

Q. So what would make that person Indian?

A. [fractional pause] He would have Indian blood [*sangre*].

Q. Indian blood?

A. Yes, his blood would still be Indian. He would be Indian.

Q. But many people around here are mixed, no? They have some Indian blood, and some ladino blood.

A. [nods] Yes, that's true.

Q. But some are known as Indians, and some are known as ladinos. What makes a person Indian?

A. Well, their customs.

Q. What customs?

A. We have our language, and our dress . . .

Q. But you tell me that you don't speak your language any more, and very few of you wear typical dress.

A. This is true.[25]

Q. So what customs are important?

A. The way we live. Our way of life [*forma de ser*].

Q. What is special about the Indian way of life? Many people here share the same customs. What makes the Indian way of life different?

A. [groping for words] Well, it is in the blood.

Q. [taking a new tack] Can you tell who is Indian and who isn't?

A. Yes, of course.

Q. How do you know? If you are working with a group of people on the road, or on a plantation, with people you've never seen before, do you know who is Indian and who isn't, without asking?

A. [general nods] Oh yes, we know. We know by their physical features. And their names. And the way they talk. One can tell. It is easy.[26]

The above exchange clearly suffered from the Nahuas' difficulties in describing subtle dimensions of identity to a North American outsider.

Nevertheless, it is revealing. Whatever their difficulty in pinning it down, these people understand indigeneity as a clear and meaningful identity, readily signaled by physical features and accent. Especially, "blood" signifies more than literal descent, referring to some essential quality, even a spiritual one. In this view, being Indian certainly entails living out a complex of racial, ethnic, and class formations that are historically associated with Indian. But no single class or cultural element by itself was, for this group, interchangeable with Indian. Rather, race and class in this setting are co-constituted, for both Indian and ladino. The pattern is hardly unfamiliar. As Franz Fanon famously wrote of settlers, in his *The Wretched of the Earth*, "you are rich because you are white, you are white because you are rich."

Hence being Indian means being poor, not because the two concepts are the same, but because ladino society has dictated ("meant") that Indians are poor, and this fate is inescapable unless a person either rebels or assimilates. (Not surprisingly, no interest in rebellion was expressed to me, the white gringa visitor. Rather, in my conversations with rural elderly individuals as well as activists, I was several times treated to lengthy explanations that ladinos would eventually receive God's justice.)

The Ethnicity Paradigm

The argument that Indian is actually an ethnic (cultural, behavioral) category is the most common reason given that it is not a racial one (and that Indians are not objects of racism).[27] The argument has several things going for it. First, in actual social interaction, Indians are not normally defined solely on the basis of physical signals (like skin and hair) but behavioral ones, like dress. Physical differences between Indians and non-Indians, particularly in rural areas, are indeed often insignificant if noticeable at all. Indians can become ladino simply by adopting the cultural norms of the ladino.[28] Nor is the "ladinized" individual then stuck socially in some intermediate racial slot, like *mulato*. Rather, she has entered the great category of mestizo, widely understood as Latin America's biological norm and even its ideological one. Hence indigenous peoples do have what Carl Degler famously called an "escape hatch," one not truly available to blacks, either in North or Latin America.[29]

Moreover, the argument that Indian is an ethnic identity reflects popular awareness that the old racial categories (and ideologies) are specious.

It therefore enjoys a certain moral authority, as an enlightened doctrine. Hence the high-minded affirmation (which has the added authority of being scientifically correct) that no Salvadoran is of pure race, that all are mixed, and therefore that no one is really Indian in any racial sense. This argument casts any counter-argument—that racial divisions do exist—as reviving wrong-headed beliefs in racial division and therefore actually racist.

And yet, for all its strengths, the ethnicity paradigm has several hidden ambiguities. Most obviously, it seriously underrates the continued importance of physical (racial) markers, as discussed above. But also, ethnic is politically loaded in ways not admitted. First, the term "ethnic group" seems to grant indigenous peoples at least innocuous political standing as elements within an ethnically diverse national community. Yet as ladinos are not usually called an ethnic group, the term casts indigenous people—*las etnias*—as ethnically exceptional, not the norm.

Second, the term ethnic group secures indigenous peoples ideologically within the nation as minorities, distinguished only by minor cultural variations. Thus it strategically detaches indigeneity from other terms—such as "people" and "nation"—which would suggest that indigenous peoples are not absorbed by the nation, and that they might still have some claim to autonomy or even sovereignty within their ancestral territories. For this reason, many indigenous movements today, seeking autonomy within those territories, find "ethnic group" insulting and politically dangerous. They argue that the term is properly applied only to those groups, mostly of European or Mediterranean origin, whose integration into Latin America's dominant ladino sector has been fairly seamless, or at least successful in class terms: Germans, Arabs, Jews, and so forth.[30] As the activist saying goes, "We are not 'ethnic groups.' Ethnic groups have restaurants!"[31]

The Strategic Interplay: Political Decapitation

The racial fusion, class, and ethnic paradigms of indigeneity all claim to be enlightened visions, liberating to indigenous people. And yet they strategically interplay to generate one crippling political effect: they exclude any educated professional from the identity of Indian. The racial fusion paradigm maintains that indigenous peoples no longer exist as distinct racial groups or, by extension, as conquered-national groups. The ethnicity paradigm associates Indian with certain behaviors. The class paradigm affirms that those behaviors are actually associated only with poverty and oppression: the village ("closed corporate community") of semi-proletariat laborers; languages associated with illiteracy in Spanish; dress that signals insulation from modernity; and so forth. Combined, these ideas mean that being Indian is to behave that way. The behaviors associated with upward mobility—say, working in an office, wearing European dress, writing books—signify not merely class change but ethnic change. That is, an individual who ascends the social ladder, shifts to working in city offices, and perhaps wears ladino clothing, ceases, by definition, to be Indian.

This assumption politically decapitates the indigenous community in a uniquely disabling way. Other racial groups, or even a peasant population, can develop a "native son" leadership because individual members can, through grit and/or luck, obtain the higher education vital to gaining meaningful political voice and influence at elite levels. In such a position, they can act as more effective representatives for their groups in the halls of state power. But Indians are prohibited from developing such an educated leadership because an educated Indian is no longer "Indian" and is not recognized as a legitimate spokesperson. This conflation of Indian with ignorance and illiteracy is, obviously, a powerful way to deny Indians access to meaningful policymaking levels. Not incidentally, that limitation secures Indian communities as a vulnerable work force.[32]

All three paradigms are therefore under direct attack by indigenous activists throughout Latin America. Especially in countries with significant indigenous elites—Mexico, Guatemala, Chile, Bolivia, Peru, Ecuador— indigenous intellectual activists are arguing for new understandings of "*lo Aymara*" or "*lo Quechua*" that will permit "indigenous" to embrace identities deriving from higher education and professional rank, to permit effective political activism at the national level. Prominent among these activists is a growing cadre of Mayan intellectuals, who are arguing for a complete reconception of *lo Maya*—"what is Maya." These heated debates about indigeneity in Guatemala are central to similar debates in El Salvador, and so are our subjects in the next chapter.

CHAPTER 4

IN THE SHADOW OF THE MAYA

"I am always sorry when any language is lost, because languages are the pedigree of nations."
—*Samuel Johnson*

" . . . the Indians [of San Salvador] have, with very few exceptions, not only entirely abandoned their heathen customs, but even forgotten the language of their forefathers."
—*Carl Scherzer, German traveler, 1854*

" . . . the Mayan people exists because it has and speaks its own languages."
—*Demetrio Cojtí Cuxil, Mayan intellectual, 1991*

ONE OF THE MOST FREQUENT REFERENCES I HEARD IN MY TRAVELS AND interviews about Salvadoran Indians was their comparison to the Maya in neighboring Guatemala. Even in the last stages of completing this book, the U.S. State Department desk officer for El Salvador assured me that Indians don't exist in El Salvador, for she had not seen any—"like those in Guatemala, with their dress and all." As the most populous and ethnically colorful indigenous people in the region, the Maya provide a regional model for being Indian that has fostered (among ladinos and foreign visitors alike) an intuitive understanding that Indians are indeed people distinguished by their characteristic dress and language. This model sweepingly defines most Salvadoran indígenas out of the Indian category. My taxi driver from chapter 1 also supplied the standard formula: in Guatemala one will see Indians; such Indians do not exist here.

In many ways, the two populations do indeed manifest to observers very differently and their comparison might therefore seem unwarranted. Officially, Guatemala has an indigenous population of some four million (about 42 percent of the entire population), but most observers consider this figure grossly low, and throughout the vast mountainous central region, the Mayan population is densely concentrated at around 90–98 percent.[1] By contrast, the highest reasonable estimates of El Salvador's indigenous population suggest at most 500,000 people, or 10 percent of the national population, and most estimates are much lower, between 2 and 5 percent. Many Guatemalan Maya live in clearly recognized communities, their towns and markets offering distinctly "Indian" landscapes; in El Salvador, the indigenous communities are fragmented and often invisible, scattered through wooded countryside dominated by ladino towns. The Guatemalan Mayan peoples are popularly distinguished by their distinctive brilliant dress and their Mayan languages; the Salvadoran Nahua and Lenca are believed to lack both. And politically, the Guatemalan Maya are sufficiently well organized to have leveraged—at least on paper—state recognition as a distinct cultural presence in the country, warranting extensive group rights. The Salvadoran indigenous peoples are far from gaining such political standing, and most doubt that they ever will.

But it is actually through their high visibility that the Maya matter so much to the Salvadoran ethnopolitics. Not only do they establish a regional model for being indigenous, they have heavily influenced the Salvadoran indigenous movement itself. Admiring the (relative) Mayan successes in gaining national and international recognition, the Salvadoran organizations have taken on many of the Maya movement's trappings. Some Nahua organizations actually define themselves as "Maya" (sometimes, "Maya-Nahuat," a formula startling to linguists and ethnohistorians; comparable to, say, "Teutonic Spanish"). At the same time, being ethnically eclipsed by the Maya, some Salvadoran indigenous activists grapple with their own sense of lacking the proper trappings of indigeneity and have tried to "revive" their ethnicity in material terms according to the Maya model, in order to gain more credibility: for example, holding classes to revive languages and weaving skills. Yet these projects are strained in the Salvadoran context, and have led to political trouble—as we will see in chapter 10.

By contrast, for many Salvadoran ladinos, the millions of Guatemalan Maya provide a negative model of a "backward" Indian population that has "burdened" Guatemalan national development for almost two centuries. Salvadoran nationalist discourse has therefore long made a point of distinguishing El Salvador from Guatemala in this respect, arguing that El Salvador is better positioned to develop due to its complete mestizaje and lack of Indians. Hence the Maya presence adds to Salvadoran ladino rejectionism toward any Salvadoran indigenous ethnic revival.

And yet, despite the shadow cast by the Maya over Salvadoran ethnopolitics, the discourse of being Maya *within* Guatemala is actually a battlefield of disagreement and competition. Contrary to stereotype, or even claims by sympathetic allies, both dress and language use are inconsistent even within the Mayan communities, and hot arguments surround their meaning for indigeneity. This turmoil over definitions suggests that the Mayan model is a more slippery basis for assessing indigeneity in El Salvador than it might appear. Its actual fluidity indeed sheds light on being Indian in El Salvador, and a quick comparison will be illuminating.[2]

The "Mayan People"

In the past fifteen years, "Mayan" politics has burst into the Guatemalan national stage with unheard-of public force. In the 1980s, new efforts to formalize Mayan languages catalyzed a broad wave of political mobilization. The award to Rigoberta Menchú of the 1993 Nobel Peace Prize reflected the early effectiveness of this movement in gaining international allies. By 1995 (when the Salvadoran movement was also rapidly expanding), six umbrella Mayan organizations were active in national politics, embracing some fifty-eight organizations, and a myriad of Mayan popular organizations were addressing children's needs, women's issues, youth activities, health and literacy concerns. Although periodically thrown into disarray and reconfiguration by changing political times (as all such efforts are), in the aggregate the Mayan "movement" continues to foster an expanding Mayan literature and linguistics, inspire new social and religious activism, and incrementally gain greater accommodation by the state and better access to national politics.[3]

In league with international pressure, all this domestic activity has forced unprecedented compromise from a Guatemalan government internationally infamous for its genocidal policies toward the indigenous peoples. Guatemala's new 1995 constitution granted explicit protections and rights to indigenous communities and culture. The 1995 Peace Accord on Indigenous Rights, signed by the Guatemalan legislature, created a formal framework for Mayan ethnic rights and formally recast Guatemala as a multinational state.[4] Later difficulties in ratifying these reforms prolonged the tortuous process of postwar ethnic renegotiations about how to run the country, and at this writing the basic racial division in Guatemala remains entrenched.[5] But for all its limitations and obstacles (government lip service, reactionary right-wing rejection, continuing violence), the Mayan movement has succeeded in reconfiguring public debate in Guatemala and has driven a sturdy wedge into national party politics.

What newcomers to the region may not realize, however, is that "Maya" is actually a very new label in this context. Until the 1990s, the term Maya was normally applied only to the pre-Columbian indigenous civilization: the panoply of lowland city-states that, between the seventh and twelfth centuries CE, generated such architectural wonders as Tikal in northern Guatemala and Copán in western Honduras. The *Ruta Maya* (Mayan route, now a tourist route) is still understood as the pattern of trade developed by this civilization throughout the Yucatán, parts of the Guatemalan highlands, and Belize. The great Mayan city-states had declined sharply and were long abandoned by the time of Spanish invasion, for reasons still debated among archaeologists and anthropologists. Accordingly, until recent years an acceptable historical question was "where did the Maya go?"

The question has become an embarrassing anachronism in light of recent Mayan ethnic thought and scholarship: the Maya live on, particularly in the Guatemalan and Mexican highlands. In the fifteenth century, the Spanish indeed found in the highlands a vibrant society of towns and ethnically distinct peoples speaking Mayan languages, whose longstanding rivalries served Spanish conquest (who conquered or struck tactical alliances with them, in turns). Ultimately, of course, all these Mayan peoples were reduced to a subordinate vassal caste (although pockets endured of indigenous political cohesion and culture, including reduced but still important indigenous aristocracies).[6] But the Mayan peoples maintain many traceable connections to that earlier era, in their cosmology, oral traditions, customs, and especially their languages. The Mayan highland peoples have been more divided than unified by their twenty-one languages, but those languages do all trace to an early Mayan form. That common linguistic heritage has recently been reimagined to support activists' arguments that all the Mayan-speaking peoples (*mayahablantes*) comprise a single Mayan People (*Pueblo Maya*, often capitalized by Mayan activists, contrary to customary usage in Spanish). In emphasizing the term Maya, the indigenous movement also deliberately re-appropriates for "indígena" the wealth of preconquest Mayan high art and architecture, helping Mayan intellectuals to insist that the identity "indígena" can legitimately include an educated and professional elite (tackling the "decapitation" problem described in chapter 3).

The Mayan People movement is indeed a *nationalist* discourse, grouping various Mayan ethnic groups under one overarching identity that claims group rights under the United Nations provision that "nations and peoples have the right to self-determination." Hence the Maya movement has taken on the trappings that political scientists have identified for nationalism: innovative print media, an intellectual community, a retooled mythohistory, public celebrations of emblematic practices such as dress, and so forth.[7] In this maneuver, the Maya are hardly unique: as Anthony Smith has observed, reconstructing multiple ethnic groups as a single people is a common maneuver to gain greater political leverage at the state level.[8] Unsurprisingly, however, the strategy has triggered a nationalist backlash among some ladino nationalist intellectuals, who see the Mayan claim to peoplehood as striking at the very heart of Guatemalan nationalism.[9]

Yet ladino arguments go beyond mere racial rejection, because definitions of the term Maya—and of indigeneity itself—are honestly understood and argued very differently by various players in Guatemalan politics. Two areas of major disagreement (not to exclude others) are the ethnic meanings of dress and language, locally understood as the banner emblems of indigenous identity. Both debates have major impact on the Salvadoran ethnic arena and their complexities are worth quick review.

Dress Among the Maya

No emblem of Latin American indigenous ethnic identity strikes the outside observer more forcefully than the brilliantly colored—and, to many eyes, very beautiful—embroidered Mayan clothing, or *traje típico* (literally, "typical suit," often shortened in conversation and academic writings to "traje"). Distinct indigenous men's dress has largely disappeared, although it remains vibrant in the area of Lake Atitlán and in more remote highland communities such as Todos Santos Cuchumatán. Mayan women throughout Guatemala, however, continue to wear traje as their preeminent ethnic signal: a long and often richly-colored corte (skirt), wrapped around or gathered at the waist and secured with yards of embroidered cloth belt, and a huipil, or embroidered pull-over blouse.[10] Given the rich colors and distinctive design of her clothes, the Mayan woman on the road or in the street is instantly recognizable as such. Moreover, designs are specific to the various Mayan peoples and towns: those in the know can, upon seeing the details of a woman's huipil, often identify not only her town but sometimes even her neighborhood of origin. But the ideas that people bring to traje differ greatly, in two general ways: first, what traje actually means for Mayan ethnic identity; and second, how consistently traje is actually used.

On its face, traje is a straightforward ethnic text. The precise colors and patterns of the huipil are "read" by other Mayans to indicate the wearer's ethnic group, her village origin, and perhaps her clan affiliations. Requiring months to weave, a fully embroidered huipil therefore serves as a woman's deeply personal expression of her identity. These meanings, especially the spiritual ones, may not be perceived by ethnic outsiders at all:

> Given the meaningfulness of these handmade garments and the highland Indian women's personal involvement with them, it is not surprising that they often saw their own garments as extensions of themselves. . . . It was on cloth destined to become a huipil that weavers generally did their most inspired and involved work, and once they had constructed and worn the garment, it embodied their very essence . . . women sometimes wore their huipiles inside out when they were in public spaces so that their true identity would not be seen and they might be protected from negative forces. At the end of their lives, they were typically buried in their best huipiles; their spirit went with them to the grave.[11]

This intimate spiritual connection of women's identity with traje has diluted somewhat in recent years. More Mayan women now purchase or commission their huipiles, and the tourist market has both increased production and softened ethnic and village boundaries for particular designs. By 2003, machine-made garments were increasingly common. And yet, traje continues to convey very strong associations of a Mayan worldview. A woman's personal use of traje is therefore bound up with her psychological attachment and political loyalty to her community. No wonder, then, that many Mayan women accustomed to wearing traje feel extremely uncomfortable when forced to change into ladino dress, and the right to wear it (in, say, schools) was therefore an important provision in the Peace Accord on Indigenous Identity and Rights (1994).

For Guatemalan ladinos, traje also remains a definitive signal of Indianness. The formula is usually literal: to wear traje is to be Indian; to be Indian is to wear traje. A woman wearing ladino clothing is considered, by definition, to have assimilated or be assimilating. Furthermore, the Guatemalan ladino's association with traje has been generally negative. It is considered primitive, not truly artistic, marking a despised, ignorant, rural Other. To the limited extent that traje does convey to ladinos some notion of its internal complexity, it has long connoted only an "uncivilized" culture: quaint but backward, riddled with superstition, resistant to progress.

Ladino discrimination against traje has accordingly been endemic and a major bone of contention for the Mayan movement. For instance, until 2003 traje was legally banned from public schools through the simple (and ostensibly ethnically neutral) expedient of requiring (ladino-style) uniforms. Mayan maids in ladino homes commonly wear their traje, but white-collar jobs (bank tellers, teachers, secretaries) normally require ladino dress, because such dress is considered professional. Even where no explicit rule exists, professional Maya working in ladino-dominated sectors often opt for ladino dress because of this stigma. Only in the tourist industry is indigenous traje regularly featured and promoted by ladino elites—although usually only in lower-end service positions at the interface of the tourist experience, like vendors, waiters, and maids. The overt message to tourists is that traje represents a distinctly Guatemalan national identity and valued ethnic attraction. But touristic display tends to confine traje to the realm of exotic, quaint, folkloric color—carefully removed from serious power and kept implicitly nonpolitical.[12] Tourism indeed has its own discourse of Mayan indigeneity as ancient and mystical. Here traje connotes a unique worldview and insights in which the tourist can partly partake by purchasing some related object, like a wall hanging made from it.

Crucial to the Salvadoran context is that traje has also become valuable for international human rights networking. Mayan activists trying to attract international support for the Mayan movement have used traje not only to obtain vital funds but also as a way to promote the existence and special value of Mayan culture to sympathetic human rights lobbyists: hence Oxfam has taken up the marketing of Mayan goods as a way to publicize internationally the assaults on Mayan culture by the Guatemalan government. As with the tourist market, however, much of the internal meanings of traje are lost or distorted in these campaigns, as sympathetic foreigners are led to associate traje with an exotic and romanticized rural culture. Human rights networks marketing traje to international sympathizers deliberately play into these imaginings, even offering misleading descriptions and photographs in order to evoke the right sympathetic and romantic response.[13] (Such meanings, again, are clearly at odds with most ladino thought—which, again, understands traje as backward and primitive.)

All these developments have fed back to interplay, in a crucial synergy, with the meanings and use of traje within Mayan communities. Its new commercial value especially has fostered its revival and expansion as an art form. For weavers, a single sale of one relatively inexpensive item, of perhaps US$6, provides a family with twice a worker's daily wage on a coffee plantation. With possibly 800,000 weavers selling in the market, this influx of cash has therefore had a tremendous impact on family and village economies, and constitutes a powerful motivation to weave (although also to weave less artistically and more cheaply).[14] At the same time, its promotion by the Mayan movement and international human rights campaigns has helped to elevate traje as a symbol of Mayan-nationalist pride, redignifying weaving as a craft and encouraging wider use of elaborate traje. This shift, coupled with the state's own revaluing of traje in its tourist promotion, has to some extent countered the weight of ladino stigma. Coupled with the changing domestic political climate fostered by the Peace Accords, in recent years traje has consequently become somewhat more socially acceptable and is more commonly seen in ladino settings like the downtown districts of the capital city.[15]

Much more could be said here about the practices and politics of traje.[16] But this quick overview should suffice to illustrate our basic concern: that traje carries different meanings in the gaze of Guatemalan ladinos, international tourists, national and foreign academics, human rights activists, and Mayan activists, who variously see it as backward, exotic, ancient, a precious cultural practice, a profitable commodity, a spiritual entity in itself, or a proud nationalist Mayan emblem. No wonder that traje itself is so powerful an ethnic symbol; it embodies the very contest over who the Maya *are*, socially and politically, in the modern nation-state—and therefore what they deserve from that state. But one major flaw pervades all these visions: the understanding that Mayan identity is indeed defined by wearing traje. For, in practice, Mayan use of traje is far less consistent.

In the countryside, Mayan women's use of traje is almost universal, but in towns and cities its use is becoming more complicated. The reasons are not necessarily ethnic-strategic. Traje is expensive (a good huipil costs the equivalent of a month's salary at minimum wage), and Mayan women working in factories, offices, or service industries do not have time to weave their own. Although they will have at least one set of traje, they may therefore protect it from daily wear to keep it clean and elegant ("western" clothing is far easier to wash). Wearing cheaper ladino clothing at work, women are therefore tending more frequently to wear pants and shirts at home as well, reserving their traje for special occasions. School is also having spin-off effects; girls exercise in gym clothes, and apparently the freedom and flexibility of the gym clothes is starting to affect afterschool clothing choices to wear pants or jeans.

In short, for urban Mayan women managing transitions among diverse social settings, traje is becoming something to wear some of the time. It remains a powerful ethnic marker in that no ladinos wear traje, and it is socially important to wear traje on Mayan holidays. But wearing traje on a daily basis is no longer absolutely mandatory for a Mayan woman to "qualify" as indigenous. Within their families and immediate communities, these choices are understood rather as a growing flexibility within the Mayan ethnic spectrum (although not without controversy; the question remains delicate and sometimes bitterly argued). Hence dress practices continue to change, as ethnic practices often do.

This natural fluidity runs counter to ladino stereotype, however, which sees traje as one part of the *substance*—not merely a signal—of indigeneity. In this view, adopting ladino dress even for part of a day signals not simply a growing flexibility with the Mayan identity but a literal loss of ethnic identity, a progressive assimilation to ladino cultural norms. This perception adds greatly to Mayan women's social and political burdens, as they so publicly bear Mayan identity on their own bodies. It has consequently been frustrating to Mayan women (and to Mayan men caught up in the controversy) who, faced with difficult choices, resent such external judgments. Mayan political activists—many of them urban intellectuals who do not wear traje due to the burden of its stigma but also as a personal style choice—have therefore fought forcefully for both the freedom to wear indigenous traje and for free choice in the matter. The Peace Accord on Indigenous Rights guaranteed the right to wear indigenous dress but did not mention the right of indigenous people to choose freely what to wear and still retain standing as an indigenous person.[17] The Accord's provision for "self-identification" might seem to cover that base, but only indirectly.[18] For indeed the question still lacks consensus within the Mayan community.

The role of traje in Mayan ethnic identity therefore remains fluid and contested. And authority over the matter is itself a point of contest. For who should be able to say what practices really make someone Mayan— or, for that matter, Nahua?

In the Mayan Shadow: Dress Among the Nahua

In the rural Nahua cantones of El Salvador (a few hours by bus from the Guatemalan highlands), the relative absence of traje among the Nahua floats in the national imagination as defining the absence of Indian identity. And yet, indigenous traje in El Salvador has much more complicated readings than its simple absence would suggest. If the Salvadoran indigenous people lived in another part of the world, perhaps this lack of traje would not matter so much to their profile as Indians; in North America, for example, dress is not a criterion. But in the shadow of the Maya, the relative lack of traje among the Nahua and Lenca cast them as "not Indian" by local ladino standards.[19]

Certainly, traje among the Nahua was once a rich internal ethnic text. Nahua women in the hot climate of western El Salvador routinely went topless when working even in public areas, and often still do in the privacy of the home. But they wore embroidered huipiles to go to market and for ceremonial occasions, and always wore what in the Salvadoran context are called *refajos*: a shorter version of the Mayan corte, the colorful, wrapped skirts. Cloth for refajos was still fabricated in the western Salvadoran town of Nahuizalco until the 1970s; the pattern was a characteristic overlay, still observable (now in faded form) on older Nahua women today. Salvadoran Nahua women also added a distinctive line of embroidery along the refajo seam, not seen in Guatemalan cortes.

During the twentieth century, however, Nahua women's use of refajos and ceremonial huipiles progressively declined. In some areas, such as Tacuba, traje was reportedly abandoned in the early twentieth century.[20] In other towns, such as Nahuizalco, it holds on today, especially among the older generation. But in the mid-1970s the last Salvadoran factory making refajos, in Nahuizalco, went out of business. Cloth for refajos was still sold into the late 1990s from a single market stand in Nahuizalco, but was imported from Guatemala. In any gathering of women in Nahuizalco or in the equally "Indian" town of Santo Domingo de Guzmán, a few mostly older women will appear in refajos. But new material is rarely seen, hand embroidery is no longer practiced, and huipiles have been replaced by unadorned ladino blouses. Very few women below the age of forty wear traje at all. (On men, the traje típico was the loose mantle and loose pants made of a rough white cotton; these have entirely disappeared.) Traje remains a powerful ethnic symbol of indigeneity, but the complex internal messages once conveyed through detailed embroidery patterns are no longer possible, and even the memory of them is fading.

For Salvadoran ladinos, as for Guatemalan ladinos, traje is not merely the signal but the substance of indigeneity. Its scarcity was the single greatest indicator cited to me that "there are no Indians in El Salvador." Only women still wearing traje are identified, by Salvadoran ladinos, as Indian, and prompt the admission that "a few Indians still exist in Nahuizalco and Izalco." Nor are foreign academics immune from this powerful association. I was told three separate stories of foreign academics who, accustomed to the Guatemalan context and skeptical of an indigenous presence in El Salvador, expressed their astonishment that "there are Indians in El Salvador!" only upon seeing western Nahua women in traje.

The scarcity of traje carries extra political importance because it is enlisted to support the idea that 1932 marked the end of any "truly" Indian presence in the country. In the 1932 Matanza, indigenous men were supposedly identified on sight as "communists" and arrested and/or shot

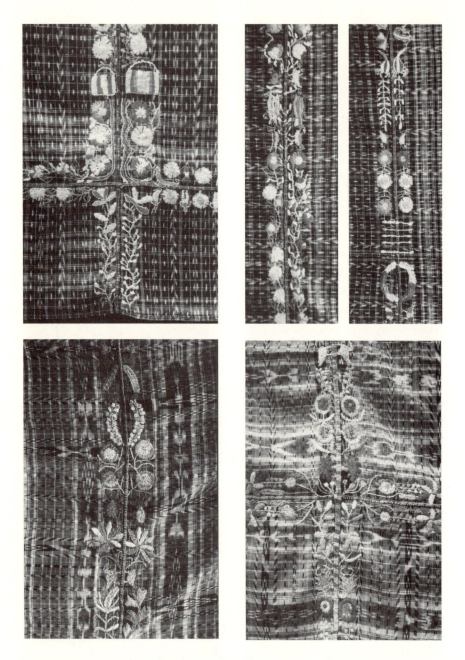

FIGURES 5A–E. Samples of Nahua embroidery, now rarely seen. Patterns run along the seam of the refajo (skirt), showing handbags, vines, flowers, scorpions, birds and other animals.

without ceremony.[21] The Indians therefore supposedly gave up their dress during this emergency in order to escape death and persecution. Oral versions also sometimes added that traje was later made illegal by the Martínez regime; this story is frequently repeated by younger indigenous activists.

None of these common ideas is supported by oral testimony among older Nahua, ethnographic evidence from their communities, or any documentation. In my own interviews with elderly Nahua in cantones surrounding Nahuizalco, men seemed entirely unfamiliar with the 1932 Matanza explanation, and drew a blank at the idea of any law, order, or rule in 1932 against traje. On the contrary, one elderly man told me a story, with many chuckles, of some poor ladinos who, after the Matanza, deliberately put on indigenous traje for a trip to the Sonsonate department governor to solicit sympathy and help. Such a tactic would have been most unlikely if traje had been made illegal or were in such disgrace as to provoke instant arrest. Instead, male traje in El Salvador probably fell into disuse in much the same way, and in the same period, that Mayan male traje in Guatemala fell into disuse, and probably for many of the same reasons: social pressures related to extensive migrant labor, generic ladino discrimination and stigma, and the availability of cheaper northern imports.[22]

Neither did older Nahua women in my interviews remember any official targeting of indigenous dress. The reason universally given by these women for the general abandonment of traje was, as for the Maya, simply its cost. Material for refajos costs some 300–600 colones (about $40–$80), equivalent to about one month's income for an entire family. In the more acute poverty of western El Salvador, this burden is especially prohibitive, especially given the far cheaper alternative of clothing donated by North American charities. A general movement of the younger generation toward Western clothing certainly also contributes to a lack of interest in traje.

But these trends are not universal. Market vendors in Nahuizalco, where use of traje is most common, told me in 1995 that sales of cloth for refajos approximated fifty per year. The same vendors hazarded that between ten and twenty women in each canton, on the average, wear traje daily. According to two local seamstresses, the number of refajos being sewn was much larger, from fabric brought in by individuals who had purchased it in Guatemala.[23] Given that refajos usually last for many years if not decades, and that most women do not wear their refajos daily, this suggests that a significant number of Nahua women may own at least one refajo. Nahua women's use of traje may therefore be more extensive than superficial visual observations on the roads or in markets may suggest.

Finally, no record—no public announcement, correspondence, telegram, notation of any kind—has been found to indicate any official policy, military order, or government decree against traje. Moreover, the fabled targeting of indigenous dress, if it took place, was reportedly directed only against men's traje. Men were, overwhelmingly, the target of the protracted killing spree of early 1932. Although victimized by the general terror, Nahua women were not targeted in the same way. Certainly there is no evidence of any hasty and systematic abandonment of women's traje in the period immediately following 1932. The survival of the refajo factory into the 1970s is one strong indicator of a much longer process of decline.

Why did the idea of an official ban against traje take such strong hold in the Salvadoran national memory? Perhaps an outright ban, by some earlier brutal regime, is a more concrete and comfortable explanation than a more diffused climate of shame and stigma, maintained against indigeneity by Salvadoran society as a whole.

So what of the other functions of traje, so important to the Guatemalan Mayan movement: its commercialization, and international human rights networking? In the 1990s, the Salvadoran indigenous organizations tried to encourage these linkages. For example, in the town of Panchimalco (the famous indigenous community south of the capital), a local priest launched a new program to revive weaving of the town's traditional checkered refajo cloth, obtaining funds for two floor looms and concentrating on training the community's youth. A belt-weaving project was also underway. Backstrap loom weaving, still a living industry in the Panchimalco cantones, was being promoted by the town's Casa de la Cultura as well as by the parochial school. In the mid-1990s the products of these efforts remained modest (weavings for sale consisted solely of small squares, of about 42 x 50 cm, selling for 30 colones or about $3.50 each). Still, both projects were a source of hope and pride to the community.

Such projects are described as *rescate*—the effort to remember, revive, and revitalize material indigenous culture. As among many ethnic groups, the material object here evokes ideas not only of a present existence but of a past existence, a set of values and meanings (a culture) authored by the community. That sense of creative authorship helps to lift the stigma attached to being indígena even as it helps to define the ethnic community for purposes of political organizing. That weaving is also a source of cash income for the community further enhances the social standing of both art and weaver.

But the synergistic effects of weaving, culture, the tourist market, and ethnopolitics so important among the Maya here work against each other. For Salvadoran weaving faces a major problem that the Maya do not confront, which is competition by the Maya themselves. The high quality and sheer volume of Mayan Guatemalan weaving outshines nascent efforts like the Panchimalco products, which—resurrected from near-demise— lack the textual richness, originality, and complexity (i.e., exotic appeal to tourists) of the Guatemalan weavings. Because Salvadoran Nahua and Lenca women are no longer identified ethnically by distinctive dress, their personal, spiritual link with weaving has indeed attenuated. The repertoire of symbols and designs (so engrossing to buyers of Mayan weavings) has mostly been lost, and such richness cannot easily be faked. Having lost both its spiritual importance and its repertoire of symbolic designs, Salvadoran weaving has lost its primary function as an internal ethnic text, and no longer serves as a font of artistic inspiration and rigor. Lacking such connections, its capacity to compete on the international market is greatly impeded.

All these factors indicate a poor prospect for a revival of Nahua traje. Without a lucrative market, incentives for weaving are low. Without income from weaving, most women cannot afford the cloth for refajos. And without the redignification of market success and tourist interest, incentives for wearing it are also low. In fact, a traje revival effort might succeed only in putting considerable ethnic pressure on women. That pressure has already had unpleasant effects: for example, one non-Indian development activist in Nahuizalco, anxious to demonstrate to an international visitor that the indigenous community truly existed, convened gatherings of Nahua women with explicit instructions that only those wearing refajos could attend, and expelled those who appeared in their charity-bin dresses. Such a crude method may seem reprehensible but reflects the real difficulty of breaking through the stereotype. Even for some Nahua activists, a certain guilt hovers around the question. One Nahua artisan and activist, viewing with satisfaction a photograph I took of her weaving a *petate* (wicker mat), lamented that for the image truly to represent her ethnic identity, the picture should show her wearing traje—which she does not own. The public ethnic symbolism of traje developed by the Maya—traje as symbol of an ancient and noble culture—is here working backwards. The absence of the *symbol* is treated as evidence of the absence of *what is symbolized*: the indigenous community itself.

The Ethnic Politics of Language

The second emblem of indigeneity in Central America is language, and it is, arguably, a far more powerful one. Traje is a powerful visual signal, but traje can be adopted or abandoned in a moment (although not without personal turmoil). Not so easily changed or mastered by outsiders, language marks ethnic boundaries with great force, limiting assimilation as well as mutual comprehension. Moreover, language not only signals the existence of an alternative worldview but enables its very conception and expression, even shaping cognition. Language is so powerful an ethnic marker that it is the most forceful argument supporting indigenous claims that they constitute distinct "peoples." For almost everyone in Central America, to make a convincing claim to be indigenous, a group must retain its indigenous language.[24] But again, the ethnic significance of indigenous languages in the Salvadoran arena is more complex than a simple equation (language equals ethnicity) would propose.

Mayan Languages and the Mayan Cultural Renaissance

Like traje, the Mayan languages are such potent ethnic markers of indigeneity that they overshadow and delegitimize the Nahua and Lencan claims of being indigenous. In 1988, the Proyecto Lingüístico Francisco Marroquín (PLFM) estimated the number of Maya-language speakers in Guatemala at 2,929,300 (about 30 percent of the country), a figure later corroborated by the 1994 census—although this figure too is often considered low.[25] Tracing to common proto-Maya roots, the twenty-one Mayan languages also distinguish and demarcate the twenty-one Mayan ethnic groups; together, they distinguish the Maya from ladinos. Especially in the highlands, Mayan languages are the first languages for much of the indigenous population, especially women. Lack of fluency and literacy in Spanish therefore continues to impede Mayas' participation in ladino-dominated society and in politics. But for the Mayan movement, the

Mayan languages are pillars not only of Mayan ethnic experience but also ethnonationalist ambitions.

The political importance of any language is indeed powerful, and particularly so for groups whose cultures are under political assault. As Demetrio Cojtí Cuxil (one of the most influential Mayan writers on Mayan-language politics) has argued, for the Maya as for all nations, languages "'crystallize' the common history, the national character and the voluntary desire to live in the nationalities which speak them."[26] They mark the ethnic boundaries of different Mayan peoples, and express each one's distinct historical experience so effectively that linguists and historians have been able to reconstruct centuries of history through the usages and traditions passed down. Since present Mayan ethnic experience is made sensible only in light of those histories (Cojtí argues), the Mayan languages constitute both a dynamic and a durable institution for the expression of the group experience as a coherent process. At the same time, Cojtí rejects ladino concerns that the diverse Mayan languages impede Guatemalan national integration. On the contrary, he argues, official recognition of the Mayan languages would relieve the pervasive sense of political alienation experienced by Mayas, who are now forced to learn a second language in order to engage in official business in what is, supposedly, their own state.

In mainstream ladino thought, however, the Mayan languages have long been understood as simply another outmoded Indian relic, incapable of expressing modern concepts and the social needs of a modern world, and so doomed to extinction. Indeed, until recent years, the Mayan languages were considered by ladino authorities not to have a literary capacity—not to have any grammar at all. Accordingly, government policy has treated the Mayan languages as an obstacle to indigenous social welfare and to the full integration (and progress) of the Guatemalan nation. The government's bilingual education program, PRONEBI, was designed to *castellanizar* (Spanish-ize) the indigenous population, not to develop Mayan language fluency. Hence the country has long seen a sweeping official neglect of the Mayan languages as living modern languages. Until the Mayan movement took hold, except for the Christian Bible and a few related tracts produced by missionaries, no books had been printed in Mayan languages.

But the Mayan movement has challenged those entrenched biases. One of the first gains of the movement was to establish the Academy for

Mayan Languages as a government institution, staffed by Maya and charged with developing and promoting the languages as living literary forms. In the last two decades, a cadre of university-trained Mayan linguists and writers has been working to analyze, systematize, and revalue the Mayan languages, and to defeat ladino views of their backwardness and incapacity.[27] The weak link in this effort, in contrast to traje, is the market for such skills—material rewards for learning the languages. This is seen as serious; hence in the 1990s some activists were urging the Guatemalan state to create a bilingual civil service, that would not only serve mayahablantes but provide jobs for people who undertook the effort of becoming literate in a Mayan language.

As with dress, however, these arguments assume that Mayan ethnic identity is identified by use of a Mayan language. In this respect (if no other), the Maya People movement is in sympathy with ladino thought: speaking Mayan language is considered a definitive element of being Maya, such that, to the extent language is lost, Mayan ethnicity is deemed to be diluted or lost. And yet, as noted above, the percentage of Guatemalans who spoke a Mayan language in the 1990s (about 30 percent) was significantly lower than the percentage of people who called themselves indigenous (about 42 percent). For more than a million people, then, language was not a mandatory ethnic marker. In other words, so far as the Maya themselves are concerned, to be Indian one does not necessarily have to speak an indigenous language.[28]

So even in Guatemala, a simplistic equation of indigeneity and language is a bit out of step with Mayan ethnic experience, in which language partly signals identity. This disjunction suggests that, as for dress, such a standard may be slippery for assessing indigeneity in El Salvador.

Language Revival Among the Nahua

Use of the Salvadoran indigenous languages has declined to the point that many people describe them as "dead" languages. The three indigenous languages still knowing some shreds of usage are Nahuat (in the west) and the Ulua languages of Cacaopera and Potón (among the eastern indigenous communities commonly called Lenca). But no fluent speakers of Cacaopera and Potón remain; use of both languages is confined to symbolic efforts (slogans, signs). Both Nahuas and ladinos believe that fluent speakers of Nahuat are also very few. A survey by the Ministry of Education in the late

1980s found no more than 200 Nahuat speakers among all of the western indigenous communities—using a very low standard of a 75-word vocabulary.[29] A survey by the National University in 1991 found no more than 130.[30]

Salvadoran ladino beliefs about the use and importance of Nahuat have not been surveyed, but in my interviews the same equation of indigeneity and language held among Guatemalan ladinos seemed salient: the supposed absence of Nahuat was commonly cited as the second major signal (after dress) that Indians have assimilated and disappeared. My interviews also suggested that the indigenous languages were less disparaged as "backward" perhaps simply because they are understood already to have disappeared. Indeed, Nahua words appearing in Salvadoran Spanish have been written up and publicly celebrated as forming one element of Salvadoran mestizaje.[31] Otherwise, government policy has been a monolith of neglect, but with the language in decline since the nineteenth century and so few speakers today, that policy is less dissonant than in Guatemala.

As with traje, the evaporation of Nahuat is commonly attributed to the trauma of the 1932 Matanza. And as with traje, the explanation is inadequate, but it carries a seed of truth. There is some testimonial evidence that Nahuat was strategically abandoned after 1932, at least in public places. Elderly indigenous informants in the Nahuizalco region remember the initial effort not to speak Nahuat in public areas, recalling that ladinos suspected it was associated with communist intrigues. For the same reason, Nahuat also supposedly disappeared from the marketplace. No longer employing the public vocabulary of work, trade, and politics, Nahua became confined to the home and to private matters, and both its vocabulary and its grammar compressed accordingly. In 1930, the linguist Schultz-Jena found ten verb forms in daily use. In 1973, Lyle Campbell found six. By the 1990s, according to Gayo Tiberia (of the National University), only three were being used. Most of the remaining vocabulary concerned private and family concerns: the language of childcare, cooking, and proverbs.[32]

The abandonment of Nahuat was not, however, initiated by the Matanza. According to some travelers' accounts, Nahuat was actually in steep decline in the mid-nineteenth century. The causes for this decline are not understood, although internal migrations may have been a factor. Nor is the Matanza blamed by most Nahua themselves. In my interviews, Nahua instead traced their language's demise to mid-twentieth century stigma: the general belief that the language itself is backward and silly. Some people especially blamed schoolteachers, who humiliated and scolded children in the 1940s through the 1960s and even expelled them from the classroom for speaking Nahuat.

Such memories indicate that Nahuat did not disappear overnight after 1932, but was still the language of the family—and of children entering schools—well into the mid-twentieth century. Indeed, widespread casual use of Nahuat persists today, and is by no means confined to the elderly. Contradicting the field studies cited above, in 1979 North American linguist Judy Maxwell found widespread use of Nahuat in markets, homes, and workplaces, as well as speakers sufficiently fluent to qualify as teachers in all the villages surveyed. In my own brief contact with the mostly indigenous canton of Pushtan, I often heard Nahuat being spoken by people other than the elderly (for example, a young mother in the road, grappling with her son's disheveled clothing, shifted in this intimate moment into Nahuat). Couples occasionally resort to Nahuat in arguments. Small phrases of greeting and good wishes are widely known and used, and phrases of Nahuat float through the marketplace. None of this casual usage appears on the language surveys mentioned above. But the surveys may underestimate the extent to which such lingering fragmented use of Nahuat remains a concealed realm of Nahua ethnic life, symbolically important to marking the indigenous community.

Far more consistent among the Nahua is a characteristically "Indian" way of speaking Spanish, a dialect sometimes incomprehensible even to urban ladino Salvadorans from the same township.[33] The western Nahua tend to convert vowels (traje becomes "truje"; *luna* becomes "lona") and consonants (*piedra* is "piegra," *traigamelo* is "traibome"). Some words alter more profoundly: for example, *niño* (child) is "ningio"; *abuelito* (grandfather) is "nollito." They also tend to use the feminine gender for masculine words. These "Indian Spanish" language patterns are pivotal to a question crucial to the Salvadoran ethnic arena: whether indigenous people, in the ordinary run of daily affairs, are socially identifiable as such. My question "How do you know who is Indian?" commonly drew mention of accent immediately after physical features and names.[34] For people in the Nahua countryside, a characteristically "Indian" way of speaking Spanish is widely understood and recognized as an indigenous ethnic marker.

Not surprisingly, the ethnic value placed on Indian Spanish is low on all sides. Ladinos view Indian Spanish as laughable and backward. Indígenas themselves understand their unique Spanish as one manifestation of their own lack of education and an obstacle to their dealings with better educated city people. "We lack the words to talk to them," they say. Nor do most rural indígenas, anxious to escape marginalization and poverty, have any interest in Nahuat outside of the occasional festival or ethnic political gathering. Nahuat is the "old language," the quaint tongue of their grandparents. If a language is coveted, it is English: the language of economic opportunity, via the vast Salvadoran northern migration. Still, Nahuat retains some symbolic value for ethnic politics. Nahuat is trotted out at celebrations, and a few famous speakers are often invited to distant villages on special occasions to perform. Nahuat revival—formal classes, for children and adults—are central projects in several organizations' proposed programs, and roughly a third of the funding proposals submitted to UNESCO's "Culture of Peace" program were for language revival (see chapter 10).

But Nahuat rescate in the 1990s was strained in ways that the Guatemalan Maya language movement is not. First, and most obviously, it lacked a critical mass of speakers on which to build. Second, the Salvadoran activists themselves were not qualified to pursue such a strategy. Proposed teachers (movement members) did not themselves use Nahuat on a daily basis, and had no formal linguistic or pedagogical training. Most lacked even the ability to write words on a blackboard; their sole qualification was enthusiasm. Nor was training available; no experts on the language existed who could offer any, partly because a standardized version of modern Nahuat has not been formulated. Differing dialects persist (e.g., among Panchimalco, Santo Domingo de Guzmán, Nahuizalco, and Izalco), and rivalries over which dialect will be "standard" are bitter and unresolved. Hopes of linguists convening local "congresses" on Nahuat (three since 1988) were dashed by the failure to mesh technical agendas with the political agendas of indigenous activists. Nor was there unity even about its alphabet: five alphabets have been constructed to date, and no consensus had been reached about which one should prevail.

Most crippling to solving all these problems was the lack of Nahua intellectuals. Mayan intellectuals have been vital to galvanizing the Mayan language movement, supplying the professional authority, ethnic leadership, and political access to convert the work of linguists into a major politicized movement. In El Salvador, only one of the indigenous activists urging Nahuat rescate (revival) had an education beyond the sixth grade, and most activists were barely literate in Spanish. No one bridged the chasm between the rural indigenous activist and the ladino university professional. Frustrations were mutual.

Hence the potential of Nahuat rescate actually to take off in popular usage seemed minimal. One cynical critic even suggested to me that Nahuat's dim future may actually have facilitated CONCULTURA's government support to the indigenous movement because the chance of any genuine language revival, which might strengthen community ethnic consciousness and political capacity, seemed so low.

So why such heavy emphasis by the Salvadoran movement on reviving Nahuat? The underlying reason is that the Salvadoran indigenous movement is trying to match criteria for indigeneity already worked out by others. The Salvadoran activists are vulnerable to an internationally hegemonic formula regarding what Indians *are*: people who maintain distinct dress, language, customs, and territory. This model is given further clout by international funding, but it is potent in any case. The Nahua are compelled to adopt outside standards for being Indian because their own discourse of indigeneity—the criteria by which they identify themselves and each other as indígenas, in their own local settings—is so unpersuasive for Salvadoran ladinos and for potential international allies. Ironically, however, in trying to emulate standards for indigeneity alien to their own experience, they are only aggravating observers' impressions of their ethnic inauthenticity, as we will see.

CHAPTER 5

REMEMBERING CUSCATLÁN

"Forgetting, and I would even say historical error, is an essential factor in the creation of a nation . . ."

—*Ernest Renan, 1882*

Reading History

AS WE SAW IN THE PREVIOUS THREE CHAPTERS, THE DISCOURSE OF INDIGENEITY in El Salvador today reflects multiple threads: interlaced ideas about race, class, and ethnicity, and expectations (stereotypes) drawn from the Guatemalan Maya. Our closer probing of those threads found that mainstream Salvadoran ladino ideas remain oddly incongruent with local Salvadoran indigenous ethnic experience and self-perceptions. And yet, these contradictions only raise a deeper question: why has the no-Indians claim become so firmly entrenched in Salvadoran national discourse? When did this claim first emerge? And what political baggage does it carry? Those questions require us to plumb the country's ethnohistory that has fostered the doctrine of erasure, which so forcefully shapes ethnic politics in the late twentieth century.

Exploring a history, in El Salvador or anywhere else, is not simply a matter of tracing events and trends: e.g., the Spanish arrival, early conquests, and later racial-caste systems. Studying how a national history has been *written* (and periodically rewritten) may be even more illuminating. History in the sense of material events, like deaths during a civil conflict, can be explored as objective reality, confirmed by excavations of graves and other empirical methods. But history as a narrative does not exist outside its telling; it is inevitably explored and interpreted according to later assumptions and biases as well as political agendas. Nation building especially involves the strategic "colonization" of history. Selectively emphasizing some events, strategically forgetting or recasting others, and glorifying (and sanitizing) selected heroes allows a nationalist doctrine to propose a noble origin for the nation, confirm its organic relationship to the modern state's territory, and inspire popular loyalty to its purported collective political values and mission.

The Salvadoran national narrative has tended to obscure the country's ethnohistory through sheer neglect, as we have seen and for reasons we will explore. But although Indians seem to be missing, Salvadoran official history is actually a narrative into which all sectors of the national society—including indigenous peoples—have been woven to fit its basic proposal of national unity. Untangling the Indian's precise configuration in that narrative requires digging through the fragmentary historical record to reconstruct how being Indian in El Salvador has been recast over time. For, as much as past material events, what shapes Salvadoran indigeneity today is how those events have been represented in the official national narrative—or omitted from it. Textbooks, the census, public rhetoric, and public symbols have guided and framed present-day popular assumptions and values about Indians. These sources therefore provide us important clues.

For instance, when we look at El Salvador's official national history through the lens of the indigenous ethnic question, we immediately find a glaring contradiction at its very foundation: official celebration of the country's origins in Cuscatlán, the Nahua city once located on the outskirts of present-day San Salvador. Salvadoran nationalist discourse has fully colonized Cuscatlán, appropriating its memory, its imagined glory, and even its conquest for the modern nation's own semimythic heritage. Salvadorans indeed often refer to the country as "Cuscatlán," especially when in more nationalist moods. The name "Cuscatlán" circulates commercially as well: it has been adopted by one of the country's largest banks, complete with sun-disk emblem. Atlacatl, supposedly the Nahua prince who led Cuscatlán's warriors against the Spanish, is also celebrated—most famously, as the name assigned to a particularly infamous army battalion.

With Indians themselves so deliberately excised from El Salvador's national self-profile, why do indigenous Cuscatlán and Atlacatl have such iconic places in the nationalist narrative? The answer takes us beyond El Salvador's boundaries. States throughout Latin America have used the romanticized memory of indigenous heroes and civilizations for nationalist narratives to help make sense of government authority in national territories—or simply to help authorize the army's grip on those territories. The same pattern has served Latin America's foreign relations: the fusion of Spanish and indigenous bloodlines is claimed to define the "Latin American" race, as explored in later chapters.

Before looking at those larger geopolitical influences, however, we first need to look quickly at the indigenous civilization that Salvadoran national mythology later appropriated for its own symbolic origins, legitimacy, and greater romance. Especially, we need to recognize how that mythology has twisted the historical record, contributing its own subtexts to being Indian today. What was the preconquest civilization like? Who were the Nahua? It is our great loss (too common in the Americas, alas) that we have only fragmented records of what the Nahua themselves said or wrote about their culture and politics, or about their experience of the Spanish invasion that destroyed them.[1] But some descriptions of the region by indigenous and Spanish commentators have survived, and from these we have a fragmentary portrait of what was destroyed. Partly to better illuminate how the Salvadoran national narrative has appropriated and distorted the collective memory of Cuscatlán, but also as a small homage to the people and civilization long destroyed and forgotten by most, some space will be dedicated here to peering back into what scholars have gleaned about that world.

The World of the Nahua-Pipiles

Today, Salvadoran references suggest that the Nahua were—especially by comparison to the Maya—a small and obscure society, even a cultural backwater, lacking great temples and great art. Even the name commonly given the Nahua—Pipiles—has long been translated as "child-like," supposedly dating from their simplified, backward use of the Nahuatl language, "like a child." But is this humble image accurate? A closer look at the territory's history offers us a very different portrait.

Human habitation in El Salvador dates back at least ten thousand years, but for present-day political purposes the country's history begins around 2000 BCE, when Mesoamerica entered into that era of extensive trade (and occasional warfare) that linked its diverse ethnic groups artistically and, to a large degree, culturally. The early peoples in present-day El Salvador formed the southern fringes of this cultural zone, trading to the north with the great Mayan city-states and as far away as central Mexico.

Today, the state's tourism literature claims proudly that these peoples were themselves Maya, but this claim rests on thin ice. The Chortí, a Mayan people, lived in the north of present-day El Salvador (in Chalatenango) in the classic period, and Mayan ceramic designs appeared in the central province of Cuscatlán during this time. Settlement patterns throughout the territory (the style and layout of homes and communities) reflect settlement patterns in Maya regions. The early peoples of El Salvador certainly participated in Mesoamerica's elite trade of jade, obsidian, and ceremonial objects, and the ceremonial center of Chalchuapa (in the northeast) was an important center in the preclassic Maya world. Mayan figures sometimes appear in painting and relief sculpture even along the eastern coastal zone.[2] Today, however, archaeologists lean toward an understanding that these Mayan influences represent flows of trade rather than people.[3] For example, Mayan settlement patterns were also shared by the Ulua (Lenca), known to be ethnically distinct from the Maya.

Whether Mayan or not, this population suffered a demographic collapse around 900–1000 CE, for reasons still unknown. Perhaps one of the region's periodic volcanic eruptions caused a mass exodus. Perhaps the disintegration of the great Mayan city-states, which collapsed around this time, contributed some additional disruption. Or perhaps a regional plague depopulated all these societies. In any case, the remaining population was ethnically transformed around the tenth century with the first arrivals of the Nahua.

The Nahua are not a Mayan people, but originate from northern Mexico, and are of the same language group (Nahuatl) as the famous Aztec (who earlier had established the lake city of Tenochtitlán, today the location of Mexico City).[4] Nahuatl-speaking groups migrated from Mexico into Pacific coastal Mesoamerica in waves, between the tenth and fourteenth centuries, settling as far south as Nicaragua. (The Nicarao were also Nahua-speakers and were culturally very similar to the Salvadoran

Nahua, although less strong militarily and apparently with a less central-ized political system.) These Nahua migrations brought northern Aztec and Toltec designs on ceramics and ritual objects into the region of later El Salvador, displacing the strikingly different Mayan motifs.

For this new Nahua population, three centers became important: Los Izalcos in the west, later famous for its cacao; Los Nonualcos, in the cen-tral region; and Cuscatlán to the east, the largest city and the seat of pri-mary military power. All three were located not on the hot coastal plain but in the more temperate valleys in the coastal mountain range, some 1200–2000 meters above the sea. Perhaps a million Nahua inhabited this region, more or less bounded on the east by the Lempa River (the people later known as the Lenca lived to the east of this barrier, in a much less centralized and today less-understood society). In this land, the Nahua developed a rich agriculture and sustained a lively long-distance trade as far north as Tenochtitlán. Cacao, cultivated in a great irrigation complex developed in the Izalcos, was especially prized, and traded throughout the Isthmus.[5] Indeed, the Izalcos' vast irrigation system—with many miles of channels, dykes, and sluices—may have contributed to the Nahuas' devel-oping such a strong central state, guarded by a standing military. By the time of the Spanish Conquest, the Spanish understood Cuscatlán to be one of the four major powers in Mesoamerica, comparable to the three great Mayan cities of the time.[6]

The Spanish called these people Pipiles, apparently because this name was used by their Mayan and/or Mexica translators, and the name has stuck (in scholarly work, partly as a handy way to distinguish the Salvado-ran Nahua from other Nahuatl language groups in the region). But some uncertainty has surrounded its translation. Today, "Pipil" is almost univer-sally translated by Salvadorans as "childish" or "child-like," a term that supposedly derived from the simplified or "childish" version of Nahuatl which the Nahua spoke in their cultural backwater. But the scholarship of this claim, which dates to a seventeenth-century Spanish historian, was always shaky (no such accent or grammar differences have ever been doc-umented).[7] "Pipil" is more probably an adaptation of the Nahua word *pip-iltin*, the plural of *pilli*, which does translate as "child" but also as "noble." All sources agree that, as among the Aztec, the pipiltin were indeed the noble class among the Nahua, who owned all the land, and controlled all politics, administration, and warfare.[8] William Fowler (the most exhaustive

FIGURES 6A AND B.
Nahua figures from the
region of Cuscatlán. Above,
ceramic effigy of the god
Tlaloc, from the ceremonial
center Cihuatán, around
1000 CE. Below, the god
Huehueteot, from the same
period. (In the collection of
the David J. Guzmán
National Museum, San
Salvador. Photographs from
El Salvador: Antiguas
Civilizaciones, courtesy
of the Banco Agricola
Comercial de El Salvador.)

researcher on the preconquest Nahua) believes that "the very name 'Pipil' ... should probably be understood as a reference to the noble lineages." In this case, the Mayan and Mexica translators were probably using "Pipil" to refer to the political elite of this major state. If so, the Nahua of Cuscatlán have been wrongly saddled with the demeaning stigma of a Spanish translator's error for the past four-and-a-half centuries.

Cuscatlán's lack of spectacular tall temples also contributes to beliefs today that the Nahua were only an Aztec backwater. In his classic history, *El Salvador*, Alastair White even assumed that the Nahua used only slash-and-burn agriculture, that their social organization was relatively "primitive," and that their inability to coordinate on any grand scale caused their defeat.[9] But Spanish reports and archaeological studies have offered quite a different picture: of a wealthy region with vast fruit orchards and cacao plantations, sophisticated irrigation systems, extensive long-distance trade networks, and a formidable standing army that repelled every Mayan military encroachment. Although their architecture did not reach the spectacular height of earlier Mayan temples, the Nahua did develop extensive ceremonial centers and towns. Spanish commentary repeatedly mentions the region's beauty and prosperity. Even a half century after the conquest, in 1576, Spanish imperial agent Diego Garcia de Palacio reported to his king that the Izalcos region was "the largest and richest province which Your Majesty possesses in these parts."[10]

From contemporary chronicles, we can be fairly sure of a few dimensions of their culture.[11] The Nahua of the Salvadoran region were divided into three general classes: the nobility, commoners, and slaves. The noble lineages—the pipiltin—had all political and administrative power and apparently owned all land, on which commoners worked. Their king or prince (possibly called the *teyte*, as among the Nahua-Nicarao to the south) normally ruled not alone but with a council of nobles, probably chosen from those close to his lineage. The commoners cultivated the crops, provided an annual tribute to the nobility, and served as warriors at need; but they could also distinguish themselves in battle and obtain status as pipiltin through great deeds. The women were the weavers—a newborn daughter had a spindle put in her hand—and the pipiltin wore finely woven and beautifully dyed cotton robes. The priests, who conducted ceremonies but also decided whether the Nahua should go to war, wore long robes of fine cotton and great two-cornered hats with a plume of quetzal feathers. (The commoners were allowed to wear only henequen cloth.) We know some of their laws: adultery and incest, for example, were punishable by death, but prostitution was acceptable and a stable public institution. People could also be sold into slavery, or sell themselves, or be made slaves as punishment for rape or robbery.[12]

We know something of their economy. Their diet was based on corn, beans, and squash, but also avocado and many other fruits and vegetables. They also raised turkeys, and hunted deer and boar. They grew great amounts of cotton and traded cacao as far away as central Mexico, also using cacao beans as money. They processed and traded balsam and indigo, and they cultivated and smoked tobacco. They worshiped the Mexican pantheon, especially the sun, the god of rain, and Xipe Totec, whose warrior cult focused on the ceremonial wearing of flagellated human skin taken from prisoners. All chroniclers agree that, like the Aztec, they practiced extensive ritual human sacrifice of war captives and of children, to celebrate a victory or the seasons—and even ritual cannibalism.

They also made war. Their standing army lived in special barracks, and was led in battle by the prince. Distinguished warriors wore plumed headdresses, jaguar-skin vests, elaborate jewelry, and their hair long and braided with red ribbon; lords of the pipiltin added a silver pendant to the braid's end. They fought their neighbors and each other, enslaved and ritually sacrificed their captives. Cuscatlán was, according to scholarly criteria for such things, a true state: able to tax its people, draft soldiers for war, and sustain a true legal code. But it was also a "conquest state," fighting and absorbing other Nahua polities and occasionally battling over territory with the Maya-Kaqchikel. In other words, Cuscatlán was not a utopia, but was morally complicated, like societies everywhere.

So what does any of this history mean for being Indian in El Salvador today?

Appropriating Cuscatlán

Being Indian in modern El Salvador today reflects all the above history, most obviously in that present-day Nahua and Lenca people are the descendents of the preconquest peoples and therefore, in collective memory, legatees of those cultures' destruction. But that legacy has been reshaped by how Cuscatlán has been reimagined, romanticized, and appropriated to ennoble the modern Salvadoran nationalist narrative.

Take, for example, Atlacatl, the indigenous princely warrior credited in the nationalist lexicon with leading Cuscatlán's resistance to the Spanish and celebrated in political rhetoric, public sculpture, nationalist poetry, and grade-school textbooks. Noble, heroic, handsome, and tragic, his mythic figure contributes to El Salvador's claim to a unique identity, but his like appears in other countries as well. Every Central American country has its iconic Conquest Indian: Lempira in Honduras (whose name was appropriated for the national currency); Tecún-Umán in Guatemala (a Mayan, visible to tourists as imposing statues in the capital); and of course Nicaragua (of the Nahua-Nicarao, whose name was appropriated for the country itself). These nationalist Conquest Indians evoke tragic defeat, but—perhaps being a more sympathetic figure than the Spanish conquerors—are celebrated in national rhetoric as the conquerors themselves are not. Conquest Indians also resonate in ways especially useful to nation building because their very indigeneity (fused into the national bloodline by mixture with European settlers) boosts the modern nation's claim to the national territory. To paraphrase Philip Deloria, appropriating the Indian warrior's tragic image allows the nation "a symbolically powerful and emotionally charged position" for claiming an identity rooted in El Salvador's landscape.[13]

In the national mythology, Atlacatl was the Prince of Cuscatlán and leader of the pipiltin and the Nahua army.[14] As noted above, the Nahua did have a princely leader who led the warriors into battle, but we know nothing specific about the one who faced Alvarado except that his name was apparently Atonal. "Atacat" was a Guatemalan town chronicled in a Kaqchikel text as having been conquered by the Spanish on their way to Cuscatlán. The town was misread as a person by a Spanish historian in 1866, who translated it by adding the "tl" construction of Mexican Nahuatl, thus inventing "Atlacatl" just in time for his insertion into the nationalist narrative as it emerged in the late nineteenth century. At some point, Atlacatl also became identified as the Nahua archer who wounded Alvarado in the thigh, a rousing but completely unfounded idea (the identity of the archer was never known).

Like Cuscatlán itself, Atlacatl was freely reimagined, romanticized, and exoticized by Salvadoran nationalist intellectuals who, at the turn of the century, were reimagining El Salvador itself partly through a small corpus of nostalgic fables, poetry, and music. An early literary journal, *La Quincena*, published a number of such works: for example, in 1903, "Tepta: Indian Legend," "Indian Rhapsody," and even a short piano piece, "Atlacatl: Indian March." One poem, "The Court of Atlacatl," exemplifies the genre (see page 94).[15]

Thus beefed up, the imaginary Atlacatl was incorporated into Salvadoran school texts and survived there until the late 1980s. His name also circulates commercially: an "Atlacatl" finance company and an "Atlacatl" trucking company operate today. Most notorious was the "Atlacatl" army battalion, which, in 1989, earned international infamy through the slaughter of six Jesuits and their housekeeper. Hence, although most Salvadoran professionals know he is a myth, any open admission that his whole historical image was bungled would embarrass too many, and he hangs on for the domestic and even the international public.[16]

Aside from Atlacatl, however, Salvadoran nationalist iconography has conspicuously neglected what we might term "conquest art": indigenous glyphs or historical depictions of preconquest indigenous culture and of the conquest itself. In Guatemala, Mayan glyphs are rampant in national sites such as public buildings, and surround the portraits of past presidents on the national currency. By contrast, Salvadoran state buildings and public pageantry never use Nahua imagery in any iconic fashion (except on the international airport, designed explicitly for tourism), while Salvadoran currency surrounds its national heroes only with empty space.[17] Rare exceptions include an impressive tile mosaic above the entrance to the Archive of the Legislative Assembly, which depicts Spanish soldiers defeating Indians (presumably Nahua) who crouch or fall in various positions of submission and death. The Nahua are dressed incorrectly, however; the images leave out the famous cotton armor. The images were taken not from the region's own history but from a famous sequence of paintings by the Kaqchikeles, whose image of indigeneity has the warriors bare-chested.

This disconnect of historical imagery from the actual Nahua is even more glaring in statues of Atlacatl. In one standing prominently in the San Salvador suburb of Antigua Cuscatlán, he is rendered as a North American plains Indian with an eagle-feather headdress. His rendition at the Atlacatl battalion's base is also of a plains Indian, modeled from a North American tobacco company logo.

FIGURE 7. Statue of Atlacatl in Antigua Cuscatlán, 1996. Shortly after this photo was taken, the municipality repainted the statue gold. (Photo by author.)

The Court of Atlacatl

In the midst of his Court,
brilliant constellation
of grave priests, of soldiers
of Princes and Elders;
is the King Atlacatl.
The June sun
inflames in gold the evening sky,
giving to Cuscatlán luminous contours
and a green more intense to its fields.
The Court is in celebration.
In censers of onyx and jasper,
perfuming the air,
the incense burns in white spirals
while a melancholy complaint
the sweet chimera gives to the air
like ah! of a woman in love.
Far from the splendor and
        brilliance of the nobles
the people are delighted
by Chichimeca artists with their agile
games and contortions. Laughter
and happy songs
resound in the streets:
merchants from distant lands
go offering the feathers of quetzales,
fragrant resins, gold dust,
black obsidian and colorful cloth.
All is animation; but one can see
in the King's visage,
like a cloud in the summer sky,
that some sadness troubles his soul:
he does not respond as before,
to the genuflections and greetings
of his vassals, with friendly smile,
a rainbow in the storm of his anger.

It is that dire messages have arrived
for the King, of miseries and disasters.
Already the children of the sun, the white men
that send the lightening, are arriving implacable
like a curse, leveling villages
and razing altars:
already the firearm resounds in his domains,
the titular gods are mocked
and wounded Cuscatlán, wavers and falls!
While the night extends
its cloak of pain over the valley
the happy throng laughs and sings
in the plazas and the streets:
its melancholy complaint
the sweet chimera gives to the air
like ah! a woman in love;
and the tom-tom falls to nothing!

Thus, in the Salvadoran national narrative, Cuscatlán remains a dreamy idyll, an exoticized icon, ill-understood but vaguely evoking a time of beauty, innocence, and nobility. Its mystical aura is evoked and celebrated in an occasional glyph or sun-disk. But its very loss also somehow infuses El Salvador's longer national memory and its own undertone of conquest and tragic fall, associated with internal conflict but also the country's vulnerability to U.S. imperialism. Such a mood is expressed in a recent three-walled mural in the main staircase of the Universidad Tecnológica (a student project, completed in 1995). Here the entire history of the country is represented metaphorically, beginning with utopian visions of the pre-Columbian indigenous people in various poses of religious worship and pastoral bliss. Blood and a cracked earthen vessel represent the conquest. The sequence then continues through various images of modern war and repression, and culminates in the reconciliation of people, the earth, and Jesus Christ, bringing the triumph of just governance and egalitarian economic development. Cuscatlán is here adapted for a larger nationalist (and anti-imperialist) vision: the original Indians in a pristine and innocent state of nature, overrun and wrecked by European weaponry, laying the country open to oppression and ruin by nefarious imperialist forces.

FIGURE 8. The Salvadoran national airport, displaying Nahua glyphs, designed in the 1970s to promote tourism. (Photo by author.)

Selling the Past

The dreamy image of Cuscatlán deployed in the national identity discourse changed markedly in the mid-1990s, when Salvadoran state discourse suddenly shifted from blanket rejection of any living indigenous presence to its active promotion. In a new flurry of brochures and public rhetoric, both living Indians and Cuscatlán were suddenly celebrated as banner emblems of the Salvadoran national identity. Both domestic and international political incentives inspired this dramatic shift. One reason was nationalistic: to imagine, and instill in the public, new ideological tenets about Salvadoran identity that could glue together a society still deeply riven by the civil war (a motive described further in chapter 10). But a second motive was more purely material: to promote El Salvador as a more seductive "destination image" for international tourism. Although clearly narrow and tokenistic, this new celebration of indigeneity (past and present) changed the country's ideological terrain for ethnopolitics and opened new possibilities for the indigenous movement, whatever its fetishizing effects on the indigenous peoples. But it also redefined the indigenous peoples according to models taken from Guatemala and from the exotic fantasies of the "native" fostered by international tourism.

Major financial interests fed this unprecedented rhetorical shift. Since the mid-1980s, international tourists have brought billions of dollars annually into Latin America, and the trend is rising. Between 1980 and 2000, for example, tourist revenues in Peru and Ecuador more than doubled, from 4.5 percent to 11.6 percent of export income and from 3.2 percent to 7.0 percent, respectively. In Guatemala, tourism rose from its low of 4.6 percent of export income in 1984 to 13.3 percent in 2000, and in 2002 was the country's leading export sector. With the Peace Accords, tourism to El Salvador also rebounded from a low of 1.8 percent in 1994 to 7 percent in 2000.

Such major revenues inspired new state efforts to promote their countries' suddenly charming and much-valued indigenous cultures for ethnic tourism. Indeed, aside from the classic "sand, sex, and sun" formula offered by the tropical coasts, and ecotourism largely to the rainforests, Central America's principal attraction for international tourists is historical tourism to the magnificent and freshly excavated Maya temple complexes in southern Mexico, Guatemala, and Honduras. But everywhere, tourists are also attracted to indigenous landscapes (charming villages, colorful markets, women in traje) and spend their currency on indigenous weavings, carvings, and other crafts. Accordingly, state development planners have switched from ignoring and sequestering their "dirty Indians," or hiding them as eyesores, to front-staging indigenous villages and crafts as attractive national scenery: that is, as foreign currency magnets.

Hence the *Mundo Maya* (Mayan World) initiative: a regional cooperative tourism venture, launched by UNESCO in the mid-1980s, among Guatemala, Belize, Honduras, El Salvador, and the southern states of Mexico. *Mundo Maya* focuses on facilitating tourism to the major archaeological sites of the classic Maya civilization as well as ecotourism of neighboring habitat, conceptualized as a *Ruta Maya* (Mayan Route) throughout the region. As explained above, El Salvador has only a feeble claim to being part of this Ruta Maya, as its territory was dominated by non-Mayan populations. Nevertheless, in the 1990s the Salvadoran Institute for Tourism (IST) issued a series of attractive travel posters labeled "*El Salvador . . . Mundo Maya,*" that soon adorned the walls of businesses around the country, and published a series of *Mundo Maya* tourist brochures that referred grandly to the country's "more than 3000 years of Mayan history."[18] The project extended to fresh promotion of Nahua and Lenca *artesanía* and craft fairs.

The *Mundo Maya* campaign, however, inserted a peculiar twist into El Salvador's ethnic environment by redefining both the Nahua and the Lenca as Maya. IST brochures subsume all pre-Columbian civilizations of El Salvador under the single rubric of "Maya" or present them only in relation to the Maya. (For example, the major Toltec and Olmec civilizations, whose art was so influential in the country's territory, are incorporated simply as "predecessors to the Maya.") El Salvador's principal tourist attraction, the seventh-century town of Joya de Ceren—a pre-Nahua site, for which the ethnic identity of the inhabitants remains unknown—is presented as a "Maya" site. When facts simply don't fit, like the non-Mayan-ness of the Nahua and Lenca, they are left out. The reasoning is pragmatic: "Maya" sells to tourists, while "Nahua" does not. (Even though it would be more accurate to do so, El Salvador could not be promoted effectively to tourists as part of the "Aztec World." Nor is "Pipil" workable, having no name recognition, and, if translated as "childish," the Pipil reference is unimpressive in any case.) All this Mayanist rhetoric has had hegemonic impact: throughout the country today, officials at every level casually believe and repeat that the Nahua are indeed Maya. Even the Nahua and Lenca now say they are Maya. In such a hearty climate of Mayan celebration, what indeed is the sense or value in *not* being Maya?

In sum, *Mundo Maya* offered some benefits to the Nahua by fostering unprecedented state patronage for the indigenous movement's efforts to publicize the indigenous presence. But its mayanization effect was detrimental in other ways. For one thing, it actually aggravated the Salvadoran indigenous peoples' appearance, both to tourists and to some professionals, as "not truly Indian" by endorsing the Guatemalan Mayan peoples as the benchmark for their indigeneity. *Mundo Maya* therefore worked against the indigenous movement's urgent efforts to overcome the not-truly-Indian stigma which remained their primary political obstacle. Worse, *Mundo Maya* informed the indigenous peoples' own identity discourse in ways that would backfire, especially in their efforts to attract international allies (a problem to which we return in chapter 10).

Indigenous Discourse

As explained in the preface, this book does not pretend to offer a comprehensive description of indigenous political thought in El Salvador: that task I leave to other writers, preferably indigenous ones. But in our examining a national narrative that attempts to be hegemonic, we must acknowledge briefly how the indigenous movement has resisted or been swayed by it. Like the state, the indigenous movement has appropriated the conquest for its mythic narrative, although obviously with opposite meanings. State discourses celebrates it as the dawn of the country's mestizaje (as in this chapter's opening quote); the indigenous movement cites it as the great historical crime, the unjust extinguishing of indigenous sovereignty that frames indigeneity and the indigenous peoples' present political predicament. Yet this indigenous counter-discourse is necessarily formulated and deployed publicly under conditions dominated by the state's discourse, and so has been steered by its twists and silences.

First, it bears note that the Salvadoran indigenous movement's emphasis on the conquest is not entirely homespun. It draws heavily from a pan-American indigenous discourse galvanized to new energies by the Quincentennial in 1992. The conquest is a pillar of indigenous ideologies throughout the Americas because it marks the moment definitive for all: when the "Indian" was created as a pan-American racial identity, immediately disparaged, targeted for extermination or expulsion, or subordinated to creole rule. For this reason, the Quincentennial (five hundredth) anniversary of Columbus's first voyage triggered hundreds of conferences within Latin America (and around the world) and fostered a proliferation of indigenous organizations. This global surge of indigenous activism eventually leveraged the General Assembly's declaration of the U.N. Decade of Indigenous Peoples (for 1993–2003) and ensured that the Nobel Prize award for 1993 be granted to Maya activist Rigoberta Menchú.[19]

Quincentennial activism brought the relatively isolated Salvadoran ethnic movement into contact with other regional indigenous activists and its rhetoric into accord with an emerging canon of pan–Latin American indigenous discourse. For example, an indigenous activist from Sonsonate wrote the following passage immediately after he attended a continental indigenous conference in Ecuador in 1990:

Since the first invasions and occupations by European adventurers that our peoples [sic] have suffered for 503 years, the history of subjugation continues. . . . We repudiate the day 12 of October, because for us the indigenous peoples that day is the day of the worst disgrace, because it marks the beginning of the invasions and occupations by the dictator Christopher Columbus and his henchmen against our indigenous peoples in order to take our lands and rob us of our wealth. Today we are completing 503 years during which we have been massacred, marginalized and exploited. That is the reason why we do not celebrate this day the 12 of October but repudiate it totally.[20]

And yet, details of the conquest, or of preconquest life, remain vague in Salvadoran indigenous rhetoric. For example, Atlacatl is a fiction that Salvadoran indigenous activists are in no position to penetrate. Reified as he is in school textbooks, military mystique, and monuments, Atlacatl is honored vaguely as an ancient hero. But he is conspicuously missing from indigenous iconography, incorporated into no logo or organization name. Rather, the icons of the modern indigenous movement are Anastasio Aquino, leader of an 1833 revolt in the Nonualcos, and Feliciano Ama, a key leader in the 1932 uprising (both discussed in later chapters). Possibly some intrinsic hollowness of the Atlacatl myth, and especially his appropriation by the state, dilutes his political resonance for activists.

Similarly, the absence of pre-Columbian indigenous art in Salvadoran public buildings and national iconography cripples indigenous efforts to utilize that art toward ethnic revival. Pre-Columbian art provides powerful symbols for most indigenous movements, partly by reattaching to "Indian" the capacity for sophisticated civilization and partly by confirming the indigenous peoples' unique cultural history—and prior sovereignty—in the territory. Symbols from pre-Columbian cosmologies can also help to inspire and guide the revival (or reinvention) of a prior religious tradition. On a more pragmatic level, such art provides models for craft-revival projects, which—given the booming tourist market—can strengthen local ethnic cohesion and economies, as discussed in chapter 3.[21]

But for indigenous activists in El Salvador, their own artistic heritage is hard to come by. The country's archaeological sites are mostly unexcavated, obscured by soil and plant growth, hardly visible to the untrained eye. Very little has been written in Spanish on the country's preconquest history, and most indigenous leaders are effectively illiterate in any case. Public access to photographs of preconquest art is almost nonexistent. In the search for their cultural roots, indigenous activists are therefore often at the mercy of ladino government pamphlets: that is, tourist brochures.

As a result, Nahua activists seeking to glorify their preconquest culture have been steered toward Mayan cosmology and imagery. An interior wall of the ANIS meeting house, for example, is illustrated with a mural displaying Mayan figures. Some Nahua in rival organizations even call themselves Maya or "Maya-Nahuat." The latter construction is politically detrimental, particularly at the international level, because it implies to knowledgeable outsiders (like United Nations officials) that the Nahua are ignorant of their own Mexican origins.[22] Indeed, the Maya-Nahuat formula even suggests that the Nahua activists are inventing their identity from misinformation in the state's tourist brochures.

In fact, the Nahuas' belief that they are a Mayan people draws on much deeper social roots. Despite Cuscatlán's preconquest history of warfare with the Maya-Kaqchikeles, the Nahua and Lenca have known the Maya as close neighbors for a millennium, and over the past five centuries old enmities have been forgotten. Regular trade and religious pilgrimages across the Guatemalan border over the centuries have kept ethnic difference soft and have sustained interethnic connections and interchanges within the old Mesoamerican cultural zone. Even typical Nahua women's dress has, for at least a century, mirrored Maya-Kaqchikel dress.[23] Nor are the differences between Nahuat and Mayan languages politically relevant; the Guatemalan Mayan peoples themselves have some twenty-one mutually unintelligible languages, and the deeper differences between the Mayan and Nahuat language groups are understood only by linguists. A conceptual jump only a few hundred more miles up the Central American isthmus might indeed grant the Nahua a politically useful affiliation with their actual linguistic brethren and the prestigious Aztec tradition. But their Mayan affiliation is actually the more socially genuine, in that they perceive their own cultural and ethnic experience as part of the Mayan orbit.

Thus invented memories and myths of Cuscatlán and the conquest infuse both Salvadoran nationalist imagery and indigenous rhetoric. By contrast, the subsequent three centuries of colonial rule are missing from both mythic narratives; they stand simply as an undifferentiated era of dispossession and oppression for the latter. Yet we need to shine some light onto those centuries in order to recognize how they set the stage for the 1932 crisis.

CHAPTER 6

FROM COLONIAL RULE TO INDEPENDENCE

YNDIOS. Drunkenness, thievery, idleness, negligence and promiscuity are vices characteristic of this species. They know no other diversion than material pleasure, and a kind of dance, with neither grace nor variety, in which they pass many hours to the unison strokes of the flute and tambourine, which they alternate with leaden representations of events that pertain to the time of their conquest. They reject no superstition or belief in material spirits and evil objects; They are very submissive toward the Spanish, especially with their superiors, to whom they endlessly direct their supplications or responses preceded by reverences and genuflections. They commonly use an indirect or impersonal manner and take great care (without ceasing to do what they want when they can) not to contradict [the Spanish] in anything: Their dwellings are merely unkempt huts, made of sticks and cane, covered with leaves, grass and yuncos; Their dress, commonly very scant, is of coarse cotton cloth, [although] they remain completely naked, both sexes, within their houses; Their common foods are corn, beans, plátano and roots, being very unscrupulous about alternating them or setting them aside in favour of all kinds of filthy animals or fruits or wild seeds, tree saps, and plant juices, of exceeding bitterness, suitable to an excessive attachment to a solitary and unsociable life . . . Their jealous and suspicious character, the early age in which they begin the propagation of their species, the facility with which they join clandestinely with no regard for social civilities, and their natural dirty dishevelment, and the bad appearance of their women, considerably slows the advancement of their people (población) . . .

—*Gutierrez y Ulloa, 1807*[1]

"They are all soldiers."

—*Mrs. Henry Foote, 1869*

IN EL SALVADOR'S NATIONALIST NARRATIVE, THE CONQUEST INDIAN OF fabled Cuscatlán is an image aglow with tragic romance: a two-dimensional action figure, frozen in heroic gesture, in an exotic fantasy landscape. By contrast, Gutierrez y Ulloa's vision of indigeneity three centuries later (above), at the dawn of El Salvador's independence, could hardly offer a starker contrast: the Indian as peon, miserable, ruined, groveling, the degraded product of colonial abuse and oppression. That vision is key to today's indigeneity because it suggests that indigenous cultures were so shattered by the conquest that their twentieth-century descendents are completely new identities. The "real" Nahua, for example, might be understood to have vanished sometime during the sixteenth or perhaps seventeenth centuries, as the last shreds of their culture were extinguished. Their immiserated descendents would therefore represent some new ethnic identity born of colonial rule itself.[2] That view, not incidentally, buttresses a politically disabling argument: that indigenous peoples today can make no political demands based on their history of extinguished sovereignty because it was another people or nation (culture), now vanished, which lost that sovereignty. Any claim by indigenous movements of an organic continuity with the preconquest cultures is, in this light, a political fantasy not worth serious consideration.

But if indigenous life was indeed transformed so profoundly by colonial rule, did that cultural break signify a complete political one? By the nineteenth century, being Indian had transformed yet again: still poor, still bound to servitude by patronage and labor laws, yet holding considerable areas of land and mobilized into (sometimes armed) militias. Despite the drastic transformations wrought by the cataclysm of conquest, by colonial rule, and by the tumult of early statehood, threads of consistent indigenous anticolonial sentiment can be traced through those centuries and into the throes of the 1932 uprising and Matanza. With a very broad view, we can follow those threads through those centuries to better understand the present.

The Colonial Cataclysm

Certainly the Spanish invasion and colonial rule was a catastrophe for indigenous peoples throughout the Americas. The epidemiological impact alone was dire, with European diseases sometimes killing a third of the population in regions well ahead of the Spanish forces, even before battles were engaged. In the Amazon, whole peoples vanished before they were encountered, their existence attested to only by rumor and remnants of villages. Cycles of further epidemics, coupled with periodic massacres, forced labor, forced relocations, and famines, reduced the continent's population to a twentieth of its size within a single century. By the mid-eighteenth century, an estimated 95 percent of the continent's native languages were lost, and possibly 90 percent of the native population had died.[3] Forced concentrations in Spanish towns (such as those orchestrated under Toledo in the Republic of Quito) demolished some ethnic identities and reconfigured others.[4] And while, in some areas, indigenous aristocracies lingered (even providing the first wives for the overwhelmingly male conquistadors), in most areas indigenous nobilities and related social hierarchies were quickly shattered.[5] In central Africa, European colonial authority came to be called "Bula Matari," the "crusher of rocks."[6] In Latin America, the "crushing" began centuries earlier, and kept rolling, and was far more complete.

But the language offered by Gutierrez y Ulloa (above)—which indeed should ring familiar to readers of colonial and slave-owner literature everywhere—gives us clues of a certain political continuity. At the turn of the nineteenth century, the conquest was still a central theme in indigenous dances. The Indians offered exaggerated public deference to the Spanish but resisted Spanish authority however and wherever possible: through deception, foot-dragging, and perhaps what James Scott would call hidden transcripts. They had sustained and adapted their customs and culture within a subaltern orbit despised by Gutierrez y Ulloa as filthy, degraded, and degenerate but also sequestered and impenetrable to outsiders. We have no record of Indian rebellions or uprisings among the Nahua or Lenca during the colonial era, but Spanish official Pedro Cortés y Larraz had perceived an abiding "hatred," on his tour of the region in 1768–69[7]:

> Of all beings that I have seen, I suppose that these people [the Indians] are the most deserving of compassion . . . some pity them because they are so reviled. Others [pity them] because, though they work hard, they never escape from want and misery, but remain naked, ill-fed, sleeping on the ground, treated as beasts of burden, masters of nothing and constantly punished at the whipping post. Others pity them for their utter submissiveness, with their gnarled hands prostrate on the ground either before their ancient gods or at the feet of their superiors. . . . It is true they are reviled but they themselves revile everybody . . . they regard the Spaniards and ladinos as foreigners and trespassers in their domain, and therefore they view them with implacable hatred. They want nothing from the Spanish: neither his religion nor customs.[8]

Hatred for an oppressor caste would hardly be surprising under such conditions, but Cortés y Larraz perceived that hatred as deriving from the Indians' domination by people they still perceived, after more than two centuries, as "foreigners." He guessed (rightly, as later events would prove) that the conquest still pervaded their political worldview. And oddly, colonial rule itself helped to preserve indigenous ethnic cohesion in ways that laid the foundations for the 1932 uprising. Can we penetrate the veil drawn by the indigenous people over their own lives—and by the silence, disdain, and distortions of Spanish records—to find the threads which connected Cuscatlán to the twentieth-century peoples who launched that uprising?

The Racial Caste System

The first such thread was the racial caste system imposed by colonial rule, administered by Spanish authorities to ensure their labor supply. Some caution about language is needed here: from the sixteenth through the mid-nineteenth centuries, "Indian" was not understood as a "racial" identity in the sense it would be later. (For one thing, races had not yet been

FIGURES 9A AND B. Barón Castro included several plates depicting Salvadoran racial "types" in his *Población de El Salvador* (San Salvador: Universidad Centroamericana José Simeón Cañas, 1940). These nineteenth-century etchings, offered as Plates 99 and 100 in his original volume, were labeled "Indigenous lad and lass" (above) and "Water carrier and mayors [alcaldes] from some small indigenous localities." (Courtesy of the publisher.)

"scientized": that is, mapped and measured.) Nevertheless, what today we would consider racial ideas remained extremely important for colonial perceptions and administration of indios: indio was an intergenerational identity, determined by descent and signaled publicly by physical appearance, which structured all social relations, determined each person's social standing, rights, and privileges in society and in law, and established the precise rules for individual or collective political behavior. Growing mixed-race sectors—the *castas*—complicated but did not eliminate this hierarchy.

For readers not familiar with it, a quick summary of the colonial racial order may be helpful here. At the top of the ladder were the Iberian-born Spanish or *peninsulares*, marked ethnically by language and dress (and sometimes privileges like riding horses) but physically by their greater height, fairer skin, longer faces, and men's beards. Immediately below the peninsulares were the creole elites (European-bred, American-born), who were marked the same way (although often with some indigenous genetic admixture). At the bottom were the conquered Indians who, by virtue of their birth, were defined as vassals and were responsible for tribute (often paid as goods or labor). The shorter, darker, glossy black-haired "Indian" phenotype was therefore associated with this tributary laboring caste. "Mestizo" (mixed-race) quickly became an intermediate legal category because mixed-race individuals (an inevitable and immediate result of settlement) were considered exempt from the tribute required of Indians. To these categories were later added the *negros*, blacks. Some black Africans were brought within decades of the conquest as slaves, but their demographic weight ballooned in the seventeenth and eighteenth centuries with the sugar boom (especially the plantation economies in the Caribbean and the Atlantic coastal states). In the Salvadoran region, blacks were considered superior to Indians, and were imported partly to supervise Indians in indigo production.

Of course, extensive miscegenation in all directions soon created a full spectrum of skin colors and somatic types. But although boundaries became blurred, the categories of *criollo*, mestizo, negro, and indio retained their distinct legal standings and relative social values in the colonial hierarchy.[9] Nor did growing racial mixture diminish the society's exquisite sensitivity to race: rather, an elaborate terminology emerged to fit all combinations. For example, Pérez de Barradas identified 103 such terms, of which he attributed sixteen to the Guatemalan context (listed below).

Racial Definitions noted by the
General Captaincy of Guatemala, 1770.

1. Spanish with Indian produces a Mestizo.
2. Spanish with Mestiza produces a Castizo.
3. Spanish with Castiza reverts to Spanish.
4. From Spanish and Negro comes the Mulato.
5. From Spanish and Mulato comes the Morisco.
6. From Morisco and Spanish, the Albino.
7. From Albino and Spanish the Turnabout [*Torno atrás*].
8. Mulato and Indian engender the Calpamulato.
9. From Calpamulato and Indian comes the Jíbaro.
10. From Negro and Indian comes the Lobo.
11. From Lobo and Indian comes the Cambujo.
12. From Indian and Cambuja comes the Sambahigo.
13. From Mulato and Mestiza comes the Cuarterón.
14. From Cuarterón and Mestiza comes the Coyote.
15. From Coyote and Morisca is born the Albarazado.
16. From Albarazado and Salta atrás [elsewhere noted as a cross of Indian with "Chino," the latter possibly a cross between Spanish and Morisca] comes the *Tente en el aire*.

Source: J. Pérez de Barradas (1948:184–85).

The term later so important in El Salvador, ladino, initially simply meant an Indian who spoke Spanish. Later, ladino came to designate an assimilated Indian, who had adopted Spanish dress and customs, and no longer partook of indigenous social life. An Indian who sought to escape the tributary laboring condition could do so only by abandoning his or her Indian identity, through marriage, lifestyle, and probably a move out of the community. Reflecting the inevitable tensions of such a move, ladinos apparently sought the greatest possible social distance from the debased Indians, and were noted by Cortés y Larraz for particularly disdainful and brutal treatment of Indians.[10] By the late nineteenth century, in both Guatemala and El Salvador, ladinos came to dominate in small towns, often controlling shops and financial institutions, and vied with Indian communities for land and for control of the *alcaldías* (town governments).[11] By the end of the century, however, the term ladino blended with mestizo to include everyone who was neither Indian nor clearly white, and so came to include most of the elite. ("Whites" in the more Caucasian or Anglo-Saxon sense never constituted more than two percent of El Salvador's population, if that.) As a result, by the early twentieth century, Salvadoran ethnoracial relations had become defined by this indio/ladino split (for more on shifting terminologies, see chapter 8). The old colonial caste system still pervaded and structured these two identities, especially in shaping patron-client relations—and enduring hatreds (discussed below).

Under colonial rule Indians were considered vassals, responsible for tribute usually paid in the form of goods or labor submitted to Spanish settlers. After a brief period of legalized slavery (generally banned by the mid-sixteenth century), the earliest form of this servitude was the *encomienda* system: a grant of land and resources, including indigenous labor, to Spanish settlers (often as a reward for military service to the Crown, which had to be paid somehow). In the region of El Salvador, indigenous labor was enlisted by *encomenderos* (people granted encomiendas) primarily for export crops, like balsam (grown in the coastal hills) and cacao (the famous Nahua export crop of the pre-Columbian era) which found a growing creole market. Paradoxically, cacao production actually provided less dire conditions for the Nahua, as Spanish authorities permitted them to retain control of the cacao plantations (including their vast irrigation system, which incorporated miles of channels, dams, sluices, and pipes) and even to sell directly to middlemen.[12] For the first century, this arrangement sustained the Nahua of the Izalcos and Nahuizalco in relative affluence and contributed to the relative ethnic cohesion of these communities that persists to this day.[13]

But by the late seventeenth century, a far more lucrative export was indigo, a deep-blue dye processed from the native jiquilite plant which originally grew wild.[14] Forced labor for indigo production had a shattering impact on the indigenous communities. The work itself—especially the mashing of the pulp, by stamping on the leaves in the vats for days and weeks—was exhausting, and the food was probably very bad. The decomposing mounds of jiquilite pulp also drew swarms of flies, which in turn spread disease.[15] So devastating was indigo production to indigenous populations that royal edicts eventually ruled against hiring Indians to process indigo, but these were largely evaded with impunity (although the ban did periodically encourage the import of African slaves).[16] As death rates mounted, Indians apparently were inspired to flee their homes rather than submit to forced labor in indigo processing. Possibly more Indians fled than died; one colonial official believed that whole villages were depopulated once an indigo *obraje* (processing plant) was located nearby.[17]

Thus, after the first two centuries of colonial rule, many Indians had fled indigo, taxes, and ladino whips to vanish into the countryside, eking a living from the forests, the unseen back areas of haciendas, and common lands.[18] By the end of the colonial period, many indigenous towns had indeed vanished altogether, while others shrank dramatically. By the early nineteenth century, as much as a quarter of the rural population was scattered invisibly amidst hills and forest where, as one visitor observed, "they enjoy living in liberty and without any subjection to any law."[19] The newly independent Salvadoran government would grapple with this problem from its earliest years: in 1838, the new government passed a law requiring that "all those dispersed among the *ejidos* and wilderness" who "could not give good account of themselves" move into their local towns.[20] (Given the weakness of the state at that juncture, the law was probably ineffective.)

Hence one major effect of colonial rule was to scatter much of the indigenous population into an archipelago of hidden hamlets. That life endures today in the matrix of forest paths that still link the hidden world of the western Nahua and their cantones. But a scattered and covert existence was far from defining the full scope of indigenous life in the territory. Three institutions would sustain a more public Indian presence: the *comunidad*, the cofradía, and the *alcalde del comun*.

Concern by the Spanish Crown to prevent the complete decimation of the Indian workforce led to provisions for the comun or comunidad (community), a legally constituted community that provided indigenous communities with collective land and corporate representation to colonial authorities. After independence, a small number of ladino comunidades developed, but during the colonial era, the comunidad was a distinctly Indian institution.[21] Their landholdings were prodigious; even fifty years after independence, in 1879, comunidades still held a quarter of the country's territory, including what would become some of its finest coffee land. The comunidades were therefore the political and legal framework through which indigenous communities retained their corporate cohesion and defended their collective interests against local ladinos and to the state.

The second layer of Indian organization was the cofradía, or lay religious brotherhood. The cofradía is a very old institution, dating to preconquest

Europe and imported to the Americas by the Catholic Church, and which persists today. Outwardly and officially, a cofradía exists for the sole purpose of organizing the annual festival of a patron saint: its members are responsible for maintaining the saint's altar, collecting church tithes and fees, supporting all the costs and labor for the celebrations on its particular saint day, and maintaining the land, livestock, or any other property that covered those costs. That property might be substantial: one survey in 1769 found that cofradía capital included 130,958 cash in pesos, 23,453 head of cattle, and 5,264 horses and mules, in addition to indigo and immovable property.[22] The same survey found that 684 cofradías were operating in El Salvador, and that the two towns of Izalco (Dolores and Asunción) had a total of 21 cofradías between them.[23] The average capital of a cofradía in the heavily indigenous Sonsonate region was "192 pesos in addition to 400 head of cattle and other goods."[24] But costs to the cofradías might also be substantial—especially if they fell under the authority of a rapacious priest (all too common a figure in the colonial era). By the late nineteenth century, humanitarians were calling for the abolition of the cofradías as exploitative, abusive, and detrimental to the Indians' welfare.

But those calls went unheeded by the indigenous communities themselves. For one thing, the cofradías allowed the indigenous communities certain kinds of local economic leverage: for example, the cofradías of Izalco controlled the famous irrigation system of Izalco even until the 1932 Matanza. The cofradías also served a political purpose crucial to any colonized people: they were a central participatory mechanism—indeed, the only formally democratic one permitted—for indigenous political life. Each *majordomo* (leader of a cofradía) was elected by the full cofradía membership; the majordomos then elected the alcalde del comun (literally, the "mayor of the public" or "mayor of the community"). The alcalde del comun was spokesperson for the entire indigenous population to the state.

The alcalde del comun was therefore a key institution in itself, because it allowed for political representation based on genuine internal indigenous hierarchies. There were always indigenous families of relative wealth, with farms, cattle, and large homes, who acted as patrons of their communities and tended to become alcaldes del comun.[25] Alcaldes del comun would be important figures in the 1932 uprising: most famously, Feliciano Ama (who would be executed for this role in the Izalcos) and an "unofficial" alcalde del comun who reportedly led the revolt in Nahuizalco. Today, both the

Izalco/Nahuizalco and Panchimalco cofradías still have alcaldes del comun. In Izalco, he is chosen in annual elections (a process fraught with factional politics). In Panchimalco, however, his election is for life, and the name for the office is, provocatively, teyte (the term used by the Nahua in Nicaragua for their highest prince, and possibly used in Cuscatlán as well).[26]

Such was the configuration of being Indian at the dawn of Salvadoran independence. The Indians were a subordinate caste whose state was reported by outsiders as extremely miserable. Still, decentralized Spanish rule—ordered through layered creole, ladino, and indigenous corporate authority—included variations and flexibility. A substantial minority of the indigenous population was scattered in isolated hamlets and forests out of reach of direct Spanish administration. But much of the indigenous population lived in comunidades that held much of the country's agricultural land, with direct collective representation to Spanish authority. The indigenous communities also sustained a fragile internal political cohesion through the elected majordomos and alcaldes del comun. And conditions eventually improved: by the early 1800s, the indigenous population was actually recovering.[27]

Nor would that population be excluded from a major role in the tumultuous history of independent Salvadoran nation building. They would comprise an essential foundation of it.

Independence

Central America made its transition to independence through a series of creole struggles with colonial forces—and with each other—mostly in the early nineteenth century: in newly independent El Salvador, rival generals would maneuver and periodically clash for decades. In their nation-building ideologies, they were inspired especially by the recent French and the U.S. revolutionary experiences (as they understood them): independence leaders, poets, and intellectuals spoke of grand new republics which, free of the colonial trade yoke and its stultifying social hierarchies, would permit the flowering of egalitarian societies, civilization, modernity, and prosperity.[28] But liberal democratic ideals fell short of seriously addressing the racial hierarchy which secured the all-important cheap labor supply. "Indian" also remained a despised social category from which most elites kept a firm social distance. The racial caste system—with its patronage, endemic rivalries, and corporate Indian resistance—would therefore persist intact especially on the haciendas and in the countryside in general.[29]

Travelers in midcentury reported that indigenous people were increasingly speaking Spanish, and were adopting ladino farming practices. "We have seen that practically each Indian who has converted, so to speak, to the Spanish race," wrote one editorialist in 1855,

> has become a hard working agriculturalist or an intelligent artisan. An example of this is precisely this capital city, now [capital] of the state. Those who years back were called Indians, who had occupations appropriate to beasts of burden and who only produced maize and beans, are now ladinos, and occupy themselves in the cultivation of sugar cane, coffee, tobacco, and other things more important than maize and beans.[30]

Despite these trends, ethnic tensions between Indians and ladinos during the independence struggles remained high. The indigenous peoples' ethnic demographic weight (and corporate cohesion) were still considerable: throughout the nineteenth century, Indians still constituted about 40–50 percent of the country's population. The cofradías still existed in undiminished numbers, assets, and local influence. Most importantly, the indigenous comunidades still held a quarter of the country's land. Ethnic tensions with ladinos—often over control of that land—would increase, and indigenous comunidades actually held the upper hand in some local ethnic rivalries. What local chroniclers called "Indian revolts" and militia activity erupted throughout the century.

Indigenous politics—and militancy—in the nineteenth century indeed offer a far richer background than is usually recognized for the famous 1932 uprising and Matanza. The first such uprising was launched immediately with independence, in 1833, with a massive Indian rebellion from the Nonualco region. All scholars of the period acknowledge this uprising as a landmark event; it has even found a niche in the mainstream Salvadoran historical canon (e.g., in the principal high school history textbook).[31] Its leader, Anastasio Aquino, is today also granted iconic importance by indigenous activists. Exploring Aquino's rebellion requires sifting through cycles of historical reproduction, uncertain sources, and murky testimony. But it also provides an illuminating glimpse of how, after three centuries of colonial rule, indigenous politics were still strong—and still secessionist—at the dawn of Salvadoran independence.[32]

The Aquino Revolt

From what we can glean, Anastasio Aquino was an influential member of the Nahua community in Zacatecoluca (in the Nonualcos region), although apparently an hacienda laborer and, like most people of his day, illiterate. During the chaotic political atmosphere surrounding the transition to independence, his entire region was in political turmoil. The Central American Federation was formed in 1821, but the federal government (based in Guatemala City) was weak and constantly challenged by revolts. The Federation would fail, and El Salvador would be declared an independent country in 1839. The transition years were riddled with local fighting that drained the federal budget and imposed rounds of new federal taxes on a politically volatile countryside. A general crisis of authority swept the territory, as local towns and aspiring leaders saw an opportunity for autonomy or leadership.

Open ethnic conflict had erupted in 1814, when Indians rebelled against the illegal continued collection of tribute and attacked the provincial capital of San Salvador. In 1832, popular revolts against the new federal taxes rocked a number of towns in the region including Zacatecoluca and Izalco. Ethnopolitical tensions were therefore already explosive when, in January of 1833, a local hacienda owner locked Aquino's brother in the hacienda's stocks. Aquino and some friends attacked the hacienda to free him, and the incident catalyzed a mass uprising. Within weeks, Aquino had attracted thousands of mostly Indian followers, seized a series of towns, and was challenging creole control of the region. By late February, according to later (possibly exaggerated) assessments, no effective obstacle existed to his seizing the capital itself.

The rebellion was certainly inspired by tax grievances, and poor ladinos also participated. But ethnic solidarity was apparently the core of Aquino's appeal. Indeed, Aquino's first major military attack, on Santiago Nonualco, was apparently triggered by a ladino massacre of the Indian garrison in San Miguel.[33] The existence of this one-hundred-man Indian garrison is intriguing: it was established by the federal government to *put down* tax revolts, pitting Indian recruits against frustrated ladino townspeople. Aquino's intervention on the side of this force therefore highlights the ethnic solidarities at work. José Antonio Cevallos also maintains that when Aquino later executed two Indian colleagues for treachery, he severely undercut confidence among his indigenous followers in his legitimacy as an ethnic leader.

Aquino's military ambitions were, however, confined to local autonomy for the heavily indigenous Nonualco region, and this narrow objective proved his undoing. Elites in the capital were able to reorganize and retaliate, and the fighting lasted little more than a month before his army was crushed by creole-led forces. Aquino himself was captured in April and executed by firing squad in July. In an excess of creole zeal, his head was (reportedly) displayed publicly in a wooden cage for three days, as a warning to his community.[34]

Racial passions and fears among ladinos regarding Aquino are more evidence that his revolt was a specifically "Indian" one. Even today, fears of "Indian revenge" pervade Central American societies where Indian populations are significant.[35] Julio Alberto Domínguez Sosa speculates that these fears were powerful in El Salvador in 1833:

> The whites and mestizos could not tolerate any prospect of the "Commander of the liberating forces of Santiago Nonualco" going free and even remaining alive. That prospect was impossible, due to the terror which the still-fresh memory of the failed indigenous uprising was causing them. For the governing Salvadoran groups, the days of January to March 1833 had been a true nightmare. The shock that the indigenous uprising caused in these groups was enormous. Many of the white property-owners of Zacatecoluca and San Vicente preferred to take their chances in the mountains rather than face the authority of the rebels. It was logical that they wanted no return to those days, even in their imagination. . . . That is the reason for the concerted and ferocious persecution of Aquino and the Nonualcos.[36]

Later demonization by historians also suggested similar racial terror. In nineteenth-century accounts, Aquino was portrayed as a violent, ignorant indio, a barbarian leading barbarians. In 1891, Cevallos described Aquino as "monstrous" and his followers as "savages." Some Salvadoran historians, like Reyes, also argued—perhaps because the notion was reassuring—that Aquino and his followers must have been inspired and guided by creole provocateurs.[37] This argument reflects a common ladino assumption (common to slaveholder classes and settler-colonial authorities everywhere) that the indios are inherently so humble, ignorant, child-like, and impulsive as to be incapable of any major organized initiative. (Similar beliefs would surface regarding "communist" incitement of Indians in the 1932 Matanza.)

Possibly because such fears eventually faded, later twentieth-century historians have been more sympathetic to Aquino, although most authors de-emphasize the revolt's ethnic dimension and stress its class character.[38] Jorge Arias Gómez saw the rebellion as doomed precisely because of Aquino's "failure" to form cross-ethnic and cross-class alliances—missing or dismissing the revolt's ethnonationalist orientation. Domínguez Sosa agreed, although he considered Aquino's campaign to be no mere revolt, but rather a true revolution.[39] Still, Aquino's movement is not viewed as evidence of a broad, rebellious indigenous stratum, whose presence impugned El Salvador's national unity. Rather, the revolt is cast as an isolated and terminal event: a last gasp of a colonial caste identity fated to vanish, with independence, into a generic peasant sector—and therefore a minor novelty in the national narrative. Alastair White openly proposes that "since these threats were usually met by a closing of [elite] ranks and were defeated," aberrations like Indian uprisings "can be thought of in isolation to the 'normal' political system."[40]

Reflecting this view, the new history textbook, *Historia de El Salvador*, (issued in 1994) described the Aquino rebellion in a special box insert that, although seeming to highlight it, actually sets his rebellion off both visually and conceptually from the chronicle of mainstream politics.[41] After explaining the entire rebellion as stemming from a narrow agenda of tax resistance, the insert offers a short extract that concludes with an event associated with the Aquino revolt that is most likely to impress Salvadoran readers as barbarous and reprehensible: the sacking and desecration of a church, and Aquino's crowning himself king (taken from a 1935 version of events by historian Manuel Vidal). Doubts that this incident ever happened have circulated throughout the canon, and yet it is presented uncritically here:[42]

The 2000 aborigines (*aborígenes*) dispersed in all directions, robbing, killing and committing all kinds of pillage. Informed that the best goods were [hidden] in the Pilar Church, Aquino went there and, breaking down the doors, seized everything within. He hurled the saints to the ground and, placing the diadem of San José on his head, proclaimed himself "King of the Nonualcos."[43]

Perhaps some version of this event did happen. If so, it would signal something dramatic: that, as Cortés y Larraz wrote sixty years earlier, Indians (who were still at least half the territory's population) still wanted neither the Spaniard's religion nor his rule. Yet in citing it so tersely, the *Historia* trivializes the deeper ethnonationalist tenor of Aquino's rebellion. Certainly for youthful readers, Aquino's ethnic agenda is likely to be delegitimized by the impression of grandiose and fleeting pretensions by a local Indian chief. The story functioned the same way at the time. As Segundo Montes later put it, "Whether he converted himself, or not, into 'king of the Nonualcos,' whether he crowned himself as such in the church of El Pilar of San Vicente, or not, is something relegated to legend and to the ideological struggle to justify his execution and the massacre of the great majority of his followers."[44]

Alastair White (who believed Aquino's uprising should properly be treated "in isolation") indeed observed the ominous context, which nineteenth-century historians also found alarming: the larger climate of indigenous rebellion which the revolt suggested, and the potential it implied for a much wider ethnic conflagration.[45] Even the unsympathetic Cevallos recorded that, from an impulsive revolt by a few dozen people, the Aquino movement swelled rapidly to include thousands, due to its widespread popularity among the "aboriginal towns" of Santiago, Cojutepeque, San Pedro Perulapán, San Martín, Soyapango, and Ilopango. These Indian communities "had understood that his [Aquino's] revolutionary goal was to raise up and superimpose the Indian caste (*casta india*) over any other that might inhabit those regions."[46] A priest who spoke with Aquino shortly before his execution also reported that Aquino stated his goal to "liberate the Indians from the slavery in which they are held by the *chapetones*."[47]

And White also notes the larger regional context: the (reported) later arrival of a Maya Indian delegation from western Guatemala, who came too late to join Aquino in launching "a general rising of Indians."

Guatemala had been suffering similar ethnic turmoil, its transition history similarly punctuated by Indian revolts.[48] As White observes,

> It is interesting to speculate how formidable such a combination might have been, particularly in view of the fact that a few years later, in 1837–38, a movement that started as a rebellion by the Indians of western Guatemala, deftly manipulated by the conservatives, ousted the liberal Guatemalan government and inaugurated the quarter of a century of rule by Rafael Carrera.[49]

So what is the significance of Aquino's revolt to our questions about indigeneity in the twentieth century? For all its gaps and contradictions, the above record suggests that indigenous politics were both vigorous and strongly secessionist as late as 1833. Were such grievances specifically ethnic? Certainly Indian ethnic tensions centered on material grievances: forced labor on the haciendas; arbitrary punishments by *hacendados*; and forced recruitment of Indians into militias, as well as extortionist taxes. But class tensions alone do not explain such mobilizations. The Indian communities, in classic settler-colonial fashion, understood these abuses to derive from the racial split in the administration of power. Aquino sought neither control of the new state, nor greater representation for his community in a new government shared with creoles. Rather, he explicitly sought liberation of his casta from slavery and recognition by the creole authorities of political autonomy for the Nonualco indigenous community. In short, Aquino's mobilization reflected the indigenous view of the "Spanish" as foreign and illegitimate rulers, which Cortés y Larraz had reported eighty years earlier and which Gutierrez had described in 1807. That view was apparently well understood by terrified creoles in the capital.

Still, the Aquino revolt has been interpreted by most Salvadoran historians as marking the end of organized Indian resistance in the country. As Alastair White later concluded, "Small Indian insurrections, about which there is little information, continued to occur sporadically during the rest of the century; but none of these constituted a threat to the established political system."[50] Segundo Montes wrote of the 1833 rebellion (in language strikingly similar to that accorded the 1932 Matanza) that the rebellion seemed to mark the demise of indigenous ethnicity itself:

The consequence [of the 1833 rebellion and its suppression] . . . was the process of ladinization of the Nonualcos . . . abandoning all that could identify them as indígenas in order not to be victims of persecution and suspicion. Dress, language, customs, and [their] previous social, cultural and political organization had to be abandoned, or relegated to a clandestine existence, if they wanted to survive. The process was irreversible for the Nonualcos, those who today retain no more than their [characteristic] facial features and a nostalgia for the past.[51]

But this interpretation overlooks the brooding ethnic politics implied by "a nostalgia for the past." And we have no evidence of a mass "ladinization" in the Nonualcos, or anywhere else in the country, in the wake of the Aquino revolt. Indeed, the 1833 rebellion was neither the last nor even the largest indigenous mobilization to convulse nineteenth-century El Salvador. Decades of Indian revolts would follow the Aquino rebellion, some of which would spread through the entire country. In the Nonualcos themselves, five rebellions would erupt in the subsequent fifteen years. Rather than evaporating after 1833, indigenous militancy throughout the century would shape the very fabric of Salvadoran politics.

Indigenous Militias and Militancy

After the Aquino revolt, nineteenth-century Salvadoran politics were a tangle of civil military struggles, invasions from Guatemala and Honduras, coups and countercoups. (As a result of these endemic struggles, the country could not launch any serious development projects like road-building until the Zaldivar regime, in 1876–85.) "Peasants" were long believed by historians to have been uninvolved in such national matters. But in the last two decades, historians have found that power struggles in Guatemala, Mexico, and Peru included extensive involvement by rural peasant communities, who—far from being ignorant and excluded—were keenly aware of their own interest in the emerging national politic arena.[52] From the little we know, El Salvador was no different.

On the face of things, Indians could hardly have been politically passive given the dramatic impact of contemporary conditions. Even at

Aquino's time, Indians were providing troops crucial to the beleaguered federal government. Much of that service was forced; recruiters rounded up Indians, tied them together by their thumbs, and marched them to the garrison. This practice was, understandably, hated by the Indian communities, not least because it sometimes turned them into cannon fodder. One goal of Anastasio Aquino's movement was indeed to eliminate such practices; "their first acts, therefore, were to attack the escorts for parties of new recruits, *freeing* the latter and seizing arms."[53]

But the indigenous communities also willingly participated, as communities, in militia service. In the absence of any secure rule of law, the Indians had a strong interest in creole patronage. Mobilizing to support some creole or mestizo commander, an indigenous community could expect reciprocal favors and protection from that commander. Indigenous militia mobilization also reflected ambitions to confirm an Indian collective presence in the emerging independent polity.[54] As historian Patricia Alvarenga has argued, "[The Indians] hoped to gain on the battlefield a space in the State that would permit them to improve the conditions that they, as the most subordinated social group, had suffered since the colonial period."[55] And it was indeed the Indian's collective life that made their military service so valuable to creole elites:

> the structure of Indian communities was much more appropriate than that of ladino communities to improvised armies. Indian military hierarchy derived from the power hierarchy that existed within each Indian town. Community power relations were used as a model to turn peasants, especially Indians, into an organized group of warriors within a short period.[56]

As a result, much of the adult male Indian population became militia irregulars. And they were impressive soldiers. Wrote one foreign observer: "The soldiers are all taken from this class, as they are a far braver and finer race of men than the Ladinos, the mixed Indian and Spanish race, and when efficiently commanded they have been known to fight well.[57]

Not all were happy about the Indian militia service, however. Ladino hacendados still needed the indigenous communities as a cheap labor force (particularly as coffee production boomed). Indian labor revolts were a constant threat, and *armed* Indians were a potential nightmare. Indian militias in the western coffee-producing regions were therefore not permitted to hold arms permanently, or to maintain any standing force.[58] A second fear was that Indian irregulars could provide military backing for some *caudillo* or local leader, in a bid for high rank or even presidential power. In the 1880s, such a configuration indeed emerged behind General José María Rivas, of heavily indigenous Cojutepeque.

Alvarenga assumes that Rivas was himself indigenous; others doubt that he was. In either case, Rivas was an ethnic patron of classic kind: his house always open to any visitor, his wealth used to support and patronize his ethnic constituency.[59] And this ethnic base helped to propel him to national prominence. Because Cojutepeque was outside the sensitive coffee region in the west, creole state leaders had allowed his indigenous followers to remain armed. Already militantly mobilized, Cojutepequeños recruited him as their military leader in 1863, and he eventually enjoyed the popular support of the entire Nonualco region. At his height, he commanded thousands of armed and intensely loyal Indian troops. Moreover, Rivas was a skilled general and an adept politician; after his successful support of the 1885 Menéndez plot, he was reported to be the most charismatic political figure in El Salvador, and was even a possible presidential contender.[60] During his career, Rivas became governor of Cuscatlán, effected the overthrow of President Dueñas through military action on the capital, and later threatened the power of the new president Menéndez whom he had helped install.

Rivas would probably have made dangerous enemies in any case, based on pure power politics. But his national popularity formed a crucial bridge to state power for his armed Indian community, and so threatened the caste system that secured indigenous political marginality and cheap labor.[61] Rivas was abandoned and attacked by his liberal elite allies, and forced to flee to Honduras. (He was later killed during an attempted comeback in 1890.) One source cited the reason for his overthrow as being precisely his having armed Cojutepeque's "ignorant mobs": that is, the Cojutepeque Indians, whose communal ethnic loyalties were an obstacle to "the civilization and the progress of the Republic."[62, 63]

Rivas was exceptional for the military strength of his organization, which propelled his national success. Other Indian militias operated on a much smaller scale than that of Rivas's proverbial "10,000 troops." But throughout the country, and the century, the indigenous communities used that militia training to their own ends.

Indian Revolts

Aside from serving in ladino-led militia action, Indian communities also mobilized on their own, in local revolts over taxes or other grievances.[64] Throughout the century, thousands of Indians periodically demonstrated or launched revolts in communities dispersed among all departments, summarized here in Table 1.[65] In some years, such as 1872, Indian uprisings swept through the entire country.

Even a quick perusal of this (partial) list and its dates explodes any illusion of Indian ethnic irrelevance or disappearance during these decades. Far from a society blurring into mestizo national unity, or uniquely exempt from ethnic strife, nineteenth-century El Salvador was so frequently punctuated by Indian uprisings as to suggest the prototypical, rather than exceptional, quality of the Aquino rebellion.

Table 1: Indigenous Revolts in El Salvador, 1771–1918

1771–73	Volcan de Santa Ana	Indian uprising; government responds by reiterating order banning slavery (*Patria del Criollo*)
1796	Cojutepeque	Indians revolt against ladinos, killing two (LS)
1798	Santiago Nonualco	Indian workers rebel against indigo employers, demanding payment in cash rather than in kind (LS)
1811	Various communities	Indian revolts against taxes; raid jails (LS)
1814–15	San Salvador, Cojutepeque	Major Indian uprising; thousands of Indians attempt to take the city of San Salvador (LS)
1825	Nahuizalco	August: Indians revolt against local priest for excessive fees, and against local cattle owners for cattle damage to Indian crops; 3 Indians killed, many wounded; in December, ladinos counterattack (LS)

Sources: Aldo Lauria-Santiago (1992, 1999a) (LS): Hector Lindo-Fuentes (LF): Martínez *Historia de Cojutepeque* (Ma); Monterrey *Historia de El Salvador* (Mo); Patricia Alvarenga (Alv).

Table 1: Indigenous Revolts in El Salvador, 1771–1918 *(continued)*

1832	Country-wide	Revolts against taxes; extensive government repression, jailings, deaths. (LS)
1833	Chalatenango, Tejutla, Nonualco, Izalco	Indians revolt against new taxes; attack and raid Sonsonate (LS).
1833	Santiago Nonualco	Indians revolt against military recruitment, poor wages; major armed uprising led by Anastasio Aquino
1835	Various communities	Indigenous uprising to support presidency of Tomas Espinoza, elected chief of state but opposed by ladino and creole population (LS)
1837	Cojutepeque, Zacatecoluca, Nonualco area, Ilobasco	Indian rebellion "rose upon the white & mulatto population murdering them and plundering their houses, under a supposition that the origin of the devastating cholera was attributable to poison thrown into the rivers and that even the medicines supplied to them were impregnated with deleterious substances." Uprising repressed by troops; all participants executed. Chatfield, dispatch to Foreign Office June 26, 1837, FO 15-19 (LF) (also Ma 208-9, Mo)[1]
1838	Santa Ana, Ahuachapan	Indians join General Rafael Carerra to fight against el Salvadoran authority. (LS)
1837–39	Santa Ana (Volcan)	Indians revolt; possibly aided by Guatemalan president Carranza (LS)
1840	Santiago Nonualco	Uprising; 50 soldiers sent to "destroy everything": many killed (LS)
1843–45	Western region	Extensive fighting; Indian populations join local forces to rebel against local authorities. (LS)
1845	Santiago Nonualco	Indians attack house of *regidor* and free a prisoner; government expresses concerns about "Indian movement" (LS)

[1] See Reyes, *Nociones de historia*, 417 on relation of these uprisings to events in Guatemala.

1846	San Juan, Santiago Nonualco	Indian uprisings; burn houses of "*ricos*" (rich people). Suppressed by government troops: town burned, numerous executions (characterized by Reyes as a "*guerra de castas*" (caste war); see *Nociones de historia* 502-3). (LS)
1848	Santiago Nonualco	Indian revolt
1851	Atiquizaya:	Indians imprisoned for seeking to title land (LS)
1863	Various communities	Indian mobilization against Barrios (see Alvarenga); violent Indian resistance against military recruitment; indigenous military leader Rivas becomes general (LS)
1865	San Pedro Perulapan	Indians attack Ladinos (LS)
1868	Cojutepeque	Indians confront garrison soldiers, (LS)
1868	Chilanga	Indian uprising (LS)
1869	Apastapeque	Indian uprising, put down by troops from San Vicente (LS)
1870	Santa Ana	Indian uprising: burn municipal building and archives, loot stores, attack army post. Suppressed by army troops from San Salvador which raid Volcan area, destroy homes, kill "many." Governors of Ahuachapán and Sonsonate increase troops and security (LS)
1870	Cojutepeque	Indians clash with local troops; leaders beaten to death (LS)
1871	Cojutepeque	400–1,000 Indians join anti-government forces, are suppressed by government troops. (LS)
1872	Apopca	revolt led by priest (LS)

Table 1: Indigenous Revolts in El Salvador, 1771–1918 *(continued)*

1872	Cojutepeque	"Four hundred Indians armed with machetes rose . . . under the battle cry of Duenas and religion" (LF)
1872	Izalco, elsewhere	August 12: Indian revolt; widespread uprisings "throughout the country throughout the country which involved mostly Indian communities. (LS)
1873	Juayua	Indians revolt against land expropriation (LS)
1875	Izalco	Izalco revolt against abolition of ejido land: assaulted town garrison (LS)
1875	San Miguel	Indian revolt of 3,000-4,000 people, characterized as "male and female fiends" (LF p 134); attack local garrison, kill governor, burn town hall and other official buildings, four days of burning and looting of private homes and businesses; suppressed by government troops from La Union (LS)
1879	Ahuachapán	Indian rebellion (see Maria Leisten-schneider Vol I 1977 p 267)
1884	Izalco and Atiquizaya	Indian revolts (LF)
1884	Nahuizalco	Indian rebellion against land privatization; burn town hall and archive, kill 14-16 people (LS) (Leistenschneider, Dr. Rafael Zaldivar, Vol 2 pp 59-60, cited in Alv; also LS)
1885	Cojutepeque, Santa Ana (Volcan), Nahuizalco, Chalchuapa, Atiquizaya, Izalco, Santiago Nonualco, Suchitoto	Indian revolt against government of Zaldivar (LS); in Atiquizaya, general uprising, municipal archive burned; in Santiago Nonualco, Indians revolt against local garrison to support Menendez bid for power, burn local archive; suppressed by troops from Zacatecoluca, who shoot rebels in town plaza without trial (LS); in Suchitoto, Cojutepeque governor Rivas calls on region's Indians to support revolt against Zaldivar regime (LS)
1887	Izalco	uprising (LS)

1889	Cojutepeque	(LF)
1890	Cojutepeque	General Rivas again musters Indians to revolt against regime of Melendez; revolt characterized Governor of Usulutan as "*levantamiento indigena*" (indigenous uprising) (LS
1898	Santa Ana province	Indian uprising (LF)
1898	Izalco	Indian uprising against ladinos moving to support General Regalado (LS)
1918	*Ligas Rojas*	Indigenous communities join *Ligas Rojas* to reassert authority against increasing ladino coercive capacities (Alv).

Is it fair to view all these revolts and uprisings as truly "Indian" uprisings? Key dimensions suggest their ethnic character. First, ladinos from the period described them as revolts by Indians explicitly—a reference which, given the long-standing racial caste system, cannot be reduced simply to its class element (recall discussion of the "class paradigm" in chapter 3). Second, the mobilizations matched the classic model of Indian revolts described by Severo Martínez Peláez: a concentrated, local uprising, reacting to tensions with a local ladino-dominated municipality, which targeted the buildings and symbols of central town authority through arson, stone-throwing, and the occasional lynching of a hated ladino town official. Caste tensions—the conflation of race and class—determine these patterns.[66] Third, race was by no means always fused with class. The rebel leaders were sometimes relatively affluent, with substantial landholdings and authority based partly on their own ability to provide patronage to their communities. (In the 1932 uprising, the relative affluence of some rebel Indian leaders would render their participation "inexplicable" to some ladinos.)

Alvarenga indeed argues that the Indian (ethnoracial) character of these revolts was one reason why the militia system was initially abolished. The crafting of a national army (a project already begun by

Zaldívar in the 1870s) would accelerate in the 1890s, and by 1910, the state was relying on the new national army, with deliberately mixed indígena and ladino battalions. For the Indians, however, this "nationalization" of the military appears to have been equally dismal. Once again, they would be rounded up, tied together by their thumbs, and marched to the barracks.[67]

The Land Reforms

Despite these troubles, throughout the nineteenth century indigenous life remained politically cohesive, largely because their comunidades still controlled some quarter of the country's land (particularly in the western region).[68] Yet by the 1870s, that control was under fresh assault: El Salvador began to emerge from its half-century of civil warfare, and in the 1870s economic development began in earnest, especially toward developing export agriculture. But a successful export economy required infrastructure that the country still lacked: especially, a major road grid to link department capitals; port and customs facilities at Acajutla; a national telegraph to link the port, the capital, and major agricultural towns; and, not least, a more professional state bureaucracy. Some major source of foreign currency to pay for these projects was vital.

At this crucial juncture, the huge profit potential of coffee was becoming apparent. Between 1865 and 1891, annual Salvadoran coffee exports to California expanded from a value of some $80,000 to $4.8 million. Coffee production in the Sonsonate region, west of San Salvador, doubled and tripled in just three years, between 1877 and 1881.[69] Expanding coffee exports were now considered essential to the progress of the Republic and the Liberal government began to pass laws promoting coffee production, offering land titles to those who grew it.[70]

Yet much of the land best suitable for coffee was still held by the comunidades and used only for subsistence agriculture. The obstacle could not be tolerated; in 1881, the state abolished the communal lands of the comunidades, arguing that

> The existence of lands under the ownership of the Comunidades impedes agricultural development, obstructs the circulation of wealth, and weakens family bonds and the independence of the

individual. Their existence is contrary to the economic and social principles that the Republic has accepted.[71]

A year later, the ejidos—land belonging to towns and administered by ladino-dominated municipalities—were also legally abolished, likewise as a "principal obstacle" to "the Nation's chief source of life and prosperity."[72] All such collective lands were to be distributed as private parcels.

The land reforms proceeded fairly peacefully, but ethnic suspicions pervaded the division and occasional violence broke out. Confusion persisted as to which lands were actually ejido lands (assigned to a town) and which were communal lands assigned to the indigenous (and the few ladino) comunidades. Land reform was also paralyzed by disputes over boundaries, by fraud or accusations of fraud, and by foot-dragging and judicial complaints by the indigenous communities.[73] Uprisings erupted as Indians perceived or suspected extensive ladino manipulations and cheating. In 1884, some two thousand Indians attacked Nahuizalco, burned the municipality building, and killed some fourteen people. In the same year, Indian revolts shook Izalco and Atiquizaya. In April 1885, recognizing that the comunidades were not only resisting the land reform but could delay it indefinitely, the government abolished the comunidades themselves.[74] The juridical framework of Indian collective life, which had so long provided for indigenous collective representation and collective land control, was formally liquidated.

Still, privatization of the Indians' communal lands was not achieved overnight. Land retitling would drag into the next century, marked by endless delays, complaints, lawsuits, and occasional open fighting.[75] The indigenous communities did not actually oppose privatization; many Indians hoped to benefit. And, in the first phases, many indigenous individuals did obtain small plots. In the Izalco region, these plots averaged only four *manzanas* (about seven acres), less than the minimum necessary to sustain a family.[76] Nevertheless, even this amount of land provided some subsistence and small cash income that cushioned families against the highly seasonal and uneven labor market of the coffee plantations. The land reform therefore pitched Indians against ladinos not due to privatization per se, but due to ladino fraud and favoritism, particularly by ladino government agents assigned to survey and distribute the private plots.

A window on these ethnic tensions is found regarding the Izalcos—the region once famous for its cacao plantations, and to this day a dense center

of indigenous population and politics. Ladinos controlled the town government, but two Indian comunidades had controlled some 6,750 hectares of
communal land, over twice the amount of land (3,240 hectares) controlled
by the ladinos. With privatization, these comunidad lands were now to be
divided among their indigenous family members, sustaining indigenous ethnic control. But the remaining lands around Izalco—private haciendas and
"empty land"—comprised 12,150 hectares, or nearly twice the indigenous
holdings. Under the terms of the reforms, "empty lands" and all unclaimed
lands were to revert to state ownership, to be parceled out to private buyers by municipal authorities.

But those authorities were ladinos, themselves often interested in the
land. And they controlled the paperwork. It was hard enough for Indians
to gain title even to the former communal lands of their own dissolved
comunidades, to which (as former members) they had legal right. Lacking
capital, credit, and literacy, individual Indians were most unlikely to gain
access to "state lands." Hence the ladinos, as a bloc, threatened to gain
ownership of some 15,390 hectares, or over twice the Indian holdings.
Indigenous resentment therefore reflected not simply loss of land but fear
of an inexorable transfer of political and economic power to ladino hands.
Tensions sometimes became violent: in 1898 an infuriated crowd of
Indians, convinced of systematic fraud, attacked the local court and cut
off the hand of the hated land reform agent.

Caste Relations Collapse

Despite the turmoil of the land reforms, in the decades immediately pre-
ceding the 1932 Matanza, ethnic relations in the Salvadoran countryside
were not uniformly hostile. For one thing, many Indians had gained or
retained some land. ("There are only four classes besides soldiers in
Salvador," Mrs. Henry Foote had written in 1869. "Great shopkeepers,
little shopkeepers, servants, and agriculturalists; the latter class are the
pure Indians, and generally have their own little piece of land and house
on it."[77]) Also, patron-client relations provided for some reciprocity
between ladinos and Indians, mitigating ethnic tensions by securing basic
Indian subsistence. In towns such as in Ataco, where landowners provided
workers with a stable food supply, the population apparently did not
mobilize in 1932 at all.

Of course, racial patron-client relations commonly seem rosier to those on top. A series of 1979 interviews by Segundo Montes conveys the pleasant hue that some ladinos perceived of the graces surrounding *compadrazgo*, the godparent system (an institution common throughout Catholic Latin America). Many Indians sought ladinos as godparents for their children, and were then beholden to the ladino godparent (*padrino*) for a host of favors and courtesies. One elderly ladino recalled the system fondly:

> For the naturales [Indians] . . . even today, yes? there is a reverence they show: "Good evening, padrino!" Even elderly men came to salute him. . . . And every Sunday they came to bless the padrino: "God give you good day, padrino!" And they would come to him to salute him, and he would give them some little gift: a fresh drink, some sweets, or whatever they were giving here; and I have heard the reverse, old men coming and bringing something for their padrinos, bringing good fruit which they took from the produce that they themselves cultivated, but good, yes? always for the padrino.[78]

Still, the colonial legacy was evident in the obsequious manners accompanying these relations (e.g., kneeling with hands on the ground) which manifested to travelers as groveling. And in fact, ethnic tensions were very high: in a series of interviews conducted by Segundo Montes in 1979, several ladinos remembered the "hatred" that once prevailed between the two groups. In any case, even the veneer of patronage evaporated as the country's economy transformed. For ladinos were obtaining new economic and political power, which made them increasingly see Indian services and cooperation as obsolete.

In the new export economy, ladinos were rapidly gaining new leverage. The development of a nationwide infrastructure (roads, railroad, telegraph, and telephone) was quickly providing them with new external sources of wealth, security, and political power. They also were gaining new instruments of outright force: the local town police, the rural police, and now the treasury police, created to secure the coffee crop. They also had the notorious National Guard, whose mission by the 1930s was primarily control of the Indian labor force (also in the interest of coffee production). Ladino hacendados regularly hired Guard members as private guards for the estates. Landlords could even deputize private citizens at will for specific purposes like pursuing a fugitive—and people could not refuse such service. Ladino landowners therefore had flexible and effectively unlimited police power, directed largely toward arresting drunks and brawlers but also toward suppressing strikes or labor resistance of any kind.[79]

Ladinos' need to sustain the old caste patronage system was therefore vanishing. They no longer needed sharecroppers; coffee provided their (rapidly rising) cash incomes. They no longer needed to appease indigenous communities with reciprocal services; they now had the Guard. They controlled the terms of credit and wages to smallholders and laborers, and those terms became more usurious each year. Indian resentment rose, and labor unrest with it—but this only increased ladinos' reliance on force. Mario Zapata (later a major player in the communist movement) recalled visiting a ladino friend who explained the lavish lunch laid out for the Guards stationed on his farm: "They are our salvation; without the guardia we could not operate."[80]

The official forums for land disputes were the courts, the governor's office, or even the president's office, and indigenous resistance to these changes was channeled into streams of complaints and petitions.[81] The ethnic (rather than simply class) sentiment of the liquidated indigenous comunidades is revealed in their language. For example, a 1903 petition from Izalco residents to the president protested that "we are not quarrelsome . . . nor do we want to recover our ancient communal lands, nor unsettle neighboring hacendados, what we want is justice and the fulfillment of the agreement." A 1904 petition called for assistance "with the type of case we have to resolve, principally that of representing an abolished society in the process of being liquidated." Far from having

FIGURES 10A–C. Plates 115, 119, and 120 from Barón Castro's volume, Población de El Salvador (San Salvador: Universidad Centroamericana José Simeón Cañas, 1940), showing the juxtaposition of contemporary racial images in his national imaginary. Top: "Pipil Indians of Nahuizalco." Bottom left: a classic romantic painting, which he titled "Young creole of El Salvador, with the typical apparel of the country's peasants." Bottom right: one image from two photos representing his contemporary national ideal, offered under the title "Young creoles of El Salvador." (Courtesy of the publisher.)

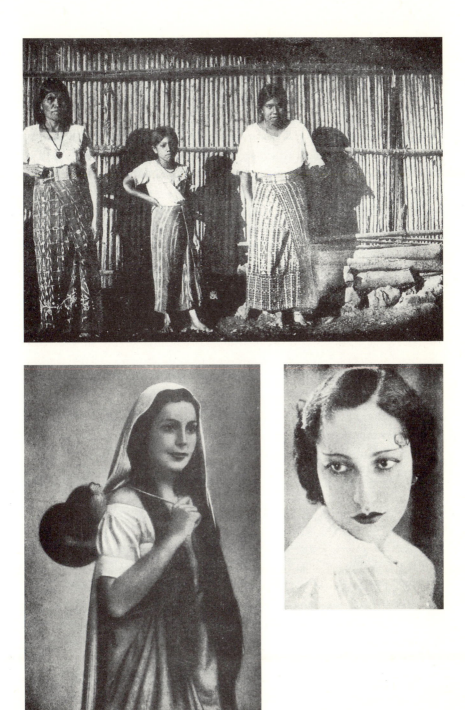

vanished with the stroke of a pen in the 1880s, the indigenous communities still considered themselves to be "in the process of being liquidated" in the early 1900s—and in fact were still functioning as corporate communities. (In Izalco, communiqués to the national government from the "Indian community" would continue into the 1940s.)

Slippery land dealing did not prevent many indigenous families from obtaining land sufficient to grow some corn, beans, and a few bags of their own coffee for sale. Yet privatization alienated far more land from the Indian communities than it provided. Worse, the privatization of once-common lands made wide tracts inaccessible to a population now growing exponentially. According to official census figures, between 1892 and 1930 the country's population doubled. One close observer estimated that the western rural population was increasing by 30,000 per year.[82] As more land was absorbed by large coffee plantations, more people—particularly subsistence cultivators, i.e., Indians—were thrown onto the wage labor market.[83]

Yet wage labor itself was becoming more unpredictable, and job conditions more grueling. Wages responded only downward to varying coffee prices; a low international market price meant lower wages, while a boom price meant no wage increase, padding the pockets of the major coffee landowners. Working conditions were onerous, with long hours and scanty food (a standard fare was two meals a day, of two tortillas and enough beans to cover them, with women receiving smaller tortillas and correspondingly less beans). Worse, this scanty ration was withheld as punishment for any infraction, including "laziness" during the long workday. Moreover, contrary to law, many *finca* (coffee plantation) owners paid their workers in their own "pesos" or scrip, usable only at the finca store, where prices were often inflated. Some coins were even assigned a value only for a specific good, like "uno refresco" (one drink).

Swelling the ranks of these unfortunate workers were Indians losing land to extortionist credit practices. In the boom years, it was routine for coffee growers, large and small, to borrow money for the planting and harvest, pay it back from ever-rising sale prices, and live on the profits, borrowing again for the following year. Reflecting this bull market but also the utter vulnerability of Indians to ladino creditors, terms of loans to smallholders were notoriously bad. Bearing in mind that a smallholder's collateral was the land itself, we can see the import of a typical contract:

Let it hereby be known that I have sold to Señor So-and-So a quintal of coffee [in advance] . . . for the sum of seventeen colones which I have received, and I promise to present [the coffee] on [date] in his place of business in this town; and I promise that, if for any reason I am not able to deliver it, I will pay to him the best price that coffee may have on that date, but in no case less than forty colones.[84]

Such terms (over 100 percent interest) were barely tolerable under conditions of boom. But within two years after the 1929 stock market crash, the international coffee market collapsed. El Salvador's exports plummeted in value from US$22.7 million in 1928 to US$6.4 million in 1932.[85] Heavily in debt, even large plantation owners went bankrupt. Small coffee producers had no hope of repaying the usurious loans, and their lands were forfeit. During the first few years after the 1929 crash, "28 percent of the coffee properties changed owners."[86] Those who lost land were hard pressed to find any other way to survive: one observer even called the debt arrangements "a new form of murder."[87]

These newly dispossessed people swelled the wage-labor market just as demand for their labor collapsed. Even the large coffee plantations (although rapidly absorbing forfeited plots) could not hire workers to harvest the bushes. In the summer of 1931, thousands of desperate, hungry workers were on the roads in Sonsonate and Ahuachapán departments, prompting newspapers in the capital to call for emergency aid measures.[88] What work did exist drew awed comment from foreigners about its terrible conditions. For instance, Canadian commander Brodeur wrote of "low wages, incredible filth, utter lack of consideration on the part of the employers, conditions in fact not far removed from slavery."[89] U.S. ambassador McCafferty observed that

Farm workers have been often miserably underpaid and have been working under conditions on some fincas which have been certainly intolerable. On the fincas of many of the richest landowners in Salvador, conditions have been the worst. Medical attention has not been available, [and] workers have been compelled to purchase their few necessities at advanced prices from stores maintained by the finca proprietors. Frequently, it has been asserted that a farm animal is of far more value to the proprietor than the worker for there is generally a plentiful supply of the latter."[90]

While all this ruin was going on, the indigenous communities were also facing rapid political erosion. The abolition of the comunidades had eliminated their formal corporate representation to the state; nationally, as a collective, they were voiceless. They were increasingly vulnerable to the various repressive police forces controlled by ladino individuals and ladino-dominated town governments. With the collapse of the coffee economy in 1930, they were rapidly losing land and facing economic desperation. By mid-1931, the conditions for a major revolt were smoldering. Some hopes for change were pinned on local elections in December. But when those elections were postponed, the die was cast.

CHAPTER 7

THE MATANZA

GENOCIDE, ETHNOCIDE . . . AUTO-ETHNOCIDE?

And then, in the glow of the burning mountain, a more ominous development was observed. Bands of Indians armed with machetes were making their way out of the ravines and tangled hills down into the towns of the area. In their eyes burned the bright light of fanatic determination. Before dawn came on the twenty-third all of the western part of the country was aflame, not with molten lava, but with revolt.
         —Thomas Anderson, 1971

We want this plague exterminated by the roots; for if it is not, it will sprout forth with new spirit, now expert and less foolish, because in new attempts they will pitch themselves against the lives of all, first, and finally slit our throats.
     —Anonymous landowner, Santa Ana, 1932

It's impossible to relate even approximately the details of the barbarism unleashed throughout the country by the repression . . . Unfortunately, the huge figures leave us cold, too, and they don't communicate the true intensity of those events, either . . .
         —Miguel Mármol, 1966

It would seem that they are going to exterminate the Indians.
     —Roy MacNaught, missionary, 1932

ON THE NIGHT OF JANUARY 22, 1932, A MASS INSURRECTION WAS LAUNCHED in El Salvador's western coffee region. Great crowds of workers, mostly Indians armed with machetes and farm tools, assembled in the roads and marched into a number of towns, and with some shooting took over the town centers from the terrified residents. For some hours or days, they engaged in a flurry of looting and drinking, celebrating what they thought was a countrywide revolution and their impending seizure of the government. But government troops were quickly sent from other departments, and within three days the last of the towns was back in ladino hands. The rebellion itself was therefore quite short; it took, at most, about a hundred lives.[1] Its repression, however, would go down in history as the bloodiest single crisis in modern Latin American history until the 1980s; the most commonly cited figure is 30,000 deaths. Most of these deaths, again, would be of Indians.

Today, the 1932 Matanza (massacre) is the most common explanation offered in El Salvador for why Indians no longer live there. Terrified by mass killings, the indigenous people supposedly gave up their dress and language in order to escape ladino suspicion and state terror, and assimilated into a generic mestizo peasant population. Yet this story remains untested, an oral tradition with no documentation, reinforced by impressions that Indians vanished and that some reason for their vanishing must exist.

It also remains an isolated myth in a national narrative otherwise devoid of ethnic references. Most histories of modern El Salvador make minor mention of Indian identity in the 1932 revolt, but until recent work by historians such as Aldo Lauria-Santiago and Patricia Alvarenga, race usually manifested merely as one additional factor aggravating "peasant" (class, sectoral) grievances over land and wages.[2] Some scholars of the 1932 crisis mention Indian ethnicity only to clarify how Indians were duped, their atavistic ethnic sentiments pumped up—with fatal consequences—by communist promises.[3] Indianness appears out of nowhere in these accounts, which make little or no mention of Indians before the revolt and certainly omit the dense history of indigenous militia service and revolts in the nineteenth century (in fairness, historians did not have access to this information until recently). As White observed of the 1833 Aquino revolt, the ethnic dimensions of the 1932 crisis therefore manifest "in isolation to the 'normal' political system."[4]

And of course, most chronicles of 1932 omit any mention of Indians after the revolt, as they are presumed to have assimilated. Instead, writers concerned with the later civil war, which peaked in the 1980s, recall the 1932 crisis as the country's tragic turning point toward open dictatorship and military rule. Rightists, by contrast, cite it as the communist insurrection that mandated that rule. Even those scholars who give some careful attention to indigenous ethnic sentiment in the uprising, like James Dunkerley, treat 1932 as the last gasp of that sentiment, after which Indian issues no longer play a part in mainstream Salvadoran national history and so require no more attention.

Only an exceptional few writers have viewed the 1932 uprising as primarily reflecting bitter indigenous resentment of the "Spanish" as foreign rulers, usurpers of Indian land and authority.[5] Until recent work by Jeff Gould, Héctor Pérez Brignoli was almost alone in identifying a primarily ethnic quality both to the revolt and to its suppression, seeing 1932 as the end of "a long and unequal struggle, begun by the Conquistadors in the sixteenth century."[6] He proposed that "there were really two insurrections . . . one an Indian and peasant insurrection, and the other a communist conspiracy"—the latter actually the weaker and less effective of the two. But his influential article has not provoked questions about the Matanza's aftermath: the ethnic question remains confined to the 1932 crisis.

Indigeneity also appears only erratically in the account universally tapped by scholars, Thomas Anderson's skillfully woven narrative, *Matanza*. Inexplicably, this book opens with a graphic image right out of a settler-colonial nightmare, of Indians filing out down jungle trails, machetes in hand, eyes ablaze with fanatical race hatred. (See the opening quote to this chapter: one can almost hear the native drums thumping.) Yet Anderson's book is far more intelligent than its theatrical beginning. He later dedicates several pages to the history of indigeneity in El Salvador and comments carefully on any indication he finds of Indian racial sentiment, as in the ambitions of certain rebel leaders. He even cites two responsible Salvadoran sources who believed that the 1932 Matanza had "the definite overtones of a race war."[7] It was also Anderson who, without elaboration, supplied the oft-cited quote regarding the Matanza, "All those of a strongly Indian cast of features . . . were considered guilty."[8] And yet, when describing the revolt itself—the taking and sacking of towns, the murders, the fear and flight of landowners—Anderson makes little mention of ethnoracial motives or hatreds. Race floats in and out of his narrative, suggesting that race contributed only some extra emotion to a crisis born of material (peasant) grievances about land and wages.

Race and class always interplay, and Salvadoran indigeneity has always interwoven them. In the 1932 revolt, the indigenous leadership was split, some ladinos joined with indigenous workers, and material grievances were certainly urgent, as in any mass rural revolt.[9] Yet such complexities always surround any ethnic revolt, and Indian revolts are no more immune from fragmentation, strategic cross-ethnic ties, and material grievances than any other ethnic upheaval. If we view the fragmentary evidence we have about the 1932 uprising through an ethnic lens, remembering also the indigenous militancy of previous decades, we find support for a conclusion long overlooked or deliberately rejected: that the 1932 revolt was so heavily shaped by racial tension, and indigenous perceptions of the "Spanish" and ladinos as invaders and occupiers, that it can be granted a long-denied place in history as one of the last great Indian uprisings of the twentieth century.

"Duped Indians"

To rediscover the Indian character of the 1932 rebellion, we must first address one disabling belief long held by the dominant ladino society about Indians generally: that they are ignorant and humble people, passion-driven and impressionable, gullible to outside agitation but requiring outsiders to mobilize at all. Such interpretations of 1932 hold that the Indians mobilized not because they grasped the communist platform, or because they had truly revolutionary goals, but because they were simply fooled into believing that the communist movement would restore their lands. In other words, they had no coherent ideology of their own, but jumped at the chance to gain material reward. In this view, indigeneity is not a political factor in itself, but only an additional factor aggravating the "peasantry's" normal gullibility.

The "duped" view was produced even at the time of the revolt, in the otherwise sympathetic report of Canadian Commander Brodeur, then in charge of two battleships that hovered at the Acajutla port during the crisis. Brodeur appears to have gained the following insights from what he considered knowledgeable ladino advisors in the country:

It appears that up to a short time ago, this low class of laborer *was content with its lot*, or at least *indifferent to the appalling conditions under which it worked*. . . . But when here and there a few managed to better themselves, *realization began to dawn* upon these latter of the unhappy, and indeed unjust, lot of their class. It was to these few *slightly superior types* that the principles of Communism . . . appealed most strongly, and it is they who helped to *spread the gospel of 'class warfare' amongst the workers*. Under these circumstances, it is hardly to be wondered at that Communism made many converts, and the number of affected Indians grew rapidly.[10] [Emphasis added.]

Jorge Schlesinger, who wrote a history of the revolt based on contemporary documents, also believed that the Indians had not realized their grievances against ladinos until they were "reminded" of it.

Among the Indians, *once such ambitions were awakened*, it was easy to *revive racial sentiment, reminding them* that they were in ancient times the owners of the land; that the present landowners were but the heirs of the usurpers, of the men who had enslaved them, and that now the hour had come to repossess the land that was theirs and that they cultivated. *Awakening* these material ambitions, the campaign began to play sentimental strings *by pointing out* that the Indian would no longer be exploited by the whites and ladinos; but that the Indian would assume direct control, elected their governors from those of their own blood and their own towns, who would understand their way of life, respect their traditions and their customs.[11] [Emphasis added.]

An indigenous people living under conditions of extreme poverty and political exclusion might be presumed to have very clear understandings of "racial sentiment." Yet ladino propensities to see Indians as politically blank or simple pawns shows up in later studies as well. For example, in Segundo Montes's famous survey of beliefs about compadrazgo, his assistants found indigenous sources from Nahuizalco unforthcoming about 1932. Naively, they deduced that these people had not been involved: "they were victims of the situation and ignorant of everything (that had occurred) up to the present, since when they are questioned one only finds fear and silence . . ."[12] Yet it is clear that the interviewees did not trust Montes's assistants. Many revealed that they themselves had lost family members in the revolt; they could hardly have been ignorant of the situation. When asked about the events of 1932, they responded as any vulnerable racial population might respond to an outside interviewer from the dominant group: by evading the question, changing the subject, claiming complete ignorance, or falling silent.[13]

Were the Indians truly duped, or so politically simple that only foreign activists could alert them to their plight? In the previous chapter, we saw evidence that the opposite was more likely true. The indigenous people had mobilized throughout the previous century, in militias following ladino patrons and in their own revolts. In the decades prior to 1932, the dissolved indigenous comunidades had sustained a keen sense of their relations, as ethnic communities, to the state. But in 1932 was this collective sentiment still Indian in character, or had it dissolved into a more generic peasant or class-based identity—as literature emphasizing a peasant mobilization suggests?

The political lens of any insurrection determines who leads, who mobilizes, what symbols are attacked, and who is killed. We can therefore glean some indication of the 1932 revolt's political lens by digging into those factors, from the few sources we have.

Who Led the Communist Party?

If Indians are mobilized only by skilled outside agitators, who might have played that role? The obvious answer is the Communist Party, especially as much of the later Matanza was directed against "communists" and "reds." And yet, although once blamed entirely for orchestrating the 1932 uprising, the Communist Party is today not credited by historians with nearly as much influence.[14]

The communists were indeed an excellent scapegoat, in the national memory, throughout the Cold War era. In the giddy decade after the Bolshevik Revolution of 1918, the international communist movement had gained ground among urban activists and worker organizations throughout Central America. The Salvadoran Communist Party (PSC, Partido Salvadoreño Comunista) took form under the guidance of legendary activists such as Augustín Farabundo Martí. By the late 1920s, the party was openly calling for the overthrow of the exploitative capitalist order. Communist activists toured the indigenous communities for at least two years prior to the uprising, providing unifying slogans and the date for a coordinated strike. Party activists also set up rural universities to diffuse communist doctrine and proletarian esprit de corps. These efforts certainly had impact in the countryside: when the rebels attacked the western towns in 1932, they shouted communist slogans, waved red flags, and were known to themselves and to others as "reds."

The Salvadoran government also considered the rebellion communist in character. All related government correspondence, both during the revolt and for years afterward, spoke only of communists, and almost never of Indians. Genuine urban perceptions probably fed this rhetoric. The indigenous comunidades had been legally dissolved decades earlier; in the capital, the ethnic tensions plaguing the coffee region were certainly a distant rural affair. School textbooks, military treatises, scholarly research and the national newspapers had already subsumed any reference to Indians within the nationalizing idea of "proletariat." In any case, the backward Indians were not thought prone to, or even capable of, mass coordinated mobilization.

Yet "communist" was a label the new government had good reasons to use. On the night of December 2, 1931, the reeling regime of President Arturo Araujo was overthrown in a military coup, and General Maximiliano Hernández Martínez had assumed power as "interim" president within days—an upheaval that added to the climate of insurrection simmering in the countryside. Initially popular even among some liberal ladino sectors, his fifteen-year rule would comprise the country's most notorious dictatorship until it was eclipsed by the brutal right-wing regime in the 1980s. Yet Martínez immediately faced international criticism for the coup and demands for restoration of an elected government. As international communism was already a U.S. hobgoblin, crushing a communist insurrection was one way for the new Martínez government to curry favor with the hemisphere's hegemon. On the other hand, the U.S. Marines were then still occupying Nicaragua in their effort to crush Sandino's famous leftist guerrilla movement and the Martínez government was very apprehensive about similar North American intervention to crush communism in El Salvador. (Indeed, a Canadian warship did dock at the port and even briefly land troops).[15] Hence the Martínez government apparently tried to avert an invasion or dreaded U.S. occupation by loudly proclaiming that the communists were already "liquidated" (a claim which prompted international alarm about excessive brutality and was retracted). Finally, both domestically and internationally, calling the rebels "communist" was a very handy way for the government to cover for the embarrassment of facing—and brutally crushing—a domestic revolt by its own dreadfully poor and abused citizens. (The same excuse would remain handy for dictatorships throughout the Cold War.) For all these reasons, "communist" discursively eclipsed "Indian" or even "peasant" in public rhetoric at the time. Even journalists reported the uprising as communist in character.[16]

But the Communist Party's role in the 1932 revolt fell far short of its own image as "vanguard of the masses." Research by historian Erik Ching in the Comintern archives in Moscow yielded up a very different portrait of the party: of confusion, insularity, and marginality, even in the view of its own organizers. Throughout 1930 and well into 1931, party members were almost completely absorbed by internal problems, such as the investigation of suspected "bourgeois reformism" among their cadres. When they felt they had achieved sufficient ideological purity to launch broader campaigns, they found themselves short of money and resources. They were unable—by their own admission—even to hold demonstrations.[17] By mid-1931, communists were also under heavy attack by the security forces, and a number of their leaders were arrested and imprisoned.

In any case, a chasm of mutual incomprehension separated the PSC from the "masses" they aspired to mobilize. Through a Marxist lens, the western coffee region had seemed prime fodder for class insurrection: a rebellious rural work force, freshly proletarianized by expanding capitalist export agriculture and now impoverished by its collapse, with a long history of class oppression. And when the PSC concentrated on narrow class goals like incremental salary increases, they did gain some popular indigenous support. But the communist platform—nationalization of private property, "dictatorship of the proletariat"—had no resonance among indigenous people concerned primarily with regaining private title to their subsistence plots. Indigenous "revolutionary" ambitions were ethnic rather than class based: to throw off ladino authority and install their own authorities, not to redesign or eliminate hierarchy altogether. Given the party's limitations (its members reported to Moscow), teaching them otherwise would take years of indoctrination before proletarian consciousness would reach the critical mass necessary for true revolution. In this modest assessment of its own local influence, the party was correct: in December 1931, their plan to enforce a boycott of the municipal elections ran counter to popular indigenous interests, and they had to call it off.[18]

Still, in its colossal ignorance of the indigenous communities, the party doubtless had little idea of the ethnic militancy it had tapped. The indigenous communities were anxious for a revolution against the rapidly strengthening ladino power structure. Now they had obtained what they thought was a powerful international alliance, which promised a glorious global revolution of the poor. With its international contacts, they believed, the PSC could help them achieve what for four centuries they had been unable to achieve: final victory over ladino government.[19] They had already begun militant mobilization under the communist banner, especially in some major and bloody demonstrations in May 1931, when thousands of Indians marched into Sonsonate.[20] As one party member reported to the Comintern in 1931, "we cannot deter the revolutionary wave . . . the masses are thirsty for blood and gold . . . these comrades are under the illusion that with their machetes they are sufficiently prepared to bring forth a movement of this class."[21]

Trying to retain some semblance of its vanguard role, the PSC did call for a general uprising, and scheduled January 22, 1932, as the fatal date. But the government learned of the insurrection and arrested Martí and other key leaders days before. As the story is usually told, those arrests demoralized the party and its members actually called off the revolt, but communist cadres in the countryside were out of touch with the urban leadership, and the insurrection could not be stopped.[22] That version implies that the problem was merely logistical, and that the party could indeed have stopped the revolt if communications had been effective, having more authority over the revolt's momentum than its own members perceived. By contrast, on the eve of the revolt, the party was still holding emergency meetings about whether to participate in a rebellion it had planned but had long since ceased to control. While they dithered, the Nahua were launching the last great Indian revolt of the century, waving red flags and shouting communist slogans. But did these slogans suggest that communist doctrine had indeed taken hold of their collective imagination, galvanizing a new class consciousness?

Jorge Schlesinger believed that the communist rhetoric of class struggle was an alien import of which the rebels had little or no real comprehension. He is the only early chronicler of the rebellion who believed the primary motive of people engaged in the revolt was not only antiladino but anti*colonial*. According to his documents, the communist slogans shouted by the rebels were coupled freely with racial slogans, which he considered the deeper matter:

> The insurgents mobilized under the influence of ancient hatreds, because in their triumphant demonstrations they shouted deafeningly: "Long live Communism! Long live the Red Botón! Down with Imperialism! Death to the Spanish! Long live the International Red League! Long live the Indians of Nahuizalco!" which demonstrated their absolute ignorance of the ends they pursued. Within them still resonated the cry of independence, and the ladinos and mestizos represented in their subconscious the bitter taste of the Spanish dominators, the cruel tyrants over the indigenous race.[23]

Even Miguel Mármol, a staunch communist organizer in 1932 (who escaped death by a miracle in the Matanza), believed that the indigenous masses wanted not proletarian revolution but simply the (to him unrevolutionary) goal of replacing elected ladino officials with people of their own kind. It appears, then, that the revolt was communist neither in its spirit nor in its goals. Did the rebels have any coherent ideology at all?

The Indigenous Leadership

The 1932 uprising was directed on the ground by indigenous people from the communities that mobilized. Some of these leaders were actual party members but most were apparently important figures in their communities who were inspired to form a tactical alliance with the communist movement. Some were ladinos who were trusted by indigenous communities. In Nahuizalco, some were known as "Los Abuelos" (the Grandfathers or Grandparents, possibly a council of elders), who were dedicated to preserving indigenous cultural life.[24] Other leaders were more scattered.

Feliciano Ama has been immortalized as the most important leader of the revolt, both by mainstream accounts and by indigenous activists who have appropriated Ama as an emblematic leader, martyr, and philosopher. His actual role in instigating it, however, is not so certain. He was the son-in-law of Patricio Shupan, who had been a very prominent indigenous leader until his death in 1924 and was described as "very rich," with extensive farms in two departments.[25] Ama himself was said to have had some eight farms at the time of the revolt. Most importantly, he was alcalde del común (see chapter 6), elected by the mayordomos of the cofradías as his community's spokesman to the government. But he also had good contacts among the ladino elite. His lasting fame in histories of the 1932 uprising stems also from a famous photograph of him taken just prior to his hanging in the town square, which has been widely reproduced.[26]

Other leaders had quite different profiles. In Juayúa, activist Chico Sanchez was less wealthy than Ama but very popular and commanded a large following among the Juayúa indigenous cantones. By contrast, Timoteo Lúe, also of Juayúa, was a self-made man who, according to one ladino source, enriched himself through extortion of his own neighbors. The relative affluence of these key activists led some ladinos to consider these men's involvement in the revolt incomprehensible, as one hacendado from Juayúa explained:

> Little has been said of Timoteo Lúe, who was a magnate of the cantón El Chaparrón. This individual, who in the beginning owned very little, was obliging his neighbors to sell him their water sources and any lands that interested him, at whatever price he might fancy. To get them, he used threats. So okay: Timoteo Lúe was an Indian (indio), owner of fine lands; he had regular assets, from which he gained much ostentation, to give himself airs of superiority over his contemporaries, who respected him like a boss. He dressed in striking style, in loud colors and gaudy cloth. He used a coat of the best quality. Having such a good economic situation, being so feared and envied by his neighbors, it is inexplicable that he should have become communist.[27]

The simple explanation for Lúe's involvement in the uprising is that he was hungry for the power promised to its leaders by the PSC. This interpretation would accord with that of others who saw all these prominent Indians as having been lured by the high official posts promised by their communist contacts.[28] It also accords with the idea that, prior to 1932, many indígenas still held land, especially in Izalco:

> The naturales had a monetary position much superior to those of many ladinos. Here all the naturales were landowners; they still are! And in that time there was not a single indigenous family that did not live in their own house, with a plot of land, with their fruit trees and their acreage where they had their corn fields, bean fields, rice and many had a small plot of coffee. There was no indígena that was not a landowner. When in 1932 the naturales were won over [by the communists], [the communists] did not offer them land precisely because they knew that this would have been rejected and that [the Indians] would have said: "hey, you're going to take what we have." Those people they won over by offering power: that is, Feliciano Ama was going to be comandante, the other was going to governor, the other was going to be mayor here, another regidor, others were going to be judges, and so they corrupted them offering them power, control of the country was going to be in their power. Now, if they had offered them lands, as in other parts, in Nahuizalco yes, in Juayúa, but here as everyone was a landowner they did not offer them land, but power.[29]

The above view interprets the leadership's motivation as personal aggrandizement, and hearkens to the duped-Indian version by stressing its corruption by promises of power. All accounts indeed suggest that, based on communist promises, the indigenous leadership had seen an opportunity to retake greater autonomy for their communities. Even Ama used some communist rhetoric in public statements. But all such alliances call for a certain tact. It must have been apparent to intelligent observers like Ama that the communist activists did not well understand the indigenous communities. Ama, at least, appears to have trodden lightly on ethnic matters when he met with Miguel Mármol in May 1931. Mármol made a point of saying that "Ama hadn't joined the struggle as an Indian, but rather as an exploited man," perhaps to reassure himself and others that Ama's class consciousness was bona fide.[30] He was impressed by the class legitimacy conveyed by Ama's having been hung up by his thumbs; to ensure this, Ama carefully showed him the scars. But Mármol also considered Ama "the last great representative of indigenous rebellion, following the tradition of Anastasio Aquino," and his own report of Ama's conversation suggests the delicate mingling of class and ethnic dimensions:[31]

> Ama had joined with communism and the purest of our countrymen had joined our ranks with him. The Regalado family, for example, had stripped him of all his land and beaten him and hung him up by his fingers. . . . We met in Sonsonate, I recall. Ama was skinny, his skin the color of copper, with big, healthy teeth. He was totally committed to the struggle and he told me about the abuses he had suffered: he showed me the scars on his fingers from the hanging. He pointed up to a small mountain to show me how far the land he still had went, and it wasn't so small either, and he told me how he was going to allot the land to the Indians who had nothing.[32]

But Ama also had good friends among Izalco's ladino elite (he would later protect some of those friends during the uprising).[33] He seems to have played the communist card carefully with these friends. He had been a staunch supporter of 1930 presidential election contender Gomez Zarate; he had headed the "Indigenous Committee" that orchestrated the Indian voting bloc for Zarate in the cantones around Izalco. After the elections were canceled, however, he abandoned national party politics and withdrew his support from Zarate in favor of the communist alliance. Shortly before the uprising, Zarate sent him a handwritten letter by private messenger, appealing to him to abandon the communists. A newspaper account after the revolt later cited Ama as telling the messengers what has become an oft-cited quote: "I do not want to have correspondence with an arrogant and exploitative bourgeois." (The quote was reproduced uncritically by Thomas Anderson to demonstrate Ama's wholesale adoption of communist jargon. Anderson adds—in "duped Indian" mode—that "One can hardly imagine that he chose this language himself").[34]

But decades later, members of Izalco's ladino elite who actually knew and socialized with Ama told a different story: that Ama never saw the messengers from his friend Zarate. Ama arranged not to do so, through the more socially graceful device of having his wife tell the messengers (also old friends and former political colleagues) that he was out of the house and could not be found. Ama did reportedly speak openly of his political outlook to Izalco's governor; much later, one ladino resident of Izalco would recall his saying: "Don Mario, you will always have my affection, because we have been friends, we are friends, and we will continue to be friends, but we are not going to be together in political matters, because you are certainly of the capitalists, and we are proletariat."[35] Although unconfirmed, the tone of this account shows a much more delicate handling of ladino authority by Ama than does the (also unconfirmed) Schlesinger account.

Indeed, although widely credited as the principal leader of the 1932 revolt, Ama seems to have been ambivalent about it. Although in a key ethnic leadership position, he tried not to alienate entirely his friends among the Izalco elite, walking a fine line toward a goal he understood mostly as ethnic liberation. He found the communist promise of international support convincing and hoped it would bear fruit, but he apparently hoped not to unleash unrestrained racial violence. In both hopes, of course, he was badly mistaken. At the end, he felt himself used by the communist movement for an agenda that had little to do with the goals or welfare of his people. Speaking of the communists, just before his hanging, he too would say that he had been "duped."

Who Mobilized?

Today, we are still largely in the dark about what the large crowds of farmers and workers were thinking when they stormed the western towns on the night of January 22, 1932. The great majority of these rebels were Indians, and their numbers were impressive. Ladino eyewitnesses reported rebel groups of 2,000–6,000 people in Izalco, 200–500 in Nahuizalco, and 80–600 in Juayúa.[36] Various smaller bands were encountered in other regions and on roads. If the entire revolt in the Sonsonate region mobilized about 4,000 people, this would be about one-seventh of the Indian population or close to the entire adult male Indian population, excluding the elderly.[37] Similar levels of involvement were reported from Ahuachapán. The governor estimated that the city itself was attacked by about 800 people from local cantones and another 600 from Atiquizaya. The mayor of Tacuba reported about 800 attackers.

Still, these numbers are round-figured estimates, often made by frightened people who confronted rebel groups on the roads or in assaults. Some sources may also have exaggerated the numbers of rebels to enhance their own bravery in confronting them, or to appeal for state government assistance (in the immediate crisis or for later reconstruction). For example, in Juayúa, where the town secretary reported six hundred rebels, rebel leader Chico Sanchez himself described only one hundred and twenty. North American missionary Roy MacNaught, who also lived in Juayúa, saw only eighty men involved in the initial attack on the telegraph office.[38] He believed that the other Indians who were said to have participated in the revolt were actually onlookers, who became involved when the rebellion turned to looting, in an almost festive atmosphere:

> That day the plunder went gaily on. The "reds" distributed their spoils with a lavish hand; in fact, they wanted all those, who were not otherwise lined up with them, to share in their ill-gotten gains, in order that they might be thus identified with their cause. Many were caught with this fatal bait. Were it not so sinful and serious the sight would have been ludicrous: men clothed in rags, carrying off fine clothes, bright colored, woolen blankets, hats, implements; women bearing proudly on their heads sheets of corrugated iron, measures of corn, bolts of cloth; children with their pockets full of candies, handkerchiefs and toys. I saw a man curiously examining a stolen camera as if it were a live thing that might bite him at any moment. Thus was the town of Juayua sacked.[39]

Many Indians seem to have joined the communists under threat.[40] MacNaught reported that, during the revolt (before the claim was politically convenient), some visiting Indian women told him that many of their husbands had been forcibly recruited by the rebels and that the women also had donned red ribbons to safeguard themselves. When three days later the town was retaken by government troops (which, MacNaught reported, was accomplished after only "a few minutes" of shooting), the same people were immediately to be seen waving blue and white ribbons, the color of the national flag. Does this rapid switch indicate that neither side held much appeal for the indigenous population? Or only that survival was a stronger motivation than party politics? Whatever the reason, the switch would avail them little; many of these people would be identified as rebels (sometimes by malicious gossip, to settle old scores) and shot.

In Nahuizalco, participation by indígenas from the cantones was much less broad. A ladino man who was twelve at the time remembers that the main group of rebels arrived from Juayúa on January 22 and seized the town, broke down shop doors, and smashed furniture. Once the terrified ladinos had fled or were in hiding, the local Indians of the cantones—most of whom had done little more than observe in amazement—found themselves facing a windfall opportunity to seize a few bags of flour, kitchen implements, or knickknacks. Like the Indians of Juayúa, many would later pay for these items with their lives.

Who Was Targeted?

The human targets of the 1932 rebellion were, in almost all cases, people specifically implicated in injuries to indigenous (not "communist") interests. Brignoli has observed that the entire uprising had the appearance of a colonial Indian revolt, and, as we have seen, the nineteenth century was also littered with such revolts.[41] As in those revolts, the rebels made little attempt actually to take over the instruments of governance. Instead, as had been done for centuries, those instruments were deliberately sacked, particularly the municipal archives that seemed the guardians of authority for ladino land grabs. (Three western towns lost their archives to arson in 1932). There was little systematic attempt to murder municipal officials qua officials, although some thirty were killed in battles for telegraph offices and the like.

The few deliberate murders in 1932 were of prominent ladino individuals hated for debt or land swindles against Indians. Contemporary ladino reports demonized such killings and beatified their victims. The much-denounced torture and execution of Mayor Redaelli is a prominent example. After his death, Redaelli was celebrated in the press as a progressive philanthropist, responsible for many good works such as bringing electricity to the town.[42] Anderson describes his appearing on the balcony to confront the rebels "with his wife and son clutching him," then of the rebels breaking in, raping his wife, and dragging him outside and around the town for a full day. Colonel Calderón (who was responsible for much of the later repression in the area) reported that, when Redaelli asked for water, the rebels urinated in his mouth (a story that Anderson repeats uncritically), and finally beat him to death.[43] This tale manifested as a particularly gruesome and irrational act by contemptible barbarians.

Government correspondence at the time, however, gives a different impression of Redaelli: that of a chronically absent mayor, who had enriched himself by arranging the electricity installation through a monopoly in his own name. He had tried so blatantly to manipulate the town's 1930 elections that the Sonsonate Governor's office was forced to ask the entire municipal government to absent itself from the proceedings, to stem violent popular protest.[44] He was even bitterly resented by other ladino politicians of the town, who in one report to the governor denounced him in scathing terms for inflating the number of the town's registered voters.[45] He was also the manager of a major coffee *beneficio* (whose role in impoverishing small coffee growers has been noted above) owned by the much-hated Daglio family, owners of the largest coffee plantations in the area. In light of this information, we may be less surprised that Redaelli was targeted specifically by the Indian rebels. He was indeed dragged about through the streets for hours and eventually beaten to death. The urination story, however, may be apocryphal: a Juayúa informant to Segundo Montes reported that, when Redaelli asked for water, one of the Indians put his foot in Redaelli's face.

Another rebel target was a General Rafael Rivas, of Tacuba, who was beheaded by the Indian forces. Described only as "a crusty old soldier" by Anderson, Rivas had been implicated in extensive land swindles.[46] A Tacuba resident later explained that

> he was hated for his conduct with the peasants; he would lend them money on the basis of their lands as guarantee, at usurious rates of interest, and at the date of payment would be absent, hide himself, disappear or refuse to see them, so that they couldn't pay him, and then he would have their lands, gathering in this way considerable property, and leaving the peasants in misery.[47]

Yet Rivas, too, was beatified. Newspaper accounts described him "blazing away" with his pistol at the rebel attack and so disposing of four campesinos before he was overwhelmed.[48] But the ladino resident of Tacuba interviewed by Segundo Montes described how Rivas was actually at home napping when the rebellion broke out.[49] He was tricked into opening his door by a rebel who persuaded him to come out in order to go dancing and drinking ("*vamos a tal parte, vamos a ir a echarnos unos tragos, vamos a ir a parrandear"*). When Rivas went out of his door, he was seized. But this is not the kind of story that the indignant ladino readers in the capital would want to hear, and the more heroic story was reported for posterity.

All these details suggest that the 1932 uprising was a true Indian uprising: building on the indigenous community's experience of paramilitary training and the dense history of Indian uprisings in prior decades. The communist movement did provide some early assistance with communications, a date, slogans, and false hopes of success of support from a worldwide revolution of the poor. This (illusory) support was the strategic advantage the Indian activists knew they lacked, and was key to their mobilization. But their goals and targets were consistent with their indigeneity: seeking not a revolution of the proletariat and the overthrow of the bourgeoisie, but freedom for an indigenous community (which had its own elite and class divisions) from ladino racial domination. The naiveté of this goal reflected the isolation of the rural indigenous population. Its anticolonial and anti-ladino flavor, however, was rooted in collective memory of the conquest. The consequences were disastrous.

Who Was Killed: The Matanza

No one knows how many people were killed in the Matanza. The most common figure is 30,000, which seems to have come from communist activist Miguel Mármol, who lived through it.[50] But it is doubtful that Mármol knew. Many army and ladino civilian groups were involved, and people were killed throughout the forested countryside where communication was difficult. Foreign and Salvadoran observers described roads littered with bodies; cartloads of bodies; and trucks filled with bodies, running nightly to dumping grounds for weeks. Several reports described people being brought into town squares to get safe passes and then machine-gunned by the hundreds, or lined up and shot in batches of 8 or of 50, for days.[51] By January 29, Matanza architect General José Tomás Calderón had claimed that 4,800 "communists" had been "liquidated," but this figure was later retracted (in the face of international alarm), leaving a void. Rudolfo Buezo claimed to have seen government reports citing 20,000 deaths, but no such reports have been found.[52] Thomas Anderson has suggested that the total number of deaths was probably dramatically lower. Relatively few troops, and limited time and ammunition, he argues, would have limited the numbers to no more than 8,000–10,000.[53] His logic is flawed, as discussed below, but all is guesswork.

Salvadoran government agencies evidently did not know, although by mid-February rumors of mass deaths were reaching government agencies in the capital. Government correspondence remains conspicuously missing, but two suggestive messages eerily survived. On February 15, the Director General of Health sent a letter warning the Sonsonate townships that mass graves with fifty bodies in them were unhealthy due to inadequate absorbency by the soil. "For reasons of public health," the message cautioned, such graves should be at least two meters deep, wide, and long, and hold no more than eight or ten bodies and only in one layer. This measure was deemed especially important for the Indian towns of Izalco, Nahuizalco, and Juayúa.[54] And on February 18, the Director General of Statistics sent out a request, carefully framed as stemming "from scientific interest," to all the Sonsonate towns, asking that they note in their monthly death reports the particulars "especially . . . of all those deaths caused by the communist action or by the public forces during the months of January and February . . ."[55] But no violent deaths were listed in the local Civil Registries in coming months. The mayor of Juayúa eventually responded that "we have conformed [to the law] in those two or three cases that have presented themselves, as we could not officially confirm peoples' deaths of which we know not when, nor at what hour, nor how they died, circumstances that the families also do not know . . . The military troops have given no information about this either."[56]

Nor are Nahua memories likely to yield solid figures, even if they could be systematically assembled. In January and February 1932, most people were in a frenzy of fear and trying desperately to find shelter—although few knew where or how to flee: the roads and backroads were full of soldiers. In Nahuizalco, survivors tell of people digging holes in the ground and hiding their men in them; and of young men (of rebel and therefore execution age) giving up their clothes, dressing in underwear, and sitting on the ground to appear like children. People remember seeing dogs and pigs eating bodies in the streets, and speak vaguely of "hundreds" killed. Some recall friends or brothers who hid with others in the barn of a ladino landowner employer, only to be betrayed by the landowner and machine-gunned en masse. After the vigilante patrols went through the cantones, families emerged from hiding places to find the bodies of neighbors on the road and hastily buried them three or five to a rough grave. Every year, fewer people remember where those graves are located.

Establishing the precise number of actual deaths is, in fact, not essential to gauging the Matanza's aggregate psychological and political impact. If a family lost one member or two members to vigilante squads, the collective sense of terror and injury among the survivors is vast in either case. Subsequent degrees of terror for a whole community do not rest on differences of a few thousand, but on the larger tenor of the Matanza—its race-war dimension. That tenor is also crucial to assessing later reports of the famous indigenous auto-ethnocide. Because it was not the army that turned the Matanza into a racial reign of terror; it was the ladino vigilante groups.

Race War

Certainly the army was a brutal actor in the Matanza. Mármol's vivid descriptions of the Matanza form the basis for many later accounts:

> In Armenia, a general named Pinto personally killed 700 peasants after his soldiers forced them to dig their own graves, one by one. General Ochoa, who was the governor of San Miguel, forced the arrested men to crawl on their knees up to where he was sitting in a chair, in the courtyard of the barracks, and he'd tell them: "Come here, smell my pistol." The prisoners begged him in the name of God and their children, crying and pleading with him, since before entering the courtyard they had heard intermittent gunshots. But the barbarian general insisted and convinced them: "If you don't sniff the pistol it's because you're a communist and afraid. The one who has nothing to hide, fears nothing." The peasant sniffed the barrel and right there the general put a bullet in his face. Then he'd say, "Send in the next one." . . .
>
> Tito Tomás Calvo machined-gunned, in the Church of the Conception in Izalco, which was a simple ranch house with a courtyard, more than two hundred persons at one go, the majority women and children. In Chanmico and Las Granidillas, the

National Guardsmen burned all the ranches in an area of twenty square kilometers and raped all the women over 10 years old . . .

From the barracks in Ahuachapán blood flowed in a river, as if it was water or horse piss. A lieutenant who was on duty there cried as he told about how peasants, as they were shot in groups in the courtyard, would sing "Holy Spirit You Will Reign." . . . Seven brothers by the name of Alfaro were falsely accused of being communists on the San José plantation along with their aging father. In the very entryway of the plantation they shot them all . . .

Terrible scenes like this recurred all over the central and western parts of the country. . . . The Air Force spent days upon days machine-gunning the rural zones: a person who moved was a person who made the planes spit fire. Filiciano [sic] Ama's people on the outskirts of Izalco were massacred in this way and by the punitive infantry . . .

. . . all the hamlets in the high regions of the Department of Ahuachapán, absolutely all, were devastated by machine-gun fire. No questions, no arrests, fire and lead were the only argument. In the case of the straw huts, they shot first and then went in to see if there were people inside. A driver who years later joined the Party and who still serves in our ranks, told us a story about how he was working on a coffee plantation in Ahuachapán and that on the 26th or 27th of January he was forced by an Army detachment to drive a truck that had a machine gun mounted in the cab. In the back was a squad of soldiers with automatic arms. They went out to go on patrol, to "maintain the order," and any group of peasants they encountered on their way, whether they were just talking or walking, without any prior warning, from a distance of thirty meters or more, they'd unload their machine guns and smaller arms on them. Afterwards, the captain who was in command, with a .45 in his hand, forced our present comrade to continue driving the truck, running over them, including the dying who were writhing in pain on the ground, screaming. This comrade went mad for nearly two years, left with the impression of how the truck tilted as it passed over the mounds of corpses. "I could just feel it when their bones were breaking or their bodies bursting under the tires," the comrade recalls. . . .

For years and years the people in the countryside kept being unpleasantly surprised all the time on seeing the skeleton of a hand, a foot, a skull cropping up out of the earth.

Mármol was not an impartial observer. The Matanza marked the catastrophic defeat of the communist movement to which he had dedicated his life. Nor did he himself witness events in the countryside, but gleaned them from oral reports possibly exaggerated. But a second source corroborates the tone of Mármol's account, that of Colonel Gregorio Bustamente Maceo, who touched on the Matanza in his *Historia militar de El Salvador* ("Military History of El Salvador"), published by the Ministry of Interior in 1951. Bustamente may be presumed not to have shared Mármol's political sentiments, but his account reproduces the impression of terror:

The machine guns began to sow panic and death in the regions of Juayua, Nahuizalco, Colón, Santa Tecla, the Santa Ana Volcano, and all the coastal villages from Jiquilisco to Acajutla. There were villages that were left completely razed and the workers in the capital were barbarically decimated. One group of naive men who reported voluntarily to the authorities, offering their services, were taken inside the barracks of the National Guard where every last one of them was mowed down in a line. The panic spread. . . . The slaughter was horrifying: children, old people, women, no one escaped; in Juayúa all the decent men who weren't communists were ordered to report to the Town Hall in order to receive safe passage, and when the public plaza was overflowing with men, women and children, they blocked off the streets and machine-gunned down that whole innocent crowd, not leaving alive even the poor dogs who faithfully follow their indigenous masters. . . . The slaughter continued at a wholesale rate, carried out by the famous "Civic Guard," which was set up by General Martínez in every town and comprised of perverse men who committed uncountable abuses against life, property and the honor of innocent girls. Daily, they reported to the Chief Executive the number of known victims in the last 24 hours, and the looting of goods was such that they even ran out of chickens.[57]

These passages chronicle a key feature of the Matanza that has buttressed the ethnocide charge: that many people were shot on sight, as Indians. The ethnic element of the Matanza is sometimes obscured by language about "peasants" but at the time the two were conflated. Hence Anderson's famous statement that "all those of a strongly Indian cast of features, or who dressed in a scruffy, campesino costume, were considered guilty" reflects the association of peasants and male Indian dress—characteristic white cotton shirts and pants.[58] Elsewhere references to peasants also clearly mean Indians. For example, when Bustamente described the notorious Juayúa plaza massacre (above), he wrote "all the decent *men* who weren't communists," but meant also "all the *Indians* who weren't communists." Their indigenous identity was too obvious to mention, emerging almost accidentally when he described the "poor dogs."

What drove this mass killing? The army is commonly blamed, and clearly it was responsible for the early mass executions: the machine-gunning of helpless prisoners by the dozens, hundreds, or thousands. But historian Erik Ching threw a dent into this story by finding that, beyond the de facto persecution of Indians in the initial repression, the army had no such *policy*.[59] After its initial action to put down the revolt (brutal and bloody as it was), the army withdrew from the area within days or weeks, sometimes over the protests of panicky ladino town governments. In later months and years, the army would deliberately refrain from acting as an agent for ladino attacks on Indian communities or lands. Indian communities even appealed to the army, or the army's supreme commander, General Martínez, to defend them from such attacks. Ching argues that, ideologically, army commanders saw the nation as being naturally composed of classes in which both elite and workers had equally important roles. In this view, the army's role was guardian of the whole society, and a mediator between the classes at need—although "mediation" was clearly in the interests of maintaining the status quo, which favored ladinos. In short, the military was complicit in the long-term subordination of the rural communities simply because its role was to maintain a stable social order which, as times changed, permitted ladino landowners and agro-commercial entrepreneurs to complete the dispossession of indigenous lands.

The agents more intent on attacking the Indian communities were indeed the ladino landowners and other rivals to indigenous economic interests.

Ladino civilians were central to the Matanza from the beginning, joining army patrols during the first assaults on the "communists." Joaquín Méndez documents such collaboration, citing the army commander of a Santa Ana troop that marched south into the uprising zone. In the following passage, note again the alternating terms "Indians" and "communists":

> we continued the march toward Nahuizalco. At the side of the road were many communists who threw stones at us and later blocked our way, brandishing machetes. Finally we reached the town, where we saw that some houses had been burned and others looted. The darkness was complete; worse, it was raining. For this reason, and knowing the rebellious spirit of the Indians, I did not send out patrols. . . . The following morning, I sent out patrols from among the forces at my command, advised by ladinos, who knew all the communist indigenous people (indígenas comunistas). These patrols were able to capture some, confiscating the goods that had been looted from shops and the red insignias that they carried. They clearly confessed their identity, and were executed.[60]

But in the weeks and months following the uprising, ladino violence took over and escalated. Ladinos formed civil patrols in all the major towns of the coffee region, allowing private ladino citizens to launch projects of ethnic vengeance. Some of these patrols would amount to vigilante bands that worked their way through the cantones for weeks, looting households and killing anyone who looked guilty. One army observer of the patrol's activities in Nahuizalco reported on March 14, in apparent disgust, that "the medicine was more deadly than the disease." Those citizens who had joined the soldiers out of "Patriotism," he said, putting the word in quotes, were actually "sowing terror and fright among ladinos and indígenas alike and discrediting the Authorities . . ."[61] My own interviews in Nahuizalco brought several references to murders by these patrols, mostly on the roads. The problem of ammunition suggested by Anderson (above) was not a significant obstacle: one Nahua woman recounted to me how her uncle was seized with his two brothers, all three tied to a fence and clubbed to death.[62]

Ladino perspectives are equally crucial to assessing the race-war dimension of the Matanza. Most often quoted is a large landowner who lived in the Salcoatitán area, near Nahuizalco, whose account appeared in a Santa Ana paper days after the revolt, at the height of the repression. Normally only his last paragraph is reproduced, but the longer passage is greatly illuminating. We can notice here, again, how he alternates the terms "masses," "workers," and "Indians" and equates the position of Salvadoran and North American Indians in modern nations:

Neither you, nor anyone who lives in the towns, in the cities, and who considers himself protected by the agents of order, can have the least idea how we have felt here, in crucial moments, to find ourselves alone, absolutely alone, in the hands and at the mercy of the masses, who are no more than a horde of infuriated savages, with demonic instincts, who shout curses at the ladino, curses at the patrones and brandish the machetes [*corvos*] with a thirst for robbery, a thirst for every kind of crime imaginable . . .

There is not one Indian [*indio*] who is not affiliated with the communist movement. Any one of them who stayed in his house was only waiting for the last notice to join their ranks. Good workers [*mozos*] whom I considered loyal and whom we had treated as part of the family were among the first to join up and to lend their contribution to the evil cause. And such is the cheek of these people, that now that they see themselves vanquished by the actions of the government, which has served to annihilate them, those same people who at one moment were making attempts on our lives and all that we possess, are those now seeking protection and swearing to us that they belonged to us [*nos pertenecían*] and that they were not involved. They want to evade the danger. But that is the penalty they have imposed on themselves . . .

They passed by here in a great crowd, on the night of Saturday the 23rd, that attacked Nahuizalco, and with no time to make mincemeat of me, since they were anxious to reach Nahuizalco; they contented themselves with blasphemous jeers and marked me out as one of the first who must fall into their hands. In the crowd, in the immense confused multitude, were all of them: about two hundred workers of mine, of my neighbors and my brothers. Those I believed humble, honorable, who had received favors of every kind on our part, [we] who granted them land for their crops without charging them any rent; whom we paid their wages with religious punctuality, which, although small, as everywhere in the country, is a wage in conformity with their abilities, since they are incapable of earning more; some barely able to perform their task, and others whom one must lead by the hand in order to teach them the simplest chores, because lazy as they are, they do not commit themselves to making themselves efficient or to improving themselves in anything. And they, who have the very germ of villainous blood, who are of a nature inferior to ours, who are of a conquered race, with little needed to incite ferocious passion against the ladino, because they hate us and they will always hate us in latent form. It has been a grave, a dangerous error to concede to them the rights of citizens. That has been enormously bad for the country. They were told that they were free, that the nation also existed for them, and that they had full rights to elect their leaders and to take charge. And they understand that "leaders" and "taking charge" as exactly equivalent to engaging in rape, robbery, scandal, desecration of property, etc., and to kill their employers. . . .

I, who always considered that I could consume ten Indians in a row, they with their machetes and I with my revolver and fifty bullets; I who had never trembled before these criminals, because I felt they were humble sheep when I saw them all well-behaved, and the villains among them I thought were subject to the force of my arm, upon our meeting their forces, when I made out the mob [*mancha*], the crowd of two hundred which came in pursuit of me, I mounted my horse and in dizzying career broke through rocky wall and precipice, ruining wire fences, until I could take shelter with my brother in his hacienda . . .

We want this plague exterminated by the roots;[63] for if it is not, it will sprout forth with new spirit, now expert and less foolish, because in new attempts they will pitch themselves against the lives of all, first, and finally slit our throats. We need the strong hand of the government [to act], without asking anyone's consent, because there are merciful people who preach pardon, because they have still not seen that their lives hang by a thread. It was well done in North America, from the beginning with them:

they [the Indians] were shot, first, before they impeded the development of progress in that nation; they [the whites] first killed the Indians, because those would never have good sentiments toward anything. We, here, we treated them like family, with every consideration, and now you have seen them in action! They have ferocious instincts.[64]

Although we have no surveys, it is probably fair to suppose that the writer's sentiments were shared by other landowners in the area. His fusion of workers and Indians was probably far wider. That fusion would explain the irregular references to communists, peasants and indios in many accounts of the revolt in the more densely Indian areas.[65]

In assessing the general mood in the countryside, the testimony of Roy MacNaught, the missionary stationed in Juayúa, is especially interesting because of his personal detachment from local race relations. The ultimate nonpartisan, he hid with his family in his house for three days during the revolt, praying to God for protection from the rebels. He was astonished to find himself under Communist rule, and relieved to find that the rebels passed his door day and night without so much as knocking. He was more relieved when the troops arrived to free the town, but the ensuing repression appalled him, and the Matanza was a source of great personal pain; his assistant was killed. "As he was a faithful worker in the gospel, he had many enemies; as he was an Indian, he had other enemies among those who consider themselves superior to this race and cannot bear to see an Indian prosper." He was horrified to find that his own Protestant converts ("believers") had been targeted and were being killed, victims of rumors that they were ringleaders of the revolt. Later he would write in his journal,

February 14: The Indians are hated now as never before. In Nahuizalco there is a defense league composed of the Ladino element. These Ladinos have rounded up all the male believers they can find and have had them shot. . . . The remainder of the Indian men in Nahuizalco have either been killed or are in hiding. . . .

March 3: We have word that there have been executed in Nahuizalco alone, 2500 men. One day they lined up 400 boys and shot them. They have tortured the women to make them tell where their husbands and brothers are. In that town there is scarcely a man to be seen now. It would seem that they are going to exterminate the Indians.[66]

The Indians' extermination seems to have been less a formal government project than a short-lived mass ladino ethos. It manifested as a brief flare of racial extremism that swept the hearts and minds of ladinos in the area, drawing normally quiet people, prone to ethnic cohabitation within a familiar caste system, into deadly participation. The Indians were now "doubly red," as Anderson put it; killing them became a defense of nation and civilization.[67]

Ethnic Battles over Land and Water

The Matanza would also signal a decisive turn in another power struggle: a dramatic transfer of land from indigenous to ladino hands after the Matanza. The repressive conditions following the uprising were a godsend to ladinos aspiring to seize indigenous plots, and the rush of land transfers proceeded around the region through a variety of devices. Again, one of Segundo Montes's interviews in Izalco about 1932 offers important oral testimony:

> There are very wicked people. And here were some lawyers from Sonsonate who had been brought to take away the lands of the Indians [naturales] they spoke to; because the guardia had robbed the naturales, truly robbed them; entered into their houses and taken everything—their corn, all their harvest for the year—all this they took, for the troops had to live and they were going to live from this [plunder]. But not only this, padre, but all the things they had, right? . . . they kept ancient necklaces, with silver crosses, and all the little things they had, and they say that all these were stolen. Afterwards, when these two [lawyers] were here, when all this had happened and those remaining were afraid, terribly afraid, those who were left alive, right? they listened to what these lawyers told them. These two lawyers came, to profit from their fear; and told them; "if you don't give me the title to your land, I won't arrange things for you, and they will come and get you, as an Indian, and shoot you." But the people, being so afraid, believed them.[68]

In Izalco, the court itself became involved, signing over to prominent ladino citizens the lands left without formal owners when the indigenous owner was killed.[69] (This transfer must have left numerous families homeless, as single male property owners are virtually unknown among the Nahua.) Other methods amounted to outright fraud. In Nahuizalco, it had been the practice among the local Nahua to give their land titles to some urban ladino for safekeeping, since their own homes—sometimes made of sticks—normally had no place to keep such documents dry or away from animals and children. With all the copies in the archive burned, it was an easy matter for those ladinos to enlist a secretary to rewrite the deed in his or her own name, and then to destroy the original.[70]

An aggravating factor during the post-Matanza period was the inability of illiterate women, especially widows of men executed as communists, to resist land expropriation or even to understand fully the consequences of handing over land deeds to patrones. Public legal matters were normally handled by men, but times were desperate. In the months after the Matanza, with husbands and brothers slain, many women found themselves destitute and their children facing starvation. Some went to local patrones asking for food. A bag of rice would indeed be granted—in exchange for the deed. The scale of this practice may never be discernible, since such transactions were normally not reported to local land registries.

In Izalco, the Matanza also set the stage for a dramatic confrontation over water. In 1932, Izalco's ladino-controlled town government still did not have control over this crucial resource. As we have seen, the irrigation system around Izalco was highly complex, channeled from distant rivers to individual plots through the miles of networked channels, dating to before the conquest, to serve the region's cacao production. Indigenous control of so vital a resource is one interesting indication of significant indigenous political power at this relatively late date. Certainly it was a source of considerable irritation to ladino farmers.

Both the cofradías and their control over Izalco's water came under direct attack by the Izalco municipality in one of its earliest meetings after the 1932 uprising. By the end of January, the indigenous community was already physically shattered by army violence. Its political profile was also in ruins, both locally and nationally, through its damning association with the "reds." On a crest of racial triumphalism, on February 3rd the ladino-controlled town council passed two resolutions. The first resolution argued that the cofradía celebrations were thinly disguised political rallies, and resolved to lock all their icons inside the church, in order to make those celebrations impossible. This assault on the cofradías apparently came to nothing, perhaps because it encroached on ancient and sacred rites of the church, which could not so easily fall prey to "red scare." But the second resolution was far more successful, striking directly at the water issue. The resolution's language also invoked the nationalist interest in export agriculture, which had buttressed the state's assault on the indigenous comunidades fifty years prior:

> that being a duty of the Corporation [of Izalco] to watch over the interests of social welfare, [and] to promote agriculture as far as possible, as the principal patrimony of these inhabitants; that encountering so much difficulty with the farms and fields which have remained controlled by the indigenous class [clase indígena] who have, by [controlling] irrigation in the dry season, always put unjustifiable obstacles against the ladino element that has dedicated itself to the cultivation of cereals, and since the recent events which occurred in this city would give opportunity for even greater difficulties because of those indigenous elements who were mixed up with the Communist affair, the Municipal Corporation resolves . . . that from this day forward, the provision of irrigation services will be encharged to the [Municipal] Corporation, [and] that we will recognize no right that the indígenas claim to have which are not regulated in conformity with the law.

By February 15th, the town council had voted to create a water board of supervisors; by mid-March, they had elaborated a new system of allowances and fees, which was, with impressive optimism, inscribed into law in April.

Implementation of the new system, however, was fraught with conflict. Apparently, many indigenous residents tapped illegally into the new system, and redirected water into clandestine pipes. Very few people paid the new fees. It can reasonably be imagined that the cofradías conspired to coordinate and shelter this subversion. But by late February, the indigenous community was feeling the impact. On February 26, Felix Turish appealed to the Sonsonate Governor, invoking the community's prior corporate privileges as confirmed by the central government (*Gobierno Supremo*):

> *Señor Gobierno Político del Departamento:* We wish to inform you that we ask the Department Government, that because of our relations that we have with the Central Government, that we comply with our duties, that we have in this municipality of Indians [Indígenas] of Asunción Izalco, because of our poverty it is with urgency that we have appealed to the esteemed General . . . to concede us some small portions of water, that always have been managed by the alcalde comunal, Indians of the Barrio de Asunción de Izalco . . . and at the same time we submit in this departmental Government that we are licensed by our Supreme Government that we can manage this water through the former customs of our ancestors and in order to have certain proof can put down in writing regarding our relations that we have with the Supreme Government . . . we leave you very sincerely . . . the Municipality of Indians of Asunción Izalco.[71]

Any government response on the water question is unclear. But indigenous resistance would remain lively. By March 1933, the town council was besieged with complaints, and was forced to appeal to the President for help in controlling the situation.[72] Nor would the matter go away. Competition between the ladino municipality and the indigenous communities over Izalco's water would persist into the 1990s: a burning ethnic confrontation still plaguing the "Indian-free" nation.

Aftermath: Ethnocide?

After 1932, the indigenous community becomes difficult to track. Any reference to Indians or indígenas effectively disappears from public debate and state record. As the story would evolve in later decades, the indigenous community self-dissolved: terrified by thousands of executions, shamed and endangered by the link to communism, the indígenas abandoned native dress and language, and disappeared as such. In most correspondence and almost all scholarly writing in ensuing decades after 1932, language about Indians was replaced by references to peasants and masses. As time passed, an impression would grow that the Indian existed no longer.

Did the indigenous communities indeed suddenly try to abandon their ethnic identity? Under a veil of silence, it is hard to tell. But Turish's direct appeal to the government regarding Izalco's water battles, cited above, suggests the opposite: that in the years after the Matanza, far from trying to hide itself, the Izalco indigenous community was trying hard to sustain its ethnic profile on the national political stage. Every year, the Asunción Izalco community ritually sent a list of the cofradías' new majordomos to the capital; in May 1935, the list included twenty cofradías and corresponding names. In November 1936, Turish sent notification of the annual election of the alcalde del comun. None of this suggests an effort to disappear. So did the indigenous peoples' political voice fade from public view because their ethnic cohesion was indeed dissolving? Or did it fade only because the dominant society wished it would and ceased to listen?

To answer these questions, we must find some way to trace ethnic identities in the indigenous communities. That project leads us to a hidden source, long overlooked in mildewed volumes sequestered in the region's municipal archives.

CHAPTER 8

ASSIMILATED OR ERASED?

ETHNOCIDE BY STATISTICS

. . . it is not the existence of the Indian that determines the definition, but the existence of a definition that determines the Indian.

—*Fernando Mires, 1991*

TO THIS DAY, THE 1932 MATANZA IS CITED AS THE HISTORICAL MOMENT when any meaningful indigenous ethnic presence vanished in El Salvador—when the indígenas abandoned their ethnicity, stopped being Indian.[1] Two core beliefs support this claim. The first, addressed in the previous chapter, is that the military regime of General Martínez launched a deliberate campaign of genocide or ethnocide against the Indian communities, first by lethal violence and subsequently by outlawing indigenous dress. The national archives told us a very different story: that after the initial murderous repression of the rebels, the military understood its role to be one of ethnic arbiter, and in the years after the Matanza sometimes even defended indigenous interests against ladino assaults.[2] Ladino vigilantes pursued a campaign of racial terror, but indigenous ethnicity actually remained a vital political asset to communities still seeking government protection against ladino pressures.

But the second of these beliefs still requires our attention: that the indigenous people nevertheless reacted to the Matanza by abandoning their ethnic dress and language, due to the climate of terror sustained through ladino vigilantism in the Matanza's immediate aftermath. The national census has contributed its authority to this idea simply by omitting any reference to race or indígenas from national census surveys since 1930. Still, an alternative source, the Civil Registry, suggests that this official silence did not so much reflect indigenous ethnic disappearance as help to affirm it. In other words, the famous indigenous ethnocide was—at least in part—orchestrated by Salvadoran officialdom on paper.

Counting Indians: The Census as Ethnic Battlefield

Any study of ethnic politics (especially of genocide or ethnocide) must engage hard numbers: the number of people claiming to be—and/or understood by others to be—members of each group. Unfortunately, counting ethnic-group membership is among the most difficult and controversial tasks associated with ethnic politics, because identities are fluid, contextual, fuzzy-boundaried, and change over time, as we have seen.[3] Counts are also notoriously politicized, as ethnic activists typically seek to maximize their own numbers (or deaths) while their opponents often seek to minimize them. Simple logistics may also impede arriving at any reliable figures: difficult terrain, a frightened population, under-equipped or under-trained surveyors.

In such situations, so fraught with controversy, the national census often becomes a highly contested discursive site. Anyone familiar with census surveys knows how difficult counting ethnic identities can be, and how much people argue about the methods, categories, and membership criteria. Also, omissions may be as politically significant as inclusions. (For example, readers may be familiar with heated arguments in the United States about whether the national census undercounted Latinos in some areas and whether it should count multiracial identities.) Such arguments are so heated because the census, ironically, carries an aura of an objective, scientific, or otherwise dispassionate authority over the matter.

In El Salvador, the census contributes to the no-Indians discourse simply by omitting any category for ethnic or racial identity. This blank record does provide some leeway for indigenous activists to make their own claims about the indigenous population's size, because such claims cannot be neatly rejected. But far more effectively, the omission suggests that no such divisions exist or matter, and that the true number of

Indians—or at least their cultural distinctiveness (Indianness)—is too low to warrant any official count. Facing this stolid rejection, suggestions to make such a count tend to appear excessive, making something of nothing. Funds for any kind of field study are therefore unforthcoming from an uninterested and overburdened state. Indigenous estimates therefore often manifest as inflated and politically motivated.

Thus any argument that an indigenous population does persist in El Salvador remains politically empty because no one knows, even within broad strokes, how large that population actually is. And estimates vary widely. U.S. government sources (the State Department, the Peace Corps) offer 1 percent or much less: "the country is ethnically homogeneous, and only a few hundred citizens identify as indigenous people" reads the State Department's 2002 *Human Rights Report*. But the Salvadoran government itself, reporting to the International Labor Organization in 1993, put the proportion of indigenous people at 2 percent, or about 124,000 people. Indigenous estimates soar by comparison: CCNIS estimates a very high 30 percent, while ANIS has proposed an indefensible 45 percent. More sober estimates hover around 10 to 12 percent, including those of CONCULTURA and the Procuradora de la Paz—although the 10 percent figure was never professionally established and has not been independently confirmed.[4] In 1990, anthropologist Mac Chapin settled on 500,000 (at the time, about 10 percent). The European Union has accepted 5 percent (at this writing, this totals about 310,000 people).

Even if a formal count were conducted, however, solid results might prove elusive. Any census must rely on consistent criteria, and—not to belabor the point—definitions of Indian in El Salvador remain contested. Is an Indian someone who speaks an indigenous language and wears characteristic embroidered dress? Or is an Indian someone who wears no shoes and cultivates rice and beans? Self-definition is the obvious solution, but given the depth of racial discrimination in El Salvador, any survey would be hampered by the social difficulty of asking Guatemala's 1994 census question, "Are you indigenous?" (a question not always so easy to ask in Guatemala, either). If posed by an outsider, timidity and shame would make a positive answer to that question difficult for many people— even for those who, in the bosom of their communities, do consider themselves indígenas. The obvious solution is to train surveyors from inside the communities, who know and are trusted by the community. But insider researchers free from bias—and with sufficient literacy to keep accurate records—would be hard to find.

All efforts since 1930 to estimate the indigenous population—or the scale of the Matanza—have therefore been forced to extrapolate from earlier material or from field studies stretched thin by a lack of resources. Even the best of these efforts confronted missing and contradictory data. In the nineteenth century, a primary obstacle was the logistical challenge of accurately counting a population scattered (or even deliberately hiding) throughout heavily forested and roadless terrain, hunkered down in backwoods to avoid taxes and labor drafts.[5] Better access to these areas after 1880 might explain one glaring discrepancy: in 1837, Irish surveyor John Galindo, reporting to the London Geographical Society, estimated the indigenous population at 22.5 percent, yet in 1884—perhaps benefiting from the new network of all-season roads?—Rafael Reyes estimated the same population at 55 percent.[6]

A second and more tenacious obstacle has been the difficulty of confirming household size. Even today, indigenous families in both El Salvador and Guatemala tend to underreport their children, and overburdened census takers (often ladinos unfamiliar with the area) are not able to undertake diligent cross-checking. In the nineteenth century, logistical obstacles to verification and lack of rigor may safely be imagined to have been far worse. An undercount of children would explain another historical conundrum: in 1807 Gutierrez y Ulloa estimated the indigenous *population* at 43 percent of the total but indigenous *families* at 55 percent. A dramatically higher Indian child-mortality rate would explain this discrepancy, but underreporting and statistical trouble are at least as likely culprits.

However contradictory they might be, all known government and travelers' estimates, from Spanish colonization to 1927, were assembled by Salvadoran scholar Rodolfo Barón Castro in the magisterial volume *La Población del Salvador* ("The Population of El Salvador"), completed in 1940.[7] Taken at face value, Barón Castro's compilation shows a flattening out of the indigenous population decline after independence, declining only two percent between 1884 and 1903, to 23 percent, and converging in the 1920s to suggest an indigenous population of about 20 percent.[8]

Among these estimates, the 1930 census is an anomaly. The last national census to attempt any count of ethnic identity, it reported a national indigenous total of only 5.6 percent, concentrated entirely in the western departments and especially Ahuachapán and Sonsonate (see Table 1). This census showed no indígenas at all in Lenca territory, in the east. These statistics have bolstered the impression, to later observers, that the indigenous population even in 1930 was in rapid decline, and seems to warrant the omission of ethnicity from subsequent census surveys.

The 1930 census figure of 5.6 percent was, however, always controversial. It strikingly contradicted the various estimates noted above. North American anthropologist Richard Adams, who conducted a demographic survey in the 1950s, described it as "startling."[9] Some critics have even speculated that the low figure reflected the ethnocidal interests of the Martínez regime, or at least of local officials. But it is more likely that the 1930 census was simply a weak census, run by an underequipped and possibly inexperienced census authority. Certainly it had a rocky history. Conducted hastily in 1930, its compilation and analysis were somehow derailed (perhaps by the transition to military rule); in 1940 the original documents were found moldering in a back room by the new Department of Statistics director. Recruiting students from the National University during their two-month winter vacation, he was able to compile and publish the census in 1941. The original documents were later consumed by a fire, so that the students' accuracy, and the methodology and general quality of the census, cannot be checked. But its other troubles are suggested elsewhere. Writing to Sonsonate Department mayoral offices during the 1932 Matanza, the Census Office asked urgently for complete lists of their cantones—the rural hamlets where most indígenas lived and where the Matanza was being pursued.[10] If the Census Office found itself with no reliable list of the cantones in 1932, its 1930 survey of these same districts is suspect.

Whatever its accuracy, the 1930 census marked the end of official attention to national ethnic demography. No subsequent census (of 1950, 1961, 1973, or 1992) addressed the question. Some Salvadorans believe that the Constitution of 1950 actually prohibited the recording of race in the census (a measure seen today as progressive), but the constitution contains no such clause—although it does call more broadly for the abolition of any form of racial discrimination.[11]

Table 2: Indigenous Population of El Salvador, 1930 Census

Department	% Indigenous	Total
Sonsonate	34.7	34,764
Ahuachapán	26.1	20,572
La Libertad	7.4	8,749
San Salvador	5.9	11,334
Santa Ana	2.6	4,751
All others:	less than one percent	
Total	5.6 percent	79,573

Source: 1930 Población de la República de El Salvador, Censo del 1o. de Mayo 1930

An Alternative Source: The Birth Records

Although the census offers little help in reconstructing ethnohistorical demographics, a second source has always existed: the Civil Registry, initiated by the central government in the 1860s. These bound, handwritten folios, in which local officials recorded births and deaths of each township, often included notation of the newborn's "race" (raza).[12] Until recently the registry has been effectively unavailable, as the original handwritten, bound volumes were scattered among town "archives" (too often, the floor of a closet, or a corner of the room), often moldy and disintegrating. Towns supposedly sent copies of their registries to the national capital at least until 1915, but that centralized data has been lost.[13] In 1992, however, in preparing for the 1996 election, the El Salvador's Supreme Electoral Tribunal microfilmed all the surviving birth and death records in the country in order to create a list of eligible voters, and the registry could be reviewed thoroughly for the first time.

Superficially, the birth records are a simple and direct source of ethnic information. A typical formula was, "*[Nombre] nació hembra indígena, hija ilegítima de . . .*" ([Name] born indigenous girl, illegitimate daughter of . . .) and so on. Sometimes the racial identity would be attached to the parents: "*[Nombre] nació hijo ilegítimo de [padre] y [madre], ladinos de esta jurisdicción . . .*" ([Name] born illegitimate son of [father] and [mother], ladinos of this jurisdiction . . .), and so on.[14] Straightforward readings of these notations allow us to make simple ethnic calculations. Hence we have registry data from 1884 published by the Government Ministry, which show a countrywide indigenous birth rate of 25.3 percent (Table 3). Salvadoran historian Salvador I. Barberena also drew on the registry to compile countrywide racial totals for 1899–1903, which indicated that about 23 percent of births were being reported as indigenous at the turn of the century (Table 4).[15]

Table 3: Indigenous Birth Proportions by Department, 1884

Department	% Indigenous	Department	% Indigenous
Sonsonate	52.0	Cabañas	11.1
Cuscatlán	50.3	Usulután	10.9
La Paz	50.0	La Union	10.7
Ahuachapán	48.9	San Vicente	7.7
San Salvador	47.8	Chalatenango	7.6
Gotera (Morazán)	34.0	San Miguel	4.4
La Libertad	15.8	Santa Ana	3.3
Average Percentage: 25.3			

Source: Memorias del Ministerio de Gobernación, 1884

Table 4: Indigenous Births by State Totals, 1899–1903

Year	% Indigenous	Total Indigenous
1899	22.5	9,012
1900	23.3	9,777
1901	22.5	9,539
1902	22.3	9,124
1903	23.0	10,053
Average Percentage: 22.9		

Source: Salvador I. Barberena, "Estudios Demográficos," *La Quincena* Vol. IV 43–45.

Read more carefully, however, the birth records are a murkier text. El Salvador's civil code never actually required notation of race (perhaps reflecting this extrajudicial quality, in some towns racial notations were carefully inserted into the margin, next to the formal entry). Town secretaries therefore entered the racial identity of newborns according to local custom and, apparently, individual biases or differing ideas about the job. In a single municipality, changes of handwriting are frequently associated with entries listing dramatically more ladinos, or more indígenas, suggesting that ethnic identities were understood (or at least recorded) differently by various secretaries. Also, inconsistent practices sometimes left gaps, where no ethnic identities were entered for months or years. In larger towns and at the national level, these variations tend to average out (as demonstrated by the consistent countrywide totals in Table 3). But in smaller *municipios*, or where one secretary's handwriting prevailed for long periods, idiosyncratic records sometimes make any confident interpretation of underlying ethnic demography impossible.

Dramatically inconsistent annual rates of indígena and ladino births also offer mysteries; for example, indigenous rates in the relatively large municipio of Izalco (which in the 1930s held a population of some 20,000) swing from 40 percent in 1930, to 36 percent in 1931, to 51 percent in 1932. Similar variations appeared for San Antonio Masahuat (see Chart 2). Sudden clusters of "indígena" notations hint that indigenous women sometimes came to the alcaldia together, perhaps for mutual support or on an important market day, and reported births from previous weeks or months.

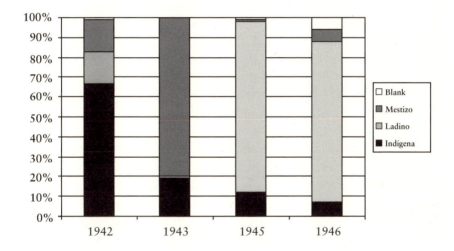

**Chart 2: Changing Ethnic Birth Labels
in San Antonio Masahuat, La Paz Department, 1942–46**

Source: Civil Registry, Birth Records, San Antonio Masahuat: Supreme Electoral Tribunal, San Salvador.

The registry also offers a temporally narrow window. Nineteenth century records are fragmented and inconsistent; civil recordkeeping in general was erratic until the 1910s. For the southwestern departments, consistent racial notations emerge primarily between 1905 and 1940. In Sonsonate and Ahuachapán, race notations peaked in the 1920s and then faded as the twentieth century progressed (with the exception of Juayúa, which dropped references to race in 1922). In La Paz department, the race category vanished abruptly, throughout all townships, between 1944 and

1947. By 1950, very few municipios still listed race routinely. The last town to do so, Nahuizalco, omitted the category in September of that year.

Finally, birth data does not equate with population data. Important information is still missing: reporting rates by the rural population; the ethnic death records, which have not yet been compiled; and differing fertility rates for the ladino and indígena populations (an urban/rural as well as a class difference). Generic undercounts of the indigenous population are very likely, given its backwoods covert existence. Until the fuller bureaucratization of the state in the mid-twentieth century, many rural people found no compelling reason to report births and indeed were motivated by labor and tax laws not to do so. (Even today, many people in the countryside do not report stillbirths.)[16] The Supreme Electoral Tribunal indeed found, in 1992, that the demographic group least recorded in the Civil Registry was western rural women: that is, women in the mostly indigenous zones. Furthermore, the decades after the 1940s brought heavy urbanization and migration resulting from industrialization and a worsening land shortage. This data therefore does not serve as a basis by which to project today's indigenous population.

Despite these important limitations, the registry offers a treasure trove of local detail and remains an invaluable source for early twentieth-century statistics on race. In the decades leading up to the Matanza, it portrays a community clearly split in racial terms. The categories were overwhelmingly either ladina or indígena (sometimes india, or *indita*). Rarely, births might be labeled *blanca* (white), or, much more rarely, mulata (mixed African-ladina or African-Indian) or negra (black, i.e., Afro-Latino). In the 1930s (notably, starting before the Matanza), the term mestizo was introduced, in ways detailed below.

One of the registry's first revelations is that the birth rates from 1884 and from 1899–1903 (cited in Tables 2 and 3) need to be treated with great caution if not skepticism. According to the registry, many towns did not record the ethnic identity of newborns at all until after 1900. In the Sonsonate department, where high indigenous populations particularly encouraged their registry, townships that omitted racial notations in 1900 included Caluco, Cuisnahuat, Nahulingo, San Antonio del Monte, and the much larger and demographically more important towns of Izalco and the departmental capital of Sonsonate itself.[17] Whether these townships found some other way to estimate and report ethnic births to the capital remains unknown, but without such information we must consider the possibility that Barberena's ethnic data from 1899–1903 seriously underestimated the total.

But the value of the birth records goes beyond such narrow questions of aggregate ethnic counts. They are a unique ethnic text because they reflect a precise public moment: the moment when the family member came to the civil registry desk of the alcaldía and self-declared, or was perceived by the official charged with making the entry, as belonging to one racial group or the other. The racial identity of the parents, even if previously inscribed in the registry, was not checked; there was no such South African apartheid-style rigor at work. The birth records therefore indicate ethnoracial perceptions at the moment of registration. And because ladino also functioned as an ethnic category, to which indígenas could assimilate through behavioral change, the registry should reveal how ethnic identity transformed through these years. That is, indigenous families which set out to assimilate ("ladino-ize") after the 1932 Matanza should appear in increasing proportions, in that official moment, as ladinos. The birth records should therefore reflect any sweeping effort by the indigenous population to hide itself—or indeed any broad experience of assimilation, or mestizaje. What we find, however, is a very different picture.

The Troubled Inscription of Mestizaje

Mestizaje is indeed traceable through the Civil Registry. The early 1930s saw the first use of the term mestizo, and its use increased steadily through the decade. By the mid-1940s, mestizo began to replace all other terms, sometimes taking over all birth records until the race category was eliminated entirely (again, in all cases, by 1950).

But what kind of social process did this *mestization* of the registry represent? In the first decades of its appearance, "mestizo" was recorded with such great inconsistency as to suggest complete confusion, at the local level, about what it meant. In some towns, mestizo suddenly replaced all other racial categories; everyone was now mestizo. In other cases it was introduced as a synonym for ladino, alternating with indígena. In still other cases, the reverse was true: it substituted for indígena, and alternated with ladino. Use of mestizo often varied with different handwritings; chart 2 shows such swings in San Antonio Masahuat, where different hands seemed to switch from using mestizo back to using ladino between 1943 and 1945. (Secretaries in that township also confusingly recorded "*ladino, raza mestizo*,"—"ladino, of mestizo race"—for a series of entries in 1944–45.) In a few towns, the term mestizo was never used at all: ladino and indígena were used until the racial category was eliminated entirely, usually in the 1940s.

In some townships, "mestizo" entered the record for a few months, then vanished (secretaries going back to recording ladino and indígena), and then returned . . . yet with obscure meaning. Table 5 shows such a pattern in Panchimalco, today the country's most famously Indian town (in the Nonualco Nahua region, south of the capital). In 1945, one handwriting consistently recorded almost all mestizos (M) up to entry 121 (noted with the ★), although the writer twice entered "mestizo indígena" (MI, underlined). This consistency would suggest that everyone had indeed assimilated to mestizo. But at that point another hand took over, reintroducing indígena (I) and seeming to use mestizo as a synonym for ladino. After that, entries became inconsistent and impossible to interpret. What, for example, are the ethnic identities of newborns in the last 50-odd entries, where mestizo increasingly alternates with blanks?

Table 5: Ethnic identity of newborns, Panchimalco, 1945

Chronology of entries is read left to right. The crucial change in handwriting at entry 121, the end of the *mestizo* sweep, is marked with a star (★). Later omissions of ethnic identity are marked by "?" a pattern of omission common to the coastal municipalities in the late 1940s. Note also the use of "*mestizo indígena*" twice, in line two, in bold underline.

Key: M = *mestizo* I = *indígena* L = *ladino* ? = ethnicity not recorded

```
? ? ? ? ? ? M M M M M M M M M M M M M M M M M M M M M M M M M M M M M M M M M
M M M M M M M M M M M M M M M M M M I M M M M M MI MI M M M M M M M M M M M M M
M M M M M M M M M M M M M M M M M M M M M M M M M M M M M M M M M M M M M ? ?
M M I M M M M M M M M M M M M M M M M M M M M I M M M M M M M M M M M M M M M
M M M ? M M M M M M M M M M M M M M M M M M M M M M M M M M M M M M M M M M M
M M M M M M M M M ? M M M M M M M M M M M M M M M M M M M M M M M M M M M M M
M M M M M M M M M ★ I I I I I I I M I M I M I M M M I I M M M M M M I I I I I ? I I I I I I I
I I M M M I I I I ? L I I M I I I I I ? I I I I I M I M M M M M I I I I ? I I I I I M M I I I I M M I I I I
I I I I I I L I M M I M M M I I I M I I I I I M M I M I I ? M M I I M I M M M I I I M M M M ? ? M
? M I M M ? I M ? ? ? ? ? ? M M I M M I ? ? I I ? ? ? I ? I M ? I ? I ? ? ? M ? ? ? ? ? I I ?
M M M M ? ? ? I ? ? M ? M ? M I ? ? I ? ? M M M ? ? M M M ? ? ? ? ? ? ? ? ? M ? M M I ? ? ? ? M
M M M M M M I M
```

These inconsistencies suggest that, at the community level, mestizaje had nothing like the social clarity or cohesion it is granted, post hoc, by modern scholarship. Rather, the records portray a muddled process of relabeling with which people grappled uncertainly and without consensus. Poorly understood or adopted inconsistently by town secretaries, the new term mestizo seems rather to have reflected some new ideological, political, or administrative agenda. That it represented a deliberate policy shift is indicated by the suddenness of its wholesale adoption between one day and the next. That it did not make full sense locally is suggested by its inconsistencies and frequent reversals. In this confused contest, a sudden takeover of a town's registry by the term mestizo—what we might call a "mestizo sweep"—simply draws a curtain over underlying local complexities, rendering the registry unreadable for purposes of ethnic demography. Yet even with these inconsistencies—or perhaps because of them—the birth records give serious trouble to the legend of the 1932 ethnocide.[18]

A Legend Set Back

Two striking findings stand out in the birth records. First, they indicate no overall drop in indigenous totals. Birth rates in Sonsonate and Ahuachapán between 1900 and 1950 show no indication that indigenous ethnic identity declined precipitously, or even noticeably, in the years immediately following the 1932 Matanza. On the contrary, in the two largest indigenous municipios of Sonsonate—Nahuizalco and Izalco—indigenous birth proportions either held rock-steady or actually rose until racial notations were abruptly eliminated from the registry, in 1945 and 1950, respectively.

Other towns show no overall pattern but rather erratic swings, some of which may be attributable to migration. For example, the decline in Ishuatán is matched by a corresponding increase in neighboring Cuisnahuat, a trend substantiated by oral history of a major ladino migration to Ishuatán during this period. Similarly, ethnic migration is suggested from Tacuba (which dropped some fourteen percentage points between 1930 and 1945) to neighboring San Francisco Menendez (which rose toward the end of that same period). When all swings are totaled, and if we project Juayúa's indigenous population forward at 45 percent, Sonsonate's department-wide indigenous birth rate also appears largely stable, even showing a slight increase from 32 percent in 1930 to 34.9 percent in 1950. (Of interest here is that even the highly suspect 1930 census of Sonsonate indicated a very close match to the registry's 1930 figure: one of 34.7 percent.)

Second, the registry reveals a substantial indigenous presence in many more townships than is commonly recognized. Table 6 indicates high indigenous birth rates in parts of Ahuachapán never cited today as having sustained high indigenous populations. Map 2 shows impressive densities of indigenous birth rates in 1940–45 throughout southern La Libertad and all of La Paz, although these townships are commonly assumed to have lost any recognizable indigenous population decades earlier. The birth data indeed suggests the persistence, into the mid-1940s, of a dense belt of indigenous communities all along El Salvador's western coastal hill zone (see map).

Table 6: Percentages of Indigenous Births
in Selected Departments and Municipios, El Salvador

Municipio	Avg % Indig in Municipio	Year/s Sampled	% Indig. in Year/s Sampled	Mun. % of Dept's Pop	% Indig. of Dept Pop
Sonsonate				100.0	34.2
Nahuizalco	86.1	1945/50	85.7/86.4	11.8	10.1
Santa Catarina Masahuat	79.9	1940/45	82.6/77.1	3.0	2.4
Santo Domingo de Guzman	69.6	940/45	71.4/67.7	1.8	1.3
Cuisnahuat	60.8	1940/4	67.1/54.5	3.2	1.9
Juayua	(45.0)	1920/25	52.5/52.3	8.7	(3.9)
Izalco	50.3	1940/45	50.2/50.3	18.5	9.3
Sonzacate	48.9	1945	48.9	1.6	0.8
San Antonio del Monte	48.8	1940/45	39.2/58.3	2.5	1.2
Acajutla	54.1	1945	54.1	5.6	2.5
San Julian	10.3	1940	10.3	5.8	0.6
Nahulingo	9.5	1940/45	14.5/4.5	1.2	0.1
Ishuatán	2.8	1940	2.8	3.6	0.1
Armenia	0.0	1935/40/45	0.0	9.7	0.0
Caluco	——	1935/40/45	——	2.0	——
Salcoatitán	——	1935/40/45	——	1.5	——
Sonsonate	——	1935/40/45	——	19.5	——

Table 6: Percentages of Indigenous Births
in Selected Departments and Municipios, El Salvador (continued)

Municipio	Avg % Indig in Municipio	Year/s Sampled	% Indig. in Year/s	Sampled	Mun. % of Dept's
Ahuachapán				100.0	47.9
San Francisco Menendez	90.9	1945/50	92.2/89.5	6.6	6.0
Guaymango	82.7	1945	82.7	6.8	5.7
Ataco	(70.0)	1920/30	75.5/73.1	7.3	(5.4)
San Pedro Puxtla	66.5	1940/45	61.2/71.8	3.8	2.6
Apaneca	55.7	1940/45	57.7/53.6	5.0	2.8
Tacuba	55.4	1940/45	57.1/53.6	9.9	5.5
Ahuachapán	(50.0)	1920/25	62.1/57.0	33.4	(17.4)
Jujutla	20.9	1940/45	8.4/33.3	7.6	2.5
El Refugio	0.0	1940/45	0.0/0.0	1.2	0.0
Atiquizaya	0.0	1940/45	0.0/0.0	15.7	0.0
Turin	0.0	1940/45	0.0/0.0	2.5	0.0
San Salvador					
Rosario de Mora	90.3	1950	90.3	1.0	0.9
Panchimalco	80.5	1940/45	79.2/81.7	4.7	3.8
Cuscatlán					
Candelaria	68.4	1939	68.4	4.5	3.1
Cojutepeque	21.6	1941/42	22.3/20.8	15.7	3.4
Santa Cruz Analquito	4.3	1944/45	2.6/6.0	1.3	0.05
San Rafael Cedras	3.3	1943/45	0.0/6.6	4.7	0.5
La Libertad				100.0	16.0
Huizucar	98.4	1944/45	97.3 / 99.5	3.6	3.6
Colón	88.8	1941/1942	82.7/94.9	6.1	5.4
Talnique	75.3	1941/42	67.9/82.6	2.0	1.5
Zaragoza	75.4	1942/43	66.3/84.5	1.5	1.1
Tepecoyo	63.2	1944	63.2	3.5	2.2
Chiltiupán	50.2	1946/50	37.1/63.3	2.1	1.1
Sacacoyo	24.8	1941/42	16.3/33.3	1.4	0.3

Table 6: Percentages of Indigenous Births
in Selected Departments and Municipios, El Salvador (continued)

Municipio	Avg % Indig in Municipio	Year/s Sampled	% Indig. in Year/s	Sampled	Mun. % of Dept's
Tamanique	24.5	1943/44	6.4/42.1	1.4	0.3
Nueva Cuscatlán	11.1	1939	11.1	1.0	0.1
Teotepeque	10.2	1943	10.2	3.1	0.3
Comasagua	0.0	1947/48	0.0/0.0	4.0	0.0
Quezaltepeque	0.0	1945	0.0	11.6	0.0
Dept. La Paz				100.0	42.4
San Francisco Chinameca	97.3	1944/45	97.3/97.2	3.3	3.2
San Miguel Tepezontes	91.5	1945/46	91.7/91.3	2.4	2.2
Tapalhuaca	84.1	1942/43	100/68.2	2.0	1.7
San Juan Tepezontes	80.4	1945/46	79.2/81.6	1.2	0.9
Santa María Ostuma	78.7	1943//44	85.1/72.2	3.5	2.8
San Pedro Nonualco	78.6	1934/35	83.8/73.4	6.0	4.7
San Antonio Masahuat	67.0	1942	67.0	2.7	1.8
San Juan Nonualco	58.3	1943/44	58.6/58.0	8.3	4.8
San Pedro Masahuat	41.1	1944/45	48.1/34.5	6.1	2.5
Zacatecoluca	38.9	1945	38.9	29.2	11.4
San Juan Talpa	38.1	1945	38.1	3.7	1.4
Santiago Nonualco	30.0	1949	30.0	12.9	3.9
Cuyultitán	28.0	1943/44	0.9/55.1	1.5	0.4
Mercedes La Ceiba	25.0	1938/39	25.0/25.0	0.4	0.1
Jerusalen	22.6	1944/45	19.0/26.1	0.9	0.2
Paraiso de Osorio	10.9	1940/41	15.2/6.5	1.2	0.1
San Rafael Obrajuela	10.1	1944/45	12.8/7.3	3.2	0.3
Olocuilta	0.0	1943/44	0.0	5.4	0.0
El Rosario	0.0	1942/43	0.0	0.0	0.0
San Luis Talpa	0.0	1944/45	0.0	0.0	0.0
San Emigdio	----	1943/44/45	----	1.1	0.0

MAP 2. Map of Indigenous Births in Selected Municipalities in El Salvador, 1940–45.

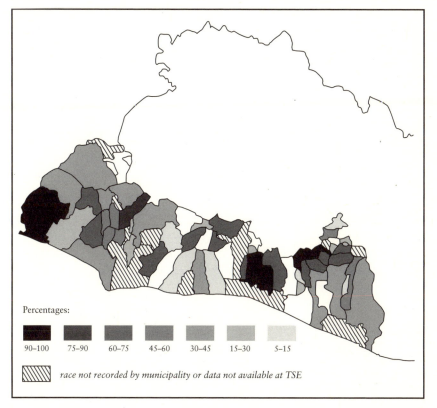

Percentages:

90–100 75–90 60–75 45–60 30–45 15–30 5–15

race not recorded by municipality or data not available at TSE

Source: Birth Records (Libros de Nacimientos) of the Salvadorean Civil Registry: Supreme Electoral Tribunal (TSE), San Salvador.

Birth records in other departments—Santa Ana, Cuscatlán, Usulután, Morazán—were too incomplete to offer conclusive portraits, but evidence peeks out of similar trends. Racial entries were very inconsistent in the northeastern department of Morazán (Lenca territory), but the townships of Guatajiagua, San Simón, and Cacaopera recorded indigenous rates of 51 percent (in 1934–35), 60 percent (in 1940), and 53 percent (in 1946–47), respectively. In Santa Ana and Usulután departments, notation of indigenous births stopped in the 1910s, but, again, often abruptly: for example, the once very rebellious indígena town of Coatepeque dropped the race category in 1916, although the indigenous proportion had held steady at about

18 percent in the 1911–15 period. In Cuscatlán department, most municipios dropped the category in the 1930s, but the department capital,
Cojutepeque, was still recording 21 percent indigenous births in 1941–42.

Whatever the underlying ethnic trends, the birth records make one
thing clear. Indigenous ethnic identity in El Salvador was administratively
erased well before its actual social demise. The famous ethnocide was to
some degree *clerical*.

So what did the term mestizo actually signify? A sincere government
effort to impose it as the politically correct term of the period? A new
term to help local administrators manage racial labels that were, with
advancing assimilation, increasingly unworkable? A term slightly ahead
of its time—a top-down reform that, at first, didn't entirely match local
perceptions? Whatever the logic, or combination of logics, administrative
fiat was intruding on established social perceptions. Especially suggestive
of this are sudden cases of mestizo sweep, usually between 1945 and 1947,
in towns still recording indigenous birth rates of 50 percent and above.
How can we read the mestizo sweep?

The Broader Range of Mestizaje

El Salvador was not alone in erasing race from the national census. By
1950, race had suddenly gone out of vogue as a census category in every
country in Central America. Costa Rica had already given up any effort
to tabulate ethnic or racial divisions, under any rubric, decades earlier.
But Panama, which kept up the race category with particular care
through the 1940 census (listing "white," "black," "mestizo" and "other
races," and going to elaborate methods to account for the small indigenous
population), made no mention at all of race in the 1950 census.[19] Like El
Salvador, Nicaragua's count of Indians had already mysteriously plummeted from 30 percent in 1906 to 4 percent in 1920; in the 1950 census,
the skin color category was switched to a language count, and even that distinction was dropped by 1963.[20] Honduras too dropped any direct mention of race or ethnicity after 1940 (although the 1950 census retained
categories of wearing shoes and eating wheat bread, proxy signals for ethnic identity). Guatemala had counted races in the 1921 census; afterward,
it continued to count the country's ladinos and indios under the new label
"ethnic groups." Mexico also switched from racial notations to linguistic

ones (grouping "indigenous languages and dialects" into twenty families, such as Maya). Some regional consensus was clearly at work, although we still do not know precisely how it was circulating. The Guatemalan census of 1950 suggests that some new knowledge was taking hold, referring in its introduction to the scientific incorrectness of race as a census category.[21]

But if race was being abandoned as a crude and scientifically specious concept, that concern was not the only force at work. A complicated history of ethnic tension, land rivalries, and nationalist anxiety also pervaded the advent of mestizaje and still pervades it today. For example, in Guatemala, anthropologist Charles R. Hale also found a pattern of mestizo sweep in the marriage records of Chimaltenango between 1986 and 1990. In 1986, the ethnic identity of most marriages was labeled "unknown." The next three years showed 80 percent indígena/indígena marriages. But in 1990, the record suddenly chronicled 50 percent ladino/ladino marriages. Hale concludes that "Since these fluctuations . . . could not possibly correspond to actual demographic shifts, the only conclusion to draw is that the civil registry was having trouble figuring out who is who."[22] Upon his inquiries, one Chimaltenango official told Hale that the local registry had given up trying to label people, and was simply returning the forms blank. A ladina official in the National Statistics Institute (NSI) further explained that the old categories had become unworkable because indigenous people no longer wanted to be identified as Indians (so apparently officials at the NSI were simply making up what they thought were more appropriate figures).

But Hale also observed the political context for these wild swings: the rise of the pan-Maya movement in the late 1980s and 1990s. Facing this challenge, some ladino voices were suddenly invoking mestizaje as a cloak for rejecting Mayan ethnic demands, casting them as scientifically specious, socially retrograde, falsely divisive, and racist. Hale concluded that these forcible assertions of mestizaje signified not so much actual changing ethnic perceptions as an "appropriation from above." "The ladino embrace of mestizaje," although it "has no single, stable political meaning," represents "a tactical shift by the relatively powerful, that may ameliorate but ultimately serves to reproduce existing racism and power inequity."[23]

In Nicaragua, too, historian Jeff Gould traced early mestizaje to ethnic economic tensions. As in El Salvador, in the 1930s land seizures by commercial ladino interests were provoking violent corporate Indian protest, particularly in the Matagalpa region. Through mestizaje, local ladino authorities and landowners could affirm the fact and moral rightness of Indian ethnic dissolution as legally incorporated communities and even as an ethnic category. As Hale found in Guatemala, in this context of ethnic rivalry, the "myth" of mestizaje "became meaningful only in the context of the real violence waged against the [indigenous] communities"[24]:

> these lawyers, poets, and caretakers could take advantage of the indigenous silence and invent a version of social history that, notwithstanding a blatant disregard for local facts, rapidly become a canon: Despite the noble efforts of their enlightened defenders, a primitive race tragically died off, victim of its inability to modernize and of unscrupulous outsiders who took advantage of its simplicity.[25]

Yet the Nicaraguan discourse of mestizaje was no more adequate in Nicaragua than it would be in El Salvador, papering over a continuing indigenous presence rather than reflecting its genuine evaporation. When, in the early 1980s, the Sandinistas carried their forced integration policies to the indigenous communities on the Atlantic Coast, based on presumptions of nationalist mestizaje, they met armed resistance. Even on the Pacific coast, where mestizaje was considered most complete, complex interweavings of indigeneity were sustained in hidden and multiple ways and an indigenous movement re-emerged in the 1990s.[26]

Hence, in all three countries, mestizaje altered inscriptions of identity but also filtered into public doctrine and popular perceptions about local ethnic experience. It also eventually obtained an aura of objective truth and moral authority, able to recast any indigenous movement that challenged it not only as retrogressive but as divisive to the nation—even seditious. But its sweeping takeover throughout Latin America, and the nationalist energies that accompany its local endorsement, signal that there is more to mestizaje's origins than local ethnic rivalries over political power and land. And there is.

CHAPTER 9

BEING MESTIZO

THE TWISTED LOGICS OF MESTIZAJE

If the United States is the Anglo-Saxon republic, . . . the constellation of democratic Republics of Latin America are . . . the cosmopolitan, the Indian, the Semite, the Greek, the Roman, the German, the Middle Easterner, they are the arm of all the races, they are the brotherhood, synthesis of all History, they are the liberty proclaimed with the heroic gesture of the wars of Independence, and of a thousand revolutions, the divine forge on which the Palladium has been revitalized, of everlasting metal, of Democracy and Republic. The rest of the nations are races. Latin America, sir, is humanity.

—Francisco Gavida, 1903

The indigenous problem consists in this: there are three million Mexicans, at the least, that do not receive the benefits of the country's progress; that form true isolates, incapable of following the pace of development in Mexico; that do not feel themselves to be Mexicans.

—Alfonso Caso, 1958

THE BIRTH RECORDS SUGGEST THAT THE IDENTITY "MESTIZO" TOOK SOME decades to embed in Salvadoran local thought. In its early years, people did not share the same idea of what it meant. Over time, however, the notation "mestizo" took over the records entirely, and by the 1950 census its universal use had rendered the category of race itself obsolete. Indian and ladino alike were now, officially, mestizo. And yet, where did this idea of universal racial mixture come from? Why did it abruptly take over some civil registries between one day and the next? And how did it so successfully come to veil—at least in government doctrine and increasingly in public perceptions—the very existence of the indigenous communities still densely situated in the cantones of the western coffee region?

As an idea about racial identity, mestizaje has a complicated history. It was not merely a new social belief about racial mixing, nor was it simply a scientific observation about biological miscegenation. Nor did it reflect purely local or domestic problems, as in Nicaragua and Guatemala. It was also a pan–Latin American doctrine that, by the 1920s, was sweeping throughout the continent. Decades before "mestizo" entered the Salvadoran Civil Registry, the project of imagining mestizaje was being pursued as a new racial-nationalist and geostrategic idea among nationalist intellectuals throughout the continent. Those thinkers were concerned with Indians but were much more concerned about what race meant for their nations' economic growth, international trade, and their ability to fend off European and North American imperialism. To trace those inner motives and the political logic of mestizaje as it entered El Salvador, we must therefore go back to those writers who became its key contributors: what some theorists might call the epistemic community on race for state builders of the day.[1]

To do so, we must temporarily leave El Salvador, and look at the larger environment of ideas in which Salvadoran racial ideas were steeping: the states rapidly gelling as a community under the name "Latin America." And that project requires that we consider the larger global environment of ideas—circulating also in Europe, Asia, and Africa—in which the identity "Latin America" itself was taking shape.

Racial Nationalism and the Anglo-Saxon Problem

The framing condition impacting Salvadoran racial thought in the early twentieth century was racial nationalism. It is often difficult for people today to appreciate the cognitive force that racial nationalism once held globally. And yet, disseminated especially by European social scientists and scientized through seemingly impressive statistical studies, its basic logic was once persuasive to nationalists all over the world. Racial identities were believed to drive mental qualities like intelligence, patience, diligence, and so forth. Those mental qualities would obviously determine each race's collective cultural predispositions and even its transcendental spiritual character (in a *volk*ish or Jungian sense). Because each race's spirit and culture were unique, each race needed and could legitimately demand its own state, in which it could establish a government to defend its unique needs and interests. But each race's innate abilities would also determine its potential and accomplishments in that state: hence some nations were racially predisposed to do better than others—and to dominate others.

Evidence for these assumptions seemed compelling. The vast British Empire (then at its territorial peak) seemed dramatic proof that the Anglo-Saxon race was distinctly superior to the multitude of peoples (races) it was dominating. The rapid expansion of the United States, understood to be steered and dominated by Anglo-Saxons, seemed to clinch this notion. By the same logic, the relative weakness of the dwindled Spanish Empire suggested Spanish racial flaws like "languor," "laziness," and "arrogance." Racial sciences therefore spun off from these apparent facts not to test them but to explain why they were true. Major studies (mostly British) attempted to measure the brain size and other features of each race, generating impressive charts of cranial, nostril, and earlobe measurements and the like.[2] Worse, some European thinkers (such as, famously, Herbert Spencer) also argued that white superiority rested on its "purity." On this argument, a nation's racial homogeneity was essential to the nation's collective political health and even to national security itself. In the 1920s and 1930s, these arguments about racial purity fed most famously into Nazi German racial mysticism and the genocidal logic of the Holocaust, as well as the equally fervent, mystical, and genocidal racial nationalism of imperial Japan. The whole package of ideas was a powerful caution to nation builders against racial mixing.

Yet racial nationalism was hardly confined to Europe or Great Power rivalries. Rapidly disseminated by European colonialist and imperialist texts, by 1900 racial nationalism had swept into nationalist thought in all corners of the world, like a great change of global weather. Latin American nationalisms were fully in its path. Hence, in 1911, Mexican intellectual Manuel Gamio referred admiringly to nationalist unity as "a solemn cry of shared blood."[3] In 1915, Argentinean sociologist José Ingenieros put the message plainly:

to say nation, is to say race; national unity is not equivalent to political unity, but to spiritual and social unity, to racial unity. . . . In summation, we speak of "race" to characterize a society homogeneous in customs and ideals which differentiate it from other societies that coexist with it in time and that limit it in space.[4]

But the scientized idea of Anglo-Saxon superiority also gave serious trouble to Latin American nationalists, because it implied that the relative weakness of Latin American states was organic: Spanish racial flaws coupled with the degenerating effects of negro and indio components. In this light, the inferior Indian corroded the national racial stock, impeding its very capacity for growth. The Indian admixture even precluded that essential "spiritual" unity which any great nation required.

Hence the dilemma facing Latin American nation builders was partly a racial one. If a nation could be truly civilized only to the extent that it was white, and any non-white blood eroded its very capacity for civilization, then to become fully civilized, Latin American nations had to be not only white but homogeneously white.[5] And of course, they were neither. One answer was to "whiten" the nations by promoting mass white European immigration. Whitening did seem viable in the Southern Cone (cleansing of the Argentinean Pampas being mostly completed, and the Chilean Mapuche being expected to dwindle away especially after the massacres of the 1880s).[6] But elsewhere, whitening loomed difficult or impossible, given heavily Indian and black demographics. The continent as a whole was variously estimated by contemporary observers as 60–75 percent indigenous. Through the racial lens then operating, the outlook for Latin America as a region appeared grim.[7]

This racial "problem" generated arguments and bitter diatribes against Indians throughout the continent. Even in Argentina, José Ingenieros mourned Spanish mixture with Indian (and Arab) blood as having "retarded the formation of new nationalities of white race [in the Southern Cone] by a century."[8] Chilean writer Guillermo Feliu Cruz later described the Chilean population in the early nineteenth century as "about three quarters constituted of Spanish-indigenous mestizaje, neither barbarian nor civilized."[9] In heavily indigenous countries like Mexico, European racial theory—and policy solutions to its ominous message—were therefore under urgent political debate.

The Indian Problem

By the late nineteenth century, race was only one pressing quandary for Latin American intellectuals as they explored ways to integrate their nations politically and socially. Those efforts were not isolated in each country, but were pursued in consultations around the continent, through books, pamphlets, letters, travel, and conferences. One central forum, for example, was provided by the International Conferences of American States, sponsored by the United States and first held in Washington, D.C. in 1899. Drawing together representatives from all states in the Americas, these conferences were concerned first with developing Latin America as a security community (called the "Organization of Peace"). But they were also concerned with trade and economic growth, and quickly expanded to address domestic matters discovered to be essential to integrating Latin American trade and cooperation. For example, at the Seventh Conference in 1933, discussions hammered out agreements on matters ranging from customs regulations to patent laws to newspaper licensing to library catalog systems. More debates addressed what delegates perceived as endemic social problems among the working classes, like crime, drunkenness, promiscuity, vagrancy, and "immorality" in general. Concerns here were humanitarian but also pragmatic: national economic development was understood to rest on developing a strong internal market, and a strong market was clearly hobbled by the poverty, ignorance, and isolation of the vast ranks of Latin America's poor.[10]

Indians were clearly central to that obstacle. Everywhere, intellectuals understood that economic growth was dragged down by the Indians' perceived backwardness, superstition, poverty, insularity, and inefficiency. Hence debates were pursued all over Latin America under the rubric of "the Indian problem." For example, even in 1864, Mexican aristocrat and *científico* Francisco Pimentel had lamented the Indian problem as an obstacle to developing even basic national infrastructure, like roads and the telegraph:

> To what end do we think so much of *things* when there are not *persons*? We want railroads, and the greater part of our population knows no way to move about except by foot; we want telegraphs, and the Indian sees the apparatus as a thing of witchcraft; we want

to introduce gas [lighting] in our cities, and almost all our compatriots illuminate [their homes] with ocote; we want to extend our commerce and there are no consumers. With reason did an illustrious foreigner who visited Mexico some years ago say: "With the improvement of the state and character of the Indians will Mexico progress; but while this has yet to come about, its most passionate admirers should have little hope of its progress and even of its existence as a nation."[11]

Certainly such visions were shared by Salvadoran thinkers. For instance, in a 1906 polemic about the Central American *patria*, Salvadoran writer Miguel Román Peña offered a more poetic vision of the Indian problem, coupling a vision of Indian suffering to a lament about their obstructing progress:[12]

In our Patria exists a great majority ignorant of the boundaries of the territory and, far more, its history. Our civilization is exotic and superficial; it has still not penetrated the heart of the people. The native of this soil, the Indian, the mulatto, has lowered his face before destiny, and with the supreme sorrow of a conquered race, lives apart in humble shack, despoiled of the lands of their fathers. Thus are the descendants of Montezuma, Atlacatl and Atahualpa; thus the legitimate sons of our Patria, covered with rags, badly nourished, such that our riches, our forests, our marvelous fauna, are exploited by strangers' hands; and those serfs [*ilotas*] of the American forests are frequently taken to the fields of battle, ignorant of the reason for such happenings; there they fertilize in bestial war, by shedding their blood, the land that they should be watering only with the sweat of their brow!

The solution, Román Peña argued, was education:

Now is the opportune time to instruct and patriotically educate our people; it is necessary to chisel out [*cincelar*] his political personality; to show him . . . the high things of life, and make him understand that to them he can fly with faith in law, in democracy and in patriotism.[13]

And intrinsic to grappling with this Indian problem was a regional effort to understand the Indian as a racial group.[14]

Although everyone involved in these debates used the term race, discussion labored under extensive confusion as to what a race actually was. Especially, people questioned whether race was more a biological fact or a social identity, and so whether the miserable situation of the Indian communities could be redeemed through educational and hygienic programs or was somehow fixed biologically, confirming their degenerated state as hopeless. Some celebratory currents were visible: some "indigenist" ideologists believed that Latin American countries should find their true character and inspiration in the original indigenous cultures.[15] But the tone of most authors was prescriptive: to find some way to make moral and scientific sense of the Indian's abysmal poverty and isolation in order to arrive at some set of remedial policies. Given the conflation of "Indian" with poverty, ignorance, superstition, and crime, and elites' desires to turn Indians into productive capitalist units, for many writers the Indian problem was actually the need to eliminate Indianness through policies consistent with a moral framework.

The nationalist dimension of the Indian problem was equally clear, for many writers recognized that Indians did not seem *interested* in the nation. Andrés Molina Enríquez, for example, recognized that the Indians sustained a plethora of local loyalties to their various groups (patrias), whose own lack of unity prevented their obtaining any larger political vision or loyalty:

> In particular the indigenous element, comprised of tribes and peoples very different among themselves, completely lacks unity. . . . The multiplicity and confusion among the traditions of origin, the differences of type, the divergences of customs, the diversities of language, and the evolutionary distances that distinguish and separate among them, are so evident as to belong to the range of public and well-known facts. . . . Each indigenous group is consequently a special patria and the units of them are considered so in reality. Only in exceptional cases of great danger, do those groups count on the others; generally they keep each to their own forces, and when they are attacked, if they cannot win, they resign themselves to death. They have, however, multiple and small indigenous patrias, that are autonomous. These are complete

patrias and not fragments of patrias. They do not have, therefore, any external orientation. The Indians will never be deliberate traitors to their own patria to the benefit of an external patria.[16]

Molina Enríquez was equally pessimistic, however, about the political dedication of Mexico's creole elites, whose class snobbery and cosmopolitan ties to their European home countries (he argued) precluded their identifying with their own (mixed-race, impoverished) nation of Mexico. Rather, he believed the mestizo—the mixed-race and mixed-cultural population—provided the foundation for Mexican nation building:

> The fundamental and inevitable base of all future labor undertaken for the good of the country, must be the continuation of the mestizos as the preponderant ethnic element and as the directive political class of the population. . . . In them truly exist a unity of origin, unity of religion, unity of type, unity of language and unity of desires, goals and aspirations. . . . All those circumstances of unity compose and translate into a firm, ardent and resolute patriotic love.[17]

Molina Enríquez was hardly alone in this view. Francisco Gavida and others had been promoting mestizo nationalism for some decades, and the idea was increasingly seizing the imagination of the emerging cadre of post-Revolutionary Mexican nation builders. One such voice was Manuel Gamio, a Boas-trained anthropologist and one of the most influential Mexican social scientists of his day. His famous *Forjando patria* (Forging the Fatherland), for example, provided a sober argument for a more systematic, pragmatic, and scientific approach to governance and to racial divisions.[18] His preface became famous as a poetic celebration of the mestizo as the veritable racial incarnation of the continent's epic history:

> In the great forge of America, on the gigantic anvil of the Andes, virile races of bronze and iron have battled for centuries and centuries. . . . When the brown arm of the Atahualpas and the Moctezumas reached the moment of mixing and confusing peoples, a miraculous link was consummated: the same blood swelled the veins of the Americans and their thought flowed in the same

paths. . . . Today it is for the revolutionaries of Mexico to take up the hammer and gird themselves with the blacksmith's apron in order to bring forth from the miraculous anvil the new patria made of mingled iron and bronze. . . . There is the iron. . . . There is the bronze. . . . Strike, brothers![19]

And he concluded his book with a phrase in uppercase letters:

FUSION OF THE RACES, CONVERGENCE AND FUSION OF CULTURAL PRACTICES, LINGUISTIC UNIFICATION AND ECONOMIC EQUILIBRIUM OF THE SOCIAL SECTORS, are concepts that summarize this book and indicate conditions which, in our opinion, must characterize the Mexican population so that it will constitute and incarnate a strong Patria and a coherent and defined Nationality.[20]

This vision of an ennobled, Spanish-Indian mestizo race galvanized imaginations not only in Mexico but throughout those parts of Latin America where whitening appeared hopeless: especially the middle Isthmus and the Andes. Intellectuals, politicians, journalists, and literati in Guatemala, Lima, Costa Rica, Caracas, and Havana found it compelling. It was a vision that included Indians in abstracted form: celebrating the Indian component for its attached mythic history and romanticized values, and rendering obsolete and "backward" the old ideas of Indian racial inferiority. The idea rapidly assumed hegemonic proportions in Mexican nationalist thought as well as in El Salvador, Nicaragua, and Honduras.[21] In all these states, racial-nationalist mestizaje conceptually incorporated the Indian heritage not simply as a fact on the ground but also as a mark of national distinction—"we all have Indian blood." The same vision called for appropriating the art and symbols of pre-Columbian indigenous societies—even the heroes who resisted Spanish Conquest—as iconic referents to the nation's origins and essential character. Hence *indo-mestizaje* inspired celebration of reinvented "Conquest Indians," such as Atlacatl, in public statues and nationalist verse, as we have already seen.

Indo-mestizaje might well have offered a framework of values through which national societies could begin to address racial divisions and prejudice more substantially, as Gamio clearly intended. But a second and equally compelling interest would create conditions for continuing patterns of racial denial, ethnic violence, and Indian marginality to the national identity.

Mestizaje as a Foreign Relations Discourse

By the late nineteenth century, Latin America as a region was facing new international pressures. Economic trade had always been dependent on primary product export to Europe and to the United States, but, with the exponential growth of commercial export agriculture, the domestic impact of that dependency rapidly intensified. El Salvador was, of course, an exemplar of this pattern: by 1910, all domestic railroad traffic was controlled by the (U.S.) United Fruit Company and all ocean shipping was controlled by a U.S. monopoly. By the 1920s, coffee accounted for 95 percent of Salvadoran exports and many of the local coffee processing plants were owned by foreigners, especially North Americans and Germans.[22] Predictably, this dependency also transformed the sociology of the Salvadoran political elite: by the 1920s, the Salvadoran government was almost entirely dominated by sugar and coffee growers with, of course, strong social and commercial ties to North American and European business sectors.[23] Similar patterns characterized the other Central American states.

Viewing the economic risks inherent in such a scenario, Latin American nationalist intellectuals had long worried about the vulnerability of their nations' economies to foreign monopoly prices and to unpredictable fluctuations in the international market.[24] But the political risks were also worrisome: especially, the region's vulnerability to growing U.S. political and military leverage. Intellectual debates became more urgent after the Spanish-American War and a series of U.S. military invasions to support U.S. trade interests; for Central Americans, the U.S. occupation of Nicaragua (1911–1933) was particularly alarming.

Solidarity among Latin American states in facing this trade and military leverage was becoming an obvious need: attacking or undermining each other clearly made all only more vulnerable to imperialist intervention. One effort among intellectuals was therefore to consolidate a shared sense of Spanish and Portuguese America as a security community: a group of states sharing common expectations of peace and mutual assistance.[25] To gain cohesion, however, that community required some shared sense of identity, which now had to be more explicitly defined. And enlisted in this project of reimagining Latin America were racial ideas of a quite different order from the indo-mestizaje of thinkers like Gamio. In part, intellectuals sought to challenge the Anglo-Saxon supremacy theory cranked out in service of European imperialism. That project found an ally among Spanish intellectuals, whose concerns for Spain's geostrategic position relative to the global "Anglo" bloc now dovetailed powerfully with Latin American racial-nationalist thought.

A century after Latin American independence, Spain was indeed the crippled core of its former imperium. The 1898 Spanish-American War had deprived Spain of its last major imperial holdings, Cuba and the Philippines; it was now shamefully reduced in comparison to its old rival Anglo Britain and now the Anglo United States. Spanish ambitions to reaffirm some organic link to its former colonies therefore inspired the counter-doctrine of "la Raza": a single Spanish-Latin American race born of Spanish colonial fusion with native American blood. In 1912, Spanish ideologues building on this doctrine managed to launch Dia de la Raza (Day of the Race), an annual holiday commemorating the arrival of Columbus in the Americas and still celebrated throughout Latin America.

Resonating so well with Latin America's nervousness about the U.S. imperialism, la Raza was immediately popular. By the early 1920s, it was of growing importance to anti-imperialist nationalist discourses throughout the continent. Influential elite advocates included Enríque Jose Varona in Cuba, Leopoldo Lugones and José Ingenieros in Argentina, and poet Gabriela Mistral in Chile. But its scope was not confined to elite discourse; it rapidly became a popular holiday down to the village level. As Salvadoran intellectual and humanitarian Albert Masferrer observed somewhat cynically in 1923:

> If one gives attention to our journalistic literature and in belligerent and nationalistic poetry—so prolific in Hispanoamerica—one will find that hardly a day passes without an article, a harangue, an ode, a sonnet, dedicated to celebrating the merits of la raza, the defense of la raza, the future of la raza; which, veiled or openly, always allude to the United States of the North. The governments and towns contribute every year, the 12 of October, with discourses, artillery salvos and glasses of champagne to wish strength, breadth, prominence and splendor to the prestige of la raza, a continental idol.[26]

But what, exactly, was the ideological position of Indians in this new idol? The indigenous peoples were supposedly included in la Raza and were even celebrated in statue and verse. But embedded within the global racial rivalry expressed by la Raza was a logic that rejected any living Indian presence. One author of that logic was Mexican intellectual José Vasconcelos, whose most famous articles, "The Cosmic Race" (1925) and "Indology" (1926), illuminate a vision of the indigenous peoples that would feed directly into Salvadoran racial thought.

The Cosmic Race

Vasconcelos did not invent the "cosmic race" notion, but in the 1920s he became, as Alan Knight has put it, "its most celebrated cultist."[27] His background offers some clues about the political motives behind his racial thought. Born in 1882 of a lower-middle-class Oaxaca family, Vasconcelos had studied law in Mexico City and by the 1920s rose to be the country's leading public statesman on education (he was appointed Secretary of Education from 1921 to 1924). He had detested Porfirio's dictatorship, and his passion for civil liberties embroiled him in the urban revolutionary movement. During periods of particular upheaval, he left the country and studied extensively in Europe and the U.S. His international exposure, his inevitable disillusionment as a liberal Mexican revolutionary, and his experience as a diplomat staving off U.S. intervention during the tumultuous revolutionary and Carranza periods, crystallized his pan-Latin American consciousness and his biting anti-*yanqui* sentiment. His cosmic race doctrine, published as several essays in the mid-1920s, detailed both his assessment of the U.S. threat and his prescription for resisting it.[28]

The core message of "The Cosmic Race" was that the American continent was essentially divided between two races: the northern *sajones* (Saxons) or whites, and the southern *latinos*—the Spanish/French amalgam that had settled the tropical regions (a category that tacitly absorbed the Portuguese).[29] Even as these two races had fought for centuries, so their rivalry persisted in Saxon ambitions to control the hemisphere, and only in this racialized context could the Latin American predicament be understood.[30] (Again, Spain's geostrategic interests are apparent here.) The Saxons had the advantage, partly because they had sustained their racial/cultural identity in league with Europe (white/Saxon England). As a consequence, the Saxon United States now enjoyed a fine political unity over a vast swath of territory, rendering it a hemispheric colossus.[31] By contrast, the creoles had made the fatal error of cutting themselves off from European (Spanish and French) mother culture/s in wrenching their independence from imperial Spain, and consequently had lost track of their glorious common heritage and had broken up politically into degenerated state fragments. (Like Gamio and many others of his time, Vasconcelos viewed the modern Latin American states as the products of caudillos, whose self-interest had disgracefully betrayed the glorious potential for latino unity sought by independence heroes, such as Bolivar.)

Vasconcelos's solution was to reconceive a grand racial unity for mixed-race Latin America as a whole. In bold contradiction to European "pure-race" theory, he argued that the whites had erred badly in so fiercely preserving their racial purity and in disdaining miscegenation with Negros and Indians. Purity ultimately meant inbreeding, and weakening; moreover, pure races were inevitably betrayed by their own hubris, and would be swept aside by history when their moment had passed. Nonracist latinos, on the other hand, had "out of love" interbred freely with Negros and Indians, and so the continent was now a vast homogeneous mixture of all the immigrant European races. Such a synthesis was unique, marvelous, and the foundation for the next great stage of human history: a single united world. "What will come," wrote Vasconcelos, "is the definitive race, the synthesis race or integral race, made of the genius and blood of all the peoples, and moreover, more capable of true brotherhood and of a truly universal vision."[32]

Vasconcelos's cosmic race concept had, however, little or nothing to do with Indians. Although citing the admixture of indigenous and black blood, he saw the true value of la Raza in its European Spanish and French—hence, "Latin"—cultural (racial) roots. In "La Raza Cósmica," his tone about Indians was indeed dismissive: those Indians not already "Spanishized" (españolizados) had "no other door to the future than the door of modern culture, nor any other future than the road already cleared by the latino civilization." His goal was to eliminate Indianness by turning Indians into latino-mestizos through cultural change, rather than truly to obviate and eliminate anti-Indian bias. Indeed, he believed that marginalizing—even eliminating—the indigenous peoples was essential to Latin America's *international* security and standing.

"La Raza Cósmica" therefore sustained and reinforced existing racial biases, arguing that the Indians, Africans, and Chinese were still distinct races and that racial defense against them was still necessary, if problematic to world peace. The need of "civilized races," he wrote, was to prevent the "lower breeds" from "multiplying madly," a brute practice that secured their poverty, which then sent them clamoring to the civilized races for succor. The high road to world peace was to help such races advance in wealth and "culture" to the point where all races could naturally interbreed as equals, creating a world system of mixed races and finally one world race. At one North American conference, Vasconcelos diplomatically lauded this future (based on biological, cultural, and "spiritual" fusion) as the ultimate road to harmonious global relations:

> If we do not wish to be overwhelmed by the wave of the Negro, of the Indian, or of the Asiatic, we shall have to see that the Negro, the Indian, and the Asiatic are raised to the higher standards of life, where reproduction becomes regulated and quality predominates over numbers. Instead of the competitive manner of life advocated by the defenders of the pure-race civilization and by the imperialists and conquerors, we shall have to adopt, then, the cooperative, collaborating manner of interracial organization . . . [33]

But when speaking to Latin American audiences, Vasconcelos assumed a much more combative tone, insisting that the immediate task for Latin America was to consolidate a Latin racial consciousness to oppose the Saxons or whites of the North. Any premature adoption of internationalism, he argued, would only secure Latin America's ultimate subordination. His geostrategic vision of world racial politics is clear:

> So as not to have to renounce the patria at some time it is necessary that we live in conformity with the highest interest of *the race*, even when this is still not the highest interest of Humanity. It is clear that the heart on its own conforms to a perfect internationalism, but, in the actual circumstances of the world, internationalism would only further the triumph of the most powerful nations; it would serve exclusively English ends. . . . It would be, then, infantile for weak

peoples like ourselves to reject all that is ours in the name of propositions that will not crystallize in reality.[34]

Hence, in this vision, Latin America's geostrategic interests rested on imagining and celebrating a *Latin* American identity, because the region's principal racial conflict was not internal—whites or creoles against Indians—but external: latinos against Saxons. The mestizo to be celebrated was therefore Latin—a model that subsumed indigenous peoples only on conditions of their effective disappearance. Indeed, in the global racial confrontation it imagined, any distinctly Indian populations were merely atavistic outliers of the "great synthetic race." Indo-mestizaje (such as promoted by Manuel Gamio) had also assumed that indigenous peoples could not be allowed to sabotage Latin America's solidarity and growth, whether by retarding Latin America's national economies or by stubbornly sustaining indigenous patrias. But latino-mestizaje proposed more: that the very presence of Indians had to be defined as insubstantial, irrelevant to the region's character and future.

Thus in the writings of these two prominent theorists, Gamio and Vasconcelos, we see examples of two versions of mestizaje, both deploying ideas of racial mixing yet grounded in antithetical precepts. Gamio's indo-mestizaje called for (at least rhetorical) celebration of Indian blood as a dignified element of the national racial stock, and set the terms for celebrating or at least accepting indigenous communities as politically innocuous ethnic groups. Vasconcelos's latino-mestizaje disparaged and rejected Indians, admitting them into la Raza only on terms of their effective ethnic disappearance through complete assimilation to latino norms. Indo-mestizaje was rooted in biological and anthropological theories of race, rejecting racism in the interest of justice, social welfare, and national unity. Latino-mestizaje was rooted in a global geostrategic competition with the Anglo-Saxons, adopting racist thought while rejecting internal racial division. Both doctrines took their political urgency from an understanding that racial fusion was essential to the integration of Latin American states, and that the unassimilated Indian was a drag on Latin America's racial-cultural competition with the Saxon United States. But one made some ideological room for indigenous peoples as living ethnic communities; the other did not. Both models played out in the mestizaje that took hold in El Salvador.

Indians in the Mestizo Nation

Records of intellectual discussions of Indians and race in early twentieth century El Salvador are scarce. But we can find some clues by again turning to the literary journal, *La Quincena*. As shown in chapter 5, this turn-of-the-century journal offered new romantic imaginings of Atlacatl and of Cuscatlán that became embedded in the nationalist mythohistory. But these romantic visions were juxtaposed with more sober essays on race and race relations that show the diversity of thought at the time. For example, the prominent Salvadoran historian Salvador I. Barberena offered in 1905 a series of scholarly essays about Latin America's races, including descriptions of negros ("hypocritical, spiteful and always disposed to revolt" but tending "to decrease every day more and more") and indios (who despite terrible treatment "conserve their mental faculties in latent state" as they could demonstrate "in exceptional circumstances"). Barberena was clearly no racial nationalist, but other writers did allude graphically to the geopolitics of race, such as Román Peña:

> Since our diplomatic and political appearance, we have lived a life of revolts and seditions; we have left in the road of republicanism many tracks of blood and of barbarity. Our *exodus to modern life* is very painful, and to date, we can say that it is still not ended. The *civilized nations* have believed, in view of our political vicissitudes, that we are incapable of governing ourselves, and *that our race, due to its moral and physical conditions, is good only to serve as slaves to the European and North American race*, superior to our own in its personal and material development. Nothing could be more unjust a judgment. . . . Our mistakes, our bankruptcies, our villainies and stupidities *are the conditions proper to the infancy of peoples*. The development of a people follows the same laws that govern the growth of the individual; as we see that *when one takes one's first steps* one often falls and suffers contusions.[35] [Emphasis added.]

But a self-image as an "infant" race (falling and suffering contusions) suggested at best a mediocre future for El Salvador as an eternally junior partner in world affairs. The new discourse of mestizaje was being developed precisely to undo such dismal visions. But as it took hold in El

Salvador, mestizaje imported the contradictory threads discussed above: acceptance and even celebration of Indian blood—yet also insistence on racial unity in ways that cast Indians (and blacks and Chinese) as unwelcome outliers.

We can see the interplay through the writings of one famous intellectual, Alberto Masferrer. Within El Salvador, Masferrer (1868–1932) was the most prominent social critic of his day: progressive, widely read, and deeply committed to the amelioration of rural poverty and the acute class divisions that created such glaring disjunctions for El Salvador. In his newspaper *Patria*, he argued for a range of social reforms that he famously bracketed as the "vital minimum": those minimal conditions (sufficient housing, food, schooling, medical care, leisure) necessary for anyone (particularly rural peasants, who usually lacked them) to pursue their own potential in life.[36] His ideas for social reforms were later labeled utopian and unrealistic, especially when ineptly adopted by President Araujo (who, partly due to the antipathy of the large landowners to such reforms, was overthrown in the December 1931 coup that brought the Martínez dictatorship to power).

But Masferrer's social commentary ranged far beyond the "vital minimum" concept, touching boldly on almost all dimensions of social thought. He almost never referred specifically to Indians, using terms like "campesinos" in denouncing abysmal rural conditions—language that can be interpreted to signal that ethnic divisions in El Salvador were obsolete and irrelevant by his day. But his writings on la Raza offer a portrait of mestizaje's complicated entry into his own nationalist thought.

In 1923, as cited above, Masferrer found the continent's rapturous rhetoric about la Raza grossly overdrawn and even absurd. The "general, constant and profound preoccupation" of Latin American elites, Masferrer argued, could be boiled down to rude terms: "What should we do so that the United States of the North will not continue putting us in its spacious pockets with such greed and speed? and, if possible, what can we do to suspend such pocketing, and even to get back what has been pocketed?"[37] But he found the la Raza concept both ill-founded and laden with disturbing implications, and he took aim. First, he argued, the Latin American mestizo was still, at most, a race in formation. Any mixed sector that did exist was (as Gamio too had emphasized) far more Indian than white, and so contradicted the largely white imagery that lay at the core of la Raza.

(For this reason Masferrer believed that "Indoamerica" was a more appropriate term for the region than "América Latina.") More ominously, however, the mestizo was not all-inclusive:

> And even supposing that that mestizo nucleus exists, already fixed and perfectly defined, one must ask our writers and sociologists *if that* is the race proposed to be defended and extolled. If so, they should begin by saying so, to see what destiny we reserve for the millions of pure Indians, of negros, of mulatos and of zambos that we have in Mexico, in the Antilles, in Central America, in all of the Caribbean, and in less but still considerable number among the peoples of the South.
>
> But no, they have not thought of such a thing, and when they speak of defending and cultivating the race, they are referring vaguely and immediately to a white or almost white nucleus; something almost Spanish or almost French, which they designate with the adjective *latino*. The fact is as false as the name. That latino nucleus is, in reality and if we refer to the vast Hispanoamerican assembly, a small minority, barely noticeable.[38]

Therefore, he argued, the implications of la Raza doctrine for everyone else were negative, because every non-white would get in the way of its claim, particularly the Indians. His view of the Indians' logical fate in the new la Raza discourse would not be widely shared for another five decades:

> if our vision and our criteria are la raza . . . then we are hindered by the thousands of Mexican and Central American Indians; we are hindered by the broken mixed-Araucano Chilenos and the Indians of diverse denominations in Venezuela and in Colombia, in Ecuador and in Bolivia; we are hindered by all that is not white, or mestizo with mostly white blood, not aboriginal; that is to say, we are hindered by, at least, half the population of the Indolatino continent.
>
> And as they hinder us, to be logical we would try to annihilate them, or at least *continue treating them as we have up to now*, as an inferior race, good only to be exploited . . . left in ignorance and in misery, and given up to Time, with the tacit and hopeful wish that we are getting rid of them.[39]

The answer to this dilemma, he argued, was not to base the continent's identity on specious ideas of a unified race but rather to create a single continent-wide culture, one that could indeed bring all races together within a common set of progressive ideas and spiritual values. Racial fusion might come about eventually, but without such a spiritual quality, he believed, Latin America had almost no reason to exist.

Such was Masferrer's view in 1923. Scarcely four years later, he had made a complete about-face. If the continent had not yet actually achieved racial unity, he wrote in the essay "Now and in You" (1927), la Raza was nevertheless emerging, infused with spiritual and nationalist mission. The "New Man" was the expression of this race: "So that *America* one day be a reality, it is necessary that it begin to live in you, *New Man* who longs to forge the future . . . that this *new race* may rise, clean, strong and vigorous."[40] In his 1927 essay "Battle Cry," he reproduced the cosmic race discourse of Vasconcelos almost intact: "America has complete territorial unity, and a unity in formation of race and of language that gives it a capacity to attempt the work of fusion that no other Continent can realize."[41] Gone entirely from Masferrer's language was any mention of Indians; the only "peoples" in America were now the state-nations themselves, forged through racial fusion into the unity that was the continent's "supreme need":

> In other Continents the mountain ranges separate. In America they unify. The Andes are the granite thread that connects twenty peoples. . . . A hundred million whites, twenty million blacks, seventy million mestizos and two million Asians, that mix their blood and their souls, clothing their spirit in two unique languages that will blend into one, form the elements of the NEW RACE, of the *cosmic race* that will forge America.
>
> . . . And so, while by birth and coming together the sum of Humanity is formed, we are forming of ourselves a consciousness, a *Continental Consciousness*, that is our supreme need: and the *new race* is forming that we must purify and refine, so that it will answer the desires of a *New and Unique Consciousness*.[42]

Masferrer was only one voice in Salvadoran intellectual thought, and hardly typical. Still, his conversion to mestizaje reflects a larger strategic shift in the state's racial-nationalist doctrine, which the sudden switch to mestizo in the birth records also reflected. The indigenous presence was being erased in records, in state doctrine, and in nationalist ideology. Moreover, mestizaje quickly transformed the standing of blacks and Chinese, *lo negro* and *lo chino*, formerly distinct racial groups who were also ultimately erased.

Los Negros: "No way!"

Only one group "doesn't exist" in El Salvador with greater force than do Indians, and that is blacks (africanos or negros). Popular belief holds that blacks have never been present in the country at all. Nor is this idea an idle observation; it serves a deep antipathy. Many Salvadorans are comfortable with the idea of Indian racial admixture, and readily admit some element of Indian blood in their family tree. (Usually, this turns out to be a grand- or great-grandmother—the implications of a male indigenous ancestor seem to be more ominous). But they find the idea of racial intermixture with blacks inadmissible, and any suggestion of it insulting. As one Salvadoran employee in the U.S. embassy (whose personal appearance, incidentally, would have cast her immediately in North America as African American) expostulated to me on being asked if negros had ever lived in El Salvador, "No way!"

This denial is buttressed by several arguments. One long-standing idea, traceable at least to the turn of the century, is that africanos can live only on the hot humid coasts of the Caribbean Basin and Brazilian tropics. They are therefore unable to live in the Central American highlands (where most ladinos live) because the highland climate is too cold for them.[43] In El Salvador (which has a hot humid coast), the explanation most commonly expressed to me in interviews was that, being situated on the Pacific coast, El Salvador was insulated from the black slave trade of the Caribbean and Atlantic coast, and so never obtained a black population during the colonial period. If a very few negros did arrive, they later died or left, leaving no communities (or unwanted genes) behind. Another belief (circulating also among people of professional rank) is that blacks were prohibited by law from entering the country under the Martínez dictatorship (in the 1930s). Another is that the 1950 Constitution actually prohibited blacks from entering the country—or from settling in it, or from gaining citizenship in it, depending on the teller.

There is no evidence to support any of these beliefs. According to colonial documents, African slaves were imported into the Salvadoran region in small but significant numbers during the early colonial period. In the sixteenth century, creole hacendados received permission from the Crown to import slaves in groups of several hundred at a time. In the Sonsonate region among others, these black slaves actually held higher social standing than the tributary Indians, working as house and personal servants on the encomiendas and later as overseers of Indian labor and as collectors of Indian tribute. In some places, they eventually obtained sizable plots of land and cattle. In indigo production (for which they were specifically destined, due to royal restrictions on the employment of Indians), they were given the less strenuous jobs of transportation and supervision.

Nor is there any evidence that these early africano populations ever left. Late in the sixteenth century, the militias assembled to repel English pirates were reportedly composed of "great numbers of Africans."[44] In 1613, a local official opposed further imports because the number of blacks was so large in his region that he feared an uprising.[45] And indeed, in the seventeenth and eighteenth centuries, revolts erupted by communities of "African slaves" numbering two thousand or more.[46] These numbers may seem small but were then equivalent to the population of many Salvadoran department capitals.

By the mid-eighteenth century, observers of festivals in the region could still observe communities singing in "the language of Guinea or of Angola." In 1799, the region was still maintaining "cuerpos de negros y pardos" (corps of blacks and mixed blacks).[47] In the early 1800s, government records still distinguished among "ladinos, indios y mulatos." In 1807, Don Antonio Gutierrez y Ulloa (chief magistrate for the Province of Guatemala) reported "four towns, eighty-two villages [aldeas] and thirty hamlets [reducciones] of Mulatos"—which he clearly distinguished from mestizos.[48] In 1829, one traveler reported his impressions of the Sonsonate district:

> Of the [creoles], there are also very few; they form, in this province [Sonsonate] not one fiftieth part, perhaps, of the population. It is, therefore, very unusual to see any but dark coloured inhabitants. Some of the finest of them, in personal appearance, are a mixture of Africans and Indians; although many of the latter, especially the young people, are interesting and handsome.[49]

Finally, no twentieth-century law or regulation ever prohibited the entry, settlement, or patriation of blacks, under the Martínez dictatorship or any other regime. Certainly the liberal 1950 Constitution, which was the first Salvadoran constitution explicitly to ban any discrimination on the basis of race, included no such clause. The only public government order that openly prohibited immigration on racial grounds was directed against the Chinese (as "Asians" or "yellows"), discussed below.

Rather, the negro made a quiet exit from the national self-portrait by the simple expedient of social amnesia: it was forgotten that blacks had been part of the mestizo spectrum. By the early 1900s, the Civil Registry only made occasional note of mulatos. By 1930, the mulato category had vanished from the census altogether, and only a count of negros was made (totaling an insignificant seventy-two).[50]

One cautionary note is due here. The perceived absence of "blackness" in El Salvador today cannot be labeled "wrong." Races are matters of collective perception, and do not exist outside it. Like "Indian," the discourse of "blackness" changes by region, and throughout Latin America, some admixture of African heritage does not make someone "black." Imposing a Northern model on a Southern society—as the correct view—could therefore rightly be denounced as a kind of racial imperialism. The disappearance of lo negro even from local popular perceptions—people's understanding of their own identity and that of their neighbors—does indicate that blackness has vanished from social experience as Indianness has not. Barón Castro assumed as much in his 1942 tome, commenting blandly that

> The black, which never reached great numbers, could not develop independently of the Indian, nor find lands in which to continue more or less pure. . . . By this chance, they mixed with the Indians, losing all [collective] personality. In those places where their concentrations were of greater importance, their traces remained more noticeable; that is all. For all practical purposes, they lacked influence in the social evolution of the country.

But later Salvadoran mestizaje did not simply assert that blacks were absorbed through racial fusion. Rather it carefully rejects any historical presence of negros, assuring Salvadorans of their collective immunity from unwanted negro blood. Moreover, this "black-free" tenet actually sustains—and obviates any need to address—a still-lively popular anti-black prejudice. Only recently have a few intellectuals begun to draw on Pedro Escalante's critique that a mere eyeball survey of El Salvador's population finds extensive suggestions of African genetic contributions, clearly visible in facial features, hair texture, and build.[51]

Hence, whatever its claim to inclusion, Salvadoran mestizaje is a black-free mestizaje. In its earliest years, mestizaje also targeted a second group deemed a racial outlier of the mestizo nation: the Chinese.

Los Chinos: "Pernicious Foreigners"

Anti-Chinese sentiment first swept through Central America at the end of the nineteenth century, probably fed by the virulent Sinophobia long promoted in the United States. With 200,000 Chinese immigrants in the western U.S. competing for subsistence wages, the federal government passed its first full ban on Chinese immigration in 1882, a restriction not lifted until 1948. In 1902, during its occupation of Cuba, the U.S. also banned Chinese immigration to that country.[52] In the 1910s, anti-Chinese sentiment was picked up enthusiastically by postrevolutionary Mexico. Although its entire Chinese population numbered only some 40,000, by the 1920s Mexico was in the full throes of Sinophobia, complete with wild rumors of satanic rituals, baby-eating, "yellow peril," and attendant pogroms.[53] Panama, Cuba, and Honduras would also be affected.

This racist anxiety rippled into El Salvador in waves. The earliest impact appears to have been in 1897, when El Salvador passed a law defining Chinese as "pernicious foreigners" (*extranjeros perniciosos*) and prohibiting any further settlement.[54] But the law was not effectively enforced, and by the 1920s a tiny yet successful Chinese business sector was established that soon gained an advantage over locally owned shops, feeding local racial irritation. Tensions increased with a sudden scare in 1923: the discovery that an undisclosed number of Chinese immigrants had entered the country illegally, by substituting the photograph of some relative or friend on smuggled travel documents. The low numbers involved in this scam—the entire Chinese population in 1930 appears to have been about 300—bore no relation to the peril perceived.[55] In a classic contradiction, the Chinese were simultaneously accused of separatist and subversive tendencies and an alarming propensity to assimilate—and to interbreed. In 1930, the government passed a law compelling Chinese who had changed their names to Spanish forms to change them back: hence a nationwide list announcing that "Miguel Quan" was to be reinscribed as "Quan Chang Tuin," "Joaquín Alonso Quant" as "Quan Joo Quian," and so forth through 244 names—which, again, totaled most of the entire Chinese population of the country.[56]

Anti-Chinese hysteria reached a peak in both Mexico and El Salvador in 1931, with the press of both countries railing about secret Chinese plots, parasitic disease, the national currency being siphoned off to China, and "yellow peril." In El Salvador, the racial cause was taken up primarily by the newspaper *Diario Latino*, which campaigned for their mass expulsion. This campaign was launched first in the name of protecting small women shopkeepers in the capital, whose businesses were threatened by "the shops of the Mongols, like the projection of the tentacles of an enormous octopus extended mercilessly through all the areas of the capital, crushing with its competition the shops of our poor women."[57] The inflamed legislature accordingly passed an exorbitant business fee of 200 colones a month, applicable only to foreigners, which essentially constituted an expulsion order. Facing ruin, many Chinese made hasty preparations to leave the country.

But some sought another solution. The only way for the overwhelmingly male Chinese businessmen to avoid the impossible fee was to marry a Salvadoran citizen. Alerted to a few scattered cases of such marriages, *Diario Latino* passionately denounced the prospect of "our women working like slaves in the fronts of shops, for Chinese owners comfortably relaxing in backyard hammocks." An even more horrible prospect was the "degeneration" of the race promised by such alliances, through the vulnerability of Salvadoran women, who, as another paper lamented,

are pressured by the able manipulation of the Asians, without recourse other than to marry individuals of the yellow race seriously compromising their health, that of their children and the future of the people [*pueblo*] to which they belong, because by mixing with elements so foreign to their race, to their customs and their traditions, they contribute to their bastardization and degeneration, giving life to individuals of a hybrid nature, manifestly inferior to that of any other race.[58]

Examining Mexican attacks on the Chinese in the same years, Alan Knight observed the "functional interdependence" of Sinophobia and Mexican mestizaje. "Thus, just as that nationalism sought to 'forge the nation' by integrating the Indian, so it also sought to cleanse the nation by expelling the Chinese (since integration, in this case, would mean racial surrender and decline)."[59] This same logic (of cleansing the national race of a racial outlier associated with another geographic region) was spelled out in 1931 by the Salvadoran newspaper *El Espectador*:

> The Departmental Governors, like all the mayors of the Republic, must cooperate effectively with [the anti-Chinese campaign], so that the [expulsion] decree will have its full effect, because it deals with the protection of *nationals* against the silent but tenacious voracity of the Chinese merchants, who are *profoundly harmful to the country*, not only because they take from our land all they can, leaving nothing useful, but also because they constitute *a true danger to the nationality*, one that has been called for some time "the yellow peril," that has wrought such havoc in Mexico, Panamá, Cuba and other countries, that have found themselves obliged to dictate energetic defensive measures like that which today we report and which do such honour to the Government of *ingeniero* don Arturo Araujo, and especially for the Minister of Government, doctor Joaquín Novoa, who has revealed himself, by his energetic and patriotic attitude against the Chinese, *as a true patriot and defender of the ideal redeemers and constructors of the nationalist creed*, that has been, is and will continue to be our creed.[60]

Sinophobia in El Salvador was not pursued without some liberal protest. When the expulsion campaign had been underway for some months, Albert Masferrer was finally moved to point out in his newspaper, *Patria*, that the Chinese businesses were more successful than Salvadoran women's shops because the latter were dirty and badly run. He commented brusquely that the Chinese were being persecuted "for the *crime* of being cleaner, more orderly, better supplied, more sociable and more punctual," and blamed local town governments for failing to instruct Salvadoran women competitors in good business techniques.[61] Masferrer's protest, however, appears to have had little actual impact on state policy.

Rather, the death knell of institutionalized Sinophobia came when it ran afoul of the U.S. government, which by mid-1931 had become concerned that penalties on "foreigners" might damage U.S. investments. On August 8, *Diario Latino* had to backpedal hastily, assuring its North American readers that no such general effect was intended. In November, the Chinese representative to Mexico came to El Salvador to smooth the waters, and the prospect of unfavorable international scrutiny apparently dampened the racist ardor of *Diario Latino*.

But Sinophobia in El Salvador would not precisely vanish—or, better, be openly discredited by antiracist protest like that of Masferrer. Rather, it would diffuse into a broader xenophobia attached to anticommunism. In the wake of the 1932 revolt, a similar failed communist insurrection in Cuba had sent a number of communist activists seeking sanctuary throughout Central America, and in 1932 some were passing through El Salvador on their way to other havens. With the aftermath of El Salvador's own January crisis still hot, in April 1932 the Director General of Police instructed the Government Ministry to confiscate the passports of all foreigners entering the country and hold them for collection, within three days, at the police station. "In this manner we can avert the invasion of pernicious and undesirable elements into our country."[62]

The port authorities obeyed, but again retreat was forced by its inadvertent impact on North Americans. This time the offended party was former U.S. military attaché Hartz, who arrived by plane from the canal zone on route to Washington only to have his passport seized. Hartz promptly sent an irate message to Washington reporting that he had been "submitted to interrogations and other absurd formalities, deprived of his passport, without being given any receipt, although he demanded one." Under the glare of the U.S. embassy, the passport rule had to be abandoned.

But anxieties about foreigners persisted. In November 1932, the Director General of Police issued an order that Russians, Poles, Syrians, Palestinians, and Chinese be denied visas even to pass through the country. Again the order ran into legal trouble, and its duration was short. (Pedro Escalante has speculated that this measure—an entirely internal department directive, never fully implemented—may be the origin of the legend that the Martínez regime once banned blacks from the country.)[63]

With partial success in having expelled the Chinese and facing these international complications, El Salvador's anti-Chinese hysteria eventually faded. A small Chinese population would persist in El Salvador, although town governments were still asked to report on their presence for some years. As time passed, intermarriage (and a low ethnic profile) reduced local tensions to a more moderate level. Similar worries would surround Muslim "Palestinians" who sometimes irritated their Christian competitors by keeping their shops open on Sundays.[64] But eventually, both identities became obsolete, subsumed by "mestizo." The chino category dissolved into a vague somatic reference, conveying vague notions of eye and face shape without attached ethnic significance—beyond the implication that chino is one step farther from the white ideal.

The Indian Non-Problem

The phobic treatment of lo negro and lo chino illuminates the racial hostilities as well as the geopolitics embedded in mestizaje. It also may illuminate the larger climate of racial-nationalist tension that surrounded the 1932 Matanza. The ladinos' genocidal backlash against the indigenous population was certainly based on the locally embedded and historically deep ladino-indio split. But it also erupted in a larger climate of racial-nationalism that included considerable tensions about foreigners and any element that might "degenerate" the national race. When the indigenous rebellion erupted in January 1932, public calls to eradicate Chinese "pollutants," in the name of patriotism, had suffused Salvadoran media and public debate for months. Although Indians were of course not foreign in the same way as were the Chinese, in the uprising's aftermath some people called for the Indians' racial cleansing in the name of the nation's welfare, as we have seen. The racial-nationalist climate may partly explain the genocidal quality of ladino vigilante violence in the Matanza—a climate of ethnic extermination that, until then, had been unknown in El Salvador.

Still, the racial homogeneity urged in mestizaje was contradicted by pluralist alternatives being promoted, especially in Mexico, where a more gradualist strategy urged some accommodation of indigenous presence toward an enlightened assimilation project. In the aftermath of the 1932 crisis, the Martinez regime may therefore have been trying to placate international opinion and affirm adherence to enlightened standards by enthusiastically endorsing the Interamerican Indigenist Institute proposed at the Conference of Interamerican States in 1940. His government even announced the forthcoming foundation of a "Salvadoran Indigenous Institute." But the Salvadoran Indigenous Institute would never be established. Instead, tensions about Indians would soon be resolved through a more elegant method: erasure. In 1955, for example, El Salvador actually hosted a "Seminar on Indigenous Problems of Central America," with delegations from Central America, Panama and Mexico, and chaired by the venerable Manuel Gamio. In the final run-down of delegates' reports, each country offered some estimate of its indigenous populations: the Honduran government offered a good-faith estimate of 100,000; the Panamanian delegation reported 45,400 indigenous people "monolingual" in their native languages; even the Costa Rican delegate dutifully reported his country's 4,000 indígenas. The Salvadoran report, however, stands out as an exercise in denial, consigning the indigenous presence to the pre-Hispanic past:

> El Salvador continued, making mention of the different groups that inhabited regions of the country in the prehispanic époque, such as the Mayas, the Mam, the Pocomam, the Chortí, the Pipiles, etc. . . . Delegate Señor Lardé y Larín noted that in his country there exists practically no indigenous problem, and that the campaign undertaken by the Government of El Salvador is to raise the level of life of the *campesino* population.[65]

At the seminar each country also reported some relevant policy regarding indigenous peoples: Panama had ceded territory to the Kuna; Costa Rica was protecting territory already ceded to indigenous peoples along the Atlantic Coast; Guatemala was providing tariff protections to Mayan textiles. El Salvador, by contrast, "with the opening of roads to all the regions of the country, is improving and homogenizing the *rural population*; which has brought about the improvement in cultivation systems and the protection and marketing of their industries."[66]

In 1956, Barón Castro reported to a conference in Madrid that El Salvador's indigenous population was some 10 percent of the whole, yet that it was "atomized" and that ethnic integration was complete. At the same conference, he also reaffirmed what would become a common cant: "El Salvador is the country that has the highest degree of mestizaje in America." In 1958, El Salvador ratified the International Labor

Organization (ILO) Convention 107 on Indigenous Populations, but with the opening disclaimer, "That insofar as in our country indigenous populations *do not exist*, nor do other Tribal and Semitribal populations that are not integrated into the national collectivity . . ."[67]

The few scholarly studies describing Salvadoran Indian communities made no dent in these claims. In the 1950s, the eminent anthropologist Alejandro Marroquín found strong indigenous ethnic sensibility in his in-depth ethnography of Panchimalco. The "cultural surveys" by Richard Adams, also in the 1950s, found widespread indigenous ethnic presence. Ethnographic surveys of western Nahua practices by Concepción Clara de Guevarra in the 1970s found a wealth of distinct spiritual beliefs and practices. And a perceptive investigation of indigenous politics by Mac Chapin in the late 1980s contradicted everything about Salvadoran mestizaje by finding not only a cohesive indigenous sector but cohesive indigenous political sentiment. But all these authorities remained marginalized: specialist esoterica, not impacting the larger national image of a country that has no Indians.

Thus Salvadoran mestizaje proposed that El Salvador was a mestizo success story, a truly unified nation, a racial exemplar of the continent. This was El Salvador's arid terrain for ethnic politics when, in the 1970s, the transnational movement of indigenous peoples began to blow a new wind into its domestic political climate.

CHAPTER 10

CELEBRATING INDIANS

. . . insofar as in our country indigenous populations do not exist, nor do other Tribal and Semitribal populations that are not integrated into the national collectivity."
—Salvadoran Legislature, Preamble to Ratification of ILO Convention 107 on Indigenous Populations, 1958[1]

The Salvadorian society has recognized the high human value of the indigenous peoples. The indigenous population should receive not only attention but also the opportunity to develop in its own way and in concert with national development. This would establish a framework in which the indigenous human element of Salvadorian society could take up its true role in the quest for a national identity.
—Salvadoran Ministry of Education, December 1993[2]

BY THE 1980S, ACCORDING TO GOVERNMENT DOCTRINE AS WELL AS POPULAR ladino impressions, El Salvador was a country without Indians. In the previous chapter, we saw how this belief emerged from racial ideas born not only of domestic tensions, such as the rivalries over land, but also international racial geopolitics. Having "the highest degree of mestizaje in America" had become a keystone of El Salvador's identity as a Latin American nation-state and was understood to confirm its respectable standing in the "family of nations."

Yet even in the 1980s that same international climate was already changing, as new values surrounding ethnic diversity began to challenge the old racial-nationalist discourses in countries around the world. By the mid-1990s, a whole new body of ideas about race and nation had filtered into El Salvador, generating the odd politics described in chapter 1, to which we can at last return: sudden celebration of the indigenous presence by El Salvador's Education Ministry, in a country where public denial of any indigenous presence was still monolithic. As in past eras, domestic and transnational forces were again intersecting in El Salvador to inspire fresh debates about the Salvadoran national identity. In doing so, they reshaped indigeneity itself, bringing new images, dignity, hopes, and opportunities . . . and new obstacles and humiliations.

Reimagining the Salvadoran National Identity

The crisis facing Salvadoran nationalism in the mid-1990s was the country's painful transition from the bloodiest period in its history. Brewing through the 1970s and cresting in the 1980s, the civil war brought not only terrible military violence (and some 80,000 deaths) but widespread terror and massive dislocations of people wrought by thousands of death-squad assassinations and informer networks. The conflict circulated around long-standing grievances: extreme economic inequality, lack of political representation for most people in the country, and harsh government repression.

But, as in any such conflict, one dimension was a metaconflict about the nature of the conflict itself, which was heavily framed by Cold War politics. According to those controlling government policy, the war struggle was best understood as a dignified community of elites taking drastic action to sustain their own benign rule, in order to defend the country as a free-trade capitalist bastion against communist infiltration. (Not incidentally, this version ensured the massive U.S. military support that so greatly increased the level of violence.) According to others, the country's struggle was one of long-suffering poor workers and peasants who, exhausted from poverty and savage brutality imposed by a self-serving oligarchy, were taking desperate and even guerilla action toward creating a more just and democratic government. (This version attracted support from an impassioned international solidarity movement.)[3]

With the end of the Cold War, however, El Salvador lost its importance to the U.S. government as an anticommunist bastion, while the guerrilla movement's dreams of leftist revolution crumbled in the ideological confusion that surrounded collapse of the Soviet Union (and the defeat of the Sandinistas in the 1990 Nicaragua election). With both sides facing military stalemate and the loss of vital external support, each was brought to sign peace accords in 1992. The goal of the accords was to create a new democratic system in which political competition could be conducted freely and in which long-excluded groups, like urban and rural workers, would gain political voice through open party politics. The first years did see a rapid democratic transition: fairly stable national elections, dramatic reduction of the notorious military, construction of a civil police force, emergence of a free press, and the almost complete cessation of political killings and state terror. But in the mid-1990s, persisting problems not only called urgently for institution building (as for the justice system) but also seemed to require a new sense of identity and direction for El Salvador itself, as a nation.[4]

As the war's metaconflict might have predicted, this ideological conundrum ran deep. Hundreds of thousands of families had been shattered physically, economically, and psychologically by warfare; possibly a million refugees were still outside the country. The guerrilla coalition, the FMLN, was now in the government, but congressional politics displayed the usual bickering and delays in promised rewards. Much of the left's former popular constituency was discouraged by this lack of progress—and by the symbolic blow of watching erstwhile leftist leaders returning to privileged middle-class existences, some to comfortable sinecures in European and U.S. universities. For its part, the right wing was demoralized by the collapse of U.S. support and the dissolution of its power base, the national army. Many professionals in both camps now held more faith in international NGOs and the managerial expertise of foreign businesses than in any domestic authority. A sense of national unity and direction, as well as the political legitimacy of the government, was gravely lacking. Yet both were essential for the consolidation of a functional party system, popular cooperation with the new rule of law, and an accountable legislature.

Moreover, the deeply damaged national economy faced a major problem with its international image. To pull the country out of poverty and debt, massive infusions of foreign capital were needed to support a shift away from primary agricultural exports and toward export-oriented industry. But El Salvador was only one, and not the most attractive, among dozens of developing countries competing for investment by Taiwan, Korea, Japan, the United States, and Europe. El Salvador's international image did have one advantage: Salvadoran workers were already seen by outsiders as particularly hardworking, a competitive edge sobering to other Central American countries equally anxious about their neoliberal survival in a globalized economy. But overshadowing this advantage was El Salvador's abysmal international reputation as a war-torn and venal dictatorship now moving toward a still fragile and precarious democracy. A better image of stability and growth was therefore deemed essential to attract investors (both domestic and international).

Yet sprucing up the country's international image itself generated difficulties. To draw investment, the government followed the neoliberal template: privatizing public industries, dropping tariffs, and creating export processing zones that attracted a growing number of maquiladora industries. Dropping tariff barriers, however, opened the country to an avalanche of imports, especially from the United States, that wiped out hundreds of local businesses. Aside from rocketing unemployment and a general mood of anxiety, people experienced this economic assault also in cultural terms. It was not merely that Salvadoran food, clothing, goods, and entertainment were being overrun by superior or cheaper American goods pouring daily into the country. People bought North American products not solely because they were (often but not always) superior but because U.S. culture itself was seen as superior: U.S. clothing, radios, and CDs carried the cachet of a U.S. lifestyle. That bias itself aggravated the uncompetitiveness of domestic industries (some Salvadoran food producers switched to English labeling for this reason). In the embittered postwar mood, however, a "buy Salvadoran" campaign would have had very little popular resonance.

Nor was it irrelevant that the country was simultaneously saturated with American rap, pop, heavy metal, and other music—all of which was understood by its critics (defined very much by generation) under the single term "rock." The older generation frequently complained that "rock" and other northern youth-culture imports were eroding "traditional" social values, leading not merely to youth rebellion but to the gang violence that was transforming many urban neighborhoods into zones of endemic fear. All this crime and alienation appeared to signal a loss of "culture" in the sense of community cohesion and shared values, which shared music had seemed to symbolize. As CONCULTURA official Freddy Leistenschneider put it somewhat sadly, "Where is the marimba, the mariachi of the old days when people could leave their doors unlocked and strangers greeted each other courteously on the street?"[5]

And yet, what resistance could be mounted to this cultural imperialism if no one was sure just what "Salvadoran culture" was? As a number of public and private officials said to me, in the current disillusioned national climate, whence comes the loyalty to choose Salvadoran products over North American products? Who will choose the local pupusa stand over McDonald's or Mister Donut, when the latter are gleaming and air-conditioned, and convey to the customer the coveted comforts of first-world middle-class ease and privilege?[6] Aside from a stream of public debate among intellectuals and in the press, CONCULTURA's own mission statement summed up the problem:

> In particular, perhaps the most urgent necessity is the search for our identity as Salvadorans, since that search is made in the context of the globalization phenomenon that presents us with alternative cultures, diverse in their quality, their good features [*bondades*] and disadvantages. The basic test, in our understanding, of any cultural system is its capacity to assimilate the best features of other cultures and peoples, without losing sight of its own ways and roots.[7]

But was the effort to reimagine El Salvador's national identity drawn purely from domestic ideas and voices?

International Pressures

The sudden concern and effort to reimagine the Salvadoran national identity reflected a conjunction of pressures. Certainly domestic intellectuals were debating the question, for all the reasons noted above. But actual government action to launch pragmatic projects toward building a new national culture would probably have languished without the clout of external actors, who contributed both specific formulas and the lure of hard funding incentives.

Especially important among these voices was UNESCO, through its "Culture of Peace Programme" (COPP). The United Nation's role as facilitator of a stable peace had been confirmed by the Peace Accords; UNESCO's consultative role—however graciously it was posed—was therefore not precisely optional for the government.[8] COPP was UNESCO's set of comprehensive reforms, designed in consultation with the government, to foster political reunification, reconciliation, and democratization. Of course, the peace accords had included provisions for free elections and the like. But UNESCO's precept in composing the COPP was that "the construction of peace" required more than institutional reforms like elections and an independent judiciary. Rather, a true and lasting peace " . . . requires the mobilization of the *values* of peace" in the population as a whole, operationalized "through a number of interrelated projects in the areas of education, science and technology, culture and communication."[9] Certainly such perceptions were shared by many caring Salvadorans who became involved with COPP, and who endorsed the premise that a constellation of measures—educational, artistic, communal, political—were necessary to reinspire and glue together the war-torn population as a cohesive national community. COPP therefore provided a crucial vector for enabling those efforts, as UNESCO provided key endorsement and a focus for domestic energies.

It was the material incentives, however, that cemented government enthusiasm: COPP was budgeted at a whopping US$32,782,000 in international grants. With such vast funds in the offing—much of it attached to projects that promised lucrative jobs (and patronage possibilities) to an underemployed professional class and an insecure civil service—not only government cooperation but a scramble for participation was guaranteed. Indeed, CONCULTURA itself was created largely to administer those funds; its new building and sizeable professional staff would absorb much of them.

COPP embraced seventy "priority action areas" grouped into four general issue areas. The first area was "democratic citizenship," which included support for "human development" as well as environmental protection and "scientific and technological development." The third area focused on education; the fourth on information and communication networking. The second issue area, however, was more explicitly discursive: "Recovery and Development of the National Identity in a Culture of Peace." Budgeted at US$10,473,000, the largest of the four areas, this part of COPP was openly intended to construct a new discourse of Salvadoran national identity. Here "identity" was understood as consisting mostly of "shared values" but also "culture" more broadly defined to include even the nation's collective mythohistory:

> This Area unites a series of actions orientated towards the recovery of *shared values*, the creation and the promotion of attitudes and consensus for tolerance, respect for life and human rights, solidarity and equity in the distribution of benefits, which are the foundation for social renovation in El Salvador.
>
> All of this will go to strengthen the reconstitution of the Salvadorian national identity. Culture, in the sense of cultivating *national and universal values*, will be the uniting element that integrates individual and collective efforts to sustain a culture of peace. *The identity of a nation* consists, to a large extent, of a *common, mythical or historically shared culture.*[10]

This quest to develop a "common, mythical or historically shared culture" included support for nine "cultural" projects, from popular culture to museums to libraries. But the last item in Area Two was unprecedented: Project 2.9, "Support to the Salvadorian Indigenous Communities," budgeted on paper for US$478,000—a huge sum by indigenous standards.[11] It was an unprecedented gesture toward an ethnic sector that, for half a century, the state had said did not exist.

How had the Salvadoran indigenous people suddenly manifested as a separate budget line item in the program of a country that had no Indians? The provision had been ushered in by UNESCO, but how had UNESCO itself obtained this interest? The answer takes us again outside the country. For while El Salvador was struggling through its decades of tortured civil war, international ideas and standards about indigeneity had changed dramatically.

International Norms and the Transnational Indigenous Peoples' Movement

Between the 1950s and the 1990s, while Salvadoran political development was stalled by various authoritarian governments and civil war, the global normative climate about racial and ethnic diversity within nations had experienced an effective reversal. The fuller history and character of that reversal goes far beyond the scope of this book, although its many historical currents make fascinating reading. In the 1960s, civil convulsions in the U.S. and Europe had violently challenged the old "melting pot" theories of ethnic assimilation and racial accord. Decolonization in Africa fed fresh global critiques about the old Eurocentric images and standards of civilization and modernity. Among specialists on development, long-standing theories that modernity would inevitably (and constructively) eradicate ethnic difference—by confining it to harmless "private" matters like dress, food, and festivals—were crumbling before the fact of persistent ethnic cohesion and conflict. Indeed, in all parts of the world racial and ethnic minorities were beginning to demand recognition both of the injustice of their own political exclusion and of their groups' unique cultural value, weaving transnational arguments about cultural diversity into their own local experience and disputes. Consultants in powerful organizations like the World Bank were being forced to reconsider just how profoundly cultural difference might run in human experience and to what extent ethnic diversity deserved (or required) appropriate public policies. It was in this fertile context of new ethnic and racial discourse that, in the 1970s, a new global movement of indigenous peoples began to take shape.

Much has also been written on the rise of indigenous ethnic politics globally, of which, again, a very broad sketch must serve us here. Especially in the Americas but also across the southern Pacific, Asia, and northern Europe, what came to be called "indigenous and tribal" groups began to consult with each other at levels hidden and public about their common predicaments of poverty, exclusion, and cultural denigration by their governments. Hundreds of organizations joined this transnational network, bringing the Guatemalan Maya in touch with the Maori of New Zealand and the Sami of Norway with the Mapuche of Chile. Each group faced unique local conditions and struggled with its own configurations of land claims and cultural demands building from its particular history; great internal debates within the movement reflected these differences. But over two decades, these global consultations began to gel into a coherent platform, emphasizing especially a common identity as peoples with rights under international law.[12]

This transnational movement emerged initially into very hostile political terrain. Of course, state governments and the dominant discourses of national societies typically considered such indigenous and tribal peoples ethnically obsolete in ways deemed important to national unity and progress, as we have seen. This stigma, as outmoded cultural relics, was indeed one common grievance on which the new indigenous movement was built. But many independent scholars, too, had believed indigenous politics to be matters of the past. (Political science literature throughout the 1970s and 1980s, for instance, tended to ignore indigenous issues with impressive confidence.) The origins of this neglect were complicated, but at least in some measure reflected politics during the Cold War. In the 1960s and 1970s, indigenous issues seemed briefly to have been absorbed by leftist class-based movements, as indigenous communities allied with (or were said to have allied with) leftist popular or guerrilla movements. The more explicitly Marxist movements deliberately contributed to this impression, as they tended to claim representative authority over an ethnically undifferentiated "peasantry" or "masses" and to dismiss specifically indigenous-ethnic concerns (like dress, language, and cosmology) as false consciousness or colonial vestiges, mere impediments to class solidarity.[13]

But over the years, many leftist alliances had begun to ring hollow to indigenous communities. For one thing, ethnic matters like dress, language, and religion were central to indigenous concerns. For another, alliances with leftist groups tended to reproduce the old ethnic hierarchies, with indigenous members remaining subordinate to nonindigenous cadres and leadership. And all too frequently, as Cold War tensions coupled with local racism to inspire new and more violent state repression, indigenous civilian communities bore the brunt of state retaliation against leftist guerillas and sometimes suffered terribly. Some reinstatement of ethnic agendas into popular movements, some more effective coupling of cultural, class, and ethnonationalist agendas, was needed.

Especially in the late 1970s and 1980s, therefore, indigenous peoples began to seek what one group in Bolivia called "our own idea." Again, internal differences required a flexible platform. But one consistent element soon became a shared understanding that indigenous politics were distinguished from other ethnic politics by the shared experience of extinguished sovereignty. Hence the transnational movement emphasized the term "peoples," which under international law granted groups the right to self-determination—a right formerly associated especially with decolonization and independent statehood but, in the indigenous movement, more commonly understood as varying degrees of political autonomy. Thus, by the 1980s, a new transnational discourse of indigeneity had emerged that framed the political platforms of what were now called, in United Nations parlance, "indigenous and tribal peoples."[14]

In its international lobbying, this new transnational discourse of indigeneity deployed a package of core grievances: extinguished sovereignty through conquest or forced absorption; denigration of their cultures and banning of their dress and languages; economic marginalization and land loss; political exclusion; and, especially, the discourses within dominant sectors of their national societies about their backwardness, savagery, and cultural obsolescence, which strategically veiled all those discriminatory practices. Yet in seeking allies and publicity, the transnational movement also strategically coupled those grievances to campaigns regarding environmental protection, human rights, and democracy, a basket that attracted a wider range of supporters. Anthropologists and other academics, human rights activists, development specialists, environmental organizations, and eventually sympathetic states (particularly the Scandinavian countries) became interested in the indigenous movement and provided technical support, political advice, plane tickets, and publicity. UNESCO itself was extensively involved in quiet yet significant support activities (the *Mundo Maya* tourist initiative discussed in chapter 2, initiated by UNESCO in 1986, was launched partly as a way to create new political space for Mayan communities in national policy). As early as 1971, the World Council of Churches had sponsored a major conference on indigenous issues in Barbados; in 1986, the Catholic Church launched its "Pastoral Indígena" program in Brazil that soon rippled throughout Latin America and into El Salvador. In 1982, the indigenous movement gained a United Nations foothold with the annual meetings of the U.N. Working Group on Indigenous Populations in Geneva, Switzerland (in 2002, these meetings matured into a "Permanent Forum," an annual event drawing hundreds of indigenous activists to New York). All this widening international attention built toward the event that drew major international attention to the indigenous movement for the first time: the 1993 Peace Prize, awarded to Guatemalan Mayan activist Rigoberta Menchú.

In 1990, the transnational indigenous movement gained an especially important bonus when the International Labor Organization (ILO) revised its Convention 107 on the Rights of Indigenous Populations. The new Convention 169 did not go as far as most indigenous observers had wanted (although recognizing them as "peoples," the text explicitly detached the term from any right to self-determination). Still, it codified common indigenous grievances and demands in unprecedented detail, and granted to indigenous rights the imprimatur of the ILO's professional and moral authority. Convention 169 therefore became a rallying point for indigenous peoples globally, as they used its ratification debates to publicize and defend their demands. Even if their governments refused to ratify it, the convention had invaluable spin-off effects for the movement. For example, in calling for consultation by indigenous peoples on development projects affecting their territories, Convention 169 inspired the World Bank, the International Development Bank, and a plethora of international NGOs working on development or the environment to revise their policies to mandate indigenous representation in their planning meetings.

In short, by the mid-1990s, state governments confronted with newly insistent indigenous movements had to sort out their responses in a very different international climate. Once-isolated indigenous peoples now had the help and endorsement of powerful new international allies on matters concrete and normative; for example, states could hardly reject indigenous demands to participate in development planning as absurd or excessive when such consultation was actually mandated by the World Bank. Even more broadly, Convention 169 signaled that the old international standards for a strong and respectable nation—racial homogeneity, ethnic unity—had shifted to ethnic pluralism and the celebration of difference. According to this new "standard of civilization," state governments trying to maintain a respectable image in international affairs (for whatever reason) were now obligated to show respect (however rhetorical) for ethnic diversity, including indigenous peoples and their needs. With indigenous peoples now representing themselves directly on the international stage, a state government's denial that such populations persisted meaningfully in the country, in the name of racial-national unity, was now—ironically—"backward."

In consequence, El Salvador's postwar effort to project a better international image required the state to give at least token recognition of the country's indigenous peoples. UNESCO's Project 2.9, "Support to the Salvadorian Indigenous Communities," reflected UNESCO's endorsement of this standard. Hence Project 2.9 was accepted by a state government that had otherwise evinced no interest whatsoever in indigenous issues or even any recognition that they existed at all. Of course, it also helped that Project 2.9 was loaded with a half-million dollars in aid; the state stood to spend most of that money on administrative support, personnel, training, and equipment—in other words, its own expenses.

And so CONCULTURA embraced CCNIS (Consejo Coordinador Nacional Indígena Salvadoreño), the coalition of indigenous organizations listed in chapter 1. At its first news conference on June 15, 1994, CCNIS leveraged this recognition by presenting itself as a coalition of Salvadoran indigenous groups formed to lobby for the government's ratification of ILO Convention 169. Spokesman Julio Alfaro (CCNIS's Secretary of National and International Relations) explained that CCNIS was established to "defend the rights of indigenous people and reclaim their own identity regarding culture and language so that they should not be confused with campesinos." A new if fragile and nascent era of cultural pluralism seemed to be forming.

But what did CCNIS, and its recognition by the government, actually signify? Re-emergence in Salvadoran public life of the long-suppressed indigenous people and new state recognition of the country's ethnic pluralism? Or only a few opportunists seeking attention and conspiring with the government to attract international funds? More was afoot than either ethnic revival or opportunism. In fact, not only state interest but CCNIS itself was a product of new transnational standards of being indigenous.

Being Indian for UNESCO

Despite the state's skimming of the budget (through CONCULTURA), the benefits of UNESCO's Project 2.9 for the indigenous peoples should have been formidable. Indigenous organizations could submit proposals to the project for specific activities and could have obtained vital funds for important projects. But Project 2.9 actually had serious limitations in the Salvadoran setting. The transnational norms that guided it, like ILO Convention 169, had been composed through consultations among some of the world's most prominent indigenous groups, like the Guatemalan Maya, the Maori of New Zealand, the Navajo of the U.S., and others who held or occupied some distinct territory and whose populations were distinguished by cultural differences mutually recognized by their dominant societies. The international standards developed in ILO Convention 169 (among other formulas) therefore reflected the needs and grievances of these peoples, such as the right to use their own languages, wear their own dress, practice their own religions, and control development in their own territories. These standards had, in effect, generated a new hegemonic model for indigeneity that worked well for peoples like the Maya. But the model did not work well for the Nahua, whose particular needs did not match up.

The specific provisions of Project 2.9 reflected this problem. UNESCO's own understanding of indigenous peoples' rights and needs reflected its long collaboration with the international indigenous movement; it saw the principal problems facing the Salvadoran peoples as "cultural." But UNESCO's concept of "culture" reflected the Maya model in focusing on matters like language, religion, arts, and artisan crafts. With the state silent and indigenous voices weak, this prefigured model was inserted into COPP with little local adjustment. Accordingly, the intended results outlined in Project 2.9 were (1) a bilingual (Nahuat-Spanish and Ulua-Spanish) education program, (2) an indigenous radio broadcast, (3) support for artisan crafts (including improving access to bank loans and marketing), (4) development of local libraries, (5) diffusion of "cultural matters" through various media, and (6) support for folklore festivals.[15]

Glaring for its absence from this list was any support for the economic needs so central to Nahua concerns, yet outside UNESCO's mandate and understanding of indigeneity: for example, corn cultivation. Corn is ethnically vital to the Salvadoran Nahuat and Lenca (as for many other indigenous peoples in the Americas) and not only because it is the mainstay of their diet and a core subsistence crop. Corn also pervades Nahua cosmology, ritual, and worldview; its cultivation also reinforces kin and communal ties.[16] Obtaining credit to plant corn, and land to plant it on, is therefore central to Nahua collective ethnic concerns.

Yet this vital social function was not recognized as "cultural" by UNESCO officials. Related indigenous concerns (micro-credit, fertilizer, market access) indeed cast their interests, as one UNESCO representative put it, as those of "mere farmers."[17] It became crucial to the indigenous organizations that a public appearance as mere farmers threatened to undermine the legitimacy of their claim to *be* indigenous peoples—and their qualification for funding. One Nahua activist became terminally frustrated by the situation:

There are those who say we should focus solely on rescuing our culture, and not on production. But I say, let those who say that first give up their comfortable homes with their television sets and stereos. Let them first give up their comfortable jobs as teachers in the town and come live in the countryside, and live and work as we do. Because there is no work. Then they will know that we must focus on production, on the close bond between us and the corn. That is the basis of our lives, us and the corn. We need credit, we need support, because when we get our piece of land, we have to be able to plant it, to begin. This capacity is what we need to strengthen ourselves, in the context of all that we are doing to strength our identity; our capacity to produce, our relation with the corn.[18]

But requests for help with corn cultivation and farming had to be abandoned, and no land-related program took its place. In the end, roughly a third of the projects proposed to Project 2.9 by Salvadoran indigenous activists concerned language revival. The remaining two-thirds concerned an array of "cultural promotion" activities: training in artisan crafts, the opening of "culture centers," festivals and ceremonies, such that the final provisions were:

1. training in the artisan production of traditional clothing;
2. establishment of ten centers serving 32 communities to train people in ceramic, wood and painting crafts;
3. a diagnostic study of "the needs and viability" of Lenca and Nahuat language revival;
4. training courses in the oral transmission of cited languages;
5. a hundred "educating actions" to promote native languages;
6. two regional artistic festivals;
7. a national artisan fair of indigenous crafts;
8. establishment of three nurseries for medicinal plants and a conference on traditional medicines.[19]

The last of these provisions bears special mention. Over the past two decades, the transnational indigenous movement has promoted a claim that indigenous people have unique expertise about their local environments. The claim is often true. But it has also been strategic, in deliberately facilitating vital alliances between indigenous peoples (as "guardians of the forest") with powerful international environmental organizations such as the World Wildlife Fund. In El Salvador, this "greening" of the transnational movement fed directly into indigenous rhetoric regarding the special connection of the Nahua and Lenca peoples with nature or "Mother Earth." And it brought the CCNIS activists some plane tickets to Central American conferences on forestry, hosted by NGOs who had already absorbed the standards of ILO Convention 169.

But the very considerable expertise of the Salvadoran peoples regarding nature actually lies in their subsistence farming ability (hence their urgent interest in fertilizer). They also have considerable knowledge of medicinal plants but no established practice of nurseries. (International interest and funding for nurseries have been greatly fed by pharmaceutical industries, which hope to patent and sell the medicines.) Nor could any Salvadoran activist in the mid-1990s articulate an environmentalist agenda in the internationally popular sense of managing rainforests or averting soil degradation. Even Point 8 of Project 2.9, therefore, did not reflect immediate local needs or interests familiar to the activists' Nahua constituencies.

In any case, the elaborate grant proposal would not work. Originally submitted to Denmark (a country known for its sympathies to Latin American indigenous peoples), the project was rejected. By summer 1996, UNESCO still held hope for Swedish funding, but even that source was ambivalent, agreeing to review the project but mentioning their doubts that any Indians still lived in El Salvador. Two years after all the labor and negotiations, the project remained unfunded. The Nahua organizations would again be frustrated despite their drastic compromises—or because of them.

For the problem they now faced was the disjunction between their own concerns and the international model of indigeneity that was opening such political doors. The same problem arose even more drastically in a second program launched by the European Union.

Being Indian for the European Union

COPP was indeed not the most important initiative to weigh in on the question of indigenous rights. In 1993, the European Union (EU) had also launched a program to support Central American indigenous peoples that, in practice, would have crippling effects on the Salvadoran indigenous movement. Called the "Program of Support for the Indigenous Peoples of Central America" (Programa de Apoyo para los Pueblos Indígenas de Centroamerica—PAPICA), the EU initiative was intended to "contribute to bettering the situation of, and to defending the rights, values and collective identity of the Indigenous Peoples, garifunas and creoles of Central America." PAPICA was to be funded at €7,500,000, to be divided among projects organized by indigenous coalitions in each of the five Central American countries.[20] Such vast sums dramatically skewed indigenous activism and reconfigured the indigenous movements throughout the region—to their detriment.

Reflecting ideals developed among the transnational movement, PAPICA was launched in a conference in San Jose, Costa Rica, in which the organizers invited indigenous representatives from the five Central American countries to consult on its program of action. (From El Salvador, Adrian Esquino Lizco and an associate of ANIS and two MAIS representatives attended.) The initial document grouped indigenous needs within three general fields: (1) enhancing collective and individual indigenous identity to counter cultural pressures by the dominant society; (2) improving collective indigenous access to national politics; and (3) improving indigenous control over the environment and natural resources in their respective territories.[21] Indigenous organizations in each country were required to form a national coordinating body or *mesa nacional* in order to qualify for funding in these categories.

As a consequence of this requirement, indigenous organizations in each country promptly formed mesas nacionales. The mesas were also to coordinate regionally, through a Central American Coordinating body (CICA), composed of representatives from each national mesa. An elaborate administrative structure was designed to maximize accountability in every direction, providing for EU monitoring while ensuring autonomous indigenous representation at every level. For example, each mesa would be advised by salaried "experts," one foreign and one indigenous from each country. (The PAPICA bureaucracy itself was therefore a kind of cash cow, in providing what were, by local standards, astronomical salaries to these local "experts.")

In El Salvador, the mesa nacional was CCNIS—the coalition supposedly formed spontaneously in 1994 to promote ILO Convention 169.

CCNIS was therefore less an autonomous domestic initiative than a direct, even mandated, product of an external funder.

And yet, within the velvet glove of PAPICA's high-minded goals was an iron-fist condition. Any indigenous organization in Central America was eligible to submit projects for funding by PAPICA but only on condition that it join the mesa nacional in its respective state, which would coordinate groups' project proposals and submit them together to PAPICA. PAPICA's intention in this requirement was partly to avert duplication of projects and to partly promote (by requiring) cooperation and information sharing among indigenous groups in each country. But more explicitly political was PAPICA's broader intent: to craft unified indigenous movements in each country. This concern was born of a superficially sensible observation: that factionalism everywhere plagues indigenous politics to its detriment and that a unified indigenous movement would carry far more political weight at the national level. With this goal in mind, PAPICA was especially determined that its funds not be channeled to one organization or faction and thereby aggravate, rather than enhance, factional rivalries.

But ruin lurked in two dimensions of the PAPICA process. The regular (mandatory) consultations among the mesas nacionales and CICA were ostensibly egalitarian, democratic, and ethnically pluralistic, an opportunity for sharing and mutual learning. But given the PAPICA directorate's control over the €628,000 payoff, "learning" in such a setting reduced to learning how to match PAPICA's expectations. And like UNESCO, PAPICA's model of indigeneity reflected Convention 169 and its emphasis on language, dress, religious, and other cultural rights. The Nahua and Lenca organizations were, again, poorly positioned to design or propose such projects, nor were those issues the most crucial to their internal needs.[22] As a result, the projects that CCNIS submitted to the PAPICA director were repeatedly rejected as badly designed and/or unpracticable. Their proposals for language revival programs lacked teachers. Their proposals for weaving programs lacked artisans. Their proposals for radio programs were beyond the capacities of all except RAIS—the ladino organization. Mechanisms for monitoring, quality control, and marketing were all missing.

In March 1996, a PAPICA delegation from Panama came to San Salvador to consult with the movement, and made clear its dissatisfaction with the Salvadoran proposals: especially, their lack of accountability, unqualified personnel, and the exclusion of other organizations like ANIS. The meeting left the delegates frustrated and bitter. The weekly meetings themselves had already become a discouraging burden on the activists as the PAPICA process dragged on without reward. After repeated failures, some Salvadoran activists found their position as supplicants offensive in principle and humiliating in practice: as some put it, just a new form of European imperialism. The situation was only more frustrating as the activists picked up quiet hints of similar judgments from Maya and other indigenous representatives in CICA. In sum, the activists found themselves confronting terms for being Indian that they were not well positioned— and were only partly motivated—to meet. By summer 1997, only the last shreds of hope for eventual funding were keeping the CCNIS group in the PAPICA process.

Even worse, PAPICA's bureaucracy, with its high-paid external and local "consultants," established privileges that were bound to cause trouble. At an early stage, the EU sent an "expert" to conduct (anonymously) a diagnostic study of the indigenous peoples' organizations in each country in order to assess the best way to assist their programs.[23] The report on El Salvador was terse but probing. The expert recognized that ANIS was still by far the largest indigenous organization in the country, but his assessment of its leader and role was acerbic:

ANIS has an unusual structure: contrary to the [practice of] the great majority of indigenous organizations, fundamental to the group is the figure of its High Chief [*Cacique Máximo*] and Spiritual Guide, A.E.L. [Adrian Esquino Lizco]; once below this summit, internal elections determine the various responsibilities and ranks, always within an inegalitarianism according to which all the associates consider themselves "brothers." Under the aegis of its *Cacique*, this organization tries to recoup the distinct culture and features of lo indio through a pan-Indianism assembled syncretically from the pictorial iconography of the North American Indians to the musical instruments of the tropical rainforest—that disappeared centuries ago in El Salvador. In its search for allies among the powerful Support Groups, it uses all mobilizing themes imaginable: communion of the Indian with Mother Earth, profound yet diffused religiosity, communitarianism, return to tradition and revalorization of pre-Columbian axiology. All this comprises a syncretic model close in its most elemental expressions to Indianist esotericism.[24]

The anonymous EU author accordingly judged that MAIS, which had split from ANIS in 1985 and was running some effective cooperatives, was the best qualified to take the role of "principal counterpart" (or paid "expert") on the PAPICA project. ANIS was to be included only on condition that it abandon its "pan-Indianist syncretism" and respect the "cultural specificities" of the local communities.[25] Accordingly, the articulate Julio Alfaro of MAIS was selected as the local indígena "expert" for El Salvador, and was promptly appointed CCNIS's "Secretary of National and International Relations" and its principal spokesman to the press. For the first year of its existence, CCNIS met in the office of a centrist labor union with which MAIS had ties. In the second year, when the union's decrepit building was demolished, CCNIS moved to meet in the new CONCULTURA building, under the auspices of the Indigenous Affairs Office.

But the entire scenario led inexorably to trouble. First, although the EU analyst had considered ANIS fundamental to CCNIS (despite its perceived sins), by reinforcing the position of an ANIS defector (MAIS) the EU strengthened the anti-ANIS posture of the new group. CCNIS became composed mostly of organizations that had split off from ANIS, bonding them in unified disaffection. The promise of vast funds now solidified this dislike into a vicious schism: especially, through an unrelentingly bitter campaign by the new chair of CCNIS, president Victor Ramos, a former president of ANIS and a particularly jealous opponent of Esquino Lizco. By 1995 ANIS was entirely excluded from CCNIS group meetings and from the elaborate €628,130 proposal that CCNIS eventually presented to the PAPICA directorate. Moreover, strengthened by his leadership role in CCNIS, Victor Ramos was propelled into greater leverage within the Salvadoran movement; soon he orchestrated a takeover of ANIS land and resources, and was widely seen to be positioning himself to take over its leadership as well.

ANIS cacique Esquino Lizco retaliated by denouncing CCNIS to both domestic and international audiences as an ARENA front group. For international audiences, ARENA was still associated with its civil war connections to army violence, the death squads, and other notorious abuses; hence the charge was the most delegitimizing political accusation that Esquino Lizco could pose. Indeed, ever since the army attack on the Las Hojas cooperative in 1983, Esquino Lizco has replayed all attacks (on ANIS or on himself) for international consumption as launched by ARENA.[26] To international solidarity networks, CCNIS was now recast as an ARENA-driven attempt to destroy ANIS, the "sole legitimate representative of El Salvador's indigenous people." Meeting in the CONCULTURA office made CCNIS more vulnerable to this charge, as the president of CONCULTURA was a former right-wing politician and CONCULTURA itself is, of course, a government agency.

The charge was specious. CCNIS included indigenous organizations well-known to have leftist ties, and MAIS, as noted, was originally associated with a centrist union. Moreover, in the postwar climate, CONCUL-TURA itself was staffed by academics who represented a full political spectrum; many were also centrists or leftists. Nevertheless, the tactic worked. Groups responded from around the world: "The Reconquest of El Salvador," lamented a headline in *Sojourner's Magazine*, and indigenous networks responded with global email campaigns.[27] By 1997 two U.S. Congressional offices were pressuring the U.S. Consulate in El Salvador to protest attacks on ANIS by "ARENA death squads" (actually Victor Ramos and some of his associates).

But international solidarity availed little. By 1997, the growing split within ANIS led the opposing faction to orchestrate the election of a new ANIS president. As "spiritual cacique," Esquino Lizco refused to step down or to vacate the ANIS offices, from which, in 1998, he was eventually expelled by the police and charged with fraud. Exonerated of fraud, he still faced expulsion from the homes his rivals believed he had obtained through graft of ANIS funds. Esquino Lizco's repeated accusations of an ARENA anti-indigenous conspiracy accompanied all these events.

Conclusion: Identity and Power

The travails of the Salvadoran indigenous movement in the mid-1990s cap this study by demonstrating the complex politics of the discourse of indigeneity that shapes and constrains being Indian. Many voices, old and new, have contributed ideas to that discourse, from international agencies brandishing newfangled notions of indigenous rights to the background echoes of forgotten historians. And many *kinds* of ideas—about ethnicity, race, nation building, foreign imperialism, modernity, and Latin America itself—have contributed to it.

All this complexity imbues every foray by indigenous activists into the public sphere. In the shadow of the Maya model, the Nahua and Lenca are seen as not truly Indian: assimilated, "ladinized," enfolded into the national mestizo culture. The Salvadoran national narrative has appropriated Cuscatlán—its indigeneity, even its conquest—for the country's mythic history, denying the Nahua their own political claim to its cultural heritage and its extinguished sovereignty. The pan-Latin American discourse of mestizaje has even linked the state's international identity to the claim that Indians have dissolved and disappeared into the national racial pool. An elaborate myth of indigenous ethnocide after 1932 has been constructed to make sense of that dissolution, and a great silence—in history books, in census statistics—has been deployed to affirm it. The edifice is daunting indeed to an underfunded and mostly illiterate ethnic movement struggling for legitimacy to represent a constituency still hunkered, forgotten and denied, in backwood hamlets.

After all this erasure, it is of dubious benefit that the state has recently rediscovered present-day Indian communities as valuable discursive assets. For tourism, the indigenous communities are living emblems of El Salvador's national ("Mayan") patrimony, valuable for their (relatively modest) tourist crafts. For the country's international image as an investment magnet, the indigenous communities are one emblem of the state's newly refurbished pluralist identity. Institutions like CONCULTURA wave the indigenous banner to signal the state's commitment to human rights and cultural pluralism and to publicize the country's rich national culture. This political utility to the state has indeed opened a small space for indigenous public politics. Yet that space is clearly very small, circumscribed by tokenism, fetishism and— not least—popular ladino cynicism. A century of erasure still frames Salvadoran state indigeneity such that a refurbished celebration of indigenous ethnicity is a mere gloss on the national façade: easily praised but just as easily viewed as contrived, a hollow state ploy to garner foreign grant money. In this climate, the best efforts by indigenous activists are readily dismissed as artificial, cheap emulations of "real" Indians like the Maya.

From all this complexity, however, one thing is clear: Salvadoran indigeneity is hardly operating in a local bubble. Although woven from local experience, being Indian in El Salvador is heavily infused with discourses drawn and adapted from Europe and North America over centuries: evolving standards of civilization; notions of modernity, rationality, and progress; and doctrines about racial unity and ethnic pluralism in the nation—not to mention evolving ideas about nationhood itself. As a result, Salvadoran indigeneity is again subject to changing patterns in the global ethnic environment that now offer unprecedented openings for the indigenous Nahua and Lenca peoples. But yet again, the Nahua and Lenca are disadvantaged. They must now struggle to satisfy the skeptical gaze of transnational indigeneity even as they labor to attract the gaze of the mestizo nation. And whose version of indigeneity will prevail?

NOTES

I use Aldo Lauria-Santiago's coding system for documents from Salvadoran archives. Those obtained from El Salvador's National Archive (Archivo General de la Nación) are denoted "AGN." Documents from the AGN's Gobernación (Government Ministry) collection for Sonsonate Department are designated "SONGOB." Researchers are cautioned that retrieval of the documents cited here may be difficult and time consuming. For further analyses of these historical records, see Aldo Lauria-Santiago, *An Agrarian Republic: Commercial Agriculture and the Politics of Peasant Communities in El Salvador, 1823–1914* (Pittsburgh: University of Pittsburgh Press, 1999); Ana Patricia Alvarenga, *Cultura y ética de la violencia: El Salvador 1880-1932* (San José, Costa Rica: EDUCA, 1996); and Erik Ching, "From Clientelism to Militarism: The State, Politics and Authoritarianism in El Salvador, 1840–1940" (Ph.D. diss., University of California at Santa Barbara, 1997).

Introduction

1. The following narrative is drawn from Alvarado's account, as excerpted in Francis Gall, "Conquista de El Salvador y fundación del primigenio San Salvador, 1524" in *Antropología e Historia de Guatemala* 18, no.1 (1966): 27–29.
2. Cited in Santiago I. Barberena, *Historia de El Salvador*, Tomo I (San Salvador: Ministerio de Educación de Publicaciones 1966 [1914]), 302.

Chapter 1

1. The term "racial formation" is taken from Omi and Winant, who summarize their definition of racial formation as ". . . the process by which social, economic and political forces determine the content and importance of racial categories, and by which they are in turn shaped by racial meanings." Michael Omi and

Howard Winant, *Racial Formation in the United States from the 1960s to the 1980s* (New York and London: Routledge and Kegan Paul, 1986), 61. For fuller discussion of racial theory and citations informing this discussion, see chapter 2.

2. On such approaches regarding indigeneity, see especially Les Field, "Who Are the Indians? Reconceptualizing Indigenous Identity, Resistance and the Role of Social Science in Latin America," *Latin American Research Review* 29, no. 3 (1994) and Edward F. Fischer, "Cultural Logic and Maya Identity: Rethinking Constructivism and Essentialism," *Current Anthropology* 40, no. 4 (August–October 1999).

3. *Burundi: Ethnocide as Discourse and Practice.* Lemarchand was inspired partly by Donald L. Horowitz's *A Democratic South Africa? Constitutional Engineering in a Divided Society* (Berkeley: University of California Press, 1991 [1985]), in which Horowitz described arguments in South Africa about how the "South African" polity should be understood (as a society divided by class, or one nation racially divided, or several nations sharing one state, or a corporate racial democracy). These arguments underlay rival proposals for the design of the post-apartheid government, and how people and groups would be represented in that government. Although he recognized the fervor with which each position was argued, Horowitz treated the metaconflict simply as an impediment to resolution of the "real" conflict, which he understood as resource redistribution and political representation.

4. René Lemarchand, *Burundi: Ethnocide as Discourse and Practice* (New York: Woodrow Wilson Center and Cambridge University Press, 1996), 17.

5. As Anthony Smith has put it, ethnic identities are neither purely invented nor freely imagined, but are periodically reconstructed to meet new political challenges. A large literature on instrumentalist, primordialist, and constructivist theories of ethnicity has explored the interplay of politics with broader social experience and cognition, but its review here would too heavily burden this discussion. See Anthony Smith, "The Nation: Invented, Imagined, Reconstructed?," *Millennium: Journal of International Studies* 20, no. 3 (1991). For my deeper discussion endorsing a heterodox approach, see Virginia Tilley, "The Terms of the Debate: Untangling Language about Ethnicity and Ethnic Movements," *Ethnic and Racial Studies* 29, no. 3 (1997); the analysis in this book demonstrates one application of that approach.

6. See debates on the "Maya" identity developed over the past decade as a new ethnonationalist formula: e.g., Demetrio Cojtí, *Configuración del pensamiento político del Pueblo Maya* [Configuration of the Political Thought of the Mayan People] (Quetzaltenango, Guatemala: Asociación de Escritores Mayances de Guatemala, 1995); Kay Warren, *Indigenous Movements and Their Critics: Pan-Maya Activism in Guatemala* (Princeton, NJ: Princeton University Press, 1998); and Walter Little, "Getting Organized: Political and Economic Dilemmas for Maya Handicrafts Vendors" (paper presented to the XXIV International Congress of Latin American Studies Association, Dallas, Texas, 2003).

7. Michel Foucault, *The Archaeology of Knowledge and the Discourse on Language* (New York: Pantheon Books 1980 [1972]), 132–33.

8. Fernando Mires, *El discurso de la indianidad* (Quito, Ecuador: Ediciones Abya-Yala, 1991), 163: translation mine.

9. James Scott, *Domination and the Arts of Resistance: Hidden Transcripts* (New Haven, CT: Yale University Press, 1990).

10. For a very different analysis of being Indian, see Judith Friedlander, *Being Indian in Hueyapan: A Study of Forced Identity in Contemporary Mexico* (New York: St. Martin's Press, 1975). Friedlander focused critically on the instrumentalist influence of urban intellectuals on hegemonic ideas of Indianness in the countryside. The later shift from instrumentalist to more constructivist approaches was represented by, for example, collected essays in Greg Urban and Joel Sherzer (eds.), *Nation-States and Indians in Latin America* (Austin: University of Texas Press, 1991), especially Thomas Abercrombie's "To Be Indian, to Be Bolivian: 'Ethnic' and 'National' Discourses of Identity"; Jean E. Jackson's "Being and Becoming an Indian in the Vaupés"; and David Maybury-Lewis's "Becoming Indian in Lowland South America."

11. See Richard N. Adams, "The Conquest Tradition of Mesoamerica," *The Americas* 46 (October 1989).

12. See discussion in chapter 11.

13. This literature exceeds citation space here: sample sources are cited in subsequent chapters. Standing out among works informative to this book are Richard Adams's many works on ethnicity and nation building in Central America; Carol Smith's landmark edited volume on Guatemalan ethnohistory and ethnopolitics; Charles R. Hale's work on Miskito politics on the Nicaraguan Atlantic coast; Kay Warren's study of the politics of ethnic representation among the Maya, *Indigenous Movements and Their Critics*; Carol Hendrickson's work on traje and ethnic representation; Greg Grandin's work on race relations in Quetzaltenango, *The Blood of Guatemala: A History of Race and Nation* (Durham, NC: Duke University Press, 2000); and analyses of Mayan weaving and weavers by R. McKenna Brown and Walter Little. Donna Lee Van Cott and Deborah Yashar were early colleagues in developing political science analysis of indigenous politics, as was Alison Brysk on the transnational dimension of indigenous political networks in her *From Tribal Village to Global Village: Indian Rights and International Relations in Latin America* (Stanford, CA: Stanford University Press, 2000). See Les Field, "Who Are the Indians?" and Richard Adams, "Works on Latin American Ethnicity, Emigration, and Indian Resistance and Survival," *Latin American Research Review* 32, no. 2 (1997) for important review articles on this literature.

14. Studies of mestizaje have expanded rapidly in recent years: on indigeneity and nationalism, most influential here are works by Florencia Mallon, "Constructing Mestizaje in Latin America: Authenticity, Marginality, and Gender in the Claiming of Ethnic Identities," *Journal of Latin American Anthropology* 2, no. 1 (1996); Charles R. Hale, "*Mestizaje*, Hybridity, and the Cultural Politics of Difference in Post-Revolutionary Central America," *Journal of Latin American Anthropology* 2, no. 1 (1996) and *Resistance and Contradiction: Miskito Indians and the Nicaraguan State, 1894–1987* (Stanford, CA: Stanford University Press, 1994); and Marisol de la Cadena, *Indigenous Mestizos: The Politics of Race and Culture in Cuzco, Peru, 1919–1991* (Durham and London: Duke University Press, 2000), as well as studies by Les Field and Diane Nelson. On blackness, see especially Michael George Hanchard's *Orpheus and Power:*

the Movimiento Negro of Rio de Janeiro and Sao Paulo, Brazil, 1945–1988 (Princeton, NJ: Princeton University Press, 1994); on Brazil, see Winthrop R. Wright's *Café con Leche: Race, Class and National Image in Venezuela* (Austin: University of Texas Press, 1990); on Venezuela, David Howard's *Coloring the Nation: Race and Ethnicity in the Dominican Republic* (Boulder: Lynne Reinner Publishers, 2001). This latter literature also hovers behind the history, presented in chapter 9, of negrophobia and Sinophobia in El Salvador.

15. This book cannot adequately reflect my intellectual and professional debt to Franke Wilmer, Alison Brysk, Donna Lee Van Cott, Deborah Yashar, and Kara Shaw, political scientists whose works and theory building largely carved out this subfield in the discipline. The deeper tradition in political science, however, is revealing: see, e.g., the ethnically blind analyses of democratization and authoritarianism in edited volumes by Seymour Martin Lipset and Aldo Solari, *Elites in Latin America* (New York: Oxford University Press, 1967); David Collier, *The New Authoritarianism in Latin America* (Princeton, NJ: Princeton University Press, 1979); and Larry Diamond, Juan J. Linz, and Seymour Martin Lipset, *Democracy in Developing Countries: Latin America* (Boulder: Lynne Reinner Publishers, 1989). This ethnic-blind tradition—whose inadequacies emerged as ethnic militancy and strikes erupted in several of the countries treated—is today being further amended by a rising new cadre of scholars: e.g., Robert Andolina and Diane Haughney.

Chapter 2

1. These include ratification of El Salvador's endorsement of the Interamerican Indigenist Institute in 1941 and ratification of the International Labor Organization's Convention on the Rights of Indigenous Populations 107; see respectively Decreto No. 18, *Diario Oficial* 130 (67): 905–8 (24 March 1941) and Decreto Legislativo No. 2709, *Diario Oficial* (2 October 1958).

2. Luis Salazar, curator, Patronato Pro-Patrimonio Cultural, San Salvador, interview with author, October 14, 1995.

3. Alejandro Marroquín, "El problema indígena en El Salvador," *América Indígena* 35 (4) (Oct–Dec 1975); Max Chapin, *La población indígena de El Salvador* (San Salvador: Ministerio de Educación, 1990); and Chapin, "The 500,000 Invisible Indians of El Salvador," *Cultural Survival Quarterly* 13 (3), (1994).

4. See Richard Adams, *Cultural Surveys of Panama, Nicaragua, Guatemala, El Salvador, Honduras* (Pan American Sanitary Bureau, World Health Organization, 1957). Citations from Blaine Ethridge edition, 1976.

5. These include Adams, *Cultural Surveys*; Alejandro Marroquín, *Panchimalco: investigación sociológica* (San Salvador: Ministerio de Educación, 1959) and *San Pedro Nonualco* (San Salvador: Editorial Universitaria, 1962); and Concepción Clara de Guevarra, *Exploración etnográfica: Departamento de Sonsonate* (San Salvador: Ministerio de Educación, 1975a). Ethnographies of the Lenca are grotesquely scarce; see Miguel Amaya Amaya, *Historias de Cacaopera* (San Salvador: Ministerio de Educación, 1985).

6. Chapin's *La población indígena* is highly recommended to readers as a concise and insightful survey.
7. For example, Tom Barry, *El Salvador: a Country Guide* (Albuquerque, NM: Inter-Hemispheric Education Resource Center, 1990).
8. For example, Tina Rosenberg, *Children of Cain: Violence and the Violent in Latin America* (New York: Penguin Press, 1992); Tommie Sue Montgomery, *Revolution in El Salvador: origins and evolution,* 2nd ed. (Boulder, CO: Westview Press, 1995); and Yvon Grenier, *The Emergence of Insurgency in El Salvador: Ideology and Political Will* (Pittsburgh: Pittsburgh University Press, 1999).
9. El IV. Congreso Linguístico/Primer Simposio "Pueblos Indígenas de El Salvador y sus Fronteras," 25–27 September 1996, coordinated by the former director of the Indigenous Affairs Office, anthropologist Gloria Mejia de Gutierrez.
10. Carlos Guzmán-Bockler and Jean-Loup Hebert, *Guatemala: una interpretación histórico-social* (Mexico: Siglo XXI, 1970); cited in Hale, "*Mestizaje,* Hybridity, and the Cultural Politics of Difference," 43.
11. See especially Chapin, *La población indígena* and "The 500,000 Invisible Indians."
12. The only recent attempt at a comprehensive description of this population was by political activist Miguel Angel Amaya Amaya, *Historias de Cacaopera.*
13. See especially Chapin, *La población indígena.*
14. Adams, *Cultural Surveys*; Marroquín, *San Pedro Nonualco*; and Clara de Guevarra, *Exploración etnográfica.*
15. Clara de Guevarra, *Exploración etnográfica.*
16. Some ladino cofradías exist but are exceptional. In Nahuizalco, one such cofradía exists. The Mayan and pan-American indigenous spiritual movement exists in some tension with the cofradías. (In Morazán, the spiritual-political Lenca movement headed by Miguel Amaya Amaya was sharply at odds with the mayordomos in the 1990s.)
17. The term "movement" often suggests more coherence that close examination here supports. On the shifting and elusive character of the Mayan movement, for example, see Santiago Bastos and Manuela Camus, *Entre el mecapal y el cielo: desarrollo del movimiento Maya en Guatemala* (Guatemala: FLACSO, 2003).
18. Adrian Esquino Lizco, interview with author, April 29, 1996. In this interview, Adrian claimed to be sixty, but the Civil Registry of San Ramón indicates that he was fifty-eight, which would have made him sixteen in 1954.
19. Dr. José Antonio Herrera, Supreme Electoral Tribunal, interview with author, May 1997.
20. Confidential interview, Indigenous Affairs Office, March 1996; also, confidential interviews, Nahua individuals in the Nahuizalco cantones, March–April 1996.

Chapter 3

1. See Bartolomé de Las Casas, *In Defense of the Indians: The Defense of the Most Reverend Lord Don Fray Bartolomé de Las Casas, of the Order of Preachers, Late Bishop of Chiapa,* trans. and ed. Stafford Poole (DeKalb, IL: Northern Illinois University Press, 1992), composed around 1550. On ulterior

church motives, see Patricia Seed, "'Are These Not Also Men?': The Indians' Humanity and Capacity for Spanish Civilization," *Journal of Latin American Studies*, 25:3 (1993).

2. Especially important to framing this section are several foundational works: especially, Vine Deloria's classic *Custer Died for Your Sins: An Indian Manifesto* (New York: MacMillan, 1969); Robert Berkhofer's *The White Man's Indian* (New York: Random House, 1979); Fergus M. Bordewich's *Killing the White Man's Indian: Reinventing Native Americans at the End of the Twentieth Century* (New York: Doubleday, 1996); and Philip Deloria's *Playing Indian* (New Haven: Yale University Press, 1998). Other observations on North American imagery here are my own.

3. On the connection of evolving images to white policy, see Berkhofer, *The White Man's Indian*; on the appropriation of Indian imagery by whites, see especially Deloria, *Playing Indian*.

4. See, for example, Richard Drinnon, *Facing West: The Metaphysics of Indian Hating and Empire Building* (New York: Schocken Books, 1990) and Berkhofer, *The White Man's Indian*.

5. On comparable exoticizing in the marketing of Mayan artesania to tourists but also human rights networks, see especially Carol Hendrickson, "Selling Guatemala: Maya Export Products in U.S. Mail-Order Catalogues," in David Howes, ed., *Commodities and Cultural Borders* (New York: Routledge, 1997).

6. Eric Wolf, "The Vicissitudes of the Closed Corporate Community," *American Ethnologist* 13, (1986): 325–29.

7. On such differing perceptions, see especially Les Field, *The Grimace of Macho Raton: Artisans, Identity and Nation in Late-Twentieth Century Nicaragua* (Durham, NC: Duke University Press, 1999).

8. These summary claims are based on my interviews among government bureaucrats in Guatemala and El Salvador as well as with upper-middle-class ladinos in the respective capitals in 1995–96, 1999, and 2003. Rejection of indigenous cultural production as "culture" in the "higher" sense was particularly notable among ladinos working in the *Casas de la Cultura*, the Guatemalan Ministry of Culture, Salvadoran museums, and in the tourist industry.

9. On such difficult negotiations, see especially Bordewich, *Killing the White Man's Indian* and Mires, *El discurso de la indianidad*.

10. A blanket neglect of ethnic or racial politics has long characterized mainstream political science literature, particularly on transitions and democratization: e.g., Samuel Huntington, *Political Order in Changing Societies* (New Haven, CT: Yale University Press, 1968); Julio Cotler, "A Structural-Historical Approach to the Breakdown of Democratic Institutions: Peru," in Juan J. Linz and Alfred Stepan, *The Breakdown of Democratic Regimes: Latin America* (Baltimore, MD: Johns Hopkins University Press, 1978); Guillermo O'Donnell and Phillipe C. Schmitter, *Transitions from Authoritarian Rule: Tentative Conclusions about Uncertain Democracies*, Vol. 4 (Baltimore, MD: The Johns Hopkins University Press, 1986); and Diamond et al., *Democracy in Developing Countries*.

11. See Omi and Winant, *Racial Formation in the United States*; also Hanchard, *Orpheus and Power*, 14.

12. See Omi and Winant, *Racial Formation in the United States*, on how racial formations characteristically obliterate internal ethnic divisions. An obvious exception is the historical North American construction of "white," which has preserved internal ethnic identities: see especially Stephen Steinberg, *The Ethnic Myth: Race, Ethnicity and Class in America* (Boston: Beacon Press, 1989) on this case. But for a rebuttal of arguments that some groups, like the Irish, became "white" only over time, see Eric Arneson, "Whiteness and the Historians' Imagination," *International Labor and Working-Class History*, no. 60 (Fall 2001).

13. See, e.g., Berkhofer, *The White Man's Indian*; also Bordewich, *Killing the White Man's Indian* and Mires, *El discurso de la indianidad*.

14. Howard Winant especially argues for this essentialized nature of race outside biological determinism: "As a consequence of centuries of inscription in the social order, racial dynamics inevitably acquire their own autonomous logic, penetrating the fabric of social life and the cultural system at every level": *Racial Conditions: Politics, Theory, Comparisons* (Minneapolis: University of Minnesota Press, 1994), 353. See also Alan Knight, "Racism, Revolution and *Indigenismo*: Mexico, 1910–1940," in Richard Graham, ed., *The Idea of Race in Latin America*, 93.

15. Omi and Winant, *Racial Formation in the United States*.

16. For a different breakdown of arguments on the same general trajectory, see the "four fallacies" identified by Warren, *Indigenous Movements and Their Critics*, 70–72.

17. Such discriminating nuances also apply to mulattos. In 1971, Carl Degler could list ten common Brazilian terms for African Americans ranging from black to virtually "white": *pretos, cabras, cabo verde, escuros, mulatos escuros, mulatos claros, pardos, srarás, morenos*, and *branco de terra*. Degler, *Neither Black Nor White*, 103.

18. Again, "Pipil" is a term dating from the pre-Columbian era that has long been accorded to the Salvadoran Nahua; for clarification, see discussion in chapter 4.

19. I use the term "blacks" here as a literal translation of *negros*, which is the term commonly used in the Central American context. The term *afro-latino* has not caught on.

20. On constructions and representations of dominant white or Spanish societies, see, for example, Keith Basso, *Portraits of "The Whiteman"* (New York and Cambridge: Cambridge University Press, 1979).

21. With some rare exceptions, e.g., Nash, "Cultural Resistance and Class Consciousness," and Findji, "From Resistance to Social Movement," social-movements literature has also largely ignored indigenous movements, on the assumption that ethnic and racial movements in Latin America are "less consequential than in some other regions of the world": see Susan Eckstein, "Power and Popular Protest in Latin America," in Eckstein, *Power and Popular Protest*, 24. On the political motivations behind social-movement research that affect this trend, see Roberts, "Beyond Romanticism." Efforts to reincorporate the politics of indigenous peoples have, however, generated a growing literature cited throughout this book: early important edited volumes include Carol Smith, *Guatemalan Indians and the State*; Graham, *The Idea of Race in Latin America*; Urban and Sherzer,

Nation-States and Indians; and Van Cott, *Indigenous Peoples and Democracy*. A second body of new literature on African American experience and movements in Brazil, the Caribbean and its rim, is building on an older literature regarding Brazilian race relations: see especially Fernández, *The Negro in Brazilian Society*; Degler, *Neither Black Nor White*; Skidmore, *Black into White*; Hanchard, *Orpheus and Power*; and Winant, "Rethinking Race in Brazil."

22. Concepción Clara de Guevarra, "El añil de los 'indios cheles,'" *América Indígena* 35, no. 4 (October 1975).

23. The 1992 Habitation Census indicates no clear correlation between poverty indicators in towns historically associated with majority indigenous populations. See the *Censo Nacionales V de Población y IV de Vivienda, 1992, El Salvador*. For Sonsonate department, see *Tomo III, Departamento de Sonsonate, Características de la Vivienda, Cuadro 3*.

24. The Nahuas' relation to class is, indeed, very similar to the historical experience of African Americans, North America's subordinate racial category. Some Indians can obtain some wealth, but the poorest social strata are associated with and dominated by Indian ethnicity. As anthropologist Alejandro Marroquín found in his 1962 study of Panchimalco, *San Pedro Nonualco*, "The social classes are crosscut by the social categories already studied, ladinos and indígenas. For example: there are in Panchimalco ladino merchants . . . and indígena merchants; there are indígena farmers and ladino farmers; but in the lower social classes, that is, among the landless campesinos and manual laborers (*peones*), only by rare exception could we find a ladino among them, as almost all of these classes are constituted of indigenous elements."

25. Although I was repeatedly told this by Nahua individuals, I am no longer convinced that this is true, and look back on my own reiteration of it here as unfortunate: see details of language patterns in chapter 4.

26. This conversation took place as part of a gathering called by a local activist organization to recruit members. After speeches by the organizers, I was asked if I had any questions. The organizers wandered away prior to this stage of the discussion. The primary respondent was a man of about thirty, who worked as a day laborer. Five other adults, a man and four women of various ages, actively engaged in the conversation by chorusing in, nodding, or providing suggestions for answers.

27. This argument is reproduced broadly throughout Latin America: for example, see Marisol de la Cadena, *Indigenous Mestizos*, 1–40, on such claims in Peru.

28. See, for example, Adams, "Ethnic Emergence and Expansion in Central America," *Texas Papers on Latin America* No. 88-08 (Austin: University of Texas Press, 1988); "Ethnic Images and Strategies in 1944," *Texas Papers on Latin America* No. 88-06; and "Strategies of Ethnic Survival in Central America," *Texas Papers on Latin America* No. 88-10.

29. Carl Degler, in *Neither Black Nor White*, described the mulatto category in Brazil as an intermediate racial category through which individuals could escape the stigma of negro and become upwardly mobile. His "escape hatch" theory was later criticized by such theorists as Nelson do Valle Silva, who argued that the objective conditions of the mulatto were no better than that of negros. For relevant statistical studies and analysis, see Hanchard, *Orpheus and Power,* 38.

For a useful essay on literature and theory on African Americans in Brazil, see Winant, "Rethinking Race in Brazil." The larger nationalist doctrines relating to "blackness" are also illuminating: see chapter 1, note 14 of this book.

30. Of course, sanguine indigenous impressions on the successful social experience of these ethnic groups are overplayed. Jews face considerable prejudice in Latin America, which has sometimes been violent: among a rich literature, see autobiographical accounts by Victor Perera, *The Cross and the Pear Tree: A Sephardic Journey* (New York: Knopf, 1995) and *Rites. A Guatemalan Boyhood* (San Francisco: Mercury House, 1994). Arabs also sense a certain pressure, and maintain protective ethnic networks. Still, such identities are positioned as subgroups within the dominant society, and their members may occupy positions in the political and economic elite. Ambitions by Jewish, Arab, and other ethnicities to obtain more, not less, access to national governance further distinguish their ethnopolitics from the nationalist bent of indigenous peoples, which combine state-centric platforms with bids for varying degrees of political autonomy.

31. This saying is often credited to Brooklyn Rivera (e.g., see Charles R. Hale, *Resistance and Contradiction: Miskito Indians and the Nicaraguan State, 1894-1987* [Stanford, CA: Stanford University Press, 1994], 214), although Rivera was not necessarily its author. Whatever its origin, it has caught on; I first heard it at the 1990 Congreso Continental de Pueblos Indígenas in Quito, and in recent years I have heard it from Nahua, K'iche', Quichua, Iroquois, Apache, and Cree activists.

32. See, for example, the discussion in Warren, *Indigenous Movements and Their Critics.*

Chapter 4

1. This statistic is from the 1994 Guatemalan census. The proportion most frequently cited to me by academics working in the highlands was 60 percent, although the methodology of the study usually cited for this figure is, at best, shaky: see Leopoldo Tzian, *Mayas y Ladinos en cifras: el caso de Guatemala* (Guatemala: Cholsamaj, 1990). Higher estimates of the countrywide proportion may reflect bias resulting from observers' experience in the densely indigenous highlands. This is not to suggest that the 1994 census was accurate. On endemic difficulties in such surveys, see chapter 8. On changes in Guatemalan ethnic population distribution, see especially Richard Adams, "Etnias y Sociedades (1930-1979)," in Héctor Pérez Brignoli, ed., *De la posguerra a la crisis (1945-1979)*, 2nd ed., Vol. 5 of *Historia general de Centroamérica* (Madrid: Comunidades Europeas and FLACSO, 1994).

2. Some such literature reflects what Les Field calls the "cultural survival" school in "Who Are the Indians?"

3. On the history of the Maya movement, see especially Bastos and Camus, *Entre el mecapal y el cielo.*

4. For the text and an analysis from the Pueblo Maya perspective of the *Acuerdo sobre Identidad y Derechos de los Pueblos Indígenas* [Accord on the Identity and Rights of the Indigenous Peoples], signed in Mexico City on 31 March

1995 and ratified a year later by the Guatemalan legislature, see *Construyendo un Futuro para Nuestro Pasado: derechos del Pueblo Maya y el Proceso de Paz* [Constructing a Future for Our Past: rights of the Maya People and the Peace Process] (Guatemala: Cholsamaj and Rajpopi' ri Mayab' Amaq,' 1995).

5. See Bastos and Camus, *Entre el mecapal y el cielo*, 205–51.

6. An especially useful study of indigenous aristocracies and related politics is Grandin, *The Blood of Guatemala*.

7. For analyses of nationalism emphasizing these dimensions, see especially E. J. Hobsbawm, *Nations and Nationalism since 1780* (Cambridge: Cambridge University Press, 1990) and Benedict Anderson, *Imagined Communities* (London: Verso, 1991).

8. On this strategy, see especially Cojtí, *Configuración del pensamiento político*; Santiago Bastos and Manuela Camus, *Abriendo caminos: las organizaciones mayas desde el Nobel hasta el Acuerdo de derechos indígenas* (Guatemala: FLACSO, 1991); Kay Warren, "Transforming Memories and Histories: The Meanings of Ethnic Resurgence for Mayan Indians," in Alfred Stepan, ed., *Americas: New Interpretive Essays* (New York: Oxford University Press, 1992), and *Indigenous Movements and Their Critics*; Nora C. England, "Linguistics and indigenous American languages: Mayan examples," *Journal of Latin American Anthropology* 1, no. 1 (1995); and Hale, "*Mestizaje*, Hybridity, and the Cultural Politics of Difference." Throughout this book, I use "reconstruction" in the sense offered by Anthony Smith, "The Nation: Invented, Imagined, Reconstructed?"; see also Tilley, "The Terms of the Debate."

9. See especially discussion in Warren, *Indigenous Movements and Their Critics*, 33–51.

10. For a comprehensive discussion of Guatemalan traje, see Carol Hendrickson, *Weaving Identities: Construction of Dress and Self in a Highland Guatemalan Town* (Austin: University of Texas Press, 1995). See also her earlier article, "Images of the Indian in Guatemala: the Role of Indigenous Dress in Indian and Ladino Constructions," in Urban and Sherzer, *Nation-States and Indians*.

11. Beverly Gordon, *Identity in Cloth: Continuity and Survival in Guatemalan Textiles* (Madison: University of Wisconsin Press, 1993), 2–3.

12. Rigoberta Menchú, *I, Rigoberta Menchú: An Indian Woman in Guatemala* (New York: Verso, 1993 [1983], 204–9) offers an illuminating description of the hypocrisy and abuse that underlie Guatemala's "Indian queen" contests.

13. See especially Hendrickson's cogent discussion of human-rights marketing strategies, "Selling Guatemala: Maya Export Products."

14. See especially Little, "Getting Organized," on market strategies and incentives among the Mayan weavers in villages surrounding the Antigua Guatemala market; see also M. Krystal, "Cultural Revitalization and Tourism at the Morería Nima' K'iche'," *Ethnology* 39, no. 3 (2000). Sheldon Annis, *God and Production in a Guatemalan Town* (Austin: University of Texas Press, 1987), 107–35, offers an analysis focused more on sectarian differences.

15. Observations are based on my research regarding international tourism in 2003.

16. See also Diane Nelson's *A Finger in the Wound: Body Politics in Quincentennial Guatemala* (Berkeley: University of California Press, 1999).

17. Government of Guatemala and the Unidad Revolucionara Nacional Guatemalteca, Peace Accord on Indigenous Identity and Rights, III, E (1995), 1.

18. Ibid., I, 2, v.

19. My own observation of Lenca dress was confirmed in interviews by Miguel Amaya Amaya: see also Amaya, *Historias de Cacaopera*.

20. Segundo Montes, *El compadrazgo: una estructura de poder en El Salvador* (San Salvador: Universidad Centroamericana José Simeón Cañas, 1979), 311.

21. Thomas Anderson, *Matanza* (Willimantic, CT: Curbstone Press, 1992 [1971]), 170.

22. The influx of charity clothes from volunteer organizations like St. Vincent de Paul's has swamped poor communities globally, providing cheap clothing but also wiping out local clothing practices, weaving, and production. One observer has called this flood the "uglification" of the world.

23. Of the two seamstresses in this small town (with a population of roughly 6,000) the one located closest to the market claimed to sew roughly 300 refajos annually; the other claimed only some 20. Both figures were quick estimates, and so should be taken with great caution, although both women clearly considered refajos a major and regular source of their income.

24. Les Field, "Who Are the Indians?" offers an important critique of this view.

25. Figures cited in *Identidad*, Proyecto *Aprendamos*, Colección *Conozcamos Guatemala*, no. 1, 13 May 1995 (Guatemala: Prensa Libre, 1995).

26. "Lingüística e Idioma Maya en Guatemala [Mayan linguistics and language in Guatemala]," in Cojtí (1995:61–105).

27. On the rise of Maya linguists, see especially England, "Linguistics and Indigenous American Languages." The language revival actually dates to the 1960s and isolated efforts to create written forms of K'iche' in the service of ethnic mobilization. The most notable effort of the period was the formation of the Academia de la Lengua Maya Ki'che', launched by Adrian Inez Chavez, whose 1969 book *Ki'che Tz'ib': Escritura Ki'che y Otras Temas* [The Book of K'iche': K'iche' writing and other themes] (Quezaltenango, Guatemala: n.p., 1969) remains an important landmark. On how this organization reflected class divisions within urban Quezaltenango indigenous society, see Bruce Foster Hupp, "The Urban Indians of Quezaltenango, Guatemala" (master's thesis, University of Texas at Austin, 1969), 139–70. On the new wave of Mayan literature in the 1990s, see especially Gail Ament, "The Postcolonial Mayan Scribe: Contemporary Indigenous Writers of Guatemala" (unpublished diss., University of Washington, Seattle, 1998).

28. The 1994 census broke with previous practice by transferring authority over "who is an Indian" from the enumerator to the respondent. Many social obstacles still impede the personal choice to declare oneself "indígena" on the census, but the technical fact of self-declaration remains relevant here.

29. Jose Miguel Cañas, interview with author, March 7, 1996. Cañas, now a technician-researcher for CONCULTURA, helped to conduct the survey.

30. Gayo Eugenio Tiberia, School of Engineering of Information Systems, National University of El Salvador, interview with author, May 15, 1996.

31. See Pedro Geoffroy Riva (1969, 1978).

32. Gayo Eugenio Tiberia, interview with author, May 15, 1996.
33. Samuel Aguirre, Nahuizalco, personal communication, April 14, 1996.
34. People disagreed about precisely how the language barrier functioned, as some people reported that nonindigenous campesinos also use "Indian Spanish" speech patterns while others insisted that they never do. The perception of an ethnic association, however, remains.

Chapter 5

1. On these sources, including indigenous ones, see the bibliographical essay in William R. Fowler, *The Cultural Evolution of Ancient Nahua Civilizations: The Pipil-Nicarao of Central America* (Norman: University of Oklahoma Press, 1989), 14–31. The Nahua did keep written archives, the fate of which is unknown. In Tenochtitlán, the soldiers of Cortéz made great piles of the Nahuatl archives and burned them. Respect or care for such sources seems no more likely from Alvarado.
2. I am very grateful to archaeologists William Fowler, Katy Sampek, and Howard Ernst for their valuable explications of these controversies.
3. William Fowler, personal communication.
4. "Aztec" was an early name for the people who eventually settled at Tenochtitlán. At the time of the Conquest, they were known as Colhua, but "Mexica" was the name used at the time of their civilizational flowering and is still used among their descendents today (Jane Hill, "In Neca Gobierno de Puebla: Mexicano Penetrations of the Mexican State," in Urban and Sherzer, *Nation-States and Indians*, 72–94). Modern scholarship is therefore shifting toward calling them Mexicas. I use both terms here, as "Aztec" is more familiar to general readers.
5. See especially William R. Fowler, "Cacao, Indigo, and Coffee: Cash Crops in the History of El Salvador," *Research in Economic Anthropology* 8 (1987), 140–44.
6. The other three were the Mayan cities of Iximche (of the Kaqchikel), Utatlan (of the K'iche'), and Atitlan (of the Tzutujil): see Fowler, *The Cultural Evolution of Ancient Nahua Civilizations*, 224.
7. See Barberena, *Historia de El Salvador*, 165.
8. Ibid. Barberena records this word as *pipiltzin*.
9. Alastair White, *El Salvador* (London: Ernest Benn Limited, 1973), 23.
10. Diego Garcia de Palacio, *Letter to the King of Spain: being a description of the ancient provinces of Guazacapan, Izalco, Cuscatlan, and Chiquimula, in the Audiencia of Guatemala, with an account of the languages, customs, and religion of their aboriginal inhabitants, and a description of the ruins of Copan*, trans. Ephraim G. Squier (Culver City, CA: Labyrinthos, 1985 [1576]), 21.
11. On these and more details, see William Fowler's exhaustive work, *The Cultural Evolution of Ancient Nahua Civilizations*.
12. These details are taken from Garcia de Palacio, *Letter to the King of Spain*.
13. Deloria, *Playing Indian*, 78.
14. At this writing, such usage still appears on some promotional Web sites: for example, "El Salvador en Imagenes" (available at: http://www.4elsalvador.com /Atlacatl.htm).

15. Reprinted in *La Quincena* vol. 1, no. 6:195 from a volume entitled "Indian Poems."
16. See, for example, Kevin Murray's *El Salvador: Peace on Trial* (Oxford: Oxfam UK and Ireland, 1997).
17. Until the 1970s, the currency was indeed dominated by images taken explicitly from European tradition, such as neo-Greek images of the goddess Ceres. Only one bill showed an idealized Indian maiden carrying fruit on her head. In 1978, the national currency did import an image of the newly reconstructed ceremonial site Tazumal onto the 100-colon bill, but this gesture remains an exception.
18. Tourist pamphlet, *Vive*, no date, available from the Salvadoran Tourism Institute.
19. For a chronicle of indigenous activism in this period, see especially Brysk's comprehensive study, *From Tribal Village to Global Village*; see also Donna Lee Van Cott, "Indigenous Peoples and Democracy: Issues for Policy-Makers," and Alison Brysk, "Acting Globally: Indian Rights and International Politics in Latin America," both in Van Cott, ed., *Indigenous Peoples and Democracy*.
20. Fidel Flores, "Tenemos 503 años de resistencia," unpublished leaflet for the Asociación Coordinadora de Comunidades Indígenas de El Salvador (ACCIES), Sonsonate, El Salvador, 1994.
21. For an example of Mayan utilization of ancient religious texts for neo-indigenist reconstruction, see Edgar Cabrera, *La cosmogonía Maya* (San José, Costa Rica: Liga Maya Internacional, 1992).
22. UNESCO program officer, confidential interview, San Salvador, 19 June 1996: see chapter 10.
23. This observation is based on historical photographs.

Chapter 6

1. Antonio Gutierrez y Ulloa, *Estado general de la Provincia de San Salvador:Reyno de Guatemala* (San Salvador: Imprenta Nacional, 1926 [1807]), 10–11.
2. See discussion of this paradigm in Les Field, "Who Are the Indians?," 239–40.
3. The "advance attack" of epidemics may also have reduced the size and fighting capacity of the Nahua army. For one careful review of the demographic impact of disease, see Suzanne Alchon, *A Pest in the Land: New World Epidemics in a Global Perspective* (Albuquerque: University of New Mexico Press, 2003); also Murdo J. MacLeod, *Spanish Central America: A Socioeconomic History, 1520–1720* (Berkeley: University of California Press, 1973), 1–20.
4. See Thomas Abercrombie, "To Be Indian, To Be Bolivian: 'Ethnic' and 'National' Discourses of Identity," in Urban and Sherzer, eds., *Nation-States and Indians*, 95–130.
5. For an analysis of such liaisons in neighboring Guatemala, see Marta Casaus Arzú, *Guatemala: linaje y racismo* (San José, Costa Rica: FLACSO, 1995); for an illuminating study of the Mayan aristocracy in Quetzaltenango, see Grandin, *The Blood of Guatemala*. For a comparative analysis of interethnic socializing and politics among Spanish and indigenous elites in colonial Cuernavaca, see Robert Haskett, *Indigenous Rulers: An Ethnohistory of Town Government in Colonial Cuernavaca* (Albuquerque: University of New Mexico Press, 1991).

6. See M. Crawford Young, *The African Colonial State in Comparative Perspective* (New Haven, CT: Yale University Press, 1997), 1.

7. Given the brisk colonial history of neighboring Maya revolts, we might suspect such uprisings: on such revolts in Guatemala, see J. Daniel Contreras, *Una rebelión indígena en el partido de Totonicapán en 1820: el indio y la independencia* (Guatemala: Ministerio de Cultura y Deportes, 1991), 16; on colonial conditions in the region of El Salvador, see especially David Browning's classic work, *El Salvador: Landscape and Society* (Oxford: Clarendon Press, 1971).

8. Cited in Browning, *El Salvador,* 116–17. The reference to religion is especially interesting at this late date.

9. In Guatemala, for example, careful cultivation of the gene pool through selective marriages preserved (although not perfectly) the "white" bloodlines of the top families: see Casaus Arzú, *Guatemala.*

10. Cited in Browning, *El Salvador,* 123: ". . . I fear the principal cause of the Indian movement to the forests and mountains is so that they might free themselves from the injustice, deceits and robberies that the ladinos harmfully inflict upon them."

11. On the emergence of ladinos as a class deliberately reinforced and deployed by elites to control indigenous labor, see Smith, *Guatemalan Indians and the State,* 84–87 and discussion in Warren, *Indigenous Movements and Their Critics,* 10–11. No such deliberate manipulations have been identified regarding ladinos in El Salvador.

12. On cacao production during the colonial period, see Fowler, "Cacao, Indigo, and Coffee," 144–47. The geographic extent of this irrigation system has still not been charted: Ernst and Sampek, interview with author, March 2, 1996. On ethnic rivalries regarding water in 1932, see chapter 7.

13. Browning, *El Salvador,* 53–54.

14. Rapidly expanding textile industries (in Spanish America as well as Europe) created a booming demand for such quality dyes, and as Atlantic piracy declined, better trans-Atlantic shipping allowed lucrative local production: see MacLeod's detailed explanation for the early slow growth of indigo, *Spanish Central America,* 176–203. For two centuries, with only brief lulls, indigo remained the principal export crop of the region, finally eclipsed only by the invention of synthetic dyes and the advent of coffee production in the latter half of the nineteenth century: see Browning, *El Salvador,* 66–67; also Fowler, "Cacao, Indigo, and Coffee."

15. Browning, *El Salvador,* 73.

16. This pattern contradicted efforts by Spanish authorities and priests, successful elsewhere, to "congregate" the indigenous populations into central towns: see MacLeod, *Spanish Central America,* 176–203; see also Browning, *El Salvador,* 41.

17. Browning, *El Salvador,* 73.

18. On the motives and success of congregación, see again discussion in MacLeod, *Spanish Central America,* 120–23, 343.

19. Cortés y Larraz, cited in Browning, *El Salvador,* 133.

20. Don Isidro Menendez, ed., *Recopilación de las Leyes del Salvador, en Centro-America,* 2nd. ed. (San Salvador: Imprenta Nacional, 1821–1855). Resistance to the law was to be punishable by imprisonment for the first offence, and double the penalty for the second. For the third offence, the house would be burned and the resisters assumed to be "protectors or auxiliaries of bandits."

21. See especially works by Aldo Lauria-Santiago, who has extensively examined the comunidades in the nineteenth century.

22. Survey by Cortés y Larraz: see Santiago Montes Mozo, *Etnohistoria de El Salvador: el guachival centroamericano* (San Salvador: Ministerio de Educación, 1977), 130–34.

23. Santiago Montes Mozo, *Etnohistoria de El Salvador*, 135.

24. Ibid., 130. "Other goods" included the images and standards of the saint around which ceremonies and processions centered. These were often made of silver, exquisitely carved by Spanish artists, and of great value. Their beauty fostered their theft or illegal sale when the international market for such antiquities boomed in the twentieth century.

25. A wealthy Maya elite has been much more visible in Guatemala, particularly in Quezaltenango, where the long heritage of the local K'iche' aristocracy is demonstrated for visitors in lavish cemetery mausoleums as well as chronicles of the city. For accounts of Quezaltenango Quiche class relations, see Hupp, "The Urban Indians of Quezaltenango, Guatemala" and Grandin, *The Blood of Guatemala*. I have not seen any comparable evidence of an Indian elite in colonial El Salvador.

26. See Fowler, *The Cultural Evolution of Ancient Nahua Civilizations*, 192.

27. William H. Durham, *Scarcity and Survival in Central America: Ecological Origins of the Soccer War* (Stanford, CA: Stanford University Press, 1979), 21–22.

28. On the Latin American independence movements, see, inter alia, Benedict Anderson, *Imagined Communities*.

29. Browning, *El Salvador*, 139–221; Smith, *Guatemalan Indians and the State*; Robert G. Williams, *States and Social Evolution: Coffee and the Rise of National Governments in Central America* (Chapel Hill: University of North Carolina Press, 1994), 105–46; David McCreery, "Wage Labor, Free Labor, and Vagrancy Laws: The Transition to Capitalism in Guatemala, 1920–1945," in William Roseberry et al, eds., *Coffee, Society and Power in Latin America* (Baltimore and London: The Johns Hopkins Press, 1995).

30. Cited in Héctor Lindo-Fuentes, *Weak Foundations: The Economy of El Salvador in the Nineteenth Century* (Berkeley: University of California Press, 1990), 72.

31. Representative scholars include Rafael Reyes, *Nociones de historia de el Salvador*, 3rd ed. (San Salvador: Imprenta R. Reyes, 1920), 75–77; Browning, *El Salvador*, 142; White, *El Salvador*, 71–74; Julio Alberto Domínguez Sosa, *Las tribus nonualcas y su caudillo Anastasio Aquino* (Costa Rica: EDUCA, 1984); Segundo Montes, "Los indígenas en El Salvador," *Boletín de Ciencias Económicas y Sociales* (Universidad Centroamericana José Simeon Cañas, 1985); and James Dunkerley, *Power in the Isthmus: A Political History of Modern Central America* (London: Verso Press, 1988), 11–13; the relevant textbook is the *Historia de El Salvador*, Vol. I (San Salvador: Ministerio de Educacion, 1994), 198.

32. A detailed (if somewhat speculative) reconstruction of events by Domínguez Sosa, *Las tribus nonualcas*, relies primarily on historian José Antonio Cevallos's *Recuerdos Salvadoreños*, Tomo I (San Salvador: Ministerio de Educación 1961 [1891]), which used primary sources not all of which are available today. White

draws on Domínguez and his sources, and also cites Coronel Julio César Calderón, *Episodios Nacionales: el indio Anastasio Aquino y el por qué de su rebelión en 1833 en Santiago Nonualco*. (San Salvador: Imp. Moreno, 1957). Observing these cycles of reproduction, historian Erik Ching rightly points out that historiography on Aquino still lacks substantial primary documentation and that our understanding of the Aquino revolt is still fragile. Given its consistency with contemporary and later indigenous mobilizations, however, I consider Domínguez's account largely credible.

33. White, *El Salvador*, 73.

34. Domínguez Sosa, *Las tribus nonualcas*, 234.

35. See also Adams, "The Conquest Tradition of Mesoamerica."

36. Domínguez Sosa, *Las tribus nonualcas*, 22.

37. Reyes, *Nociones de historia de el Salvador*, 76.

38. Jorge Arias Gómez, *El proceso político Centroamericano*, Seminario de Historia Contemporánea de Centro América (San Salvador: Editorial Universitaria, 1964); Domínguez Sosa, *Las tribus nonualcas*; Montes, "Los indígenas en El Salvador."

39. Arias Gómez, *El proceso político Centroamericano*; Domínguez Sosa, *Las tribus nonualcas*, 102.

40. White, *El Salvador*, 71.

41. This completely revised two-volume textbook, made possible by the newly open political climate, is the first truly professional history textbook the country has known. The writing team was drawn internationally from the finest scholars in the field and coordinated by Knut Walter and Héctor Lindo-Fuentes, whose credentials as historians of Salvadoran history are unmatched. I critique the discursive politics of this work, therefore, with a grateful nod to these scholars.

42. Cevallos, *Recuerdos Salvadoreños*, 217; Arias Gómez, *El proceso político Centroamericano*, 42; Domínguez Sosa, *Las tribus nonualcas*, 110–11; White, *El Salvador*, 72; Montes, "Los indígenas en El Salvador," 150.

43. *Historia de El Salvador*, 198.

44. Montes, "Los indígenas en El Salvador," 150. A fascinating comparison study is Jan Rus's "Whose Caste War? Indians, Ladinos, and the Chiapas "Caste War" of 1869," in Murdo J. MacLeod and Robert Wasserstrom, eds., *Spaniards and Indians in Southeastern Mesoamerica: Essays on the History of Ethnic Relations* (Lincoln: University of Nebraska Press, 1983), which describes how an indigenous uprising was recharacterized and demonized by nineteenth-century historians in Chiapas whose versions were then reproduced uncritically in later works.

45. White, *El Salvador*, 71–74.

46. Cited in Domínguez Sosa, *Las tribus nonualcas*, 217.

47. Ibid., 234. Cevallos was writing some half-century later and may have relied partly on oral traditions. His account may well have been imbued with late nineteenth-century constructions of events and of the "Indian." But I disagree with Aldo Lauria-Santiago, "An Agrarian Republic: Production, Politics and the Peasantry in El Salvador, 1840–1920" (Ph.D. diss., University of Chicago, 1992), that Cevallos is therefore less revealing; rather, his biases indicate that elite intellectuals were still interested in demonizing Aquino at that later date, and so his account suggests ongoing ethnic tensions.

48. For example, rebellions in Totonicapán broke out in 1803, 1813, 1820, and almost continuously from 1821 to 1824. These rebellions were not seen as "symptoms of a national infirmity that should be cured from its roots, but as simple 'Indian revolts' that had to be suppressed because they would damage the economy of the country": see Contreras, *Una rebelión indígena*.

49. White, *El Salvador*, 74; see also Smith, *Guatemalan Indians and the State*.

50. White, *El Salvador*, 74.

51. Montes, "Los indígenas en El Salvador," 151, emphasis added.

52. Carol Smith, "Origins of the National Question in Guatemala: A Hypothesis," in Smith, ed., *Guatemalan Indians and the State*; Mallon, "Constructing Mestizaje in Latin America."

53. White, *El Salvador*, 73, emphasis added.

54. The widespread scholarly idea that Indians typically lack any appreciation of the nation, and form loyalties only to individual patrons, persists to the present day. Mallon was an early voice to debunk this notion, in her important comparative study of Peru and Mexico, "Constructing Mestizaje in Latin America."

55. Ana Patricia Alvarenga, *Cultura y ética de la violencia: El Salvador 1880-1932* (San Salvador: EDUCA, 1994), 36.

56. Alvarenga, *Cultura y ética de la violencia*, 36–37.

57. Mrs. Henry Foote, *Recollections of Central America and the West Coast of Africa* (London: T. C. Newby, 1869), 61.

58. Alvarenga, *Cultura y ética de la violencia*, 47–48.

59. Dispatches from the U.S. Consul, cited in Alvarenga, *Cultura y ética de la violencia*, 49–50. I concur with Alvarenga that Rivas himself was probably of Indian ethnicity, not only because of the particularly intense ethnic quality of his Cojutepequeño following and the racist tension expressed by his rivals who sought his removal from power, but because his personal largesse and open house reflects indigenous leadership norms.

60. Alvarenga, *Cultura y ética de la violencia*, 52.

61. Lowell Gudmundson, *Central America, 1821-1887: Liberalism before Liberal Reform* (Tuscaloosa: University of Alabama Press, 1995), 246–48, offers a cogent discussion of attitudes about racial mixture among the elite during this period. For a different perspective, see the analysis by Casaus Arzú of the Guatemalan elite, an influential segment of which deliberately resisted racial mixture through careful marriage strategies.

62. Lauria-Santiago, "An Agrarian Republic," 495.

63. Citation is from Francisco Castañeda, *El General Menéndez y sus victimarios* (San Salvador: Ministerio de Educación, Dirección de Publicaciones, 1966); see Alvarenga, *Cultura y ética de la violencia*, 53.

64. This data was unearthed through exhaustive archival work by historian Lauria-Santiago, published in his "An Agrarian Republic." The pattern of indigenous revolts is entirely omitted from most secondary accounts. Hector Pérez Brignoli, who offered a very insightful analysis of Indian ethnic sentiment in 1932 and pointedly observed the similarities of the 1932 uprising with colonial revolts (unspecified), entirely overlooked the occurrence of indigenous revolts in the nineteenth century: see "Indians, Communists, and Peasants: The 1932

Rebellion in El Salvador," in Roseberry et al, eds., *Coffee, Society and Power in Latin America*. Even Patricia Alvarenga, who has provided the most nuanced analysis of racial-caste relations in the nineteenth century, left the phenomenon of Indian revolts mostly unexplored.

65. I cite Lauria-Santiago's original unpublished dissertation, "An Agrarian Republic," on these revolts because it includes a fuller chronicle of these revolts than does the published version.

66. Alvarenga has also pointed out an ethnic dimension in the punishment of such revolts in her *Cultura y ética de la violencia*. Whipping was a punishment regularly accorded to Indians and capital punishment by whipping was the fate of some Indian revolt leaders. Whipping was so associated with indigeneity that one ladino prisoner from a respected family contemplated suicide rather than submit to the shame of it.

67. Alvarenga, *Cultura y ética de la violencia*, 158.

68. In 1880, the state recognized forty such comunidades (of which only three were ladino). This pattern is recognized in the country's new high school textbook: see the *Historia de El Salvador* II, 16, map.

69. Browning, *El Salvador,* 161–62.

70. Lindo-Fuentes, *Weak Foundations*; Williams, *States and Social Evolution*.

71. Acuerdo Legislativo, *Diario Oficial*, February 26, 1881. I would be grateful to anyone who can help illuminate the logic behind the "weakens family bonds" formula.

72. Passed on March 2, 1882. See Decreto Legislativo of that date, in Alberto Mens, *Recopilación de disposiciones legales vígentes relacionadas con la agricultura* (Santa Tecla: n.p., 1904), cited in Browning, *El Salvador*, 208. Although his research has been considerably expanded and corrected by researchers like Aldo Lauria-Santiago and Lindo-Fuentes, Browning remains a wonderful source on this period.

73. On this process, beginning earlier in the century, see Aldo Lauria-Santiago, "Land, Community, and Revolt in Indian Izalco, 1860–1900," *Hispanic American Historical Review* 79, no. 3 (August 1999).

74. "The Legislative Assembly, considering that despite the many efforts made during previous Administrations to extinguish the comunidades and all kind of communal connection (vinculación), the expected result has not been obtained, as there still exist great portions of communal land not distributed, this causing delay prejudicial to the progress of agriculture. That experience has demonstrated that the extinction of ejidal lands has multiplied hundredfold the value of the [affected] real property and has terminated in a peaceful manner the various questions over land that have affected the tranquility of some property owners, has decreed that: Art. 1 All comunidades be extinguished . . . " *Diario Oficial*, February 27, 1881.

75. For details, see especially Aldo Lauria-Santiago's excellent studies of this complicated history; also Alvarenga, *Cultura y ética de la violencia*.

76. Everett Alan Wilson, "The Crisis of National Integration in El Salvador, 1919–1935" (Ph.D. diss., Stanford University, 1970).

77. Foote, *Recollections of Central America*, 61.

78. Montes, *El compadrazgo*, 261.

79. On this system of repression, see especially Alvarenga, *Cultura y ética de la violencia*, 79–150.
80. Cited in Anderson, *Matanza*, 100.
81. Aldo Lauria-Santiago has pointed out that many disputes broke out also between indigenous communities and so lacked an ethnic component. It is not my intention to obscure such disputes or to imply uniform indigenous solidarity but to focus on how ethnic tensions transformed in a changing juridical environment. Accordingly, I neglect the full range of land conflicts here.
82. Durham, *Scarcity and Survival in Central America*, 21–22, 43.
83. For an analysis of how land shortage contributed to the so-called "Soccer War" of 1967, and of the socioeconomic policies that so greatly aggravated that shortage, see Durham, *Scarcity and Survival in Central America*.
84. Cited in Wilson, "The Crisis of National Integration," 118.
85. Durham, *Scarcity and Survival in Central America*, 44.
86. Marroquín, n.d., cited in Durham, *Scarcity and Survival in Central America*: on debt defaults, see also "Un Documento," *Patria*, April 13, 1929, cited in Wilson, "The Crisis of National Integration," 118.
87. See also "Un Documento," *Patria*, April 13, 1929, cited in Wilson, "The Crisis of National Integration," 118.
88. *La Prensa*, July 2, 1931. On July 7, the same paper observed that communist propagandists "are profiting from the distressful situation of the peasants and illiterate people" in the western departments, to whom they were distributing communist information.
89. Cited in Leon Zamosc, "The Landing That Never Was: Canadian Marines and the Salvadorean Insurrection of 1932," *Canadian Journal of Latin American and Caribbean Studies* 9, no. 21 (1987), 136.
90. Cited in Brignoli, "Indians, Communists, and Peasants," 232.

Chapter 7

1. Anderson, *Matanza*, 2nd ed., 176. Citations of Anderson here are from the second edition published in 1992; his first edition was published in 1971.
2. For sources that omit the indigenous factor, see Shawn L. Bird and Philip J. Williams, "El Salvador: Revolt and Negotiated Transition," in Thomas Walker and Ariel Armony, eds., *Repression, Resistance, and Democratic Transition in Central America* (Wilmington, DE: Scholarly Resources, 2000); Robert Armstrong and Janet Shenk, *El Salvador: The Face of Revolution* (Boston: South End Press, 1982); Rosenberg, *Children of Cain*; and Montgomery, *Revolution in El Salvador*. For sources that treat indigenous sentiment as tertiary aggravating factors, see, for example, White, *El Salvador*, 101; Roqué Dalton, *Miguel Mármol* (Willimantic, CT: Curbstone Press, 1986); Montgomery, *Revolution in El Salvador*; A. Douglas Kincaid, "Peasants into Rebels: Community and Class in Rural El Salvador," in David H. Levine, ed., *Constructing Culture and Power in Latin America* (Ann Arbor: University of Michigan Press, 1993); and Dunkerley, *Power in the Isthmus*, 96–97.

3. Joaquín Méndez, *Los sucesos comunistas en El Salvador* (San Salvador: Funes and Ungo, 1932); Anderson, *Matanza*, 2nd ed.; White, *El Salvador*, 101.

4. White, *El Salvador*, 71.

5. Jorge Schlesinger, *Revolución Comunista* (Guatemala: Union Tipografica Castañeda, Avila y Cia, 1946), 26; Alvarenga, *Cultura y ética de la violencia*; Brignoli, "Indians, Communists, and Peasants." Works in Spanish most important to later interpretations are the eyewitness accounts of Méndez, *Los sucesos comunistas* and Miguel Mármol (Dalton, *Miguel Mármol*). Shorter but influential studies include those by Jorge Arias Gómez, *El proceso político Centroamericano* (San Salvador: Editorial Universitaria, 1964); White, *El Salvador;* and Montes, "Los indígenas en El Salvador." The new *Historia de El Salvador* textbook gives the 1932 crisis careful treatment. Important English-language sources include Alvarenga, *Cultura y ética de la violencia* and Kincaid, "Peasants into Rebels."

6. Brignoli, "Indians, Communists, and Peasants," 256.

7. Anderson, *Matanza*, 2nd ed., 31.

8. Anderson, *Matanza*, 2nd ed., 170.

9. An important study of ethnic and class interests in 1932, also drawing on oral testimony as well as contemporary documentation, is Aldo Lauria-Santiago and Jeffrey L. Gould, "They Call Us Thieves and Steal Our Wage: Toward a Reinterpretation of the Salvadoran Rural Mobilization, 1929–1931," *The Hispanic American Historical Review* 84, no. 2 (May 2004). These historians reject the idea that the 1932 Matanza represented an "ethnic conflict *tout court*" but do not elaborate their understanding of "tout court." Their evidence, in my view, supports the analysis here.

10. Cited in Zamosc, "The Landing That Never Was," 136, emphasis added.

11. Schlesinger, *Revolución Comunista*, 25, emphasis added.

12. Montes, *El compadrazgo*, 330. In my own conversations with indigenous residents in the Nahuizalco cantones, I found people to be voluble and forthcoming about 1932 if I was accompanied by a trusted member of the community.

13. Ibid. These eyewitness interviews, transcribed at length in Montes's Appendices, comprise an invaluable and underutilized source on the 1932 crisis; Montes's book can even be read as a cover for publishing this politically sensitive material.

14. Erik Ching's pivotal research remains the central source on this revision: "In Search of the Party: The Communist Party, the Comintern, and the Peasant Rebellion of 1932 in El Salvador," *Americas* 55, no. 2 (1998). See also Virginia Tilley and Erik Ching, "Indians, the Military, and the 1932 Rebellion in El Salvador," *Journal of Latin American Studies* 30, no. 1 (1998).

15. One of the most interesting accounts of the revolt was provided by the commander of a Canadian ship anchored at Acajutla: see Zamosc, "The Landing That Never Was." Later, some would argue that Martínez's worries about foreign intervention contributed heavily to the brutality of the repression, including General Calderón's famous notification to U.S. and Canadian officials after three days that 4,800 communists had been "liquidated" (scandalized reactions from U.S. and Canadian diplomats would inspire Calderón's rapid but unconvincing backpedaling on this claim).

16. See Méndez, *Los sucesos comunistas* as well as Anderson, *Matanza*, 2nd ed. This is also the version offered by El Salvador's revised textbook, the *Historia de El Salvador* II, 122.
17. Ching, "In Search of the Party," 218–23.
18. Ibid., 223.
19. That anticolonialism was still central to indigenous perspectives has been suggested earlier; Schlesinger also deduced this motive: *Revolución Comunista*, 25.
20. Anderson, *Matanza*, 2nd ed., 102–5.
21. Cited in Ching, "In Search of the Party," 224.
22. Anderson, *Matanza*, 2nd ed.
23. Schlesinger, *Revolución Comunista*, 190.
24. Lauria-Santiago and Gould, "They Call Us Thieves."
25. Anderson, *Matanza*, 2nd ed., 95.
26. See, e.g., the high school history textbook, *Historia de El Salvador* II, 135. The indigenous organization ANIS reproduced the famous photograph as a large wall poster with an attached quote, "'They will assassinate me but my ideas will remain in the thought of the Nations: Mayas, Lencas and Nahuat'—Feliciano Ama." In 1996, ANIS director Esquino Lizco cited the source of this quote by tapping his own temple.
27. Méndez, *Los sucesos comunistas*, 61.
28. See interview with "A" in Montes, *El compadrazgo*, 283; also Anderson, *Matanza*, 2nd ed., 97.
29. Montes, *El compadrazgo*, 265. Although valuable for expressing ladino perceptions, and probably not entirely wrong regarding widespread Indian smallholding, this quote is likely unreliable as evidence of social conditions. It parallels my experience of Guatemalan ladino tendencies to generalize universal Indian affluence from the existence of a small (Maya) elite. Land loss in the Izalco area prior to 1932 was also a problem, although possibly less grave than in other areas.
30. Dalton, *Miguel Mármol*, 307.
31. An unexplored dimension of Ama's present importance to indigenous activist ideology is how Mármol's account established Ama's role for the leftist canon. Since the left was responsible for extensive rural organizing in the 1970s and 1980s, Ama may well have been preserved popularly as "the leader of greatest importance" (*"el dirigente indígena de mayor peso," Historia de El Salvador* II, 123) partly because of his legitimization by Mármol, whose leftist credentials were impeccable.
32. Dalton, *Miguel Mármol*, 307.
33. Montes, *El compadrazgo*, 270, 274–75. The connections between Ama and prominent Izalco ladinos are described in the extraordinary interview by Montes with "A," probably Barrientos. "A" said that, had Ama's ladino friends been in town (most had fled to San Salvador), they would have prevented his hanging, believing that he had saved their lives during the revolt.
34. Anderson, *Matanza*, 2nd ed., 97.
35. "Don Mario, usted siempre tendré mi cariño, porque hemos sido amigos, somos amigos y seguiremos siendo amigos, pero no vamos a ir ya juntos en las cosas políticas, porque usted es ya de los capitalistas, y nosotros el proletariado": cited in Montes, *El compadrazgo*, 274.

36. Montes, *El compadrazgo*, 270; Méndez, *Los sucesos comunistas*.

37. In chapter 8, I show figures to support my estimate of the indigenous population of Sonsonate department in 1932 at about 32,000 people, based on the municipal birth records. The very unreliable 1930 census also put the department's indigenous proportion at 34.7 percent, or about 35,000 people, and the total population of the department as 100,217.

38. MacNaught, "Horrors of Communism in Central America," *The Central American Bulletin* 181 (March 1932), 8.

39. Ibid., 8–9.

40. In my interviews in the Nahuizalco cantones, three respondents (each in a different canton) claimed that many people had signed onto the communist voting lists (that would later be used to identify and execute people) simply to be nice to communist activists or under the general impression that it was the correct thing to do. This may be a revisionist story, constructed later to deny culpability. Systematic interviews might shed considerable light on indigenous perceptions of the communists in this period. Lists apparently were for the presidential campaign, as municipal elections were not held in Nahuizalco that year; see Letter from Sonsonate Governor to Government Ministry, February 9, 1932, AGN-SONGOB-3.

41. Brignoli, "Indians, Communists, and Peasants," 251.

42. Redaelli was the author of one progressive measure some months earlier: the inclusion of the father's name in the registry of illegitimate births, so that the child would be provided for. An editorial in the conservative newspaper *Diario Latino* called this measure "unprecedented" and highly humane, and urged that it be adopted throughout the country (November 2, 1931). This action may have been an effort to salvage his local reputation.

43. Anderson, *Matanza*, 2nd ed., 136.

44. Letter from Carlos Estrada M. to Sonsonate Governor, November 28, 1931; also correspondence from Mayor Redaelli to Sonsonate Governor, December 18 and 23, 1931, AGN-SONGOB-3.

45. Letter to Sonsonate Governor, November 28, 1931, AGN-SONGOB-3.

46. Anderson, *Matanza*, 2nd ed., 151.

47. Montes, *El compadrazgo*, 311.

48. Cited in Anderson, *Matanza*, 2nd ed., 151.

49. Montes, *El compadrazgo*, 318.

50. Dalton, *Miguel Mármol*, 304.

51. The machine-gunning of thousands of peasants closed off in a town square was placed by Anderson in Izalco; Mármol placed it in Juayúa.

52. Rudolfo Buezo, *Sangre de Hermanos* (Havana, n.d.); cited in Anderson, *Matanza*, 2nd ed., 174.

53. Anderson also relies for his lower death figures on sources who were involved in inflicting them, such as the head of the Civil Guard, oddly claiming that this source was credible because he was "in a position to know": see *Matanza*, 2nd ed., 174–75.

54. Message to Alcaldes from Sonsonate Governor, forwarding Note 699 from Director General of Health D.C. Escalante, sent to Sonsonate from the National Palace on February 13, 1932. AGN-SONGOB-3, emphasis added.

55. Message to Sonsonate Governor from Director General of Statistics Felix de J. Osegueda, February 18, 1932. AGN-SONGOB-3.

56. Letter from Juayúa alcalde to Sonsonate Governor, May 14, 1932, AGN-SONGOB.

57. Gregorio Bustamente Maceo, *Historia militar de El Salvador* (San Salvador: Ministerio del Interior, 1951), translation from Dalton, *Miguel Mármol*, 311.

58. Anderson, *Matanza*, 2nd ed., 170, emphasis added. Interestingly, a number of Salvadorans who told me that Indians deliberately assimilated after 1932 referred me to Anderson's book when I asked for their source.

59. For details, see Tilley and Ching, "Indians, the Military, and the 1932 Rebellion."

60. Méndez, *Los sucesos comunistas*, 141, emphasis added.

61. Enrique Uribe, March 4, 1932: see further discussion in Tilley and Ching, "Indians, the Military, and the 1932 Rebellion," 149.

62. Extensive use of clubs and machetes in the 1994 Rwandan genocide, in which nearly a million Tutsis were killed, also offers recent graphic evidence that very large-scale massacres can be effected without modern weaponry.

63. "*Deseamos que se extermine de raíz la plaga . . .*" This line has often been mistranslated as "It is our wish that this race be exterminated": for example, Brignoli, "Indians, Communists, and Peasants," 255.

64. Cited in Méndez, *Los sucesos comunistas*, 100–105.

65. José Rivas, who took over as mayor of Juayúa after Redaelli's murder, would later write a biting critique of the large coffee plantation owners, whose short-term planning and carelessness with their finances left them so vulnerable to market fluctuations that they periodically threw whole communities into destitution: Report 578 to the Sonsonate Governor, 23 August 1933, AGN-SONGOB-3.

66. MacNaught, "Horrors of Communism," 26–27.

67. Provocative parallels can be drawn between the rush of popular ladino zeal in killing Indians in 1932, the zeal of Hutu citizens of Rwanda in killing Tutsi in 1994, and the zeal of private German citizens in killing Jews during Nazi era. In all these cases, long-standing racism apparently combined with a particular configuration of national and international political interests to galvanize widespread involvement by normally passive people in genocidal acts.

68. Montes, *El compadrazgo*, 276.

69. The case of Pascuala Tula, widow of Paschaca, discussed in correspondence between the Sonsonate Governor's office and Izalco Alcalde M. Vega of September 11–13, 1934. She argued that the land of her husband's uncle had been handed to a private Izalco citizen, who in turn handed it over to the charge of a hospital, from whom she was trying to reclaim it on behalf of his heirs, her children. The case indicates the nature of this judicial mechanism and suggests further research but we do not know the scale of these transfers. AGN-SONGOB.

70. One Nahuizalco ladino informant named specific families whose wealth today traces from this practice, but confirmation is lacking. Indians from Cuisnahuat told me that they believe that the archive in that town was burned by ladinos in 1932 precisely to facilitate such fraud.

71. Letter to Señor Governador [sic] de Departmento de Sonsonate, February 26, 1933, AGN-SONGOB. Both the handwriting and the spelling in the original are

bad and difficult to decipher. One phrase reads *"para tener cierta comprobanza puede tomar redacciones por nuestros asuntos que tenemos con el Supremo Govierno . . ."*

72. In 1961, the water system would pass into the hands of the national water authority, but water conflicts would persist. In June 1996, Izalco was again seething with internal factional politics over water rights, with the indigenous community again polarized against the alcaldia.

Chapter 8

1. Some material from this chapter was presented in Tilley and Ching, "Indians, the Military and the 1932 Rebellion." Editorial advice from Erik Ching and the anonymous reviewer regarding that article is reflected here; this chapter, however, offers a different formulation, and any flaws are my sole responsibility.

2. For a fuller treatment of the army's policies after 1932, see analysis in Tilley and Ching, "Indians, the Military, and the 1932 Rebellion," and Erik Ching, "From Clientelism to Militarism: the State, Politics and Authoritarianism in El Salvador, 1840–1940" (Ph.D. diss., University of California at Santa Barbara, 1997).

3. See, for example, David Laitin's critique of the ELF database, "The Implications of Constructivism for Constructing Ethnic Fractionalization Indices," *Symposium: Cumulative Findings in the Study of Ethnic Politics,* American Political Science Association, Comparative Politics Newsletter (Winter 2001).

4. The 10 percent figure was supplied by Pedro Ticas and Marta Benavides, *Presencia indígena en El Salvador* (Mexico: Praxis Ediciones, 1993). Ticas does not report his methodology and, in an interview with me, reported he had lost his field notes. Indigenous individuals who collaborated with Ticas's study told me that his method was to ask them their own impressions of indigenous population size. Although his final estimate may be roughly accurate, I do not consider that it represents more than guesswork.

5. Lindo-Fuentes, *Weak Foundations,* 73–78, 169; see again Cortés y Larraz, cited in Browning, *El Salvador,* 120–21, 123, 125, 133.

6. Lindo-Fuentes prefers the lower of these figures, asserting that "Even before independence, the Indian population comprised less than half of the total": *Weak Foundations,* 72. He considers the higher estimates of Reyes in 1884 to reflect economic competition with ladinos that reconsigned "assimilated Indians" to "Indian" status. He accepts the 22.5 percent estimate of John Galindo, in a survey for the London Geographical Society in 1837. I believe Galindo's figures not to deserve such faith; he also estimated the "white" population at 20 percent, a figure certainly greatly inflated or at least not reflecting other contemporary concepts of "white": see Rodolfo Barón Castro, *La población de El Salvador* (San Salvador: Universidad Centroamericana José Simeón Cañas, 1942), 453.

7. Barón Castro, *La población de El Salvador.* While his volume remains very valuable, Barón Castro's interpretation of preconquest ethnic migrations and identities has been contradicted by later archaeological discoveries: see especially William R. Fowler, "La distribución prehistórica e histórica de los pipiles," *Mesoamerica* 4, no. 6 (December 1983), and "Cacao, indigo, and coffee."

8. This figure was sustained through a 1927 report by Don Pedro S. Fonseca and a 1931 report in the *Almanach de Gotha*, both of which estimated the indigenous population at 20 percent. Barón Castro himself accepted 20 percent in 1940, but admitted to the very rough methodology he used to obtain this figure. He observed that a 1927 census had found the department of San Salvador to be 7.3 percent indigenous. Since San Salvador included the capital and so was disproportionately "white" (whites including both creoles and foreigners) he reasoned that the rest of the country must be *less* white and more mestizo, and so he hazarded a countrywide indigenous average of 20 percent, signifying about 350,000 people: see *La población de El Salvador*, 524–32. He also observed that the figure might well be lower, noting that the 1933 *South American Handbook* had reported 10 percent.

9. Adams, *Cultural Surveys*. In the mid-1950s, Adams still found approximately 20 percent of the Salvadoran population to be indigenous (although he defined that 20 percent by various degrees of "ladinization" or cultural assimilation).

10. Letter to the Governor of Sonsonate from the Director General of the Census, dated February 12, 1932, requesting such a list "*a la mayor brevedad posible*" (as quickly as possible): AGN-SONGOB.

11. See Constitución Política de la Republica de El Salvador, Article 150 (San Salvador: 1950): "*Todos los hombres son iguales ante la ley. Para el goce de los derechos civiles no se podra establecer restricciones que se basen en diferencias de nacionalidad, raza, sexo o religion.*" ("All men are equal before the law. In regard to the enjoyment of civil rights, no restrictions can be established which are based on differences of nationality, race, sex or religion.") The 1950 Constitution did rule against recording the civil status of the newborn's parents (Article 181), a practice that often attached an "illegitimate" stigma to people for life. This clause may have been promoted by President Oscar Osorio, who was himself illegitimate and, reputedly, bitterly resented the trouble that the public record had cost him.

12. The Catholic Church also sometimes recorded the ethnic identity of newborns in the baptismal records. This practice, never consistent, was generally abandoned by the end of the nineteenth century, possibly for progressive reasons. In 1869, the Parish of Asunción (Izalco) listed 66.9 percent indigenous births (53 out of a total of 80).

13. Until 1915, many townships totaled the indigenous births in a separate table at the end of each month or year. That these totals were sent separately to the capital is suggested by Santiago Barberena's report, "Estudios Demographicos" [Demographic Studies], *La Quincena* 4, no. 43 (1904).

14. The vast majority of births during this period were illegitimate, a stigmatizing status not expunged from the Civil Registry until 1950: see note 11.

15. Barberena, "Estudios Demographicos," 43–45. Barberena also noted that the birth rate for ladinos was 3.37 times the death rate, and for indígenas was 3.12 times the death rate.

16. Susan Greenblatt (health worker), interview with author, San Salvador, April 1996.

17. Birth records in Nahuizalco, Salcoatitán, and Sonzacate were lost to arson in 1932.

18. In this study of the microfilms in the Tribuno Supremo Electoral, I counted indigenous births in all municipios in Sonsonate and Ahuachapán, the heart of the Matanza zone, at five-year intervals from 1900 to 1950. Comparable data was collected from the famous indigenous municipalities south of the capital in San Salvador department: Panchimalco and its southern neighbor, Rosario de Mora. I then counted indigenous births in most of the municipios in La Libertad and La Paz departments for the latest years in which race was recorded, usually the early 1940s. To reduce small-sample distortions, in the latter series I tried to collect data from two years, consecutive if possible, and averaged them. Consecutive years were not always obtainable; in almost all yearly samples, some records omitted the race category and where omissions exceeded 10 percent of the total I excluded the year. Even with the 90 percent standard, this method could over- or underestimate the indigenous population by up to 9.9 percent. For this and other reasons explained in the text, all the birth record totals must be taken as suggestive. Most samples offered here, however, did not have 10 percent missing entries; the average was closer to 4 percent.

19. Panama's largest racial minority was "blacks." Due to non-cooperation and high migration rates, census-takers had a very difficult time counting the Indian population, a problem finally officialized in the 1940 census by regenerating two figures for the censuses of 1911, 1920, 1930, and 1940: "Population without Indians" and "Total Population," the latter extrapolated from population density. This method suggested an indigenous population of about one percent higher for the country as a whole. The 1940 census defined "Indians" as "those Indians that live in tribes"; Indians living in settlements were subsumed into the "civil population." See "Cuadro No. 1: Población Total de la Provincia de Panamá, por Distrito," República de Panamá, *Censo de Poblacion 1940* Vol. I (Contraloría General de la República, Oficina del Censo), 27, n. 1. The Panama case is especially interesting because the indigenous Kuna population, formerly considered so negligible, would succeed in gaining 9 percent of Panama's territory as an autonomy zone in 1996.

20. Nicaragua's 1950 census found that only 3.23 percent of the population spoke indigenous languages in the home; categories included only Miskito and Sumo (both communities on the Atlantic coast), with counts of 20,723 and 747 respectively. See Cuadro. No. 18, *Censo General de Población de la República de Nicaragua, Mayo 1950* (Managua, August 1954), 126. The reliability of language criteria to ethnic population counts must here be treated very cautiously, as these peoples too would later gain a major autonomy zone: see especially Hale, *Resistance and Contradiction*.

21. Explaining the switch to "ethnic group," the 1950 census emphasized that the long-established census categories of ladino, indígena, amarilla ("yellow" or Asian), and negro were "not strictly racial" and that "the Statistics office has tried to maintain solely the concept of ethnic group, far from any racial consideration." It also specified that the term "ladino" was not considered a racial unit, "but more as a conjunction of cultural characteristics." In 1950, no provision was made for any other "ethnic" category than "ladino" and "indígena." *Sexto Censo de Población 1950*, Introduction, section (f) (Guatemala: Dirección General de Estadística), xi–xii.

22. Hale "*Mestizaje*, Hybridity, and the Cultural Politics of Difference," 44.
23. Ibid., 45.
24. Ibid.
25. Jeffrey Gould, "'Vana Ilusión!' The highlands Indians and the myth of Nicaragua mestiza, 1880–1925," *Hispanic American Historical Review* 73, no. 3 1993), 429.
26. I necessarily abuse complexities in this short treatment. Regarding ethnic and especially Miskito politics on the Atlantic coast, see especially Hale, *Resistance and Contradiction.* On the multiple weavings of identity among Nicaraguan artisan communities, see especially Les Field, *The Grimace of Macho Ratón*; for a provocative study of enduring indigenous identity and ethnopolitics in the central Nicaraguan highlands, see Timothy C. Brown, *The Real Contra War: Highlander Peasant Resistance in Nicaragua* (Norman: University of Oklahoma Press, 2001).

Chapter 9

1. See Emanuel Adler's discussion of transnational epistemic communities, "Cognitive Evolution: A Dynamic Approach for the Study of International Relations and Their Progress," in Emanuel Adler and Beverly Crawford, eds., *Progress in Postwar International Relations* (New York: Columbia University Press, 1991).
2. For a history of these studies, see especially Stephen Jay Gould's *The Mismeasure of Man* (New York: W. W. Norton & Company, 1996).
3. Manuel Gamio, *Forjando patria* (Mexico: Editorial Porrúa, 1960 [1916]), 21.
4. José Ingenieros, "La formación de una raza argentina," *Revista de Filosofía* 11 (1915), 466.
5. For a detailed analysis of civilization as a European discourse related to empire-building and international hegemony, see Gerrit W. Gong, *The Standard of Civilization in International Society* (Oxford: Clarendon Press, 1984).
6. Both Chilean and Argentinean sociologists, with a few notable exceptions like Manuel Ugarte, *The destiny of a Continent* (New York: Alfred A. Knopf, 1925), leaned toward "whitening" as a solution to resulting backwardness.
7. For instance, in 1916 Manuel Gamio estimated the indigenous population of Mexico at eight to ten million, and the population "of European origin" at four to six million: *Forjando patria*, 9.
8. Ingenieros, "La formación de una raza," 471.
9. Guillermo Feliu Cruz, *Un esquema de la evolución social en Chile en el siglo XIX* (Santiago, Chile: Editorial Nascimento, 1941), 6.
10. See the "Minutes and Antecedents," Vol. 7, *Seventh International Conference of American States* (Montevideo, 1933).
11. Francisco Pimentel, "Memoria sobre las causas que han originado la situación actual de la raza indígena de México y medios de remediarla," reprinted in *Dos Obras de Francisco Pimentel* (Xoco, CP, Mexico: Consejo Nacional Para la Cultura y las Artes, 1995 [1864]), 163. The editors report that the closing quote is from Brantz Mayer, *Mexico As It Was and As It Is.*
12. Then and now, loyalty to the old Central American Federation remains a strong theme in Salvadoran political thought.

13. Román Peña, "Bosquejo," *La Quincena* 8, no. 87 (November 15, 1906), 78. The "patria" in this case is not El Salvador but the failed Central American Union, still understood as the proper patria by many Salvadoran intellectuals and politicians in this period.

14. Theorizing throughout the continent included debates in Brazil and the Southern Cone: e.g., among Argentine writers, the racial typologies and "whitening" theory elaborated by sociologist Domingo Faustino Sarmiento in the 1880s; the racial fusion theory of lawyer-educator Carlos Octavio Bunge, published most famously in his *Nuestra América* (Buenos Aires: Casa Vaccaro, 1903); and the nationalist racial doctrine of sociologist José Ingenieros, as in his *Sociología Argentina* (Buenos Aires: Editorial Losada, 1946). In identifying these theorists as important to Argentinean scholarship, I rely on Aline Helg, "Race in Argentina and Cuba, 1880–1930: theory, policies, and popular reaction," in Graham, *The Idea of Race in Latin America*.

15. On these debates, see also Martin S. Stabb, "Indigenism and Racism in Mexican Thought: 1857–1911," *Journal of Inter-American Studies* 1 (1959); T. G. Powell, "Mexican Intellectuals and the Indian Question, 1876–1911," *Hispanic American Historical Review* (February 1969); and Alexander Dawson, "From Models for the Nation to Model Citizens: Indigenismo and the 'Revindication' of the Mexican Indian, 1920–40," *Journal of Latin American Studies* 30, no. 2 (May 1998).

16. Andrés Molina Enríquez, *Los grandes problemas nacionales* (Mexico: Ediciones Era, 1978 [1909]), 380.

17. Ibid., 357, 393. For a very different interpretation of indigenous political engagement with nationalist thought, see Mallon, "Constructing Mestizaje in Latin America."

18. On Gamio's role, see also Stabb, "Indigenism and Racism"; Powell, "Mexican Intellectuals"; Knight, "Racism, Revolution and *Indigenismo*"; and David A. Brading, "Manuel Gamio and Official Indigenismo in Mexico," *Bulletin of Latin American Research* 7, no. 1 (1998), 75–89.

19. Manuel Gamio, *Forjando patria*, 5–6. The image of a forge predates Gamio; see the quote at the beginning of this chapter from Francisco Gavida, "El porvenir de la América Latina" [The future of Latin America], *La Quincena* 1, no. 1 (1903).

20. Gamio, *Forjando patria*, 183, emphasis in original.

21. The Ecuadorian state also resorted to mestizaje when under pressure by indigenous collective protest: for an example from the 1970s, see Norman Whitten's classic account in *Sacha Runa: Ethnicity and Adaptation of Ecuadorian Jungle Quichua* (Urbana: University of Illinois Press, 1976), chapter 9.

22. On Salvadoran development in this period, see especially Lindo-Fuentes, *Weak Foundations*.

23. On the sociology of the Salvadoran elite in comparative context of Central American economic development, see especially Williams, *States and Social Evolution* and Ching, "From Clientelism to Militarism."

24. For a socioeconomic and ethnic history of Salvadoran concerns about monocrop agriculture in the nineteenth century in ethnohistorical perspective, see Browning, *El Salvador*.

25. A security community, in the writings of Karl Deutch, is a group of states that "possess a compatibility of core values derived from common institutions, and mutual responsiveness—a matter of mutual identity and loyalty, a sense of 'we-ness,' and are integrated to the point that they entertain 'dependable expectations of peaceful change'": Emanuel Adler and Michael Barnett, "Governing Anarchy: a Research Agenda for the Study of Security Communities," *Ethics and International Affairs* 10 (1998), 7. The concept has recently been revived in international relations theory to explain new alliance patterns and identity politics among states in the post–Cold War era.

26. Alberto Masferrer, "La Defensa de la Raza," *Paginas Escogidas* Viñeta de Antonio Flores Hernández (San Salvador: Ministerio de Educación Departamento Editorial, 1961 [1923]).

27. Knight, "Racism, Revolution and *Indigenismo*," 86.

28. Vasconcelos expounded the cosmic race doctrine most pointedly in "La Raza Cósmica" (1925), published simultaneously in Barcelona and Paris, and "Indología" (1926b), published in Barcelona. Citations for both texts are taken from Justina Sarabia, ed., *José Vasconcelos* (Madrid: Ediciones de Cultura Hispánica, 1989). Biographical information is also from this source.

29. Although Vasconcelos emphasized a generally "tropical" quality to la raza, other authors imagined a more elaborate relation to climate. Argentinean nationalist José Ingenieros believed that white demographics had naturally concentrated in temperate "septentrional" North America and temperate "meridional" southern South America (the Southern Cone), while the "intertropical" zone, being inimical to whites, retained a predominantly indigenous racial character. Sarabia, *José Vasconcelos,* 471.

30. Vasconcelos also sometimes uses the term "ethnic groups": e.g., ". . . still one must add to the physical differences the profound peculiarities of history and of race that characterize each of the great ethnic groups of contemporary America [apparently, English, Dutch, French and Spanish], since, as all the world knows, we proceed from a hispanic and latino culture and those of the North are continuers of a Saxon and German tradition. Of those ethnic differences are derived, as is natural, matrices and variations of spirit that are impossible to enumerate exactly": Sarabia, "Indología," *José Vasconcelos,* 46.

31. Vasconcelos also blamed Napoleon for U.S. hegemony. If Napoleon had not foolishly shattered the power of France, he argued, the U.S. could never have absorbed the Louisiana territories and so could never have launched the conquest of Texas and California. See Sarabia, "La Raza Cósmica," *José Vasconcelos,* 33.

32. Sarabia, "La Raza Cósmica," *José Vasconcelos,* 38.

33. Vasconcelos and Gamio, *Aspects of Mexican Civilization,* 100-102.

34. Sarabia, "La Raza Cósmica," *José Vasconcelos,* 33, emphasis added. The parallels with contemporary nationalist intellectual thought in other world regions are striking; for example, Sun Yat-Sen made the same critique of European cosmopolitanism, in the same year.

35. Peña, "Bosquejo" ["Sketch"]: emphasis added.

36. Masferrer, "El Mínimum Vital," in *Paginas Escogidas.*

37. Masferrer, "La Misión de América: La Defensa de la Raza," in *Paginas Escogidas*, 249.
38 Masferrer, *Paginas Escogidas*, 253.
39. Ibid., 255, emphasis in original.
40. Alberto Masferrer, "Ahora y en Tí Mismo" in *Paginas Escogidas*, 257, emphasis in original. On his "New Man" concept, contemporary Leninist thought may also have been an inspiration.
41. Masferrer, "El Grito de Batalla" [Battle Cry], in *Paginas Escogidas*, 262.
42. Ibid., 263, emphases in original.
43. Barberena proposed this idea to explain "the almost total disappearance of the black race in America": "Ladinos e Indios," 12. In Antigua Guatemala, one middle-class ladino gave me the same reason to explain blacks' confinement to the coast, as well as (what he supposed) to the southern (hot and humid) regions of the United States.
44. Pedro Antonio Escalante Arce, "Apuntes sobre presencia africana en la historia Salvadoreña," unpublished manuscript (n.d.), 12.
45. García Peláez, *Memorias para la historia del antiguo reyno de Guatemala*, II, 31; cited in Barón Castro, *La población de El Salvador*, 155.
46. Escalante Arce, "Apuntes sobre presencia africana," 6; Lauria-Santiago, "An Agrarian Republic," 434.
47. Menéndez, *Recopilación de las Leyes*, Book 9, Title 8, Law 3, Chapter 11, Article 1 (1956 [1799]), 339.
48. Antonio Gutierrez y Ulloa, *Ensayo historico-politico del Rno. de la Nueva Calacia con notas politicas y estadisticas de la Provincia de Guadalaxara* (Guadalajara, Jalisco, Mexico, 1983 [1816]), 9. I am grateful to researcher Ann Hutchinson, who has worked extensively in the Guatemala City archives, for her advice that "mulato" was sometimes used interchangeably with "mestizo" to indicate mixed race generally. Lauria-Santiago and Gould, "They Call Us Thieves," found the same usage in Salvadoran oral accounts of 1932. Inconsistent usage, sometimes by travelers using labels gleaned from other regions, makes the interpretation of the region's nineteenth-century demography especially difficult.
49. George Thompson, *Narrative of an Official Visit to Guatemala from Mexico* (London: J. Murray, 1829), 73–74.
50. The poor quality of the 1930 census, and its tendency dramatically to undercount the indigenous population, should also be kept in mind: see discussion in chapter 8. The stigma of negro and mulato might also have influenced people to deny such identity to the census official even if they privately held it. Such a tendency toward "self-whitening" the 1990 census in Brazil was the subject of a deliberate campaign to counteract it: see Winant "Rethinking Race in Brazil," 355.
51. Pedro Antonio Escalante Arce, "Apuntes sobre presencia Africana en la historia Salvadoreña."
52. Helg, "Race in Argentina and Cuba," 54.
53. Knight, "Racism, Revolution and *Indigenismo*," 96–97.
54. Reforms to the Ley de Extranjería, 22 May 1897, Article 52: "También serán considerados como extranjeros perniciosos para no permitirles su establecimiento

en el país á los indígenas ó originarios de la China. Esta disposición no comprenderá á los ya establecidos en el país" ("Also those who are indigenous to or originating in China will be considered pernicious foreigners not allowed to establish themselves in the country. This provision will not include those already established in the country."

55. The National Archive contains a file of confiscated travel documents, all dated 1917, each showing a formal portrait of a Chinese man or boy. Some appear stiffly in western suits and ties; some children are in Chinese jackets.

56. Executive Order of February 25, 1930, from the Minister of Exterior Relations to the Government Ministry, published in *Diario Official* on February 27, 1930.

57. *Diario Latino*, June 26, 1931.

58. *El Espectador*, July 21, 1931. In emphasizing the inferiority of human hybrids, the paper reproduces turn-of-the-century European notions about the superiority of racial purity: see Powell, "Mexican Intellectuals."

59. Knight, "Racism, Revolution and *Indigenismo*," 97.

60. *El Espectador*, July 21, 1931, emphasis added.

61. Albert Masferrer, "*En defenso de los Chinos* [In defense of the Chinese]," *Patria*, October 22 and 23, 1931, his emphasis. Masferrer also made a wry comparison with foreign-owned coffee processing plants, noting that U.S. and German ownership of most *beneficios* implied Salvadoran's "INCAPACITY for the work" (his emphasis).

62. Note 843, April 15, 1932, SONGOB.

63. Pedro Escalante, interview with author, January 27, 1996.

64. Salvadoran references to "Palestinians" in the 1920s and 1930s probably signified people from modern Lebanon, then a region still contiguous with historic Palestine. Steep economic decline and famine under Turkish rule caused some 160,000 Lebanese to emigrate between 1860 and 1914, and many came to Latin America at that time. One common racial term for "Arabs" in Latin America, then and now, is "Turks" (*Turcos*).

65. *Seminario sobre Problemas Indígenas de Centroamérica, celebrado en San Salvador, El Salvador 27 de junio a 2 de julio de 1955* (Mexico: Ediciones del Instituto Indigenista Interamericano, 1955), 14, emphasis added.

66. Ibid., emphasis added.

67. Decreto Legislativo No. 2709.

Chapter 10

1. Decreto Legislativo No. 2709.

2. *Culture of Peace Programme in El Salvador*, elaborated by the Ministry of Education and other Governmental and Non-Governmental Organizations with the cooperation of UNESCO (1993), 53, emphasis added. All English citations are from the unofficial English edition, translated by UNESCO; spellings like "Salvadorian" are UNESCO's.

3. Among a rich literature on the civil war, see, for example, Montgomery, *Revolution in El Salvador*; on elite perspectives particularly, see Rosenberg, *Children of Cain*.

4. For a recent intelligent appraisal of these obstacles particularly regarding the judicial system, see Margaret Popkin, *Peace Without Justice: Obstacles to Building the rule of Law in El Salvador* (University Park, PA: Pennsylvania State University Press, 2000).

5. Freddy Leistenschneider, director, Casas de la Cultura (CONCULTURA), interview with author, May 7, 1996.

6. Ernesto Magaña, director, Fomento Cultural, Banco Agrícola Comercial, interview with author, January 24, 1996; Leistenschneider, interview with author, May 7, 1996; José Manuel Bonilla Alvarado, director, Promoción Cultural, CONCULTURA, interview with author, December 8, 1995.

7. Mission Statement of CONCULTURA: *Presentación: CONCULTURA: Institucionalidad y Organización 1991–1994,* Part IV "El Futuro de CONCULTURA."

8. On the United Nations' role, see Kimbra L. Fishel, "The United Nations Involvement in the Salvadoran Peace Process," *World Affairs* (Spring 1998).

9. *Culture of Peace Programme in El Salvador,* 5–6.

10. *Culture of Peace Programme in El Salvador,* emphasis added.

11. *Culture of Peace Programme in El Salvador,* 89–91.

12. My analysis here of the transnational movement draws primarily from my own participation in it between 1988 and 1992; see preface and chapter 1. For a comprehensive and theoretically informed analysis of the transnational movement, see especially Brysk, *From Tribal Village to Global Village.* Studies of indigenous movements in Latin America continue to expand: valuable early review articles include Field, "Who Are the Indians?" and Richard N. Adams, "Works on Latin American Ethnicity, Emigration, and Indian Resistance and Survival," *Latin American Research Review* 32, no. 2 (1997). On debates within the movement about indigenous sovereignty and international law, see especially S. James Anaya, *Indigenous Peoples in International Law* (New York, Oxford: Oxford University Press, 1996); Duncan Ivison, Paul Patton, and Will Sanders, eds., *Political Theory and the Rights of Indigenous Peoples* (Cambridge University Press, 2000); and Curtis Cook and Juan D. Lindau, *Aboriginal Rights and Self-Government* (Montreal: McGill-Queen's University Press, 2000).

13. For one perspective on these paradigmatic tensions in the larger context of scholarship on identity politics, see Charles R. Hale, "Cultural Politics of Identity in Latin America," *Annual Review of Anthropology* 26 (1997), 567–90.

14. The term "tribal" accrued to peoples especially in south and southeast Asia, whose discursive situation mirrored those of indigenous peoples in settler-colonial societies but for whom the concept "indigenous" had no political meaning given equally "indigenous" dominant ethnicities: see Brysk, *From Tribal Village to Global Village.*

15. Programa Cultura de Paz en El Salvador: Documento de Proyecto, "Apoyo a las Comunidades Indígenas de El Salvador (Perfil 2.9)," 90.

16. On the spiritual connection of indigenous Salvadoran communities to corn cultivation in historical perspective, see Browning, *El Salvador.* For a survey of spiritual concepts and rituals attached to its cultivation among the Nahua, see Concepción Clara de Guevarra, coorda, "El añil de los 'indios cheles,'" *América Indígena* 35, no. 4 (October 1975).

17. UNESCO program officer, confidential interview, San Salvador, June 19, 1996.
18. Kenneth Bell, interview with author, March 10, 1996.
19. Programa Cultura de Paz en El Salvador, 13–18.
20. Later, the EU agreed that FUNDESCA (Foundation for Social and Economic Development in Central America) would coordinate the PAPICA program.
21. Convenio de Financiación entre la Comunidad Europea y la Fundación para el Desarollo Económico y Social de Centroamerica (FUNDESCA), Convenio No. AC-B7-3010/93/172, Anexo A Reg/ Indigêne/ DTA.
22. Victor Ramos and Leopoldo Tzian, COMG, interview with author, January 15, 1996.
23. "Identificación de un programa dirigido a la problematica indígena en Centro-America," no date.
24. Ibid., 197. By "Indianist" the report apparently refers to that subset of Indian advocates who celebrate all things Indian within a romanticized, utopianist framework.
25. The EU diagnostic accepted the common Salvadoran indigenous claim that indigenous ethnicities in El Salvador include Nahua (*nahoa*), Lenca and Maya, although the actual location of any Maya population is always left unspecified. Consequently, the EU investigator was concerned that ANIS was not respecting "non-Nahua" ethnic groups in the country.
26. ARENA was formed in 1981 by the notorious right-wing extremist and death-squad leader, Roberto D'Aubuisson. The party "brought together oligarchs, rightists, conservative professionals, and military hardliners around the themes of virulent anticommunism and nationalism" (Barry, *El Salvador*, 17), but is best known for its assassins of leftists and human rights activists that decimated its opposition and terrorized the country.
27. Aaron Gallegos, "The Reconquest of El Salvador," *Sojourner Magazine* (May–June, 1997). See also, for example, "Written statement submitted by the International Indian Treaty Council," United Nations Economic and Social Council, E/CN.4/1999/NGO/76, 5 March 1999; and the urgent call for action on the Tino-rangtiratanga email group by the South and Meso American Indian Rights Center (SAIIC) of September 22, 1998.

BIBLIOGRAPHY AND SOURCES

Note on documents:
I use Aldo Lauria-Santiago's coding system for documents from Salvadoran archives. Those obtained from El Salvador's National Archive (Archivo General de la Nación) are denoted "AGN." Documents from the AGN's Gobernación (Government Ministry) collection for Sonsonate Department are designated "SONGOB." Researchers are cautioned that retrieval of the documents cited here may be difficult and time consuming.

Interviews

My method relied primarily on unstructured rather than formal interviews. For reasons discussed in the Preface, some interviews among the rural Nahua are kept confidential.

Guatemala

Apolinario Chile Pixtún, "naturopath" and Maya priest, Chimaltenango, July 8, 1996.

José Lopez y Lopez, regional coordinator of Bilingual Education for Region 6, January 9, 1996.

Alberto Baten Ajenal, director of PRONEBI (government bilingual program) for Quetzaltenango Department, January 9, 1996.

Quemé Chay, mayor, Quetzaltenango, Guatemala, November 16, 1995.

Leopoldo Tzian, president, Coordinadora de Organizaciones Mayenses de Guatemala, Chimaltenango, Guatemala, January 15, 1996.

Carlos Isaías García, Executive Director, Association of Mayan Writers of Guatemala (Asociación de Escritores Mayances de Guatemala), Quetzaltenango, October 20, 1995.

Mora Herwig, Rolando Otoniel, director, TRAMA Textiles, Quetzaltenango, October 3, 1995.

274

El Salvador
Principal Indigenous Activists ongoing contacts, January–June, 1996
(refer to Chart 1):
ANIS—Adrian Esquino Lizco, "spiritual *cacique*"
ACCIES—Fidel Flores Hernández, president
ACOCPINSA—Victor Ramos, president, Salvadora Ramos, vice-president
ADESCOIN—Manuel Vasces, Ambrosio, Margarito
ALNITISA—Jorge Perez, president, Felipe Pais, treasurer
CODECA—Mauricio Piñeda, president
COMUPRIN—Salvadora Ramos, president
CONAIS—Richardo Maye, president
MAIS—Julio Alfaro, representative
RAIS—Maria Eugenia Alguilar de Vasces, Manuel Vasces

Formal Interviews
Aguilar, Antonio, director, Economic, Social and Cultural Rights, Procuraduría of Human Rights, May 14, 1995.

Amaya Amaya, Miguel Angel, Ulua activist, Cacaopera, El Salvador, May 17–18, 1996.

Arias, Miguel, Mayordomo, Cofradía de Niños, Nahuizalco, February 17, 1996.

Auxiliadara, Maria, schoolteacher, Nahuizalco, February 4, 1996.

Bell, Kenneth, representative for PAPICA project from the European Union (San José, Costa Rica), March 10, 1996 and June 6, 1996.

Bonilla Alvarado, José Manuel, Director of Cultural Promotion, CONCULTURA (ongoing consultations, January–June, 1996).

Cañas, José Miguel, technician, CONCULTURA, San Salvador, March 7, 1996.

Candanedo, Diana, coordinator of Indigenous Affairs, representative to PAPICA project from FUNDESCA, Panama, January 15, 1996.

Clara de Guevarra, Concepción, anthropologist, Santa Tecla, El Salvador, March 1, 1996.

Camacho, Jorge Ruiz, director, COLAPRODHES, San Salvador, June 26, 1996.

Cordeiro, Joaquín, European director, Artisan Development Program (PRODESAR, co-run by European Union and Salvadoran government), June 25, 1996.

Dada, Hector, director, FLACSO, San Salvador, February 2, 1996.

de Choussy, Ana Vilma P., Director, Patronato Pro-Patrimonia Cultural, San Salvador, February 11, 1996.

Duncan, William, Human Rights Officer, United States Embassy, June 5, 1996.

Ernst, Howard and Katy Sampek, archaeologists, Santa Tecla, March 2, 1996.

Escalante, Pedro, independent scholar, January 27, 1996.

Esquino Lizco, Adrian, cacique, Associación Nacional Indígena de El Salvador, April 29, 1996.

Fowler, William, archaeologist, February 10, 1996.

González, Francisco Manuel, mayor of Izalco, March 12, 1996.

Greenblatt, Susan, health worker, San Salvador, April 1996.

Guerra, Padre Walter, San Antonio del Monte, February 21, 1996.

Guzman, Odilia, director, Casa de la Cultura, Panchimalco, March 14, 1996.

Herrera, José Antonio, lawyer, Supreme Electoral Tribunal, San Salvador.

Lara Martínez, Carlos Benjamín, CONCULTURA, May 23, 1996.

Leistenschneider, Freddy, director, Casas de la Cultura, CONCULTURA, San Salvador, March 7, 1996.

Lourenço, Mirta Edith, program specialist, Culture of Peace Program, UNESCO, June 19, 1996.

Magaña, Ernesto, director, Cultural Promotion, Banco Agricola Comercial, San Salvador, January 24, 1996.

Martínez, Antonio Alguilar, chief of Department of Economic, Social and Cultural Rights Department, Procuraduría de Derechos Humanos, May 14, 1996.

Mejía de Gutierrez, Gloria, director, Indigenous Affairs, CONCULTURA, February 14, 1996.

Salazar, Luis, curator, Patronato Pro-Patrimonio Cultural, San Salvador, October 14, 1995.

Solar, Raul, vice-president, Instituto Salvadoreño de Turismo, June 25, 1996.

Tiberia, Gayo Eugenio, professor of linguistics, School of Information Technology Systems, National University of El Salvador, May 15, 1996.

Vargas, Padre Ismael, Jujutla, June 20, 1996.

Books, Documents, and Articles

Abercrombie, Thomas. "To Be Indian, To Be Bolivian: 'Ethnic' and 'National' Discourses of Identity," in Greg Urban and Joel Sherzer, eds., *Nation-States and Indians in Latin America*, 1991, 95–130.

Adams, Richard N. *Cultural Surveys of Panama, Nicaragua, Guatemala, El Salvador, Honduras*. Pan American Sanitary Bureau, World Health Organization, 1957. Citations from Blaine Ethridge edition, 1976.

———. "The Conquest Tradition of Mesoamerica." *The Americas* 46 (October 1989).

———. "Etnias y Sociedades (1930–1979)." In Héctor Pérez Brignoli, ed., *De la posguerra a la crisis (1945–1979)*. 2nd ed., Vol. 5 of *Historia General de Centroamérica*. Madrid: Comunidades Europeas and FLACSO, 1994.

———. "Ethnic Emergence and Expansion in Central America." *Texas Papers on Latin America* no. 88-08. Austin: University of Texas Press, 1988.

———. "Ethnic Images and Strategies in 1944." *Texas Papers on Latin America* no. 88-06. Austin: University of Texas Press, 1988.

———. *Etnicidad en el ejército de la Guatemala Liberal (1870–1950)*. Guatemala: FLACSO, 1995.

———. 1967. "Nationalization," *Handbook of Middle American Peoples*, 6. Austin: University of Texas Press, 469–89.

———. "Strategies of Ethnic Survival in Central America." *Texas Papers on Latin America* no. 88-10. Austin: University of Texas Press, 1988.

———. "Works on Latin American Ethnicity, Emigration, and Indian Resistance and Survival." *Latin American Research Review* 32, no. 2 (1997).

Adler, Emanuel. "Cognitive Evolution: A Dynamic Approach for the Study of International Relations and Their Progress." In Emanuel Adler and Beverly Crawford, eds., *Progress in Postwar International Relations*. New York: Columbia University Press, 1991.

Adler, Emanuel and Michael Barnett. "Governing Anarchy: a research agenda for the study of security communities." *Ethics and International Affairs* 10 (1996).

Alchon, Suzanne Austin. *A Pest in the Land: New World Epidemics in a Global Perspective*. Albuquerque: University of New Mexico Press, 2003.

Almond, Gabriel A. and Sidney Verba. *The Civic Culture*. Princeton, NJ: Princeton University Press, 1963.

Alvarenga, Ana Patricia. *Cultura y ética de la violencia: El Salvador 1880–1932*. EDUCA, 1996.

Amaya Amaya, Miguel Angel. *Historias de Cacaopera*. San Salvador: Ministerio de Educación, 1985.

Ament, Gail. "The Postcolonial Mayan Scribe: Contemporary Indigenous Writers of Guatemala." Unpublished dissertation, University of Washington-Seattle, 1998.

Anaya, S. James. *Indigenous Peoples in International Law*. New York: Oxford University Press, 1996.

Anderson, Benedict. *Imagined Communities*. London: Verso, 1991.

Anderson, Thomas P. *Matanza*. Willimantic, CT: Curbstone Press, 1971. Second ed. published by Curbstone Press in 1992.

Annis, Sheldon. *God and Production in a Guatemalan Town*. Austin: University of Texas Press, 1987, 107–35.

Arias Gómez, Jorge. Ponencia. *El Proceso Político Centroamericano*. Seminario de Historia Contemporánea de Centro América. San Salvador: Editorial Universitaria, 1964.

Armstrong, Robert and Janet Shenk. *El Salvador: The Face of Revolution*. Boston: South End Press, 1982.

Arneson, Eric. "Whiteness and the Historians' Imagination." *International Labor and Working-Class History*, no. 60 (Fall 2001).

Ballesteros-Gaibrois, Manuel and Julia Ulloa Suarez. *Indigenismo Americano*. Madrid: Ediciones Cultura Hispanica, 1961.

Barberena, Santiago I. *Historia de El Salvador*. Tomo I. 1914. Reprint, San Salvador: Ministerio de Educación de Publicaciones, 1966.

———."Estudios Demographicos." *La Quincena* IV, no. 43 (1904).

———. "Ladinos e Indios." *La Quincena* 5, no. 49 (April 11, 1905).

Barón Castro, Rodolfo. *La población de El Salvador*. San Salvador: Universidad Centroamericana José Simeón Cañas, 1942.

Barry, Tom. *El Salvador: a Country Guide*. Albuquerque, NM: Inter-Hemispheric Education Resource Center, 1990.

Basso, Keith. *Portraits of "The Whiteman."* New York and Cambridge: Cambridge University Press, 1979.

Bastos, Santiago and Manuela Camus. *Abriendo caminos: las organizaciones mayas desde el Nobel hasta el Acuerdo de derechos indígenas*. Guatemala: FLACSO, 1995.

———. *Entre el mecapal y el cielo: desarrollo del movimiento Maya en Guatemala*. Guatemala: FLACSO, 2003.

Berkhofer, Robert F. *The White Man's Indian*. New York: Random House, 1979.

Bird, Shawn L. and Philip J. Williams. "El Salvador: Revolt and Negotiated Transition." In Thomas Walker and Ariel Armony, eds., *Repression, Resistance, and Democratic Transition in Central America.* Wilmington, DE: Scholarly Resources, 2000.

Bordewich, Fergus M. *Killing the White Man's Indian: Reinventing Native Americans at the End of the Twentieth Century.* New York: Doubleday, 1996.

Brading, David A. "Manuel Gamio and Official Indigenismo in Mexico." *Bulletin of Latin American Research* 7, no. 1 (1988): 75–89.

Bremmer, Ian and Ray Taras, eds. *Nations and Politics in the Soviet Successor States.* Cambridge: Cambridge University Press, 1993.

Brignoli, Hector Pérez. "Indians, Communists, and Peasants: The 1932 Rebellion in El Salvador." In William Roseberry et al, eds., *Coffee, Society and Power in Latin America.* Baltimore and London: The Johns Hopkins University Press, 1995.

Brown, Timothy C. *The Real Contra War: Highlander Peasant Resistance in Nicaragua.* Norman: University of Oklahoma Press, 2001.

Browning, David. *El Salvador: Landscape and Society.* Oxford: Clarendon Press, 1971.

Brysk, Alison. "Acting Globally: Indian Rights and International Politics in Latin America." In Donna Lee Van Cott, ed., *Indigenous Peoples and Democracy in Latin America.* New York: The Inter-American Dialogue, 1995.

———. *From Tribal Village to Global Village: Indian Rights and International Relations in Latin America.* Stanford, CA: Stanford University Press, 2000.

Bunge, Carlos Octavio. *Nuestra América.* Buenos Aires: Casa Vaccaro, 1903.

Bustamente Maceo, Gregorio. *Historia militar de El Salvador.* San Salvador: Ministerio del Interior, 1951.

Cabrera, Edgar. *La cosmogonía Maya.* San José, Costa Rica: Liga Maya Internacional, 1992.

Calderón, Coronel Julio César. *Episodios nacionales: el indio Anastasio Aquino y el por qué de su rebelión en 1833 en Santiago Nonualco.* San Salvador: Imp. Moreno, 1957.

Carmack, R. M. *Harvest of Violence: The Maya Indians and the Guatemalan Crisis.* Norman: University of Oklahoma Press, 1983.

Casaus Arzú, Marta. *Guatemala: linaje y racismo.* San José, Costa Rica: FLACSO, 1995.

Caso, Alfonso. *Alfonso Caso: la comunidad indígena.* Mexico City: SepSetentas Diana, 1980.

Castañeda, Francisco. *El General Menéndez y sus victimarios.* San Salvador: Ministerio de Educación, Dirección de Publicaciones, 1966.

Censo Nacionales V de Población y IV de Vivienda, 1992, El Salvador. Tomo III, Departamento de Sonsonate, Características de la Vivienda, Cuadro 3.

Cevallos, José Antonio. *Recuerdos Salvadoreños.* Tomo I. 1891. Reprint, San Salvador: Ministerio de Educación, 1961.

Chapin, Mac. "The 500,000 Invisible Indians of El Salvador." *Cultural Survival Quarterly* 13, no. 3 (1994).

———. *La población indígena de El Salvador.* San Salvador: Ministerio de Educación, 1990.

Ching, Erik. "From Clientelism to Militarism: The State, Politics and Authoritarianism in El Salvador, 1840–1940." Ph.D. diss., University of California at Santa Barbara, 1997.

———. "In Search of the Party: The Communist Party, the Comintern, and the Peasant Rebellion of 1932 in El Salvador." *Americas* 55, no. 2 (1998).

Ching, Erik and Jussi Pakkasvirta. "Latin American Materials in the Comintern Archive." *Latin American Research Review* 35, no. 1 (2000).

Clara de Guevarra, Concepción, coorda. "El añil de los 'indios cheles.'" *América Indígena* 35, no. 4 (October 1975).

———. *Exploración Etnográfica: Departamento de Sonsonate.* San Salvador: Ministerio de Educación, 1975.

Cojtí Cuxil, Demetrio. *Configuración del pensamiento político del Pueblo Maya.* Quetzaltenango, Guatemala: Asociación de Escritores Mayances de Guatemala, 1991.

———. "Linguística e Idioma Maya en Guatemala," 1995.

———. [Waqi' Q'anil]. *Ub'aniik ri una'ooj uchomab'aal ri maya' tinamit/ Configuración del pensamiento político del Pueblo Maya, 2da. Parte.* Guatemala: CHOLSAMAJ-SPEM [Seminario Permanente de Estudios Mayas], 1995.

Collier, David, ed. *The New Authoritarianism in Latin America.* Princeton, NJ: Princeton University Press, 1979.

Comité Técnico Multisectorial para los Pueblos Indígenas de El Salvador. *Perfil de los Pueblos Indígenas de El Salvador.* CONCULTURA. San Salvador: Ministerio de Educación, 2003.

Construyendo un futuro para nuestro pasado: derechos del Pueblo Maya y el proceso de paz. Guatemala: Cholsamaj and Rajpopi' ri Mayab' Amaq', 1995.

Contreras, J. Daniel. *Una rebelión indígena en el partido de Totonicapán en 1820: el indio y la independencia.* Guatemala: Ministerio de Cultura y Deportes, 1991.

Cook, Curtis and Juan D. Lindau. *Aboriginal Rights and Self-Government.* Montreal: McGill-Queen's University Press, 2000.

Cotler, Julio. "A Structural-Historical Approach to the Breakdown of Democratic Institutions: Peru." In Juan J. Linz and Alfred Stepan, eds., *The Breakdown of Democratic Regimes: Latin America.* Baltimore, MD: Johns Hopkins University Press, 1978.

Dalton, Roqué. *Miguel Mármol.* Willimantic, CT: Curbstone Press, 1982.

Davis, Shelton H. "Agrarian Structure and Ethnic Resistance: The Indian in Guatemalan and Salvadoran National Politics." In Remo Guidieri, Francesco Fellizzi and Stanley J. Tambiah, eds., *Ethnicities and Nations: Processes of Interethnic Relations in Latin America, Southeast Asia and the Pacific.* Austin: University of Texas Press, 1988.

Dawson, Alexander S. "From Models for the Nation to Model Citizens: Indigenismo and the 'Revindication' of the Mexican Indian, 1920–40." *Journal of Latin American Studies* 30, no. 2 (May 1998).

De la Cadena, Marisol. *Indigenous Mestizos: The Politics of Race and Culture in Cuzco, Peru, 1919–1991.* Durham, NC: Duke University Press, 2000.

Degler, Carl N. *Neither Black Nor White: Slavery and Race Relations in Brazil and the United States.* New York: The MacMillan Company, 1971.

Deloria, Philip. *Playing Indian.* New Haven, CT: Yale University Press, 1998.

Deloria, Jr., Vine. *Custer Died for Your Sins: An Indian Manifesto*. New York: MacMillan, 1969.

Diamond, Larry, Juan J. Linz, and Seymour Martin Lipset, eds. *Democracy in Developing Countries: Latin America*. Boulder: Lynne Reinner Publishers, 1989.

Domínguez, Jorge I. *Race and Ethnicity in Latin America*. New York: Garland Publishing, Inc., 1994.

Dominguez Sosa, Julio Alberto. *Las tribus nonualcas y su caudillo Anastasio Aquino*. Costa Rica: EDUCA, 1984.

Drinnon, Richard. *Facing West: The Metaphysics of Indian Hating and Empire Building*. New York: Schocken Books, 1990.

Dunkerley, James. *Power in the Isthmus: A Political History of Modern Central America*. London, New York: Verso Press, 1988.

Durham, William H. *Scarcity and Survival in Central America: Ecological Origins of the Soccer War*. Stanford, CA: Stanford University Press, 1979.

Eckstein, Susan. "Power and Popular Protest in Latin America." In Susan Eckstein, ed., *Power and Popular Protest: Latin American Social Movements*. Berkeley: University of California Press, 1989.

England, Nora C. "Linguistics and Indigenous American Languages: Mayan Examples." *Journal of Latin American Anthropology* 1, no. 1 (1995).

Epp, Roger. "At the Wood's Edge: Toward a Theoretical Clearing for Indigenous Diplomacies in International Relations." In Robert M. A. Crawford and Darryl S. L. Jarvis, eds., *International Relations—Still an American Social Science?: Toward Diversity in International Thought*. New York: SUNY Press, 2001.

Escalante Arce, Pedro Antonio. "Apuntes sobre presencia africana en la historia Salvadoreña." Unpublished manuscript, n.d.

Escobar, Arturo and Sonia E. Alvarez, eds. *The Making of Social Movements in Latin America: Identity, Strategy and Democracy*. Boulder, CO: Westview Press, 1992.

Feliu Cruz, Guillermo. *Un esquema de la evolución social en Chile en el siglo XIX*. Santiago, Chile: Editorial Nascimento, 1941.

Fernández, Florestan. *The Negro in Brazilian Society*. New York: Columbia University Press, 1969.

Field, Les W. "Blood and Traits: Preliminary Observations on the Analysis of Mestizo and Indigenous Identities in Latin America vs. the U.S." *Journal of Latin American Anthropology* 7, no. 1 (2002).

———. *The Grimace of Macho Ratón: Artisans, Identity and Nation in Late-Twentieth Century Nicaragua*. Durham, NC: Duke University Press, 1999.

———. "Post-Sandinista Ethnic Identities in Western Nicaragua." *American Anthropologist* 100, no. 2 (1998).

———. "Who Are the Indians? Reconceptualizing Indigenous Identity, Resistance and the Role of Social Science in Latin America." *Latin American Research Review* 29, no. 3 (1994).

Findji, María Teresa. "From Resistance to Social Movement: The Indigenous Authorities Movement in Colombia." In Escobar and Alvarez, eds., *The Making of Social Movements in Latin America*.

Fishel, Kimbra L. "The United Nations Involvement in the Salvadoran Peace Process." *World Affairs* (Spring 1998).

Fischer, Edward F. "Cultural Logic and Maya Identity: Rethinking Constructivism and Essentialism." *Current Anthropology* 40, no. 4 (August–October 1999).

Flores, Fidel. "Tenemos 503 años de resistencia." Unpublished leaflet for the Asociación Coordinadora de Comunidades Indígenas de El Salvador (ACCIES). Sonsonate, El Salvador, 1994(?).

Foote, Henry Grant, Mrs. *Recollections of Central America and the West Coast of Africa*. London: T. C. Newby, 1869.

Foucault, Michel. *The Archaeology of Knowledge and the Discourse on Language*. New York: Pantheon Books, 1972.

———. *The Order of Things: An Archaeology of the Human Sciences*. 1970. Reprint, New York: Vintage Books, 1994.

———. *Power/Knowledge: Selected Interviews and Other Writings, 1972–1977*. New York: Pantheon Books, 1980.

Fowler, William R. "Cacao, Indigo, and Coffee: Cash Crops in the History of El Salvador." *Research in Economic Anthropology* 8 (1987).

———. *The Cultural Evolution of Ancient Nahua Civilizations: The Pipil-Nicarao of Central America*. Norman, OK: University of Oklahoma Press, 1989.

———. "La distribución prehistórica e histórica de los pipiles." *Mesoamerica* 4, no. 6. (December 1983).

Friedlander, Judith. *Being Indian in Hueyapan: A Study of Forced Identity in Contemporary Mexico*. New York: St. Martin's Press, 1975.

Gall, Francis. "Conquista de El Salvador y fundación del primigenio San Salvador, 1524." *Antropología e Historia de Guatemala* 18, no. 1 (1966).

Gallegos, Aaron. "The Reconquest of El Salvador." *Sojourner Magazine* (May–June, 1997).

Gamio, Manuel. *Forjando patria*. 1916. Reprint, Mexico: Editorial Porrúa, 1960.

Garcia de Palacio, Diego. *Letter to the King of Spain: being a description of the ancient provinces of Guazacapan, Izalco, Cuscatlan, and Chiquimula, in the Audiencia of Guatemala, with an account of the languages, customs, and religion of their aboriginal inhabitants, and a description of the ruins of Copan*. 1576. Translated and with notes by Ephraim G. Squier, with additional notes by Alexander von Frantzius and Frank E. Comparato. Reprint, Culver City, CA: Labyrinthos, 1985.

Gavida, Francisco. "El Porvenir de la América Latina." *La Quincena* 1, no. 1 (1903).

Geertz, Clifford. "Thick Description: Toward an Interpretive Theory of Culture." In *The Interpretation of Cultures*. New York: Basic Books, Inc., 1973.

Gong, Gerrit W. *The Standard of Civilization in International Society*. Oxford: Clarendon Press, 1984.

González Navarro, Moisés. "Las ideas raciales de los científicos." *Historia Mexicana* 37, no. 4 (1988).

Gordon, Beverly. *Identity in Cloth: Continuity and Survival in Guatemalan Textiles*. Madison: University of Wisconsin Press, 1993.

Gould, Jeffrey L. "Gender, Politics, and the Triumph of Mestizaje in Early 20th Century Nicaragua." *Journal of Latin American Anthropology* 2, no. 1 (1996).

———. "'Vana Ilusión!' The highlands Indians and the myth of Nicaragua mestiza, 1880–1925." *Hispanic American Historical Review* 73, no. 3 (1993).

Gould, Stephen J. *The Mismeasure of Man*. New York: W. W. Norton & Company, 1996.

Government of Guatemala and the Unidad Revolucionara Nacional Guatemalteca, Peace Accord on Indigenous Identity and Rights (1995). Available at: http://www.c-r.org/accord/guat/accord2/indigen.shtml.

Graham, Richard, ed. *The Idea of Race in Latin America, 1870–1940*. Austin: University of Texas Press, 1990.

Grandin, Greg. *The Blood of Guatemala: A History of Race and Nation*. Durham and London: Duke University Press, 2000.

Grenier, Yvon. *The Emergence of Insurgency in El Salvador: Ideology and Political Will*. Pittsburgh: Pittsburgh University Press, 1999.

Guatemala General Administration of Statistics. Introduction, section (f). *Sexto Censo de Población 1950*. Guatemala: Dirección General de Estadística, xi–xii.

Gudmundson, Lowell. *Central America, 1821–1887: Liberalism before Liberal Reform*. Tuscaloosa: University of Alabama Press, 1995.

Gutierrez y Ulloa, Antonio. *Ensayo historico-politico del Rno. de la Nueva Calacia con notas políticas y estadísticas de la Provincia de Guadalaxara*. 1816. Reprint, Guadalajara, Jalisco, Mexico, 1983.

———. *Estado general de la Provincia de San Salvador: Reyno de Guatemala*. 1807. Reprint, San Salvador: Imprenta Nacional, 1926, 10–11.

Hale, Charles A. *The Transformation of Liberalism in Late Nineteenth-Century Mexico*. Princeton, NJ: Princeton University Press, 1989.

Hale, Charles R. "Cultural Politics of Identity in Latin America." *Annual Review of Anthropology* 26 (1997): 567–90.

———. "*Mestizaje*, Hybridity, and the Cultural Politics of Difference in Post-Revolutionary Central America." *Journal of Latin American Anthropology* 2, no. 1 (1996).

———. *Resistance and Contradiction: Miskito Indians and the Nicaraguan State, 1894-1987*. Stanford, CA: Stanford University Press, 1994.

Hanchard, Michael George. *Orpheus and Power: the Movimiento Negro of Rio de Janeiro and Sao Paulo, Brazil, 1945–1988*. Princeton, NJ: Princeton University Press, 1994.

Hanke, Lewis. *Aristotle and the American Indians: A Study of Race Prejudice in the Modern World*. Chicago: Henry Regnery Company, 1959.

———. *The Spanish Struggle for Justice in the Conquest of America*. Philadelphia: University of Pennsylvania Press, 1949.

Haskett, Robert. *Indigenous Rulers: An Ethnohistory of Town Government in Colonial Cuernavaca*. Albuquerque: University of New Mexico Press, 1991.

Helg, Aline. *Our Rightful Share: The Afro-Cuban Struggle for Equality, 1886–1912*. Raleigh: University of North Carolina Press, 1995.

———. "Race in Argentina and Cuba, 1880–1930: Theory, Policies, and Popular Reaction." In Richard Graham, ed., *The Idea of Race in Latin America*.

Hendrickson, Carol. "Images of the Indian in Guatemala: the Role of Indigenous Dress in Indian and Ladino Constructions." In Greg Urban and Joel Sherzer, eds., *Nation-States and Indians in Latin America*.

————. "Selling Guatemala: Maya Export Products in U.S. Mail-Order Catalogues." In David Howes, ed., *Cross-Cultural Consumption: Global Markets, Local Realities*. New York: Routledge, 1997.

————. *Weaving Identities: Construction of Dress and Self in a Highland Guatemalan Town*. Austin: University of Texas Press, 1995.

Herrera Vega, Adolfo. *El indio occidental de El Salvador y su incorporación social por la escuela*. Santa Ana, El Salvador, 1935.

Hill, Jane H. "In Neca Gobierno de Puebla: Mexicano Penetrations of the Mexican State." In Greg Urban and Joel Sherzer, eds., *Nation-States and Indians in Latin America*, 72–94.

Hobsbawm, E. J. *Nations and Nationalism since 1780*. Cambridge: Cambridge University Press, 1990.

Horowitz, Donald L. *A Democratic South Africa? Constitutional Engineering in a Divided Society*. 1985. Reprint, Berkeley: University of California Press, 1991.

Howard, David. *Coloring the Nation: Race and Ethnicity in the Dominican Republic*. Boulder, CO: Lynne Reinner Publishers, 2001.

Hunt, Michael H. *Ideology and U.S. Foreign Policy*. New Haven, CT: Yale University Press, 1987.

Huntington, Samuel. *Political Order in Changing Societies*. New Haven, CT: Yale University Press, 1968.

Hupp, Bruce Foster. "The Urban Indians of Quezaltenango, Guatemala." Unpublished master's thesis, University of Texas at Austin, 1969.

Ingenieros, José. "La formación de una raza argentina." *Revista de Filosofía* 11 (1915).

————. *Por la unión Latino Americana*. Buenos Aires: L. J. Rosso y Cia, 1922.

————. *Sociologia Argentina*. Buenos Aires: Editorial Losada, 1946.

Instituto Indigenista Nacional. *Qué es el indio?* Guatemala: Ministerio de Educación, n.d.

Ivison, Duncan, Paul Patton, and Will Sanders, eds. *Political Theory and the Rights of Indigenous Peoples*. Cambridge: Cambridge University Press, 2000.

Jackson, Jean E. "Being and Becoming an Indian in the Vaupés." In Urban and Sherzer, eds., *Nation-States and Indians in Latin America*.

Keck, Margaret and Kathryn Sikkink. *Activists Beyond Borders: Advocacy Networks in International Politics*. Ithaca, NY: Cornell University Press, 1998.

Kincaid, A. Douglas. "Peasants into Rebels: Community and Class in Rural El Salvador." In David H. Levine, ed., *Constructing Culture and Power in Latin America*. Ann Arbor, MI: University of Michigan Press, 1993.

Knight, Alan. "Racism, Revolution and *Indigenismo*: Mexico, 1910–1940." In Richard Graham, ed., *The Idea of Race in Latin America*, 1990.

Krystal, M. "Cultural Revitalization and Tourism at the Morería Nima' K'iche'." *Ethnology* 39, no. 3 (2000).

Lainfiesta, Franciso. *Apuntamientos para la historia de Guatemala*. 1865. Reprint, Sociedad de Geografia e Historia de Guatemala, 1975.

Laitin, David. "The Implications of Constructivism for Constructing Ethnic Fractionalization Indices." *Symposium: Cumulative Findings in the Study of Ethnic Politics*. American Political Science Association, Comparative Politics Newsletter (Winter 2001).

Las Casas, Bartolomé de. *In Defense of the Indians: The Defense of the Most Reverend Lord Don Fray Bartolomé de Las Casas, of the Order of Preachers, Late Bishop of Chiapa.* Circa 1550. Reprint, translated and edited by Stafford Poole. DeKalb, IL: Northern Illinois University Press, 1992.

Lauria-Santiago, Aldo. *An Agrarian Republic: Commercial Agriculture and the Politics of Peasant Communities in El Salvador, 1823–1914.* Pittsburgh: University of Pittsburgh Press, 1999.

———. "An Agrarian Republic: Production, Politics and the Peasantry in El Salvador, 1840–1920." Ph.D. diss., University of Chicago, 1992.

———. "Land, Community, and Revolt in Indian Izalco, 1860–1900." *Hispanic American Historical Review*, 79, no. 3 (August 1999).

Lauria-Santiago, Aldo and Jeffrey L. Gould. "They Call Us Thieves and Steal Our Wage": Toward a Reinterpretation of the Salvadoran Rural Mobilization, 1929–1931." *The Hispanic American Historical Review*, 84, no. 2 (May 2004).

Lemarchand, René. *Burundi: Ethnocide as Discourse and Practice.* New York: Woodrow Wilson Center and Cambridge University Press, 1996.

Lindo-Fuentes, Héctor. *Weak Foundations: The Economy of El Salvador in the Nineteenth Century.* Berkeley, Los Angeles, Oxford: University of California Press, 1990.

Lipset, Seymour Martin and Aldo Solari. *Elites in Latin America.* New York: Oxford University Press, 1967.

Little, Walter. "Getting Organized: Political and Economic Dilemmas for Maya Handicrafts Vendors." Paper presented to the XXIV International Congress of Latin American Studies Association, Dallas, Texas, 2003.

Lovell, W. George. *A Beauty That Hurts: Life and Death in Guatemala.* Toronto: Between the Lines, 1995.

MacLeod, Murdo. *Spanish Central America: A Socioeconomic History, 1520–1720.* Berkeley, Los Angeles, London: University of California Press, 1973.

Mallon, Florencia E. "Constructing mestizaje in Latin America: Authenticity, Marginality, and Gender in the Claiming of Ethnic Identities." *Journal of Latin American Anthropology* 2, no. 1 (1996).

———. *Peasant and Nation.* Berkeley: University of California Press, 1994.

Marroquín, Alejandro D. *Panchimalco: investigación sociológica.* San Salvador: Ministerio de Educación, 1959.

———. "El problema indígena en El Salvador." *América Indígena* 35, no. 4 (Oct.–Dec. 1975).

———. *San Pedro Nonualco.* San Salvador: Editorial Universitaria, 1962.

Martin, Percy F. *Salvador of the Twentieth Century.* London: Edward Arnold, 1911.

Martínez Peláez, Severo. *Motines de indios: la violencia colonial en Centroamerica y Chiapas.* Mexico: Universidad Autonoma de Puebla, 1976.

Masferrer, Alberto. "En defenso de los Chinos" *Patria*, October 22 and 23, 1931.

———. *Paginas escogidas.* 1923, 1927. Reprint, San Salvador: Ministerio de Educación Departamento Editorial, 1961.

MacLeod, Murdo J. *Spanish Central America: A socioeconomic history, 1520–1720.* Berkeley, Los Angeles, London: University of California Press, 1973.

MacNaught, A. Roy. "Horrors of Communism in Central America." *The Central American Bulletin* 181 (March 1932).

McCreery, David. "Wage Labor, Free Labor, and Vagrancy Laws: The Transition to Capitalism in Guatemala, 1920–1945." In William Roseberry, Lowell Gudmundson, and Mario Samper Kutschbach, eds., *Coffee, Society and Power in Latin America*. Baltimore and London: The Johns Hopkins University Press, 1995.

Menchú, Rigoberta Tum. *I, Rigoberta Menchú: An Indian Woman in Guatemala*. 1983. Reprint, New York: Verso, 1993.

Méndez, Joaquín. *Los sucesos comunistas en El Salvador*. San Salvador: Funes and Ungo, 1932.

Menendez, Don Isidro, ed. *Recopilación de las Leyes del Salvador, en Centro-America*. Second edition. San Salvador: Imprenta Nacional, 1821–1855.

Mens, Alberto. *Recopilación de disposiciones legales vígentes relacionadas con la agricultura*. Santa Tecla: n.p., 1904.

Ministerio de Educacion. *Historia de El Salvador*. 2 Vols. San Salvador: Ministerio de Educacion, 1994.

Pan-American Union. *Seventh International Conference of American States*. Montevideo, Uruguay. Vol. 7. Baltimore, MD: The Sun Book and Job Printing Office, 1933.

Mires, Fernando. *El discurso de la indianidad*. Quito, Ecuador: Ediciones Abya-Yala, 1991.

Molina Enríquez, Andrés. *Los grandes problemas nacionales*. 1909. Reprint, Mexico: Ediciones Era, 1978.

Montes Mozo, Santiago. *Etnohistoria de El Salvador: el guachival centroamericano*. San Salvador: Ministerio de Educación, 1977.

Montes, Segundo. *El Compadrazgo: una estructura de poder en El Salvador*. San Salvador: Universidad Centroamericana José Simeón Cañas, 1979.

———. "Los indígenas en El Salvador." In *Boletín de Ciencias Económicas y Sociales*. San Salvador: Universidad Centroamericana José Simeon Cañas, 1985.

Montes, Segundo and Juan José Garcia Vasquez. *Salvadoran Migration to the United States: An Exploratory Study*. Washington, D.C.: Hemispheric Migration Project, Center for Immigration Policy and Refugee Assistance, Georgetown University, 1988.

Montgomery, Tommie Sue. *Revolution in El Salvador: Origins and Evolution*. 2nd edition. Boulder, CO: Westview Press, 1995.

Morner, Magnus, ed. *Race and Class in Latin America*. New York and London: Columbia University Press, 1970.

Murray, Kevin. *El Salvador: Peace on Trial*. Oxford: Oxfam UK and Ireland, 1997.

Nash, June. "Cultural Resistance and Class Consciousness in Bolivian Tin-Mining Communities." In Susan Eckstein, ed., *Power and Popular Protest: Latin American Social Movements*. Berkeley and Los Angeles: University of California Press, 1989.

Nelson, Diane. *A Finger in the Wound: Body Politics in Quincentennial Guatemala*. Berkeley: University of California Press, 1999.

O'Donnell, Guillermo and Philippe C. Schmitter. *Transitions from Authoritarian Rule: Tentative Conclusions about Uncertain Democracies*. Volume 4. Baltimore and London: The Johns Hopkins University Press, 1986.

Omi, Michael and Howard Winant. *Racial Formation in the United States from the 1960s to the 1980s*. New York and London: Routledge and Kegan Paul, 1986.

Peña, Román. "Bosquejo." *La Quincena* 8, no. 87 (November 15, 1906), 78.

Perera, Victor. *The Cross and the Pear Tree: A Sephardic Journey*. New York: Knopf, 1995.

———. *Rites: A Guatemalan Boyhood*. San Francisco: Mercury House, 1994.

Pérez de Barradas, José. *Los Mestizos de América*. Madrid: Aguirrebeña, 1948.

Pierson, Donald. *Negroes in Brazil: A Study of Race Contact at Bahia*. Chicago: The University of Chicago Press, 1942.

Pimentel, Francisco. "Memoria sobre las causas que han originado la situación actual de la raza indígena de México y medios de remediarla." 1864. Reprinted in *Dos Obras de Francisco Pimentel*. Xoco, CP, Mexico: Consejo Nacional Para la Cultura y las Artes, 1995.

Popkin, Margaret. *Peace Without Justice: Obstacles to Building the Rule of Law in El Salvador*. University Park: Pennsylvania State University Press, 2000.

Powell, T. G. "Mexican Intellectuals and the Indian Question, 1876–1911." *Hispanic American Historical Review* 48, no. 1 (February 1968).

Prizel, Ilya. *National Identity and Foreign Policy : Nationalism and Leadership in Poland, Russia and Ukraine*. New York and Cambridge: Cambridge University Press, 1998.

República de Nicaragua. Dirección General de Estadística y Censo. Cuadro. No. 18, *Censo General de Población de la República de Nicaragua, Mayo 1950*. Managua, Nicaragua: n.p., August 1954.

República de Panamá. "Cuadro No. 1: Población Total de la Provincia de Panamá, por Distrito." *Censo de Poblacion 1940* Vol. I. Contraloría General de la República. [Ciudad de Panamá]: Oficina del Censo, 1943–45.

Reyes, Rafael. *Nociones de historia de el Salvador*. Third Edition. San Salvador: Imprenta R. Reyes, 1920.

Riva, Pedro Geoffroy. *El Español que hablamos en El Salvador*. San Salvador: Ministerio de Educación, 1969.

———. *La lengua salvadoreña*. San Salvador: Ministerio de Educación, 1978.

Rivas, Ramón D. *Pueblos indígenas y garífuna de Honduras: una caracterización*. Tegucigalpa: Editorial Guaymuras, 1993.

Roberts, Kenneth M. "Beyond Romanticism: Social Movements and the Study of Political Change in Latin America." *Latin American Research Review* 32, no. 2 (1997).

Roseberry, William, Lowell Gudmundson and Mario Samper Kutschbach eds. *Coffee, Society and Power in Latin America*. Baltimore and London: The Johns Hopkins Press, 1995.

Rosenberg, Tina. *Children of Cain: Violence and the Violent in Latin America*. New York: Penguin Press, 1992.

Rus, Jan. "Whose Caste War? Indians, Ladinos, and the Chiapas "Caste War" of 1869." In Murdo J. MacLeod and Robert Wasserstrom, eds., *Spaniards and Indians in Southeastern Mesoamerica: Essays on the History of Ethnic Relations*. Lincoln and London: University of Nebraska Press, 1983.

Sarabia, Justina, ed. *José Vasconcelos*. Madrid: Ediciones de Cultura Hispánica, 1989.

Schlesinger, Jorge. *Revolución Comunista*. Guatemala: Union Tipografica Castañeda, Avila y Cia, 1946.

Scott, James. *Domination and the Arts of Resistance: Hidden Transcripts*. New Haven, CT: Yale University Press, 1990.

Seed, Patricia. "'Are These Not Also Men?': The Indians' Humanity and Capacity for Spanish Civilization." *Latin American Studies* 25, no. 3 (October 1993).

Seminario sobre problemas indígenas de Centroamérica. Celebrado en San Salvador, El Salvador 27 de junio a 2 de julio de 1955. Mexico: Ediciones del Instituto Indigenista Interamericano, 1955.

Shaw, Karena. "Leviathan's Angels: Indigenous Peoples and the Limits of the Political." Ph.D. diss., Johns Hopkins University, 1999.

Sikkink, Kathryn. *Ideas and Institutions: Developmentalism in Brazil and Argentina*. Ithaca, NY: Cornell University Press, 1991.

———. "The Origins and Continuity of International Human Rights Policies in the United States and Western Europe." In Judith Goldstein and Robert Keohane, eds., *Ideas and Foreign Policy: Beliefs, Institutions, and Political Change*. Ithaca, NY: Cornell University Press, 1993.

Skidmore, Thomas E. *Black into White: Race and Nationality in Brazilian Thought*. New York: Oxford University Press, 1974.

Smith, Anthony. *The Ethnic Origins of Nations*. Oxford: Blackwell, 1986.

———. "The Nation: Invented, Imagined, Reconstructed?" *Millennium: Journal of International Studies* 20, no. 3 (1991).

Smith, Carol A. "Local History in Global Context: Social and Economic Transitions in Western Guatemala." In David H. Levine, ed., *Constructing Culture and Power in Latin America*. Ann Arbor: University of Michigan Press, 1993.

Smith, Carol A., ed. *Guatemalan Indians and the State: 1540–1988*. Austin: University of Texas Press, 1990.

———. "Origins of the National Question in Guatemala: A Hypothesis." In Carol Smith, ed., *Guatemalan Indians and the State*.

Smith, Richard Chase. "Liberal Ideology and Indigenous Communities in Post-Independence Peru." *Journal of International Affairs* 36, no. 1 (1982).

Stabb, Martin S. "Indigenism and Racism in Mexican Thought: 1857–1911." *Journal of Inter-American Studies* 1 (1959).

Steinberg, Stephen. *The Ethnic Myth: Race, Ethnicity and Class in America*. Boston: Beacon Press, 1989.

Stephens, John L. *Incidentes de Viaje en Centroamerica, Chiapas y Yucatán*. Vols. I and II. 1841. Reprint, Editorial Universitario Centroamericana, 1971.

Stern, Steve J. "Feudalism, Capitalism and the World System in the Perspective of Latin America and the Caribbean." In Frederick Cooper et al, eds., *Confronting Historical Paradigms: Peasants, Labor and the Capitalist World System in Africa and Latin America*. Madison: University of Wisconsin Press, 1993.

Stern, Steve J., ed. *Resistance, Rebellion and Consciousness in the Andean Peasant World: 18th to 20th centuries*. Madison: University of Wisconsin Press, 1987.

Thompson, George. *Narrative of an Official Visit to Guatemala from Mexico*. London: J. Murray, 1829.

Ticas, Pedro and Marta Benavides. *Presencia indígena en El Salvador*. Mexico: Praxis Ediciones, 1993.

Tilley, Virginia. "Neo-Confucianism: The Culturalist Explanation for the East Asian Tigers." *Asian Thought and Society: An International Review* 21 (1996): 61–62.

―――. "New Help or New Hegemony? The Transnational Indigenous People's Movement and 'Being Indian' in El Salvador." *Journal of Latin American Studies* 34, no. 3 (2002).

―――. "The Terms of the Debate: Untangling Language About Ethnicity and Ethnic Movements." *Ethnic and Racial Studies* 29 no. 3 (July 1997).

Tilley, Virginia and Eric Ching. "Indians, the Military, and the 1932 Rebellion in El Salvador." *Journal of Latin American Studies* 30, no. 1 (1998).

Tzian, Leopoldo. *Mayas y Ladinos en cifras: el caso de Guatemala*. Guatemala: Cholsamaj, 1990.

Ugarte, Manuel. *The Destiny of a Continent*. New York: Alfred A. Knopf, 1925.

―――. *El porvenir de la América Latina*. Valencia: F. Sempere y Compañia, 1910.

Urban, Greg and Joel Sherzer. *Nation-States and Indians in Latin America*. Austin: University of Texas Press, 1991.

Van Cott, Donna Lee, ed. *Indigenous Peoples and Democracy in Latin America*. New York: The Inter-American Dialogue, 1995.

Vasconcelos, José. *Aspects of Mexican Civilization*. Chicago: University of Chicago Press.

―――. "Indología." 1926. Reprinted in Justina Sarabia, ed., *José Vasconcelos*.

―――. 1926. "Prólogo a la obra 'Breve historia de México.'" 1938. Reprinted in Justina Sarabia, ed., *José Vasconcelos*.

―――."La raza cósmica." 1925. Reprinted in Justina Sarabia, ed., *José Vasconcelos*.

Vasconcelos, José and Manuel Gamio. *Aspects of Mexican Civilization*. Chicago: The University of Chicago Press, 1926.

Vitoria, Francisco de. *Relectio de Indis: carta magna de los indios*. 1539. Reprint, Madrid: Consejo Superior de Investigaciones Científicas, 1989.

Warren, Kay. *Indigenous Movements and Their Critics: Pan-Maya Activism in Guatemala*. Princeton, NJ: Princeton University Press, 1998.

―――. "Transforming memories and histories: the meanings of ethnic resurgence for Mayan Indians." In Alfred Stepan, ed., *Americas: New Interpretive Essays*. New York: Oxford University Press, 1992.

White, Alastair. *El Salvador*. London and Tonbridge: Ernest Benn Limited, 1973.

Whitten, Norman. *Sacha Runa: Ethnicity and Adaptation of Ecuadorian Jungle Quichua*. Urbana: University of Illinois Press, 1976.

Williams, Robert G. *States and Social Evolution: Coffee and the Rise of National Governments in Central America*. Chapel Hill, NC: University of North Carolina Press, 1994.

Wilson, Everett Alan. "The Crisis of National Integration in El Salvador, 1919-1935." Unpublished Ph.D. diss., Stanford University, 1970.

Wilmer, Franke. *The Indigenous Voice in World Politics: From Time Immemorial*. Newbury Park, CA: Sage, 1993.

Winant, Howard. *Racial Conditions: Politics, Theory, Comparisons*. Minneapolis: University of Minnesota Press, 1994.

―――. "Rethinking Race in Brazil." In Domínguez, ed. *Race and Ethnicity in Latin America*, 1994.

Wolf, Eric. *Sons of the Shaking Earth*. Chicago: University of Chicago Press, 1959.

―――. "The Vicissitudes of the Closed Corporate Community." *American Ethnologist* 13 (1986): 325–29.

Wright, Winthrop R. *Cafe con Leçhe: Race, Class and National Image in Venezuela.* Austin: University of Texas Press, 1990.

Young, M. Crawford. *The African Colonial State in Comparative Perspective.* New Haven and London: Yale University Press, 1997.

Zamosc, Leon. "The landing that never was: Canadian marines and the Salvadorean insurrection of 1932." *Canadian Journal of Latin American and Caribbean Studies* 9, no. 21 (1987).

INDEX

Academia de la Lengua Maya Ki'che', 251n27
Adams, Richard, 173, 217, 243n13, 265n9
Alcalde del comun, 111–13, 168
Alianza Republicana Nacionalista (ARENA), 236–37, 273n26
Alfaro, Julio, 229, 236
Alvarado, Diego de, 2, 6
Alvarado, Pedro de, 1–6, 91, 241n1, 252n1
Alvarenga, Patricia, 121–22, 127, 138, 257n59, 258n64, 258n66, 259n79
Ama, Feliciano, 100, 112, 146–50, 157, 261n26, 261n31, 261n33
Amaya Amaya, Miguel, 245n12, 245n16, 251n19
Ament, Gail, 251n27
Anderson, Thomas, 137, 139, 149, 152–54, 159–60, 164, 259n1, 262n51, 262n53, 263n58
Andolina, Robert, 244
Apaches (native Americans), 11, 47, 249n31
Aquino, Anastasio, 100, 114–21, 123–24, 149, 256n32, 256n47
Arabs, 53, 59, 192, 249n30, 271n64. *See also* Palestinians

Araujo, Arturo, 143, 205, 213
Arneson, Eric, 247n12
Asociación Nacional de Indígenas Salvadoreños (ANIS), 37–39, 101, 171, 233, 235–37, 261n26, 273n25
Atlacatl, 84–85, 91–95, 100, 194, 197, 204
Atonal, 91. *See also* Atlacatl
Aztec, 2, 4, 35, 86–87, 89–90, 98, 101, 252
Barberena, Salvador I., 175, 179, 204, 252n8, 265n13, 265n14, 270n43
Barón Castro, Rodolfo, 107, 132, 172, 210, 216, 264n7, 265n8
Basso, Keith, 247n20
Birth records, 174–86, 189, 208, 262n37. *See also* Census, Civil Registry
Blacks (in El Salvador), 208–11
Brignoli, Héctor Pérez, 139, 152, 257n64
Browning, David, 258n71
Brysk, Alison, 243n13, 244n15, 253n19, 272n12
Buezo, Rudolfo, 158–59
Bustamente Maceo, Gregorio, 158

Cacao, 90, 110; production in Izalco region, 2, 87, 89, 110, 129, 165, 254n12

Cacaopera (language), 35, 78

Cacaopera (town), 35, 185

Calderón, Tomás (Colonel), 152, 154, 260n15

Cañas, José Miguel, 251n29

Casaus Arzú, Marta, 257n61

Caso, Alfonso, 189, 196

Caste. See Race

Catholic Church, 37, 112, 131, 227, 265

Census, racial notations in Brazil, 270n50; in Central America, 186–87; in El Salvador, 14–15, 31, 54, 84, 134, 170–74, 182, 186, 210, 238, 262n37, 270n50; in Guatemala, 76, 187, 249n1, 251n28, 265n8, 266n21; in Honduras, 186; in Mexico, 186–87; in Nicaragua, 186–88, 266n20; in Panama, 186, 266n19. See also Birth Records, Civil Registry

Cevallos, José Antonio, 116, 118, 255n32, 256n47

Chapin, Mac, 32, 171, 217, 245n6

Chavez, Adrian Inez, 251n27

Cherokee, 46

Chinese, 211–15. See also Sinophobia

Ching, Erik, 144, 159, 256n32, 260n14, 264n1

Civil Guard. See Guardia Civil

Civil Registry, 31, 170, 174, 178, 190, 210, 245n18, 265n14; in Guatemala, 187. See also Birth Records, Census

Civil War, 9, 27, 31–32, 36, 96, 139, 237; reconstruction following, 219–24

Clara de Guevarra, Concepción, 217, 272n16

Coffee, 50, 114, 153; conditions in western zone of, 31–32, 35, 122, 143–44, 160, 162, 190; debt and production of, 134–36; labor for, 48, 68, 121, 129; production of, 128, 132, 148, 166, 198, 254n14, 271n61; state measures to increase, 111, 131; violence relating to production of, 138, 143, 153, 157, 160, 263n65

Cofradias, 37, 111–14, 147, 165–66, 168, 245n16

Cojtí Cuxil, Demetrio, 61, 77

Cojutepeque, 118, 122, 124, 126–27, 183, 186, 257n59

Communists, 9, 21, 79, 117, 132, 214, 219–20, 262n40; involvement in 1932 uprising, 31, 71, 138–40, 142–52, 154–61, 163, 165–66, 260n15; Salvadoran Communist Party, 142–46

Comunidad, abolition of, 128–30, 132, 136, 142–43, 166, 255n21, 258n68, 258n74; ethno-political function of, 111, 113–14

Conference of Interamerican States, 215

Congreso Continental de Pueblos Indígenas (Quito), 249n31

Consejo Coordinadora Nacional de Indígenas Salvadoreños (CCNIS), 56, 171, 229, 232–37; composition profile, 39–41

Consejo Nacional de Cultura y Artes (CONCULTURA), 33–34, 41, 82, 171, 222–23, 229, 236–38, 251n29

Coordinadora Indígena Centroamericana (CICA), 233–35

Cortéz, Hernando, 2–4, 252n1

Cortéz y Larraz, Pedro, 106, 109, 118–19

Cosmic Race doctrine. See Race

Cree (native Americans), 249n31

Cruz, Guillermo Feliu, 192

Cuisnahuat, 178, 181–82, 263n70

Culture of Peace Program (COPP). See UNESCO

Cuscatlán (modern department), 122; birth records in, 175, 183, 185–86

Cuscatlán (pre-Spanish city), 2–3, 5–6,
35, 106, 113; pre-Spanish history
of, 86–90, 101; reimagined for
nationalist discourse, 84–85,
91–95, 104, 204, 238; reimagined
for tourism, 96–97

D'Aubuisson, Roberto, 273
Dalton, Roqué, 30
Degler, Carl, 58, 247n17, 248n29
Deloria, Philip, 91
Día de la Raza, 199
Domínguez Sosa, Julio Alberto,
116–17, 255n32
Dress. *See* Nahua and Maya
Dunkerley, James, 139

Education Ministry, Salvadoran
Government, 33, 78, 218–19
Escalante, Pedro, 26, 211, 214
Esquino Lizco, Adrian, 37–38, 57, 233,
235, 245n18
Ethnicity, 14, 21, 32, 83, 242n5,
243n13; census surveys of, 173,
186; class paradigm and, 55,
248n24; mestizo, 30; Maya model
for Nahua, 62, 76, 78, 98, 101;
paradigm for indigeneity, 52,
58–59; Salvadoran indigenous, 8–9,
23, 35, 169, 238, 257n59; state-
building and, 16–18. *See also*
Indian, Indigeneity, Mestizaje
European Union (EU), 24, 33, 171,
232–36, 273n20, 273n25

Farabundo Martí Liberación Nacional
(FMLN), 220
Field, Les, xi, 249n2
Fonseca, Don Pedro S., 265n8
Foote, Mrs. Henry, 104
Fowler, William, 87, 252n1, 252n10,
254n12
Foucault, Michel, 18–19
Foundation for Social and Economic
Development in Central America
(FUNDESCA), 273n20
Friedlander, Judith, 243n10

Galindo, John, 172, 264n6
Gamio, Manuel, 191, 196–97, 199,
201, 203, 205, 216, 267n7,
268n18, 268n19
Garcia de Palacio, Diego, 89
Gavida, Francisco, 189
Gould, Jeff, 21–22, 139, 187, 260n9,
270n8
Grandin, Greg, 243n13, 250n6
Guardia Civil, 132, 164, 262n53
Guatemala, 2–6, 21, 101, 109, 115,
118–20, 209, 216, 249n4, 253n5,
255n25; census, 171–72, 186–88,
190, 249n1; indigeneity and racial
thought in, 31, 36, 47, 49, 60–63,
108, 250n12, 254n9, 257n61,
261n29, 270n43, 48; mestizaje in,
197. *See also* Maya
Gudmundson, Lowell, 257n61
Gutierrez y Ulloa, Antonio, 104–5,
119, 172, 209

Hale, Charles R., xi, 187–88, 243n13
Halle, Louis J., 7
Haughney, Diane, 244n15
Hendrickson, Carol, 243n13, 250n13
Honduras, 64, 97, 120, 122; Conquest
Indian in, 91; racial doctrine in,
187, 197; "yellow peril" in, 211
Hoopa (native Americans), 46
Horowitz, Donald L., 242n3
Hupp, Bruce Foster, 251n27, 255n25

Indian, as identity discourse, 11–24;
census counts of, 186, 266n19;
class dimensions of, 55–58,
248n24; Conquest Indians, 91,
197; differing definitions of, 42–43,
82; ethnic dimensions of, 58–59;
Guatemalan concepts of, 61–70,
76–78; "Indian problem," 190,
193–98; indigenous self-identity as,
34–36; Latin American concepts of,
42–45, 192–203; North American
concepts of, 45–47; official erasure
of, 216–17, 238; racial and caste
dimensions of, 13, 50–59, 106–10;

Salvadoran scholarly views of, 104–6, 204–10; Salvadoran ladino perceptions of, 26–32, 47–50, 95, 140–41, 147, 161–63; Salvadoran official references to, 27, 30–34, 84–85, 96, 138–39, 143, 167–68, 170–71, 215–17. *See also* indigeneity, Maya, mestizaje, Nahua, Indian militancy, Indian revolts, Anastasio Aquino

Indian militancy, 120–29

Indian revolts, 123–28. *See also* Anastasio Aquino, Matanza

Indianness. *See* Indigeneity

Indigeneity, as discourse, 18–22, 24, 44; in El Salvador, 47–50, 83–84, 119, 138, 169; in Guatemala, 61–82; in the United States, 45–47; indigenous political movement and, 99–102; nationalist discourse and, 84, 91; tourism and, 96–98. *See also* Indian, Maya, Nahua

Indigo, 90, 108, 209, 254n14; impact on indigenous population, 55, 110–12, 123

Ingenieros, José, 191–92, 199, 268n14, 269n29

Instituto para el Rescate Ancestrales Indígena Salvadoreña (RAIS), 39, 234

Interamerican Indigenist Institute, 215, 244n1

International Labor Organization (ILO), 171; Convention on the Rights of Indigenous Populations, 216–18, 227–30, 232–33, 244n1

Iroquois (native Americans), 46, 249n31

Izalco (los Izalcos), 2, 8, 26, 37, 71, 81, 87, 89, 110, 112–13, 115, 149–50, 167; birth records in, 177–82, 265n12; Indian revolts in, 126–27, 129; indigenous land holdings and conflict in, 129–30, 132, 134, 148, 164–65, 261n29, 263n69; Matanza in, 150, 155–57, 261n33, 262n51; water disputes in, 37, 112, 165–68, 264n72. *See also* Cacao

Jews, 53, 59, 249n30, 263n67

Joya de Cerén, 98

Juayúa, 263n65; birth records in, 177, 181–82; revolts in, 126; 1932 uprising and Matanza in, 147–48, 150–53, 155, 158–59, 163, 262n51

Kaqchikeles, 2–4, 90–92, 101, 252n6

K'iche', 2, 249n31, 252n6; 255n25; language revival among, 241n27

Knight, Alan, 21–22, 200, 213

Laitin, David, 264n3

Land, reforms 128–30, shortage, 130–36; swindles, 152, 164–65, 263n69, 263n70

Language, as symbol of indigeneity, 12–14, 47–48, 57, 60–62, 82, 171, 195–96; census tabulations of, 186–87; importance to indigenous politics, 61, 226–27, 229–31, 234; in Latin American unity, 207; use and politics of, among Maya, 61–78; use and politics of, among Nahua, 8, 9, 13, 31, 78–82. *See also* Maya, Nahua, Nahuat, Ulua, Potón

Las Casas, Bartolomé de, 4–5

Las Hojas (cooperative), 237

Lauria-Santiago, Aldo, 138, 241, 255n21, 256n47, 257n64, 258n65, 258n72, 258n75, 259n81, 260n9, 248n70, 274

Leistenschneider, Freddy, 222

Lemarchand, René, 15

Lempira, 91

Lenca, 8, 38–39, 62, 90, 98, 106, 230–32, 234, 238–39, 244n5, 245n16, 273n25; census records among, 173, 185; dress and language use among, 70, 75–76, 78, 98, 101, 251n19; pre-Spanish history, 86–87; profile of, 35–36. *See also* Ulua, Potón

Lindo-Fuentes, Hector, 256n41, 258n72, 264n6

Little, Walter, 243n13, 250n14

Lúe, Timoteo, 147

Lugones, Leopoldo, 199

MacLeod, Murdo J., 254n14
MacNaught, Roy, 137, 151, 163
McKenna Brown, R., 243n13
Makah, 46
Mallon, Florencia, 257n54
Maori, 225, 229
Mapuche, 192, 225
Mármol, Miguel, 137, 146, 148, 154, 156, 158, 261n31, 262n51
Marroquín, Alejandro, 217, 248n24
Martí, Augustin Farabundo, 143
Martínez, Maximiliano Hernández (General), 158–59, 260n15; regime of, 73, 143–44, 169, 173, 205, 208, 210, 214–15
Martínez Peláez, Severo, 127
Masferrer, Albert, 199, 205–7, 213–14, 271n61
Matanza, 9–10, 16, 18, 20, 25, 35–36, 105, 112, 113, 117; communist party role in, 142–46; indigenous deaths in, 154–56, 172–73; impact of, on Nahua use of dress and language, 73–74, 79, 167; impact of, on indigenous land and water control, 164–67; impact of, on indigenous ethnic identity, 179, 181–86: leadership of, 146–50; mass participation in, 150–52; military's role in, 169; myth of ethnocide, 31, 71–73, 79–80, 119, 138, 167–69, 179, 181; preconditions of, 130; race-war character of, 20, 138–39, 156–64, 169, 178, 215, 260n9; targets of, 152–54. See also Birth records
Maya, 6, 14, 38, 61–63, 83, 85, 99, 187, 216, 225, 229, 243n13, 252n6, 253n5, 261n29; as ethnic model for Nahua, 61–63, 86, 98, 101, 230, 238; class components of identity for, 49, 60; dress and weaving among, 14, 80, 65–70, 75–76, 246n5, 250n14; history, 2, 6, 254n7, 255n25; language use among, 14, 61, 76–78, 81–82, 251n27; Maya-Nahuat formula,

xvii, 62, 101; Mayan political movement, 62–65, 187, 242n6, 245n16, 245n17, 249n3, 253n21; Nahua relations with, 35, 86–87, 89–90, 118, 235, 273n25. See also Mundo Maya
Mayanization, 98
Mejia de Gutierrez, Gloria, 245n9
Mejia Vides, José, 30
Menchú Tum, Rigoberta, 63, 99, 227, 250n12
Mestizaje, 20–21, 53, 188, 238, 261n14; indo- and latino- versions of, 203; international geopolitics of, 22–23, 198–204; nation-building and, 190–98; in Ecuador, 268n14; in El Salvador, 63, 79, 99, 179, 181, 204–18; in Guatemala, 187; in Nicaragua, 187–88
Metaconflict, defined, 15–16, 242n3; in Salvadoran ethnic relations, 19, 24, 26, 41; in Salvadoran civil war, 219–20
Mexica, 2, 87, 252n4
Mexico, 97, 120, 200, 206; ethnic and racial discourse in, 20–22, 30, 60, 186, 192, 194, 196–97, 215–16; indigenous communities in, 189, Nahua origins in, 86; pre-Spanish Nahua relations to, 86, 90; Sinophobia in, 211–14
Minera, Camino, 30
Mires, Fernando, 19
Mistral, Gabriela, 199
Molina Enríquez, Andrés, 195–96
Montes, Segundo, 118–19, 131, 141–42, 153, 164, 260n13, 261n33
Movimiento Autóctono Indígena Salvadoreño (MAIS), 39–41, 233, 236–37
Mundo Maya, 97–98, 227. See also Tourism

Nahua, 32, 35–36, 38; cantons of, 26, 36, 70, 111, 208; cantons, Ahuachapán, 150; cantons, Izalco, 149; cantons, Juayúa, 147; cantons,

Nahuizalco, xii, 73, 152, 156, 260n12, 262n40; cantons, Panchimalco, 74; caste relations with ladinos, 130–36; customs, 230; history of, prior to Spanish arrival, 84–90, 104; history of, post-conquest, 103–30, 252n1, 253n3; identity and class, 248n24; identity, indigenous discourse, 56–57, 99; identity, relative to Guatemalan Maya, 14; identity, Salvadoran nationalist discourse, 37, 90–96, 238; identity, tourist discourse, 96–98; identity, transnational discourse, 229–30, 239; Maya-Nahuat identity, 62, 101; political movement of, 38–39, 229–39; spiritual beliefs, 37, 217, 230; sweatlodge of, 39; term, use of, xvii–xviii; use of traditional dress, 36, 70–76, 101; weaving, 71, 74–75, 234. *See also* Nahuat, Matanza

Nahuat (language), 30, 35–36; as signal of indigenous identity, 79–80, 171; dialects and standardization of, 81; efforts to revive, 230–31, 234; relationship to Mayan language, 101; stigma on, 85–87; use by Nahua, 62, 76, 78–82, 120, 138, 167, 169, 248n25; use by nonindigenous people, 56

Nahuat (language-speaking group), 6, 31, 35, 37, 101

Nahuatl, 35, 85–87, 91, 252n1

Nahuizalco, 8, 26, 28–29, 36–37, 56, 110, 113, 132, 146, 148, 260n 12; birth records in, 178, 181–82; cofradias in, 113, 245n16; dress and language use in, 71, 73, 75, 79, 81; land holdings and conflict in, 165, 263n70; Matanza in, 155, 158, 160–61, 163, 262n40; revolts in, 112, 123–24, 126, 129, 150, 152

Nationalism, 113, 202, 243n14, 250n7; among Maya, 65; mestizaje and, 21; racial nationalism, 190–91, 196, 213, 215; Salvadoran, 219, 273n26

Navajo (native Americans), 41, 47, 229

Nicaragua, 35, 86, 113, 143, 198, 220, 243n13, 266n20, 267n26; Conquest Indian in, 91; racial doctrine in, 22, 186–88, 190, 197

Nicarao, 86, 89, 91

Nonualco (Los Nonualcos), 39, 87, 100, 114–16, 118–20, 180; revolts in, 122–26

Ojibwa (native Americans), 46

Omi, Michael, 52, 241n1

Osorio, Oscar (President), 265n11

Palestinians, 214–15, 271n64. *See also* Arabs

Panchimalco, 8, 26, 36, 74–75, 81, 217, 248n24; birth records in, 180, 183, 266n18; cofradias in, 113

Peace Accords, in El Salvador, 97, 220, 223; Accord on Indigenous Rights (Guatemala), 64, 67–68, 70

Perera, Victor, 249n30

Pimentel, Francisco, 193

Pipil, 216; as term for Nahua, xvii, 35, 54, 85, 87, 98, 247n18, 252n8; chronicled in Spanish conquest, 1–6

Pipiltin, 87, 89–91

Population, black in El Salvador, 208–9; Chinese in El Salvador, 211–12; indigenous in El Salvador, 34, 62, 113, 134, 170–74, 181–86, 216, 248n23, 262n37, 264n4, 264n6, 265n8, 265n9, 270n50; indigenous in Guatemala, 186, 249n1; indigenous in Honduras, 186; indigenous in Mexico, 186–87, 267n7; indigenous in Nicaragua, 186–87, 266n20; indigenous in Panamá, 186, 266n19; indigenous mobilization in 1932, 150; methodology in birth records, 266n18; white in El Salvador, 110, 264n6. *See also* Birth Records, Census, Civil Registry

Potón, 35, 78

Powell, T. G., 21
Programa de Apoyo para los Pueblos
    Indígenas de Centroamerica (PAPI-
    CA), 233–36, 273n20
Proyecto Linguístico Francisco
    Marroquín, 76

Quichua, 249n31
Quincentennial, 99

Race, as international relations dis-
    course, 22–24, 198–203; as pan-
    Latin American identity discourse,
    189–92; as Salvadoran national
    identity discourse, 204–17; "cosmic
    race" doctrine, 23, 200–203;
    defined, 50–52; "Indian problem"
    and, 50–55, 195–98; notation in
    birth records, 173–79; notation in
    census, 170–73, 186–88; racial caste
    system, 44, 83, 106–10, 113,
    117–18, 122, 125, 127, 132, 164,
    258n64; typology in Guatemala, 109
Ramos, Victor, 39, 236–37
Redaelli, Don Emilio, 152–53, 262n42,
    263n65
Reyes, Rafael, 117, 172, 264n6
Rigoberta Menchú Foundation, 33–34
Rivas, José (Mayor), 263n65
Rivas, José María (General), 122, 125,
    127, 257n59
Rivas, Rafael, 153–54
Rivera, Brooklyn, 249n31
Román Peña, Miguel, 194, 204

Salvadoran Institute for Tourism (SIT),
    97–98, 253n18. See also Mundo
    Maya, Tourism
Sanchez, Chico, 147, 151
Santo Domingo de Guzmán, 8, 26, 37,
    39, 71 81, 182
Schlesinger, Jorge, 141, 146, 150,
    261n19
Scott, James, 105
Seneca (Native Americans), 46

Shaw, Kara, 244n15
Shupan, Patricio, 147
Sinophobia, 23, 211, 213–14, 244n14.
    See also Chinese
Smith, Anthony, 65, 242n5, 250n8
Smith, Carol, 243n13
Sonsonate, 36–37, 73, 99, 209; coffee
    production in, 128; cofradias in,
    112; ethnic population of, 173–75,
    177–78, 181–82, 209, 262n37,
    266n18; Indian revolts in, 124–25;
    land and water conflict in, 164–67;
    municipal politics in, 153; 1932
    rebellion and Matanza in, 135,
    145, 149–50, 155
Spencer, Herbert, 191
Stabb, Martin, 21

Tecún-Umán, 91
Ticas, Pedro, 264n4
Totonicapán, 257n48
Tourism, 8, 32, 46, 48, 50, 67–69, 75,
    86, 92, 96–98, 100–101, 238,
    246n5, 246n8. See also Mundo
    Maya
Transnational Indigenous Peoples
    Movement, 224–28
Tula, Pascuala, 263n69
Turish, Felix, 166, 168

Ulua, 35, 37, 230. See also Lenca
United Fruit Company, 198
United Nations, 14, 65, 101, 227,
    272n8; Working Group on
    Indigenous Populations, 38, 227.
    See also United Nations Economic
    and Social Council
United Nations Economic and Social
    Council (UNESCO), 23, 33, 81, 97;
    Culture of Peace Program (COPP),
    222–24, 227–32, 234
United States, 10, 23, 95, 171, 189,
    191, 193, 211, 214, 219, 221,
    260n15, 269n30; as Anglo-Saxon
    nation, 22, 201, 203; census

politics in, 170; racial discourse and policy in, 45–49, 52, 56, 211, 225, 270n43; relations with El Salvador, 113, 143–44, 135, 198–200, 214, 219–20, 237, 271; Sinophobia in, 211

Valle Silva, Nelson do, 248n29
Van Cott, Donna Lee, 243n13, 244n15
Varona, Enríque Jose, 199
Vasconcelos, José, 200–203, 207, 269n28–31

Walter, Knut, 256n41
Warren, Kay, 243n13, 247n16, 249n32
Water, conflicts regarding, 37, 165–68, 264n72

Weaving, 97, 251n22; as emblem of indigeneity, 48; as ethnic project, 62; in El Salvador, 74–75, 234; in Guatemala, 68, 75, 243n13. *See also* Nahua, Maya
White, Alistair, 89, 117–19, 138, 255n32
Wilmer, Franke, 244n15
Winant, Howard, 52, 241n1, 247n14
World Council of Churches, 227
World Wildlife Fund, 232

Yashar, Debra, 243n13, 244n15

Zacatecoluca, 115–16, 124, 125, 184
Zarate, Gomez, 149